A CONVENIEN HATRED: THE HISTORY OF ANTISEMITISM

A CONVENIENT HATRED: THE HISTORY OF ANTISEMITISM

Phyllis Goldstein

Foreword by
Sir Harold Evans

Facing History and Ourselves is an international educational and professional development organization whose mission is to engage students of diverse backgrounds in an examination of racism, prejudice, and antisemitism in order to promote the development of a more humane and informed citizenry. By studying the historical development of the Holocaust and other examples of genocide, students make the essential connection between history and the moral choices they confront in their own lives. For more information about Facing History and Ourselves, please visit our website at *www.facinghistory.org.*

Copyright © 2012 by Facing History and Ourselves National Foundation.
Foreword copyright © 2012 by Sir Harold Evans.

Glossy insert credits: *Arch of Titus,* © Werner Forman/TopFoto/The Image Works; *antisemitic map,* © Albert Harlingue/Roger-Viollet/The Image Works; *Vienna,* © Mary Evans Picture Library/The Image Works; *St. Petersburg,* © Print Collector/HIP/The Image Works; *passport,* © Mary Evans Picture Library/The Image Works; *star,* © Artmedia/HIP/The Image Works; *Survivors of the Holocaust,* © Mary Evans/Robert Hunt Collection/The Image Works; *Algerian refugees,* © akg-images/Paul Almasy/The Image Works

ISBN: 978-0-9819543-8-7

eBook ISBN: 978-0-9837870-1-3

Printed in the United States of America.

10 9 8 7 6 5 4 3 2 1

Library of Congress Control Number: 2011935882

Printed on acid-free paper.

16 Hurd Road
Brookline, MA 02445-6919

FACING
HISTORY
AND
OURSELVES

FOREWORD

BY SIR HAROLD EVANS

I came late to an awareness of antisemitism. I grew up during wartime in a nonreligious but Protestant, working-class family in Manchester, Britain. We were a little uneasy about neighbors who were Catholic. We were barely aware of Jews. They were concentrated across town in Cheetham Hill. I played in a table tennis league for Manchester YMCA against Jewish youth clubs, but in the tensest matches I never heard the derogatory terms of *yid* and *kike*. I certainly never came across hatred of Jews from anyone in my family or the wider, evolving circle of friends and workmates. I suppose what emotional reservoirs of hate we had were exhausted by thinking about the German bombers overhead.

I first heard of antisemitism only later, when my father told me how Oswald Mosley had fomented riots in the thirties by marching his paramilitary Fascist thugs called "Blackshirts" through Jewish districts in London's East End. It disgusted him. Mosley's line was that it was only "big Jews" he hated, not the "little Jews." The "big Jews" were conspiring to get Britain into war with Germany, whereas the "little Jews" were harmless. But Mosley did nothing to stop his thugs from hurling bricks through the windows of humble houses displaying lighted Sabbath candles.

My first personal experience of what antisemitism could do was in 1946–47. Britain came into conflict with radical Zionists because in the exercise of its mandate it tried to limit immigration to Palestine. The Irgun hanged two British soldiers and bombed the King David Hotel. A natural patriotism inspired antisemitic riots in my native Manchester and a number of other cities.

My first encounters with the stereotype of the Jew were literary—the villainous Fagin in *Oliver Twist*, and then the subtler Shylock in *The Merchant of Venice*. Thanks to *A Convenient Hatred*, I have a better appreciation of why Jews so often attracted odium as usurious creditors. I learned there was not much else they were allowed to do. In much of Europe, Jews were denied ownership of land and property, denied entry to craft guilds and the like, and actually encouraged to take up money lending, which scripture prohibited for Christians.

If Shylock and Fagin imprinted a cartoon on my subconscious, it was obliterated when I plunged into reading histories of the 1930s and World War II, of Germany's descent from grotesque caricatures of Jews to genocide. I became interested in stereotypes. Reporting from the American Deep South in the 1950s for what was then the *Manchester Guardian*, I saw how the stereotypical "cunning Jews" were portrayed as responsible for black protests, i.e., for stirring up blacks to seek the rights guaranteed by the U.S. Constitution. Blacks, too, were stereotyped as ignorant by the very people who denied them fair and equal education. They were stereotyped, as subversive communists undermining freedom by those denying them the right to vote, and as lawless by the lynch mobs who went home for supper scot-free.

By the time I returned to the United Kingdom to become a newspaper editor in Britain, the new state of Israel was widely admired for making the desert flower. There is no doubt I paid too little thought to the Palestinians who'd been displaced, but I certainly tried to be fair to all when I edited *The Sunday Times* and *The Times* (1967–82). I resolved that the newspapers must treat Israel as we would any other country, neither more harshly nor less. Israeli Prime Minister Menachem Begin's government was angry with me in 1977 for publishing in *The Sunday Times* the critical results of a five-month investigation of the ill-treatment of Palestinian prisoners (which the State Department subsequently confirmed). The Israeli government could not have been angrier than I was at the Israeli army's facilitating role in the Christian Phalangists 1982 massacre of hundreds in the Sabra and Shatila refugee camps during the Lebanese civil war. The subsequent outcry from the people of Israel and the investigation by the Israeli government did something to redeem the reputation of the state—a reputation that the Israel Defense Forces (IDF) had damaged badly by betraying the state's founding ideals.

At the same time, I did not hesitate to condemn the British media's hysterical treatment of Israel when it retaliated for unprovoked rocket assaults from Jenin, the Palestinian refugee camp in the West Bank. In April 2002, the IDF sealed off the town, which the Palestinians had booby-trapped with hundreds of explosives. Since the press could not immediately get in, they listened to stories of atrocities from Palestinian Authority spokesmen. There was a frenzy of indictments of Israel. The IDF was portrayed as murdering 3,000 defenseless Palestinians and then burying the victims in secret mass graves.

My old newspaper, *The Guardian*, was moved to write the editorial opinion that Israel's attack was "every bit as repellent" as Osama Bin Laden's on New York on September 11, 2001.[1] Come again? In fact, a gullible press published a cataract of lies. Tom Gross[2] of Mideast Media Analysis produced a scalding review and was vindicated when both a United Nations investigation and Human Rights Watch later concluded that there had been no massacre, no secret mass graves. It was a military engagement in which the death toll was 54, of whom half were Palestinian combatants, about the same number as Israeli fatalities.

In June 2002, I was invited to speak at the 50th anniversary celebrations of Index on Censorship. Since 1972 when it first campaigned for writers suppressed in the Soviet Union and Warsaw Pact countries, Index has been Britain's leading organization promoting freedom of expression. As a newspaper editor who'd been a defendant in a fair share of secrecy prosecutions, I got the opportunity from the Index editors to compare my editing experiences in London with those over 20 years in the United States, and especially to gauge the advances in regressions on British press freedom in the 28 years since I'd given a lecture entitled "The Half Free Press." The invitation came months after Jenin and nine months after Arab hijackers flew planes into the World Trade Center and the Pentagon.

But instead of reexamining the freedoms of the press, I found my mind obsessed by the paradox that a new freedom had brought with it new corruptions. The Internet has connected the world as never before, but much of what travels at the speed of light now is half-truth masquerading as knowingness, and vast amounts of disinformation and misinformation. I was intrigued, in particular, by a report that went viral on the Internet immediately after 9/11: 4,000 Jews with jobs at the World Trade Center stayed away that morning because they had been tipped off by Mossad, Israel's intelligence agency. It was all a brilliant Jewish plot to vilify Muslims and pave the way for a joint Israeli-U.S. military operation not just against Osama bin Laden but also against militants in Palestine. Sheikh Muhammed Gemeaha at the Cairo Centre of Islamic Learning at al-Azhar University explained it for dummies: "only the Jews" were capable of toppling the World Trade Center. If the conspiracy became known to the American people, "they would have done to the Jews what Hitler did."[5]

Of course, Jews and Israelis (400 of them) and Muslims and Catholics and Buddhists and Presbyterians who had jobs at the World Trade Center did what everybody employed there did on 9/11: they showed up for work and died for good timekeeping. There were among the 2,752 victims 77 nationalities of all religions (with some 60 Muslims) who earned their living as clerks, busboys, bond traders, cooks, accountants, managers, secretaries, and technicians. The attempt to shuffle off the guilt of the outrage seemed to have had effect. Gallup sampled opinion in nine predominantly Islamic countries—Pakistan, Iran, Indonesia, Turkey, Lebanon, Morocco, Kuwait, Jordan, and Saudi Arabia. It reported that some two-thirds of those polled found the 9/11 attack morally unjustified. Only in Turkey, by 46 to 43 percent, did they believe that groups of Arabs had carried out the attacks. In Pakistan, only 4 percent accepted that the hijackers were Arabs.

Who could be crazy enough or malign enough to invent and disseminate as truth the odious fiction of a Jewish plot? And how did it convince so many people so fast? Following a lead by the investigative journalist Bryan Curtis, then at Slate, I tracked down the original disseminator of the conspiracy, Syed Adeeb, a Pakistani living in Alexandria, Virginia, who edits a website called *Information Times* (now *Information Press*). I asked him for his evidence and how he'd verified his story. He told me he had a reliable source. It was *Al-Manar* Television in Lebanon. He was not at all fazed when I pointed out that *Al-Manar* proclaims that it exists to "stage an effective psychological warfare with the Zionist enemy."

Once upon a time, Adeeb and his like would be sending out smudged cyclostyled sheets to a handful of people. But *Al-Manar's* story of a Mossad conspiracy and variations of it, endlessly recycled, had a big play in the Islamic world through the Web and word of mouth and made it into print. The newspaper *Ad-Dustour* in Jordan reported that the Twin Towers attack was "the act of the great Jewish Zionist mastermind that controls the world's economy, media, and politics."

The respected journalist Syed Talat Hussain was frank about the proliferation of the story in Pakistan: "In a country where there is a void of information, newspapers resort to rumors. In addition, there is an abiding tradition in the Pakistani print media deliberately to prove that whatever goes wrong is the work of Jews and the Hindus." Tom Friedman, the *New York Times* columnist, reported an interview with an Indonesian from Jakarta who was worried that hostility toward Christians and Jews was being fed by what he called an insidious digital divide. The article said, "Internet users are only 5 percent of the population—but these 5 percent spread rumors to everyone else. They say, 'He got it from the Internet.' They think it's the Bible."[4]

The technical accomplishment of the Internet, its speed, its reach, its infinite space, may indeed confer a spurious authenticity on nuttiness. It also, however, affords us an unprecedented degree of knowledge about what is being retailed, what people are being told, and what they may believe, especially when imprisoned by illiteracy. One thinks of Socrates's allegory of a people who live all their lives chained to the blank wall of a cave. All they ever see in the darkness are the play of shadows. Only Socrates's philosopher, released into a bright day, can see that the shadows do not represent reality.

In doing the research for the Index lecture, I caught sight of many moving shadows on the wall that were alarming when seen in the light. I was looking at nothing less than the globalization of hate. There were thousands of antisemitic stories expressed with a vehemence as astounding as the contempt for history and scholarship, to the effect that the Holocaust was a Zionist invention, a "hoax," a "lie," a Jewish "marketing operation" (Hiri Manzour, in the official Palestinian Authority newspaper *al-Hayat al Jadida*), and a "huge Israeli plot aimed at extorting the German government . . . if only you [Hitler] had done it, brother, if only it had really happened, so that the world could sigh in relief without their evil and sin" (a columnist in *Al-Akhbar,* an Egyptian government daily).

Much of the sewage had obviously seeped out from the *Protocols of the Elders of Zion,* the forgery concocted by the tsar's secret police in 1903 that contrives to represent every disaster as a Jewish plot. The ignorant credulity of the peasants in Russia might be excused for believing their troubles were the result of a plot by Jewish elders, overheard by two Christians hiding in a Jewish cemetery at midnight. But how are we to understand educated Egyptians making a multimillion dollar thirty-part dramatic series based on this fraud? Or how do we equate our joy at seeing the thousands of Egyptians speaking up for freedom in the square in Cairo in 2011 with the fact that every corner bookstore in Cairo sells as "history" copies of this fraud in Arabic, French, and English?

I looked forward to the Index event as an escape from the effluent to the affluent. An address to educated, middle-class audiences normally found at the Hay-on-Wye literary festival sponsored by *The Guardian* was an opportunity to assess my anxieties and discuss what might be done. I called the talk "The View from Ground Zero" and made it clear I was as critical of Islamophobia as I was of antisemitism.

In the green hospitality room, the night before I was to speak, I was cheered to meet three friends of intellectual distinction, two women and a man I'd known since my days in London—let's say a literary critic, a cultural innovator, and a novelist. "What are you going to talk about tomorrow?" asked the critic. I told them.

"You're not going to criticize suicide bombers, are you?"

I thought the question was satirical. It wasn't. When I owned up that

I really thought so, and strongly, they were aghast. I appealed to their reverence for the English language. I argued that a *Guardian* headline I'd seen referring to suicide bombers as "martyrs" was surely a stunning corruption of the word. Was not a martyr someone who gives up his life to save others, not to randomly kill babes in arms, old men in wheelchairs, mothers and fathers going about their innocuous ways (19 were victims at a Passover seder)? To describe murderers as martyrs was to be emotionally complicit in what Islam itself regards as a double transgression, suicide and murder.

I only inflamed their emotions. Critic and cultural innovator joined in a duet of denunciation. Suicide bombs were all the poor Palestinians could do to protest the cruelties of the Israelis. What had happened to my conscience?

I demurred. I did sympathize with refugees. I began to say the suicide bombings were just pure evil, like the beheading of Daniel Pearl of the Wall Street Journal (that February) just for being a Jew. Another mistake. I was not in some academic seminar. I was swept away in a tide of emotion about Palestinians.

"You should be ashamed of yourself, Harry. You've lived too long in America! You should get back to America!"

I looked to the novelist to stem the flow. He kept silent throughout. Later the same evening, I mentioned the outburst to James (Jamie) Rubin, the former U.S. assistant secretary of state for public affairs, who was then living in London. "You'd better be ready for more of the same when you speak," he said.

I guess there were 500 people in the tent the next day. I spoke for my allotted hour without interruption, and then there was silence. And silence. To my anxious state, it seemed to last forever. It was probably no more than seven or eight seconds. Then people stood, and they applauded, and they all kept on applauding. I was relieved and gratified, but I have no doubt the reaction was a deeply felt expression of empathy for the victims (67 of them were British) and a disgust at the political exploitation of the tragedy I'd described. Tolerance is a deep vein in British culture, so the intellectuals' vote for suicide bombers troubled me. My assailants never uttered the word "Jew," only "Israelis." Were they antisemitic? Perhaps not, but a British Parliamentary inquiry reported in 2006 that antisemitism was no longer confined to the Far Right but was manifest in a variety of ways on the Left—in the media, on the Internet, among fringe and extremist Islamists (small in number yet radical), and on campuses where a few academics and students defame Israel as an apartheid state.[5] Marie Brenner reported a similar trend in France.[6]

Antisemitism is a very peculiar pathology that recognizes no national borders. It is a mental condition conducive to paranoia and impervious to truth. Its lexicon has no word for individuality. It is fixated on group identity. It is necessarily dehumanizing when people become abstractions. Once an emotional stereotype has been created—of the Jews, of blacks, of Catholics, of Muslims—it is readily absorbed in the bones like strontium 90, an enduring poison that distorts the perceptions of the victims. All minority groups have suffered, but none have been stereotyped more heinously and more durably than Jews.

One of the reasons A Convenient Hatred is such an important and timely publication is that we can see how the poison proliferates in receptive minds, where it congeals into an unyielding conviction. As the eighteenth- century author Jonathan Swift wrote, you cannot reason someone out of something he has not been reasoned into. Shock succeeds shock on so many levels in this book. I came to think of reading each chapter from the year 586 BCE to our times as akin to entering a complex of caves and receding chambers, each harboring its own Minotaur demanding human sacrifices. We cannot summon the Theseus of myth to rid us altogether of a Minotaur that in one form or another has survived for centuries, this monster of antisemitism gorging on regular infusions of hate. But we can discern the dark and dangerous twists and turns of the labyrinth of men's minds that mutate from fear of a difference—difference of faith, of economic status, of custom, of language, of ritual, of culture—to an atrophy of ethical sense and the abyss of unreasoning hate.

Even the summaries of a cascade of cruelties that Phyllis Goldstein documents over centuries make one's blood run cold. Jew or non-Jew, what sentient being could not but be appalled by just a few of the crimes against the innocent Jews? Eight hundred put to the sword in the Rhineland town of Worms (1096), some mothers and fathers choosing suicide for themselves and their children rather than face the butchery. Over thirty men and women burned alive in Blois (1171). Hundreds murdered in their homes in Seville, buried alive in Toledo, and drowned in the Tagus (1391–1420). Two hundred thousand people expelled from their homes in Spain (1492), tens of thousands dying on the way out. Babies torn to pieces by frenzied mobs in Kishinev in what is now Moldavia (1903), 600,000 uprooted by the tsar's army in 1915. Old men, women, children, and infants in arms massacred at

Proskurov (1919). A group of 33,771 men, women, and children shot and buried in the ravine known as Babi Yar near Kiev (September 29–30, 1941). And on into the nightmare years of the other Nazi programs of mass annihilation and to Auschwitz and beyond.

In addition to these better-known atrocities, one of the greatest shocks, for me, was the active antisemitism of the Christian church, both Catholic and Protestant, including Martin Luther. I feel shame that I was so little aware of it, never thought of how the stories and values I'd absorbed in the Episcopal church had to be reconciled with a barbarous history. As a schoolboy, I'd exulted in the adventures of the armored knights, banners flying with the cross of St. George, riding to free Jerusalem from the Turks. I didn't know—how many people do?—that the crusaders, as they rode south through Europe to Jerusalem, were as keen to hunt down and kill as many Jews as they could find.

Oppression is a commonplace fate of minorities. The Jews are hardly unique in this regard: the majority has often had good cause to fear insurgency. Indeed, Jews, being not visibly different from the rest of the population, are generally exposed to less prejudice than members of more distinctive minorities. What I had not appreciated, however, until I read A Convenient Hatred, is how long Jews have uniquely been the subject of campaigns of intimidation and discrimination—since long before the creation of Israel, long before the Holocaust, long before the Spanish Inquisition, even before the Romans crucified Jesus. As striking as the persistence of the pathology is how Jews have maintained their identity, and many of them their faith, in the face of unparalleled defamation and assault. There are heroes in the story as well; more of their stories should be known.

Harold Evans is editor-at-large of Thomson Reuters, the world's largest international multimedia news provider. He is also the author of two critically acclaimed best-selling histories of America: The American Century *and* They Made America. *His most recent book is his memoir,* My Paper Chase, *which covers his early life and his years as editor of* The Sunday Times *and* The Times *of London. On the 50th anniversary of the founding of the International Press Institute, Evans was honored as one of 50 World Press Heroes.*

---

[1] "The Battle for Truth: What Really Happened in Jenin Camp?" *The Guardian*, April 17, 2002.

[2] Tom Gross, "Jeningrad," in *Those Who Forget the Past: The Question of Anti-Semitism*, ed. Ron Rosenbaum (New York: Random House, 2004), 135–144.

[3] Jonathan Rosen, "The Uncomfortable Question of Antisemitism," *The New York Times*, November 4, 2001.

[4] Thomas L. Friedman, "Global Village Idiocy," *The New York Times*, May 12, 2002.

[5] "Report of the All-Party Parliamentary Inquiry into Antisemitism," (London: The Stationery Office, 2006), 63.

[6] Marie Brenner, "France's Scarlet Letter," in *Those Who Forget the Past: The Question of Anti-Semitism*, ed. Ron Rosenbaum (New York: Random House, 2004), 220.

TO VICTIMS OF PREJUDICE

Having received a modern Jewish education more than a half century ago, I slowly came to realize that I, like almost all of my friends, had only the most limited knowledge of the history of antisemitism. Growing up right after World War II, with the horrors of the Holocaust exposed, we naively thought that the scourge of antisemitism would finally fade in our lifetime.

Yet, in our supposedly enlightened age, antisemitism has found new ways to assert itself, reviving old myths and inspiring new ones. I became haunted by the epigraph from Santayana quoted in William Shirer's *The Rise and Fall of the Third Reich*: "Those who do not remember the past are condemned to relive it."

Thus, almost a decade ago, I started thinking about a different kind of book about antisemitism, one that would cover its entire history over the millennia. I convened a series of meetings with some of the foremost scholars of Jewish history, seeking advice and, perhaps among them, an author to write this book. Yet even these eminent experts demonstrated significant gaps in their knowledge of the subject. It was at that point that I turned to Facing History and Ourselves, a nondenominational organization dedicated to understanding and fighting not only antisemitism but also other evils of intolerance. The organization shared my belief in the need for an exhaustively researched, comprehensive history of antisemitism, clearly and simply written for the widest audience possible.

It has been my honor to commit the financial resources needed to support the research and writing of this important book. Neither Facing History and Ourselves nor I have applied any ideological or intellectual strictures to the project. The result, after almost a decade of work and careful scholarship, is the publication of an extraordinary book that threads its way through more than 2,000 years of uninterrupted antisemitism.

Hopefully readers of all faiths and nationalities will achieve new insights and understanding from this book about the causes and myths that bind ancient and modern antisemitism to intolerance in our own time.

Leonard Stern

CONTENTS

INTRODUCTION

In 2001, I, like many other Jews, awakened to the fact that antisemitism was not a relic of the past but a current event. In late August of that year, we watched on TV as protesters harassed Jews at the U.N. World Conference against Racism in Durban, South Africa. It was a surreal moment. Men and women who prided themselves on their staunch opposition to all forms of racism assaulted Jews and shouted antisemitic slurs, flaunting signs, posters, and leaflets emblazoned with antisemitic stereotypes and myths. Although most people at the conference did not participate in those outbursts, very few spoke out against the assaults or the blatantly racist rhetoric.

On September 11, just two days after the Durban conference ended, 19 men hijacked four passenger planes; they flew two of the planes into the World Trade Center in New York City and one into the Pentagon in Washington, D.C. The fourth crashed into a field in Pennsylvania. Despite the fact that al-Qaeda took credit for the attacks, rumors claiming that "the Jews" were responsible spread like wildfire. Far too many people believed the lie simply because they saw it on the Internet or heard about it in the media.

In the months that followed, there would be more rumors and more attacks on Jews. Antisemitism was on the rise once again. For me, it was a sobering realization. I was not a stranger to antisemitism, personally or professionally. Although the word was rarely used when I was growing up in northwest Indiana, I knew that a hatred of Jews stood at the heart of many of the stories my parents and grandparents told, and those stories in turn were reinforced by my own experiences as a Jewish child in an overwhelmingly Christian community.

Antisemitism has also played a significant role in my professional life as senior writer at Facing History and Ourselves. Indeed, not long after the events of September 11, Margot Stern Strom, the founder of Facing History and its executive director, asked me to write a series of lessons about modern-day antisemitism for our website to supplement our work on the historical roots of antisemitism. The project heightened my awareness of this ancient hatred.

At about this time, philanthropist Leonard Stern came to Facing History with an idea for a book that would trace the history of antisemitism from ancient times to the present. It would allow us to expand the scope of the work we were already doing and deepen our understanding of this pernicious hatred. I was asked to be the author with Margot as my primary editor, a role she plays on almost every project.

From the start, the book was firmly rooted in the mission of Facing History and Ourselves. For more than 35 years, the organization has been helping people of all ages confront the events that led to the Holocaust—a history that raises profound questions about the nature of evil, the power of stereotypes and myths, and the importance of prevention. *A Convenient Hatred: The History of Antisemitism* evolved in large part from those questions. Like other Facing History publications, the book uses memorable stories to link the past to the moral questions we face today, foster empathy, and promote thoughtful conversations. In confronting the complexities and nuances of this history, we had to choose which stories to cover and what to emphasize, and that is always tricky. Our aim was not to include every incident but to feature moments where there might have been a different outcome. The hope is to sensitize the reader to this history and to encourage further investigation. This book is in many ways a primer. There will always be people who would have made different choices.

As I researched the book, I came across a memoir by Meyer Levin, an American war correspondent during World War II. In the spring of 1945, he witnessed the consequences of German antisemitism at a recently liberated concentration camp. After describing the horrors he saw on his tour, he concluded, "This was the source of the fear and guilt in every human who remained alive. For human beings had had it in them to do this, and we were of the species."[1] His words served as a powerful reminder that antisemitism is not just a Jewish story or even a European one, but it is a human story that touches us all. He also helped me understand that we cannot overcome this hatred or any other until we face it. This book provides a starting point. The more we know about the characteristics of antisemitism, how it has been adapted to new situations, and the ways it has been transmitted from place to place and generation to generation, the more likely we are to find ways to end it.

As I studied this ugly, hateful history, I encountered in every age men and women who dared to challenge the conventional wisdom, resist efforts to demonize and dehumanize Jews, and courageously choose uncomfortable truths over convenient lies. Their stories led me to wonder why such individuals have always been so few in number and, most importantly, why antisemitism has persisted despite their heroic efforts to end it.

The writings of Rabbi Abraham Joshua Heschel, a noted Jewish scholar, provided one answer to those questions. He noted, "[T]he Holocaust did not begin with the building of crematoria, and Hitler did not come to power with tanks and guns; it all began with uttering evil words, with defamation,

---

[1] Meyer Levin, *In Search* (New York: Horizon Press, 1950), 232–233.

with language and propaganda." He believed that such words, "once having been uttered, gain eternity and can never be withdrawn."[2]

Nevertheless, no one is born knowing those words. As Facing History has long taught, hatreds are learned, and because they are learned, neither antisemitism nor any other hatred is inevitable. People learn to fear and to hate in much the way they learn every other part of their culture. They are taught directly and indirectly, consciously and unconsciously, in small places close to home. Those teachings are often bolstered by the media and by various groups in a society, sometimes overtly and sometimes very subtly. Once the stereotypes and myths have become firmly embedded in an individual, an institution, or a classroom, it has always been relatively easy for a ruler, a general, a charismatic preacher, a rabble-rouser, or a disgruntled neighbor to get a crowd going. All that is needed is a crisis, and suddenly the cry is heard: "The Jews are to blame!"

As Margot read and reread chapters, she pointed out the role such individuals have played in keeping that hatred alive. They seemed to regard antisemitism as a convenient way of uniting their own followers and recruiting new ones by turning "us" against "them." It also allowed them to divert attention from their own shortcomings by scapegoating "the Jews."

My efforts to trace this history took me to a number of libraries (Facing History's own collection as well as the specialized ones I found at places such as Hebrew College and Harvard University). I also used the Internet to follow current reporting related to antisemitism and to explore a variety of archives now available online. The more I read, the more questions I had. I began to meet with scholars in the United States and in Israel, where I studied for a time at Yad Vashem. These early efforts were helpful in creating a working outline of the book as well as in gathering a team of advisers to ensure its accuracy and integrity. Such noted scholars as Yehuda Bauer, Michael Berenbaum, Lawrence Langer, and John Stendahl read and critiqued outlines and early drafts as well as the final manuscript. They did not always agree with one another or with everything I wrote, but their strong opinions and wise recommendations strengthened the book and deepened my understanding of this important history.

A number of other scholars reviewed portions of the manuscript and offered suggestions related to their areas of expertise. Among them were Paula Fredriksen, who shared her knowledge of early Judaism and Christianity; Mary C. Boys, who consulted with us on the history and teachings of the Roman Catholic Church; and Ahmed al-Rahim, who advised us on the history and teachings of Islam.

---

[2] Susannah Heschel, "Introduction," in Abraham Joshua Heschel, *Moral Grandeur and Spiritual Audacity*, ed. Susannah Heschel (New York: Farrar, Straus & Giroux, 1996), viii–ix.

Throughout our work on this book, Leonard Stern has been an amazing partner. He was incredibly patient with the lengthy process of researching, writing, and revising chapters. He was also more than willing to share his considerable knowledge of publishing in general and this history in particular. Most importantly, he encouraged us to tell this important story from our perspective in our voice.

As the manuscript took shape, Margot invited Seth Klarman, the chair of our board of directors, and a group of our colleagues to read the book. Their suggestions, questions, criticisms, and concerns influenced the final product in small ways and large. So did helpful comments from other interested educators and theologians. As the book neared completion, Margot began to involve Facing History's entire staff and board in the work. They too raised questions and offered meaningful advice.

The deep conversations that resulted from these reviews turned the process into a true Facing History experience. As always, the goal was not to agree on every point but to expand our understanding of this important history and its impact on our own identities. It is only through a deep confrontation with a particular history that we gain insights into universal themes. My hope is that this book will spark more insights, further conversation, and additional learning. Only by facing history and ourselves can we begin to meet the challenges of the present and build a more just and tolerant future.

Phyllis Goldstein

ABOUT FACING HISTORY AND OURSELVES

"I faced history one day and found myself."

—a Facing History and Ourselves student

Facing History and Ourselves is a leader in history and civic education. The organization's quality resources, professional development, and public forums provide opportunities for people of all ages to explore the connection between history and their own lives.

For more than 35 years, Facing History has been linking the past to the moral and ethical questions of our time through a rigorous examination of the root causes of antisemitism, racism, and other hatreds. History matters. The world we live in did not just happen; it is the result of choices made by countless individuals and groups. Even the smallest of those decisions can have enormous consequences.

Facing History and Ourselves has grown from an innovative course taught in a single school system to an international organization with nine offices in North America, an international hub in London, and partnerships that span the globe. By harnessing the latest technology, the organization has been able to increase its impact and extend its reach.

Facing History publications include *Facing History and Ourselves: Holocaust and Human Behavior; Fundamental Freedoms: Eleanor Roosevelt and the Universal Declaration of Human Rights; Identity and Belonging in a Changing Great Britain; Stories of Identity: Religion, Migration, and Belonging in a Changing World; What Do We Do with a Difference? France and the Debate over Headscarves in Schools;* and *Race and Membership in American History: The Eugenics Movement.*

For additional information about Facing History and Ourselves and its timely and relevant publications, visit the interactive website at *www.facinghistory.org* or follow the organization on Facebook and Twitter.

1

Beginnings

(586 BCE–135 CE)

The Middle East is the only place in the world where three continents come together. It is a crossroads that links Asia, Africa, and Europe. Life at a crossroads can be dangerous. In ancient times, the Middle East was often in turmoil, much as it is today. The armies of one group after another conquered all or part of the region and then imposed their own way of life on the people they conquered. Many cultures disappeared completely during those years. Yet Jewish culture survived and even flourished. Still, some historians believe that the hatred of Jews that is known today as antisemitism began in the Middle East in ancient times. If so, where and when did it begin? What caused it? To what extent was it similar to antisemitism in modern times?

PEOPLE ON THE MOVE

In the centuries before the Common Era,* it was not unusual for Jews as well as other peoples to move from one country to another. Some felt they had no choice—they were fleeing an invading army, or perhaps they were being forced into slavery or exile after their homeland was conquered. Most, however, packed up their belongings in order to escape poverty at home or to seek opportunities abroad, just as people do today. Unlike most people today, people in ancient times usually migrated as part of a large extended family. The newcomers would negotiate with local rulers for the right to establish roots in a new land.

The process of moving must have been as unsettling then as it is now. Newcomers in an unfamiliar place are often fearful and anxious: Will they be accepted? How will they fit in and find their own place in this new setting? We can hear these concerns in the book of Psalms, one of the

---

* History has been recorded with the use of many calendars, but the one that is most widely used today is based on a Christian calculation (probably several years off) of the birth of Jesus. The method of dating in relation to that event now uses the terms *Common Era*, or CE, for the time after Jesus's birth and BCE for the years before the Common Era.

oldest books of the Hebrew Scriptures (writings included in the Christian Bible as the Old Testament), when the author of Psalm 137 asks, "How shall we sing the Lord's song in a strange land?"

In the ancient world, Jews were not easily distinguished from their neighbors. They did the same kinds of work, built similar homes, and in many ways lived similar lives. Yet there was at least one important difference: Jews worshipped the one God—invisible and indivisible—at a time when most people prayed to a wide array of gods who looked like animals or humans. In such a world, the Jews' devotion to the one God was seen as strange or odd. Monotheism was still a new idea.

When one group defeated another, the newly conquered people were expected to accept the gods of the victor. After all, the new gods had triumphed and were therefore entitled to praise and honor. But most Jews, committed to the one God, refused to pay their respects to the gods of their conquerors. Their stubborn refusal raised questions for their conquered neighbors as well as their conquerors: Why did Jews refuse to worship the same gods everyone else did? Why did they stand apart? Their allegiance to God made Jews seem like outsiders who refused to conform to the dominant group's beliefs. Their behavior almost always aroused curiosity; sometimes it also provoked suspicion and charges of disloyalty.

Some scholars have traced the beginnings of antisemitism to the experiences of Jews in the Diaspora—a Greek word that means "scattering." The word has come to describe the communities Jews established beyond Israel, which was the kingdom established by Saul, David, and Solomon in biblical times (in about the eleventh and tenth centuries BCE). After Solomon's death, quarrels among the twelve tribes of Israel led to the creation of two separate kingdoms. Ten of the twelve tribes formed a kingdom known as Israel in the north and the other two tribes built a kingdom in the south called Judea.

In 721 BCE, Assyria, a neighboring empire, captured Samaria, the capital of Israel, the northern kingdom. The Assyrians forced members of the ten tribes from their land, and eventually they disappeared from history, probably absorbed into other groups. About 135 years later, in 586 BCE, the Babylonians conquered Judea, the southern kingdom. They destroyed the Temple in Jerusalem and forced thousands of Jews into exile in Babylonia. These Judean Jews did not disappear from history.

The exiled Jews who settled in Babylonia were able to maintain their identity, in part because they were allowed to practice their religion. They not only kept their beliefs but also deepened and enriched their understanding of those beliefs by beginning to compile and write down the Torah (the Pentateuch, or Five Books of Moses, which are also the first five books of the Christian Bible's Old Testament).

Little is known about the day-to-day lives of these Babylonian Jews. We do know that in 538 BCE, soon after the Persians (people who lived in what is now Iran) conquered Babylonia, their emperor, Cyrus, allowed Jews to return to Judea and rebuild the Temple in Jerusalem. Only a small minority left; many families had by this time put down roots in Babylonia and decided to remain there. It had become their home.

Those families were part of the growing number of Jews who lived outside Judea. Although they differed from one another in many ways, most of them struggled to maintain a Jewish identity even as they built new loyalties. Two incidents that took place in Egypt more than 400 years apart—one on the island of Elephantine and the other in Alexandria, a bustling port in the northern part of Egypt—show some of the difficulties of divided loyalties.

ANTISEMITISM IN ELEPHANTINE?

Elephantine is an island in the Nile River in southern Egypt. By 600 BCE, well before the Babylonian conquest of Judea, Jewish families had already been living on Elephantine for generations. They were not exiles or refugees. They had chosen to leave their homeland and could have returned if they wished to do so. In those days, emperors often hired foreign soldiers to protect their borders because they did not want to arm their own people. They preferred to place their trust in outsiders who were well paid to be loyal to their employer. Like neighboring rulers, Egypt's pharaohs had hired companies of Jewish, Syrian, and other foreign soldiers to protect their lands. And some of those soldiers had been stationed on Elephantine.

In order to obtain certain religious and civil rights, Jewish soldiers negotiated with the pharaohs who hired them to guard Egypt's borders. Those rights were honored not only by succeeding pharaohs but also by each of Egypt's conquerors. For example, after Persia conquered Egypt in 525 BCE, the Jewish soldiers on Elephantine transferred their loyalty to the new ruler. Because soldiers were in great demand, the Jews and other foreign soldiers who served the Persians received land as well as salaries. They and their families built permanent homes on the island.

JEWISH COMMUNITIES IN THE DIASPORA (500 BCE–100 CE)

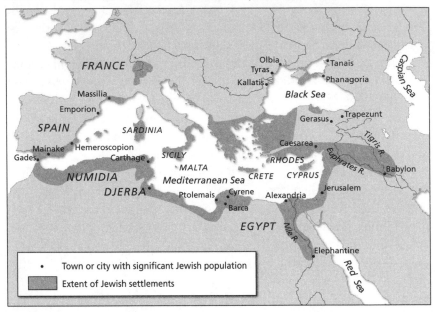

In ancient times, most Jewish settlements in the Diaspora–the area beyond Judea–were on the shores of the Mediterranean Sea.

Much of what is known about the "Jewish force" comes from the Elephantine archives that date to about 500 BCE. These documents show an established Jewish community. There are records of marriages, births, and deaths, as well as wills and purchase agreements.

For example, a deed dated 437 BCE reveals that Ananiah, an official at the Jewish temple on the island, and his wife, Tamut, an Egyptian slave owned by a man named Mueshullam, purchased a two-story mud-brick house. The seller was a Persian soldier. The family's new neighbors included other Persians and an Egyptian who managed the garden at a local temple dedicated to Khnum, an Egyptian god. Letters are also part of the archives. Some of these letters boast of accomplishments, while others demand protection of religious and civil rights.

The documents in the archives suggest that the Jews of Elephantine maintained their identity as Jews and that their religious life centered on the temple they had built on the island. They probably kept the dietary laws of Judaism, meaning they would not eat certain foods, and they probably did not work on one day each week, their Sabbath—a custom that did not exist in Egyptian society.

However, the Jews of Elephantine did not strictly follow what we have come to know as Jewish law. They sacrificed animals, such as sheep and goats, in their temple, even though the high priests in Judea had ruled many years earlier that such sacrifices could take place only in the Temple in Jerusalem. No one knows why Jews on Elephantine chose to disobey the high priests in Jerusalem. Their temple may have been built before the ruling was issued. Or the Jews who settled on the island may have left Judea in the first place because they disagreed with the high priests. What is known is that the sacrifices the Jews of Elephantine made in their temple were a source of conflict with Egyptians as well as with other Jews.

The Jews and the Egyptians were often at odds because the Egyptians worshipped Khnum, the ram-god who they believed controlled the annual flooding of the Nile River—an event essential to Egypt's survival. Elephantine was the center of Khnum's worship, and the Egyptian priests who served him were outraged that Jews included rams among their sacrifices. The Egyptians considered the practice blasphemy—open contempt for their god. However, as long as the rulers of Egypt protected the religious rights of the Jews, the Egyptians were silent.

Then, in the spring of 410 BCE, a group of Egyptians saw an opportunity to force out the Persian conquerors and the Jews who worked for them. That summer, with the support of a local ruler named Vidranga, the rebels made a point of burning the Jewish temple and several nearby homes on the island. The Jews fought back, killing a number of Egyptians.

Three years later, the rebellion was history. But the Jews of Elephantine did not yet have permission to rebuild their temple. Their anxious leaders sent a petition to the Persians, reminding them of the long history of the "Jewish force" on the island and its loyalty to Persia during the recent rebellion.[1]

The Persians did not immediately respond to the petition, perhaps because they knew that both the Egyptian priests on the island and the Jewish high priests in Jerusalem strongly objected to the sacrifices that were carried out on Elephantine. They may have feared that granting permission to rebuild the temple would lead to more conflict. So they looked for a compromise. In the end, the Persians allowed the Jews to restore their temple but ruled that they could no longer sacrifice animals there. Only the high priests at the Temple in Jerusalem were to have that privilege.

Was the destruction of the temple an act of hatred toward Jews? Was it retaliation for the Jews' religious sacrifices that Egyptians saw as insults to their god? Or was the attack motivated by the loyalty of Elephantine's

A portion of the petition sent by the Jews of Elephantine to the Persian governor in what was later known as Palestine.

Jews to Egypt's hated Persian conquerors? It is not uncommon for people to act out their anger toward a powerful ruler by attacking a weaker person or group allied with that ruler. Most historians believe that the incident arose from a clash of cultures, political disagreements that were expressed in religious form, or a combination of the two, rather than from antisemitism as we think of it today. They point out that once the Persians resolved the issue of temple sacrifices, life on Elephantine returned to normal.

Yet Jews continued to differ from their neighbors on Elephantine in important ways. They continued to worship God rather than the gods of the Egyptians, and they continued to work as soldiers for the Persians. From the Egyptians' point of view, it must have seemed that Jews were choosing to be outsiders.

ANTISEMITISM IN ALEXANDRIA?

Whole families, husbands with their wives, infant children with their parents, were burnt in the heart of the city by these supremely ruthless men who showed no pity for old age nor youth, nor the innocent years of childhood.[2]

The author of this powerful statement is Philo, a Jewish philosopher who lived in Alexandria, Egypt. He wrote an eyewitness account of the violence against Jews in the city in 38 CE—more than 400 years after the destruction of the Jewish temple on Elephantine. Who were the "supremely ruthless men who showed no pity"? Why did they attack Jews?

By 38 CE, the city of Alexandria was more than 300 years old. It had prospered because of its unique location; it was a bustling port on the Mediterranean Sea, linked by a canal to the Nile River. In 38 CE, Alexandria, like the rest of Egypt, was part of the Roman Empire. Many in the city resented Roman rule, particularly their Roman governor, Avillius Flaccus. He had won the job because he was a friend of Tiberius, the Roman emperor. Nevertheless, in his first years in office, Flaccus managed to keep the peace and make important reforms. Then, in the year 37 CE, Tiberius had died and a new emperor took the throne. Flaccus was now understandably anxious about his future.

The new Roman emperor was Caligula, widely known as the "mad emperor." (The writers of his time all mention his insanity.) Caligula demanded that everyone in his empire worship him as a god. This was not an unusual demand from Roman emperors, but it put Jews, with their belief in the one God, in an impossible situation.

Meanwhile, a few Alexandrians of Greek descent—who considered themselves the only true Alexandrians—saw Caligula's madness and Flaccus's uncertainty as an opportunity to regain control of the city. They also wanted to limit the political and economic power of Alexandria's Jews. To achieve those goals, they needed to stir up tensions in the city.

Why were there Greeks in an Egyptian city? They were descendants of the city's founders, who had arrived when Alexander the Great conquered Egypt in about 331 BCE. The Greeks took pride in the fact that Alexandria had become a major center of Greek culture. It was home to two of the world's earliest and largest public libraries—one in a temple to the Greek god Zeus and the other in a museum. The two buildings housed at least 500,000 scrolls at a time when each scroll was painstakingly written by hand. The first university in the Middle East developed around the museum and attracted scholars in mathematics, medicine, and literature from Asia, Africa, and Europe.

The Jews of Alexandria were equally proud of the city. They too saw themselves as true Alexandrians, and they made up about 40 percent of the city's population. During the 300 years that the Greeks ruled Egypt, Jews had taken an active part in the city's economic, political, and cultural life. Among them were merchants, scholars, bankers, government officials, and army officers. A few Jews had become generals and trusted advisers to Egypt's Greek rulers; many more were ordinary people—peasant farmers, artisans, sailors, soldiers, and traders.

In many respects, the Jews of Alexandria, like the Jews of Elephantine 400 years earlier, could not be distinguished from their neighbors, particularly their Greek neighbors. They too had Greek names, wore Greek clothing, and spoke the Greek language. In fact, so many Jews in Alexandria spoke only Greek that the Hebrew Scriptures were translated into Greek for their benefit. Yet they remained Jews.

After the Romans conquered Egypt in 30 BCE, Roman emperors continued to recognize the right of Jews to practice their religion, even though this meant that they would not honor the many gods of Rome. Jews, like other groups in the city, also had some political rights, including a degree of self-government as a separate ethnic group within Alexandria. But they were not full citizens; only Greeks and Romans had that status under Roman law.

© The Israel Museum, by David Harris

A glass base from Alexandria. The Greeks and later the Romans welcomed Jews to Alexandria and other cities because of their skill as glassmakers. In Alexandria, Jews turned that craft into a major industry.

Alexandria's Jews were, however, permitted to send money to Jerusalem for the upkeep of the Temple. Many of them also made the long, often dangerous journey to Jerusalem for Passover, Shavuot, or Sukkot—the great pilgrimage festivals of ancient Judaism.

Some Egyptians lived in Alexandria as well, and they too considered themselves the only true Alexandrians even though they had even fewer rights than Greeks or Jews. As a result, they were increasingly resentful of their Roman conquerors and also of the Jews, Greeks, and other foreigners who supported those conquerors. They were outraged that outsiders had a higher status than they did.

Over the years, religious issues had heightened political tensions among these various groups in Alexandria. For example, Jews regarded the story of their ancestors' exodus from Egypt, led by Moses, as a key event in their history. Each year at Passover, then as now, Jews recalled the days when they were slaves of the pharaoh in Egypt.

Not surprisingly, many Egyptians disliked this story; it made their ruler, the pharaoh, seem weak. In fact, in the third century BCE, Manetho, an Egyptian priest in Alexandria, wrote an alternative version of history in which the pharaoh was the hero and Moses the villain. It was the first of several such accounts by Egyptian writers that conflicted with Jewish beliefs.

In the first decades of the Common Era, Apion, a Greek lawyer in Alexandria, wrote and spoke against Jews. He claimed that they were a "diseased race of lepers" and a "godless" people who worshipped the head of an ass in their Temple in Jerusalem. He insisted that once a year, Jews kidnapped a Greek and fattened him up so that he could be sacrificed to their deity.[3] These and other false charges would find their way from Alexandria to Rome and, eventually, into the works of Roman and, later, Christian writers.

But even as some Greeks, like Apion, concocted false accusations about the Jews, many other Greeks were attracted to Jewish life. In much of the Middle East, life, particularly public life, was lived outdoors. When Jews gathered to pray or read from the Torah, they often did so in Greek, not Hebrew. Passersby could not only listen to the service but also understand its meaning. Many non-Jews attended Jewish services regularly, and a number of them traveled to Jerusalem for the great pilgrimage festivals. The Temple even had a special section set aside for their use. Some non-Jews in Alexandria and elsewhere became Jews; others observed Jewish festivals and commandments without a formal conversion.

A few Greeks and, later, Romans were alarmed by the interest of ordinary Alexandrians in Jewish religious practice. They viewed that interest as a threat to the state. They expected everyone in the city to pay homage to the emperor's gods as an expression of loyalty. They saw the refusal of Jews—and, later, Christians—to participate as both foolish and potentially disloyal.

Still, many historians note that for the most part, neither Greek nor Roman writers singled out Jews as targets for hatred; they had similarly negative views of other minority groups. Historians also point out that most writers at that time, including Jewish writers, tended to praise the virtues of their own group while denying the virtues of others. It was part of the usual style of rhetoric of the times, and, indeed, the same kind of hate-filled rhetoric can be heard today in places where groups are in conflict.

Nevertheless, Jews were different in certain ways from the people around them. They were the only group that consistently refused to acknowledge the gods of their neighbors, send gifts to their temples, or participate in festivals honoring those gods. Jews alone insisted on worshipping the one God. And they alone refused to work on one particular day each week; to some outsiders, Jews' insistence on observing their Sabbath was a sign of laziness or even religious absurdity. Perhaps it is not surprising, then, that malicious lies about Jews gained acceptance among many people.

Tension between Jews and their neighbors was heightened in August of 38 CE, when Agrippa I, the Roman-appointed Jewish king of Judea, stopped in Alexandria on his way to Rome. Jews celebrated his visit, but Greeks and Egyptians responded with riots and demonstrations. According to Philo, three prominent Greeks in the city—Isidoros, Dionysios, and Lampon—told Flaccus, the city's Roman governor, that Agrippa's visit was a sign that Flaccus's own days in power were numbered. They accused Agrippa and other Jews of causing trouble and questioned their loyalty to Rome.

Flaccus, worried about his own relationship with Caligula, the new emperor, did nothing to stop the violence that the Greeks incited. In fact, he encouraged it by ordering that statues of Caligula be placed in every Jewish house of worship. The Jews of Alexandria were outraged; they closed their synagogues rather than allow them to be desecrated in this way. Flaccus retaliated by taking away the political and religious privileges that Jews had enjoyed for more than 300 years. He declared that Jews were aliens in Alexandria—which meant that they were considered outsiders with no right to government protection.

The Greeks and Egyptians in Alexandria understood Flaccus's announcement to mean that they could now treat Jews as they pleased.

After all, people without rights cannot appeal to the authorities for help or seek justice on their own. In the days that followed, well-organized mobs attacked Jews with stones and clubs and forced them into a single section of the city. According to Philo, Flaccus encouraged the rioting by publicly executing a number of Jewish leaders.

When the emperor Caligula learned what was happening in Alexandria, he ordered Flaccus's arrest. Flaccus was brought to Rome, where he was tried and convicted. To the surprise of many, his main accusers were Isidoros, Dionysios, and Lampon, the same Greeks from Alexandria who had encouraged his attacks on the Jews. The attack on the Jews and the one on Flaccus were part of an effort to restore power to the city's Greek community.

The removal of Flaccus did not calm Alexandria. Both the Jews and the Greeks sent delegations to Rome to plead their case before the emperor. For Jews, the issue centered on their political and religious rights. They had been second-class citizens under the Greeks. Many now wanted to become full citizens of Alexandria.

While the delegations were still in Rome, Caligula was assassinated and a new emperor, Claudius, was named. Alexandrians responded to the news by resuming the violence. This time, the Jews armed themselves and fought back. The fighting was so ferocious that some have called it a war. Determined to end the conflict, Claudius issued an order addressed to the people of Alexandria in 41 CE; his words were read aloud throughout the city. The order stated, in part:

> *With regard to the responsibility for the disturbances and rioting, or rather, to speak the truth, the war, against the Jews, although your ambassadors, particularly Dionysios the son of Theon, argued vigorously and at length in the disputation, I have not wished to make an exact inquiry, but I harbor within me a store of immutable indignation against those who renewed the conflict. I merely say that, unless you stop this destructive and obstinate mutual enmity, I shall be forced to show what a benevolent ruler can be when he is turned to righteous indignation. Even now, therefore, I [urge] the Alexandrians to behave gently and kindly toward the Jews who have inhabited the same city for many years, and not to dishonor any of their customs in their worship of their god, but to allow them to keep their own ways, as they did in the time of the god Augustus and as I too, having heard both sides, have confirmed.*

The Jews, on the other hand, I order not to aim at more than they have previously had, . . . and not to intrude themselves into the games presided over by the [Greeks], since they enjoy what is their own, and in a city which is not their own they possess an abundance of all good things. Nor are they to bring in or invite Jews coming from Syria or [other parts of] Egypt, or I shall be forced to conceive graver suspicions. If they disobey, I shall proceed against them in every way as seeking to spread a sort of public sickness throughout the world.

If you both give up your present ways and are willing to live in gentleness and kindness with one another, I for my part will do for the city as much as I can, as one that has long been closely connected with us.[4]

Despite Claudius's edict, Greeks, Jews, and Egyptians continued to jockey for power in Alexandria. And the rhetoric that had roused such strong feelings in Alexandria resonated throughout the Roman Empire. As a result, the violence that began in Alexandria in 38 CE spread to other parts of the empire, including Judea.

WARS WITH ROME

Roman emperors recognized the right of Jews to practice their religion because it predated the Roman Empire, but they failed to understand why Jews stubbornly refused to accept Roman gods. So, from time to time, an emperor would try to force Jews to accept him as a god, as Caligula had done. Jews were outraged by such demands. Many of them came to view the Roman conquest as a religious insult. The Romans, in turn, often regarded the Jews' refusal to accept Roman gods as an act of disloyalty.

An incident that took place in 4 BCE reveals how swiftly and brutally the Romans responded to any sign of rebellion. That year, several Jewish groups in Judea mounted small uprisings. Roman soldiers responded by sweeping through the countryside, raping women, killing villagers, and destroying nearly everything in their path. In Jerusalem, the Romans executed anyone even suspected of taking part in the uprisings. They killed the rebels by nailing them to crosses and then leaving them to die a slow and horrific death. According to Josephus Flavius, a Jewish general who sided with the Romans and later became a historian, the Romans erected 2,000 crosses just outside the gates of Jerusalem after putting down the revolt. On each cross hung a Jew. The message was clear.

In 66 CE, 25 years after Claudius's edict to the Alexandrians, Jews in Judea once again launched a revolt against Rome. Known as the Great Rebellion, it was a fight that many Jews were convinced they could not win; they had too few soldiers, weapons, and other resources. They were also divided among themselves, each group with its own view of Jewish law and its own ideas about the best way to handle Rome. Some Jews believed that they had to go to war to stop the Romans from violating the Temple. Others thought a war would be suicidal. Like so many rebellions in history, a struggle for liberation became a civil war as Jews fought each other as well as the Romans.

The war ended with the destruction of the second Temple on the ninth day of the Jewish month of Av in 70 CE. Josephus, who witnessed the fighting, described what happened that day:

> *While the holy house was on fire, everything was plundered that came to hand, and ten thousand of those that were caught were slain; nor was there a commiseration of any age, or any reverence of gravity; but children, and old men, and profane persons, and priests, were all slain in the same manner. . . . The flame was also carried a long way, and made an echo, together with the groans of those that were slain; and because this hill was high, and the works at the temple were very great, one would have thought that the whole city had been on fire. Nor can one imagine anything either greater or more terrible than this noise; for there was at once a shout of the Roman legions, who were marching all together, and a sad clamour of the seditious, who were now surrounded with fire and sword.*[5]

Anger over the Romans' disrespect for Jewish customs and beliefs continued to smolder for decades. Between 115 and 117 CE, Jews in Alexandria and other cities along the coast of North Africa began their own rebellions against Rome. Like the Great Rebellion in Judea, these ended in defeat. A few years later, in 123 CE, Jews in Judea once again tried to break away from Rome by launching a series of surprise attacks. The Romans responded by sending to Judea an army legion (a force of 3,000 to about 6,000 soldiers) to put down the rebellion.

Then, in about 132 CE, the emperor Hadrian announced a plan to rename Jerusalem Aelia Capitolina, in part to honor the Roman god Jupiter Capitolinus. Hadrian also planned to build a temple in honor of Jupiter where the Jewish Temple had stood. These and other acts of contempt toward Jews and their religion prompted a new rebellion.

Jewish rebels under the leadership of Shimon Bar-Kokhba captured 50 fortified Jewish towns and 985 undefended villages and towns, including Jerusalem. Jews from other countries and even some non-Jews joined the anti-Roman rebels. Early victories inspired Jews to mint coins with slogans such as "The freedom of Israel" written in Hebrew. But the war was not over.

The turning point came when Hadrian sent to Judea one of his best generals, Julius Severus. His army included soldiers from Egypt, Britain, Syria, and other parts of the empire. Because of the size of the rebellion, Severus did not attack directly. Instead, he surrounded the fortresses to keep food and water from reaching the people who lived behind the walls. Only when hunger had weakened the rebels did the Romans attack. In the end, they destroyed every single fortress and village held by the rebels.

The final battle of the war took place at Bethar, the city where Bar-Kokhba had his headquarters. Bethar was a military stronghold because of its strategic location on the main road to Jerusalem. It also housed the Sanhedrin (the Jewish high court). In 135 CE, Hadrian's army laid siege to the city. Its walls are said to have fallen on the ninth day in the Hebrew month of Av, the Jewish fast day that commemorates the destruction of the first and second Temples. Every Jew in the city was slaughtered—children, women, and men.

The Jewish war was now essentially over. Hadrian changed the country's name from Judea to Palestine. He also demolished the city of Jerusalem and forced thousands of Jews into slavery. According to a Roman decree, Jews could not rebuild the city or live there. Only Romans had that right. Jews were permitted to enter only on the ninth day of Av to mourn the loss of the Temple.

ANTISEMITISM IN THE ROMAN EMPIRE?

In the first and second centuries, the Romans ruled an empire that was greater than any the world had yet known. It included not only much of the Middle East but also a large part of Europe. Within that empire, many groups continuously competed for power and influence. The Romans sometimes encouraged these rivalries, because this helped them maintain control of their empire.

Statements about Jews like those made by Egyptians, Greeks, and Romans sound strongly antisemitic today. But it is not clear that people in those days were antisemitic in the sense that the term is currently used. In some ways it appears that Jews were treated no differently from other groups conquered by the Romans, even though the customs and practices that set Jews apart from other groups, such as their monotheism, were a recurring source of tension and even hostility.

Still, many of the key elements that define modern antisemitism can be traced to this time in history. A variety of stereotypes and myths lie at the heart of every hatred, including antisemitism. Stereotypes are the labels "we" attach to "them" and the assumptions "we" make about "them"— sometimes without ever meeting "them." In this context, myths are lies based on those faulty assumptions, and they tend to endure because they appeal to strong emotions rather than to reason.

Both the Greeks and the Romans created stereotypes that dehumanized and demonized Jews as a group. Those stereotypes persisted long after the empires of Greece and Rome had crumbled. The Romans also claimed that Jews were conspiring to take over their empire, even though Jews in the ancient Middle East were a small minority with few allies. Over the course of many centuries, that myth would acquire a deadly force that undermined the usual "live and let live" attitudes of many rulers.

---

[1] Peter Schäfer, *Judeophobia: Attitudes toward the Jews in the Ancient World* (Cambridge, MA: Harvard University Press, 1997), 123.

[2] Philo, *Against Flaccus*, 66–68, quoted in Joseph Mélèze Modrzejewski, *The Jews of Egypt from Ramses II to Emperor Hadrian*, trans. Robert Cornman (Philadelphia: Jewish Publication Society, 1995), 148.

[3] *Contra Apionem*, trans. H. St. J. Thackeray, LCL, 2: 91–96 in Schäfer, *Judeophobia*, 63–4.

[4] London Papyrus VI 1912, CP Jud., 2:153, lines 73–104, quoted Modrzejewski, *The Jews of Egypt from Ramses II to Emperor Hadrian*, 182.

[5] William Whiston, trans., "The Wars of the Jews," in Flavius Josephus, *The Complete Works of Josephus* (Grand Rapids: Kregel Publications, 1960), 581.

2

Separation: Synagogue and Church,
Jew and Christian

(29–414 CE)

In the first century of the Common Era, Jesus of Nazareth lived as a Jew among Jews. He prayed in the synagogue, observed Jewish laws (including the dietary laws), and probably wore the fringes on his clothing (*tzitziot* in Hebrew) as required for Jewish men. His earliest followers did the same. Yet by the end of the fourth century, Jesus's followers had left the synagogue and established a new religion known as Christianity. (The word *Christianity* refers to a religion based on the life and teachings of Jesus Christ. *Christ* was not part of Jesus's name, though his followers soon began using it that way. It is a title that comes from the Greek word meaning "anointed" or "chosen." The English word *messiah* comes from a Hebrew word that has the same meaning.)

The separation of Christianity from Judaism did not happen simply or quickly. It was not a single event but rather a sometimes painful process that took generations to complete. And in this separation can be found the roots of hostility between Jews and Christians and the roots of some aspects of modern antisemitism.

JESUS AND HIS FOLLOWERS

Little is known about the early life of Jesus. He was raised in the Jewish town of Nazareth, less than 100 miles north of Jerusalem in the area known as Galilee. By all accounts, Jesus lived as a Jew and, like other Jews, obeyed the laws of the Torah. At about the age of 30, he began his ministry and was often referred to as "rabbi" (meaning "teacher").

Jesus was also killed as a Jew. Crucifixion was a method of execution commonly used by the Romans. In 4 BCE, the Romans crushed a Jewish revolt and crucified 2,000 Jewish rebels outside the walls of Jerusalem (see Chapter 1). It was the Romans, in fact, who crucified Jesus as a Jewish troublemaker.

For centuries, "the Jews" have been held responsible for Jesus's death. Did they actually play any part in it? Many scholars point out that only the Romans had the power or authority to put Jesus to death. Furthermore, the very question suggests that Jews were a united people with some influence over Rome in the first century of the Common Era. But in fact, Jews at that time were deeply divided over issues of faith and practice. Jews who held similar views banded together; many of these groups were intolerant of Jews with different views. Only a few had ties to the Romans.

If any Jews were involved in Jesus's death, they were probably Sadducees—a group associated with the high priests and other leaders of the Temple in Jerusalem. But the Sadducees certainly did not speak or act for the Pharisees, who seem to have been scrupulous in observance of traditional Jewish laws and whose concern for common people put them in opposition to the Sadducees. Nor did they speak for the Essenes, who abandoned Jerusalem in protest against the way the Temple was being run.

Each of these and many other groups had its own idea of what it meant to be faithful to God's will and its own plan for the future of the Jewish people. Perhaps that is why Jesus's closest followers did not blame "the Jews" as a group for his death. They were Jews themselves and continued to live as Jews.

Many of Jesus's closest followers believed that God would intervene in history at the "end of days" by crushing injustice and evil and establishing peace on Earth. Then the dead would rise and the scattered people of Israel would return to their homeland. As the "end of days" neared, righteous Jews, as opposed to those who were sinful, would at first be in danger but would ultimately prevail under the leadership of a messiah. The followers of Jesus often reminded their fellow Jews that after the destruction of the first Temple in 586 BCE, the prophets had envisioned such a time.

After Jesus's crucifixion, those followers were more certain than ever before that they were living in the "end of days." They proclaimed amazing news: they had seen Jesus and he had talked with them and eaten with them. They believed his tomb was empty and he had been resurrected— that is, after God had raised Jesus from the dead, he ascended to heaven. These convictions gave new energy to the movement. Earlier, it had centered on Jesus's teachings. Now his followers reminded other Jews of the words of the prophets and insisted that Jesus was the "anointed one," the "son of God" who would return to fulfill those promises.

In the months and years that followed Jesus's death, small groups of Jews met regularly to pray together and discuss his teachings. Among them were James and Peter, two of Jesus's disciples, or followers. They tried to share their understanding of their messiah with fellow Jews in synagogues and other gathering places. Convinced that the Day of Judgment was near, they urgently sought not only to be faithful to Jesus's teachings but also to persuade as many people as possible to join in their hope and expectations. In doing so, they reached out to gentiles, or non-Jews, as well as to their fellow Jews. Gradually, the Jesus movement became one that included both Jews and gentiles.

The main leader in the effort to bring Jesus's teachings to non-Jews was Paul. Originally named Saul, Paul was a devout Jew who had studied with the great Pharisee sages. He described himself as "a Hebrew born of Hebrews." He had been a fierce opponent of the Jesus movement in its early years and had tried to stamp it out as heresy, until a vision led him to embrace the very faith that he had previously condemned. Eventually Paul brought the message about Jesus to Jews and non-Jews in major cities around the eastern Mediterranean and the Aegean Sea.

Some of Paul's ideas were controversial. For example, he thought that he and other Jewish believers in Jesus, later called Christians, should continue to honor many of the laws of Judaism, but gentiles did not have to convert to Judaism in order to become Christians. Paul did not say that Christianity should replace Judaism, even though others later claimed that he had said this. Instead he spoke of the mystery of God's working for the salvation of all. And even though he did compare Jews who rejected Jesus to branches cut off from the tree that had nurtured them, Paul cautioned non-Jewish Christians to show respect to Jews as a people who had a covenant, or agreement, with God.

At first many Christian leaders disagreed with Paul's ideas on conversion, but they eventually agreed that converts to Christianity did not have to come to God through the Torah as Jews did but could reach God directly through Jesus. Paul's explanation of what it meant to be a Christian opened the new religion to many more people, and Christianity began to grow rapidly in the large cities of the Roman Empire.

A GROWING SEPARATION

When the Romans destroyed the second Temple in 70 CE, about 40 to 45 years after Jesus's death, some Christians saw the destruction as a sign from God. In their view, it confirmed their belief that as Christians, they were now the "true Israel." They believed that God had allowed the Temple to be destroyed in order to punish Jews for rejecting Jesus.

Other Jews also saw the destruction of the Temple as a sign from God, but they interpreted that sign differently. They took it to mean that Jews needed to atone for their sins by rededicating themselves to a stricter observance of Jewish law. They believed the destruction was proof that the bitter arguments and divisions among Jews had only served to harm the Jewish people as a whole and strengthen the power of Rome. They called for a return to traditional Jewish rituals and practices, emphasizing moral values and the rule of law.

In the years after the destruction of the second Temple, only two major Jewish groups, or sects, survived—the Pharisees and the followers of Jesus. The Pharisees' emphasis on traditional Jewish law contributed to the development of rabbinic Judaism—the Judaism practiced in homes and synagogues by many Jews in the world today. Rabbinic Judaism places great importance on what Jews call "the tradition of the fathers"—the non-biblical laws and customs passed down orally and by example from one generation to the next.

As part of his mission to spread and explain the teachings of Jesus, Paul wrote letters, or epistles, to Christians throughout the Roman Empire. Scholars have used those letters, along with other New Testament writings, to trace changes in the relationship between Jews and early Christians. The Gospels, which are the first four books in the New Testament, describe Jesus' life. Most scholars believe the four books were written between 68 and 100 CE—40 to 70 years after the crucifixion. Paul's epistles were written somewhat earlier, between 50 and 60 CE.

Paul wrote mainly about the meaning and the effects of Jesus's teaching, often in response to questions from and crises in the communities to whom his letters were addressed. The Gospels, on the other hand, are compilations of oral material about Jesus's teachings and about his life, death, and resurrection. It is customary to attribute each of the Gospels to individual early Christians called Matthew, Mark, Luke, and John, but most scholars now believe that none of the Gospels actually had a single author or even a single editor.

Jesus did not write down his teachings. He spoke Aramaic—the everyday language of Jews in Galilee in his day. The authors and editors of the Gospels most likely lived in the large Greek-speaking cities of the Diaspora, and they wrote in Greek. When stories are translated from one language to another, changes inevitably occur, and when those stories are passed on orally, the changes are even more numerous. No original manuscripts of the Gospels survive; the earliest existing versions are small portions of handwritten copies made in the second and third

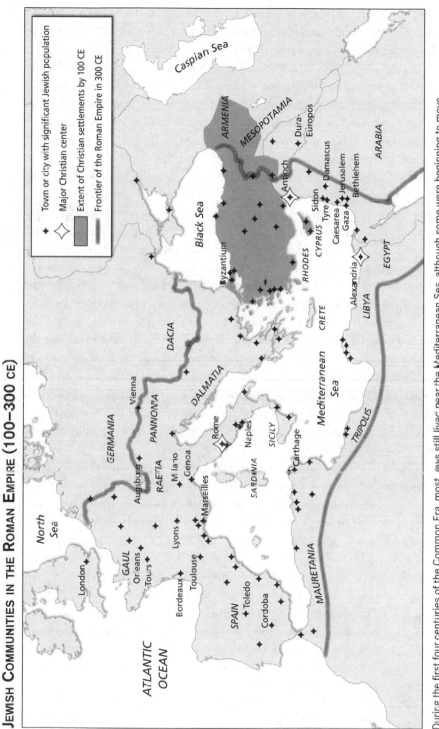

JEWISH COMMUNITIES IN THE ROMAN EMPIRE (100–300 CE)

Legend:
- Town or city with significant Jewish population
- Major Christian center
- Extent of Christian settlements by 100 CE
- Frontier of the Roman Empire in 300 CE

During the first four centuries of the Common Era, most Jews still lived near the Mediterranean Sea, although some were beginning to move into western Europe.

centuries CE. As a result, the texts that have come down from the early centuries are usually copies of copies of copies, each with different scribes who sometimes produced differing wordings at key places.

Each Gospel tells approximately the same story, emphasizing different ideas and sometimes interpreting the same events in different ways. At one time there were as many as twenty Gospels. The early church chose the four that it believed were the most authentic, along with other writings from its own history, to form the New Testament. Those four Gospels are referred to as the "canonical" Gospels.

The Gospel according to John, the last of the four Gospels, differs significantly from those of Matthew, Mark, and Luke. In the earlier Gospels, Jesus is shown debating questions of Jewish law with the Pharisees. Although these disagreements are depicted as often heated, they take place within Judaism among Jews. Jesus acts as a rabbi; he is not portrayed as separating himself from Jews whose views differ from his. The Gospel of John, however, portrays Jesus as the revelation of God and views those who disagree with him as enemies of God, choosing the darkness over the light.

The earliest Gospels suggest that a number of Jewish groups, or sects, collaborated with Pontius Pilate, the Roman governor, in calling for the death of Jesus. In John's Gospel, the story shifts from a description of Jesus's disputes with individuals and groups—Pharisees, scribes, and high priests—to an angry attack on "the Jews" and their beliefs. Some historians think that change in tone may reflect the experience of the community in which John's Gospel arose. Jews may have expelled that community from the synagogue because of its beliefs about Jesus.

Other historians think that the change in tone may reflect the times. By the end of the first century, when the Gospel of John was probably written, some Christians no longer saw themselves as Jews; indeed, by this time, many Christians never had been Jews. The churches were becoming more gentile and less Jewish. It is possible, too, that the writers of this Gospel hoped to prevent Roman persecution of Christians and perhaps even to convert Romans to the teachings of Jesus. Thus, they may have thought it would be helpful to place the responsibility for Jesus's death on someone other than the Roman governor—namely, "the Jews." Yet many Christians at that time were aware that Jews lacked the power or authority to kill Jesus or any other "troublemaker." Furthermore, only the Romans used crucifixions to deal with their enemies. Jews saw the practice as contrary to their traditions and beliefs.

Rome allowed Jews to practice their religion, even though many Roman leaders considered Jews barbaric and superstitious. And as long as Christians were considered a group within Judaism, they had the same rights as other Jews. But as Christians separated from Judaism, many Jews began to insist that Christians could no longer claim to be Jews. As a result, the Romans began persecuting Christians as a threat to the empire. After all, Christians were proclaiming the teachings of Jesus, a man the Romans had crucified as a troublemaker.

Many scholars believe that Jews began to view Christians as outsiders at least partly because they felt betrayed by Jewish believers-in-Jesus who had left Jerusalem for the safer countryside during the rebellion of 66–70 CE that led to the destruction of the second Temple. Most early Christians, influenced by the example of Jesus, believed in nonviolence and therefore refused to fight under any circumstances. Some also believed that fighting would be useless because the terrible events of that time were the inevitable beginning of the "end of days"—the period just before the coming of the messiah.

Another sign of the times is the way the Pharisees are described in the Gospels. They are shown as rigid, overly pious, and often hypocritical. The Pharisees were only one of several Jewish sects in Jesus's time, yet they are often portrayed as his major opponents, even though some scholars believe they were the group with whom he had the most in common. The high priests who belonged to the Jewish sect known as the Sadducees were Jesus's more likely opponents, but many of them were killed during the wars with Rome. It was only after the destruction of the Temple in

The menorah indicates that this sarcophagus (stone coffin) belonged to a Jew—in this case, one who lived in Rome in the first century of the Common Era.

© Erich Lessing / Art Resource, NY

70 CE that the Pharisees gained religious supremacy. At the time that the early Gospels were written, the Pharisees and the early Christians were competing for the hearts and minds of their fellow Jews.

In the years after 70 CE, Jewish survivors of the war with Rome tried to unite all Jews under the leadership of rabbis and sages. Terms like *Pharisee* or *Sadducee* tended to divide Jews rather than bring them together, and they were now used much less often. Synagogues and houses of study became more central to Jewish life, as prayer and study replaced the animal sacrifices that had been the focus of worship in the destroyed Temple.

During those years, rabbis and sages began to collect and edit the non-biblical laws and customs that made up the oral traditions of Judaism. The work they created is known as the Mishnah—a vast collection of centuries' worth of oral laws and customs. It was completed in Palestine in 200 CE. Jewish scholars in Palestine and Babylonia also began to compile commentaries on the Torah and the Mishnah. Those commentaries are known as the Talmud.

Although the rabbis rarely spoke of Christians in their writing and preaching, they, like many Jews, had strong feelings about them, particularly as the number of gentiles associated with the Christian movement increased. The war with Rome in 66–70 CE was one of several critical events that shaped the relationship between Christians and Jews. The process of separation did not happen everywhere in the same way or even at the same time.

A few scholars trace the formal separation to a decision made in Yavne, a town in Palestine, in 80 CE. Rabbis and sages, continuing the earlier work of the Pharisees, had gathered there to compile the Mishnah. They added a new blessing to the *Shemoneh Esreh*, the Eighteen Benedictions (blessings) that observant Jews recite three times a day. This new blessing referred to Jews who still practiced Judaism but believed that Jesus was the messiah as heretics. Some scholars believe that this condemnation may have contributed to the growing separation between the new and old religions.

Other scholars disagree. They argue that the prayer has had many variations in wording over the centuries and it is unlikely that Jews recited it in exactly the same way in every synagogue in Palestine or anywhere else. Many also note that in some places, Christians continued to worship in both synagogues and churches well into the third century of the Common Era.

Nevertheless, gradually, slowly, what had begun as a debate among Jews was becoming a disagreement between members of two separate religions. Both Christians and Jews began to define themselves and their religion by emphasizing the differences between the two groups. One of the first Christian writers to do so was Melito, a bishop in Sardis, a city in what is now Turkey.

In about 167 CE, Melito gave a sermon entitled "Homily on the Passover." He argued that by "crucifying Jesus," "the Jews" had "murdered God," and therefore the Jewish people as a whole were guilty of the crime. His homily is the first known use of the deicide charge (as the accusation was later known). His goal was not to incite violence against Jews but to strengthen the Christian identity of his parishioners by turning "us" against "them." At the time, Christians in Sardis and other parts of the Roman Empire were an often-persecuted minority with virtually no power. Only in later centuries, when Christians actually had political power, would Melito's words be used to justify discrimination, persecution, and murder.

At the end of the second century CE and the beginning of the third, Jews and Christians often lived side by side in the major cities of the Roman Empire. The Romans determined how each group was regarded, and attitudes toward both groups varied greatly. In the early years of the second century, the Roman historian Tacitus had described Jews as "vulgar" and "superstitious." But by the beginning of the third century, another Roman historian, Dio Cassius, noted that although Jews had "frequently been persecuted," they had prospered. He also wrote:

> *They succeeded in winning the right to observe their laws freely. They are distinguished from the rest of mankind in practically every detail of their way of life, and especially in that they honor none of the other gods, but show extreme reverence for one particular deity. They never had a statue of him even in Jerusalem itself, but believing him to be unnamable and invisible they worship him in the most extravagant way among humans. They built him a large and splendid temple . . . and dedicated to him the day called the day of Saturn [Saturday] on which, among many other most peculiar observances, they undertake no serious occupation.*[1]

THE FOURTH CENTURY: A TURNING POINT

In 312 CE, a battle for control of the Roman Empire had a profound impact on relationships among Christians, Jews, and Romans. As one version of the story goes, on the night before the soon-to-be-emperor Constantine planned to attack a rival for the throne, he saw a cross in the sky. Above that cross were these words: "In this sign, conquer." Constantine, who was not a Christian, interpreted the vision as a sign that the Christian God would bring him victory in his fight for control of the western part of the empire. The next day his troops won the battle and Constantine ordered his men to continue to fight under the sign of the cross.

Though some scholars think that the story of Constantine's vision is more legend than fact, it is clear that the new emperor wanted to end Roman persecution of Christians. In 314 CE, Constantine and Licinius Augustus (the two men ruled the empire jointly) proclaimed a new law. Known as the Edict of Milan, it states, in part:

> *When I, Constantine Augustus, as well as I, Licinius Augustus, had fortunately met near Mediolanurn (Milan), and were considering everything that pertained to the public welfare and security, we thought that, among other things which we saw would be for the good of many, those regulations pertaining to the reverence of the Divinity ought certainly to be made first, so that we might grant to the Christians and to all others full authority to observe that religion which each preferred. . . . [I]t has pleased us to remove all conditions whatsoever . . . concerning the Christians, and now any one of these who wishes to observe the Christian religion may do so freely and openly, without any disturbance or molestation. We thought it fit to commend these things most fully to your care that you may know that we have given to those Christians free and unrestricted opportunity of religious worship. When you see that this has been granted to them by us, [you] will know that we have also conceded to other religions the right of open and free observance of their worship for the sake of the peace of our times, that each one may have the free opportunity to worship as he pleases; this regulation is made that we may not seem to detract . . . from any dignity or any religion.[2]*

Constantine's edict gave Christians the right to openly practice their faith. Until then, they had met in the homes of fellow believers. Within a year of the edict, Constantine ordered the building of churches throughout the empire. With new churches came a more formal organization.

Although some Christians worried about the future of the church if it became too closely identified with the empire, most Christians were pleased with Constantine's edict. It meant an end to the persecutions they had suffered from time to time and new access to power and influence. Other groups saw reason to worry. The only people the edict mentioned by name were the Christians, and the laws that came afterward radically limited the rights of Jews as citizens of the Roman Empire. For example, in the year 315, Constantine issued the following edict:

> *We wish to make it known to the Jews and their elders and their patri-archs that if, after the enactment of this law, any one of them dares to attack with stones or some other manifestation of anger another who has fled their dangerous sect and attached himself to the worship of God [Christianity], he must speedily be given to flames and burn— together with all his accomplices.*

> *Moreover, if any one of the population should join their abominable sect and attend their meetings, he will bear with them the deserved penalties.*[3]

This law had two purposes. One was to prevent Jews from interfering with relatives or friends who converted to Christianity. The other was to discourage Christians from converting to Judaism.

Constantine's description of Judaism as "dangerous" and "abominable" is very different from the opinions expressed a century earlier by Dio Cassius, who seemed to regard Jews with respect, toleration, and curiosity. Edicts issued by later emperors reflected Constantine's views. Increasingly, Jews were regarded with disrespect, intolerance, and disgust.

By 325 CE, Constantine had absolute power in Rome; in ancient times this meant both political and religious power. That year he summoned 250 Christian bishops to a council in Nicaea, a city in present-day Turkey. The council began by adopting a creed—a statement of common beliefs. The Nicene Creed expresses a belief in God, in Jesus Christ as the son of God, and in the Holy Spirit. But the bishops of the church went beyond simply defining what Christians believe. At this and later councils, they also moved to distinguish Christianity from Judaism. For example, early Christians, like other Jews, had observed the Sabbath on the seventh day of the week and then celebrated Jesus's resurrection with special gather- ings and meals on the first day of the week (Saturday night or Sunday). Now the council insisted that Christians would observe only Sunday and not the traditional Jewish Sabbath. The bishops also separated Christian commemorations of Easter from Jewish observances of Passover (the Jewish festival during which Jesus was crucified).

Today it seems clear that Christians were creating a separation between the two faiths and that Jews were undoubtedly doing the same.

To Christians, Jews, and other groups in the fourth century, the significance of the separation was probably not so obvious.

In the 300s, the anti-Jewish laws issued by Constantine and his successors were rarely enforced. To confuse matters further, a number of later emperors granted Jews new privileges even as they issued laws that took away older privileges. Constantine himself gave rabbis and other Jewish religious leaders a status equal to that of Christian religious leaders.

Then, in 361 CE, the unthinkable happened. A man who did not consider himself a Christian became emperor of Rome. Julian, who had studied both Christianity and Greek philosophy, declared an end to the Christian empire of Constantine and set out to restore Rome to its traditional gods. It was a move that appealed to many people in the empire. In the fourth century, Christians were by no means in the majority.

As part of his return to traditional ways, Julian tried to undermine the Christian claim that Christianity had replaced Judaism. One way to do this was to rebuild the Temple in Jerusalem. Julian opened Jerusalem to Jews again and allowed them to govern themselves. They had just begun work on the Temple when he died during an invasion of Persia in 363.

Valentian, the new emperor, was a Christian who quickly took away the rights and privileges Julian had granted Jews and restored those of Christians. Nevertheless, Julian's reign had frightened many Christians. They worried that it might signal the beginning of a new anti-Christian era. As a result of these fears, they renewed their efforts to convert pagans and, at the same time, launched new attacks on Jews.

In 388, for example, a mob of Christians led by their bishop set fire to a synagogue in Callinicum, a town on the Euphrates River in what is now Iraq. When Theodosius (who was then emperor) learned of the incident, he ordered the bishop of Callinicum to rebuild the synagogue and to punish those who had participated in the incident. When Ambrose (later St. Ambrose), the powerful bishop of Milan, learned of the emperor's stand, he sent a letter scolding Theodosius for favoring the synagogue, a "home of unbelief, a house of impiety, a receptacle of folly." Laws that protected synagogues were wrong, he thundered, and should be annulled or disobeyed. Ambrose announced that he would not give the sacraments to Theodosius unless the emperor canceled his order. Reluctant to challenge the bishop, Theodosius did as Ambrose wished.

Historians sometimes use this incident to show how the status of Jews in the fourth century deteriorated. However, the truth is more complicated. Five years later, in 393, Theodosius issued a rescript—a legally binding command that corrects an earlier decision. In it, he said that "the sect of the Jews is forbidden by no law." Explaining this decision, he said that it was prompted by the efforts of some Christians in the east to "destroy and despoil the synagogues." This new ruling not only affirmed the right of Jews to assemble and to build synagogues but also prescribed punishments for those who attacked synagogues.

JEWISH CHRISTIANS AND JUDAIZING CHRISTIANS

The fourth century was a confusing time for other reasons as well. Not everyone participated in the mutual hostility between Jews and Christians. A number of Christians believed that a commitment to Christianity did not mean turning away from Jewish customs and traditions; they thought of such traditions as a connection to Jesus and his life. Among these people were both Jewish Christians—that is, Jews who believed in Jesus but continued to observe Jewish law—and Judaizing Christians, gentiles who adopted some Jewish practices.

Many leaders in the church, however, believed it was essential to widen the gap between followers of the two religions. They did not want Jewish Christians or Judaizing Christians to see value in Jewish customs and traditions. No Christian attacked the "Judaizing tendencies" within the church more vigorously than John Chrysostom (later St. John Chrysostom).

Chrysostom was born about 347 CE and lived in Antioch, a city founded by the Greeks in Syria in 300 BCE. He was considered the most persuasive preacher of his time; in fact, his title *Chrysostomos* is Greek for "golden-mouthed." He is remembered by many Christians for his courage in criticizing the rich and powerful and his compassion for the poor. In many of his sermons, he challenged injustice and denounced the comfortable arrogance of the wealthy.

Chrysostom also used his skill as an orator to attack, with vigor, the openness of many Christians to Jewish practices and faith—an openness that in Chrysostom's eyes meant a weakening of their specifically Christian identity. By the fourth century, Jews had been living in Antioch for more than 600 years and Christians for more than 200 years. Both groups were well established, with strong ties to one another. In fiery speeches, Chrysostom set out to cut those ties. He viciously attacked members of his own congregation—Christians who attended synagogues and observed Jewish festivals. He wanted to arouse in them a fear and disgust that would discourage any desire to Judaize.

How, Chrysostom asked, can Christians "have the slightest converse" with Jews, "the most miserable of all men"? He went on to describe Jews

© Art Resource, NY

Moses gives water to the tribes of Israel. The fresco was found in the remains of a synagogue in Syria. It dates to the third century, as does a nearby church. At that time, Jews and Christians often lived and prayed side by side.

as "inveterate murderers, destroyers, men possessed by the devil." To him, the synagogue was "a place of shame and ridicule," "the domicile of the devil." Indeed, he told his congregation that Jews worshipped the devil with rites that are "criminal and impure" and that the synagogue was "an assembly of criminals," "a den of thieves," and "a cavern of devils."

Why did Chrysostom believe Jews were degenerate? Because of their "odious assassination of Christ." And for this crime, Chrysostom declared, there was "no expiation possible, no indulgence, no pardon." In his view, the rejection and dispersal of the Jews was the work of God, not of emperors. He insisted that God had always hated the Jews, and therefore, on Judgment Day, God would say to Judaizers, "Depart from Me, for you have had dealings with murderers."[4]

Chrysostom's attacks had little to do with Jewish practice or belief. He was not interested in real Jews; it was the "Judaizing" Christians he was attacking. In opposing them, however, he demonized "the Jews." And he was not alone. Other Christian leaders in Chrysostom's day wrote in similar ways about Jews. Sophronius Eusebius Heironymus (later St. Jerome) was a monk who translated the Old Testament (the Christian name for the Hebrew scriptures) and the New Testament from Greek to Latin. His rhetoric was more subdued than Chrysostom's, but his message was similar: "The Jews . . . seek nothing but to have children, possess riches, and be healthy. They seek all earthly things but think nothing of heavenly things; for this reason they are mercenaries."[5]

Aurelius Augustinus (later St. Augustine), a leading theologian of the early church who lived about 50 years after Chrysostom, took a more complex view of Jews—a view that would have major consequences for the Jews of Europe. Augustine wrote that God had dispersed the Jews but had not destroyed them. In his view, God had kept Jews alive as a permanent reminder that Christianity had replaced Judaism as the true faith. He argued that the humiliated, defeated Jews showed what happens to those who reject God's truth.

Although Augustine did not want the Jews to be murdered, he did want them to suffer for what he claimed they had done to Jesus. And he wanted them to be present at the "end of days," when Jesus returned, so that they could see that they had been wrong. Like Chrysostom, Augustine described and defined Jews in terms of the purpose he thought they served for Christians—examples of the punishment inflicted by God on non-Christian believers. Such a view of Jews tended to deny their humanity and their existence as people with their own beliefs and purposes.

The language used by Chrysostom, Augustine, and other church leaders was designed to persuade Christians to cut all ties between themselves and Judaism. It had the desired effect. That language shaped attitudes and supported opinions long after the fourth century ended. It was also reflected in numerous acts of violence against Jews. As early as 414, church leaders in Alexandria led an assault on synagogues that destroyed the city's Jewish community for a time. Similar events occurred in other parts of the empire. The perpetrators were rarely punished. Increasingly, the tightening links between the political power of the Roman emperors and the religious power of church leaders left Jews isolated and vulnerable. More and more, they were viewed as outsiders—a status that would have a profound effect on Jewish life at other times and in other places.

[1] Dio Cassius, 37.17, quoted in Robert L. Wilken, *John Chrysostom and the Jews: Rhetoric and Reality in the Late 4th Century* (Berkeley: University of California Press, 1983), 47–48.

[2] "Edict of Milan (313 A. D.), Lactantius, De Mort. Pers., ch. 48. Opera, ed. O. F. Fritzsche, II, p. 288 sq. (Bibl. Patr. Ecc. Lat. XI). Latin," quoted in *Translations and Reprints from the Original Sources of European History,* vol. 4 (Philadelphia: The Department of History of the University of Pennsylvania, 1897–1907), 29.

[3] "Laws of Constantine the Great, October 18, 315: Concerning Jews, Heaven-Worshippers, And Samaritans" from "Jews and Later Roman Law, 315–531 CE," *Internet Jewish History Sourcebook,* Fordham University, Paul Halsall, http://www.fordham.edu/halsall/jewish/jews-romanlaw.html.

[4] John Chrysostom, "Chrysostom's Homilies Against the Jews."

[5] St. Jerome, quoted in Juster, *op. cit.,* II, 312, in Edward H. Flannery, *The Anguish of the Jews: Twenty-Three Centuries of Antisemitism,* rev. ed. (New York: Stimulus, 1999), 309.

3

Conquests and Consequences

(395–750 CE)

The way a people (whether an ethnic group, a nation, or a religious community) defines itself has enormous significance. That definition indicates who holds power in the group (such as rabbis or priests, kings and noblemen, or men in general) and how the group as a whole sees itself in relation to the larger world. It also determines who belongs and who does not. From the fourth through the eighth centuries of the Common Era, Jews in the Middle East and beyond were increasingly seen as outsiders—people who do not belong. That view had consequences in a world in which politics and religion were tightly linked.

WARRING EMPIRES

In 395 CE, the Roman Empire was formally divided into two parts. People in the western part, which included much of North Africa and parts of Spain, spoke mainly Latin; those in the east spoke mainly Greek. Although the western part of the empire eventually collapsed, the eastern part managed to survive and even expand. It became known as the Byzantine Empire, and its capital was Constantinople. (Byzantium was the site on which Constantine built Constantinople, which is now known as Istanbul.) To its east was the Persian Empire, which had dominated western Asia for more than a thousand years.

In the sixth and seventh centuries, the Byzantine and Persian Empires competed for land and power. To defeat its enemy, each needed money and armies. Each also demanded the loyalty of its people. In the Byzantine Empire, demands for loyalty were connected to an insistence on belonging to the dominant religion—Christianity. The two kinds of loyalty, religious and political, were intertwined. For example, the Christian governor of Carthage, a city located near modern-day Tunis in Tunisia, challenged the loyalty of his subjects with these words: "Are you servants of the emperor? If you are, you must be baptized."

Fragment of a bowl from the early Byzantine Empire. Both details, including a shofar (a ram's horn blown on some Jewish holidays) and an ark used to store the Torah, indicate it was made by or for Jews.

Byzantine rulers issued laws aimed at eliminating "the madness of Jewish impiety," "all heresies, all perfidies, and schisms," and "the error and insanity of stupid paganism." But many of these laws, though harsh, were not always enforced. In an empire that by the sixth century stretched from what is now Iraq in the east to Egypt and beyond in the west, there was always a gap between the written law and its enforcement.

However, when laws were enforced, punishments were swift and without mercy. For example, after riots broke out in Constantinople in 532, the emperor Justinian sent in troops to massacre all those involved— more than 30,000 people in all. Little is known about these riots or the people who participated in them. However, we do know how the emperor felt about the massacre. Procopius, a historian of the time, wrote that "Justinian did not see [the massacre] as murder if the victims did not share his own beliefs."

In the seventh century, similar riots took place within the Byzantine Empire; they provided the Persians with an opportunity to expand their own empire at the expense of their neighbor. In 611, the Persian army poured into what is now Syria and Palestine. In that year, they conquered Antioch; in 613, Damascus; and by 614, they were threatening Palestine. Throughout the region, the soldiers devastated cities and burned churches.

Many Jews in the Byzantine Empire welcomed the Persians. Some saw their arrival as an opportunity to win independence or even just a little more freedom. The official religion of the Persian Empire was Zoroastrianism (Zoroastrians are followers of the Iranian prophet Spitaman Zarathushtra, who lived and preached near the Aral Sea about 3,500 years ago). But the empire was home to many Jews, Christians, and Buddhists as well as Zoroastrians and pagans. So many Jews served in the Persian army that Persian commanders avoided going into battle on Jewish holy days. As a result, an Armenian historian named Sebeos observed, "As the Persians approached Palestine, the remnants of the Jewish nation rose against the Christians, joined the Persians and made common cause with them."[1]

In Jerusalem, the Persians, with the help of their Jewish allies, murdered about 60,000 Christians and sold 35,000 into slavery. It was a horrible massacre, one that Christians throughout the region vowed never to forget. They were also outraged by the outcome of the battle: the Persians handed over the city to the Jews. The Jews, in turn, expelled all Christians from Jerusalem. But Jewish rule lasted just three years. In 617, the Persians made peace with the Christians and agreed to return Palestine to Byzantine rule. When Jews in Palestine refused to accept the peace agreement, the Persians attacked them.

By 629, the Byzantines were in control of Jerusalem again. Although Jews scrambled to make peace with the authorities, Christian religious leaders demanded that the Jews be punished for their earlier disloyalty. Some were put to death, while others fled to the desert or to Persian territory. As the Byzantines launched campaigns to convert the Jews by force, many more Jews fled the empire.

OASES IN THE DESERT

In this age of empires, Jews' insistence on maintaining their own religion and their own cultural traditions made them outsiders in both the Persian and the Byzantine Empires. Where could Jews find a place to freely practice their religion? A few found a haven beyond the borders of the great empires in the harsh desert of the Arabian Peninsula. Little is known about when the first Jews arrived in the region, but certainly some Jewish families were living there before the destruction of the second Temple in 70 CE. Their numbers increased during the various struggles for power under Roman rule. Over the centuries, they were also joined by Arabs who had converted to Judaism.

Like other groups in Arabia, Jews settled in places in the desert that were watered by natural springs. In these oases, they grew dates and other crops and traded with their fellow townspeople and the Bedouin nomads of the desert. Over time, they organized themselves into tribes and clans much like those of their Arab neighbors.

To survive in a place with little or no government, a group needs allies. Jewish tribes formed alliances with Arab tribes and participated in the frequent raids and feuds among tribes. By the sixth century, Jews were so well established on the peninsula that the king of Yemen converted to Judaism.

Despite their integration into Arabian society, Jews for the most part remained distinct: they worshipped one God, observed the Sabbath on Saturday, followed Jewish dietary laws, and prayed three times a day. Some Christians—particularly those who were considered heretics by church leaders in Rome and/or Constantinople—also settled in Arabia. Like Jews, they too formed distinct communities, even though they were also well integrated into the local culture.

In the seventh century, around the time the Byzantines regained control of Jerusalem, a new religion called Islam developed in Arabia. It was influenced by both Judaism and Christianity, and it profoundly altered life throughout the Arabian Peninsula.

THE PROPHET MUHAMMAD

Islam began with the teachings of Muhammad, an Arab who was born around 570 CE and who made his home in Mecca in southwestern Arabia. An orphan, he was a poor member of the Quraysh, a wealthy tribe in Mecca. Like other tribes in that area, the Quraysh had grown rich from the caravan routes that crisscrossed the desert. Camel trains loaded with goods of all kinds made regular stops in Mecca. The city was also an important religious center. People from all parts of Arabia came there to worship the hundreds of stone idols kept in a temple known as the Kaaba.

Muhammad earned his living by managing a camel caravan for a wealthy widow, whom he later married. When he was in his forties, he began to travel into the desert to meditate. While there, Muhammad had a revelation that changed not only his own life but also the lives of many people worldwide over the past 1,300 years. The revelation that Muhammad shared with his family and friends was that Allah (the Arabic word for God) was the one, only, and almighty God, full of compassion and kindness; that he, Muhammad, had been called to spread God's message; and that the Day of Judgment was coming, and when it arrived, those who did not serve God faithfully would be engulfed in flames.

To his followers, Muhammad was a prophet sent by God. They saw him as the last in a long line of prophets that included Abraham, Moses, and Jesus. Like earlier prophets, Muhammad preached that there is but one God, whose commandments must be obeyed. For this reason, a follower of Muhammad is known as a *Muslim*: in Arabic, the word means "one who submits to God." The religion a Muslim follows is called *Islam*, which means "surrender or submission to the will of God."

Muhammad preached to anyone in Mecca who would listen. Although he had some success, many people mocked him, including some members of his own tribe. They feared that if Muhammad's message gained wide acceptance, people would stop coming to Mecca to worship at the Kaaba and to trade in the markets; this would mean a loss of income and economic power.

Eventually, Muhammad decided to leave Mecca because so many people there were opposed to his teachings. The Islamic calendar begins in 622, the year Muhammad and his followers left Mecca for the city of Medina, located at an oasis about 280 miles to the north.

JEWISH TRIBES IN MEDINA

In Muhammad's day, Jews made up about half of Medina's population. Most were farmers or jewelers. Some also made weapons and armor for a living. Although Jews had probably lived in Medina longer than the Arabs, they did not control the city; it was dominated by two large confederations of tribes that worshipped many gods—the Aws and the Khazraj. Both groups had settled in Medina sometime during the fifth century and had long battled for control of the city.

Jewish tribes in Medina took sides in the feud between the Aws and Khazraj. The three largest Jewish tribes were the Nadīr, the Qurayza, and the Qaynuqā. The Nadīr and the Qurayza sided with the Aws, while the Qaynuqā were allied with the Khazraj. By the seventh century, many people in Medina were exhausted from the almost constant warfare.

In June of the year 622, representatives of the Aws and Khazraj met twice with Muhammad near Mecca to ask for his help in making peace in Medina. At the second meeting, 75 tribal leaders swore allegiance to him and accepted Islam as their faith. In giving their loyalty to Muhammad and to Islam, the two groups of tribes renounced all of their previous agree-ments and alliances. In desert communities such as Medina, those who were not protected by an alliance had no rights.

When Muhammad arrived in Medina in September with his followers, he was aware that he did not have the support of everyone in the city. So he set out to strengthen his position. It is believed that he created a document that defined relationships among the various groups in Medina. Today that document is often referred to as the Constitution of Medina. It begins with these words:

> In the name of Allah, the Merciful, the Beneficent.

> This is a document from Muhammad the Prophet [governing the relationships] between the Believers and Muslims of Quraysh [Muhammad's tribe] and Yathrib [Medina], and whoever follows them and are attached to them and strives with them. They are a single community in the face of all other men. . . .

> A Believer shall not kill a Believer for the sake of an unbeliever, nor shall he aid an unbeliever against a Believer.

> Allah's protection is one; He grants protection even to the least among them. The Believers are responsible for one another in the face of all other men.[2]

The document treats all "Believers" as brothers with duties and responsibilities toward one another. In the past, people in Arabia had been loyal only to their families, clans, and tribes. Now they had a new, more inclusive loyalty. They were not permitted to fight other believers. The document continues:

> The peace of the Believers is one. No Believer shall conclude a separate peace from another Believer fighting in the Path of Allah. Rather it shall be for all equally. . . .

> The Believers should avenge each other's blood when it is spilled in the Path of Allah.[3]

The document focuses on the rights and responsibilities of "Believers." Those who worshipped many gods were now outsiders. But what about the Jews in Medina? Were they part of the community? (No Christians lived in the city.) The constitution states:

> *Any Jew who follows us shall have aid and comfort. Such a Jew shall not be oppressed nor his enemies aided against him. . . .*

> *The Jews of the [tribes in Medina] are a community with the Believers. The Jews have their religion, and the Muslims have theirs. This applies to their clients and themselves, except those who act wrongfully and sin, for they bring destruction upon themselves and their households.*[4]

The document also contains the following statement:

> *If they [the Jews] are called to make peace and maintain it, they must do so. And if they call upon the Believers for the like of this, it is within their rights, except where one is fighting for the sake of the Faith.*[5]

The document places Jews within the new alliance. They could count on the support of the community in matters of justice. Yet at the same time, only Muslims had the right to demand or to make a separate peace when they were fighting for sake of Islam. In other words, if Muslims were fighting for their religion, they could negotiate in wartime without taking into account the interests of their non-Muslim allies. In that sense, Jews (and Christians in other places) were not equal participants in the larger community. They were tolerated minorities.

Many historians think that the constitution was not written immediately after Muhammad's arrival in Medina. He probably needed time to establish his authority before he could define relationships among groups in the oasis. An opportunity came in 624, when the people of Mecca who opposed Muhammad and his teachings sent an army to attack him. A battle took place at Badr, which is about halfway between Mecca and Medina. To the surprise of many, the Muslims won the battle. It was a turning point for Muhammad. He now had the power and the prestige to consolidate his position in Medina.

Some historians believe that Muhammad expected Jews to accept Islam and its teachings. If so, he was disappointed. Some Jews were prepared to accept his leadership. After all, life had become almost intolerable in the oasis as a result of years of fighting. But many others joined Muhammad's opponents; still others remained neutral.

Jews opposed Muhammad for a variety of reasons. Many believed that the days of prophecy were over, so they doubted that Muhammad was a prophet. Other Jews felt that he had misinterpreted their religion. On the other hand, Muhammad believed that Jews and Christians had distorted God's revelations to Moses and later to Jesus. And he chastised them for not being true to their own religious laws.

Jews in Medina were also motivated by political considerations. In the past, they had won power by supporting one warring Arab tribe over another. Muhammad's efforts to join the two main groups in Medina into a kind of super-tribe, and the renunciation of the Arab tribes' alliances with the Jewish tribes, left many Jews uneasy about their own future in the city.

Muhammad was also uneasy. He believed there were traitors in Medina who were informing his enemies of his plans. By 624, he was convinced that the Qaynuqā (members of one of the largest Jewish tribes) were the traitors, so he and his followers attacked their forts. After a short siege, during which no other group came to its aid, the tribe surrendered. Only then did the chief of the Khazrajī, a group that had long been an ally of the Qaynuqā, ask Muhammad to spare the Qaynuqā. He agreed but expelled members of the tribe from the city and divided their lands and many of their other possessions among his followers. The Qaynuqā eventually made their way to a settlement in what is now Jordan near the border with Syria.

Why did none of the other Jewish tribes come to the aid of the Qaynuqā? Today it seems clear that if one Jewish tribe was under attack, the others were possibly in danger as well. At the time, it was not that obvious. Attacks on one tribe or another had long been part of life in Arabia. Most attacks were motivated by political or tribal disputes. Also, the Jews themselves were by no means united. The Qaynuqā had been allied to an enemy of the Nadīr and Qurayza, the two other major Jewish tribes in Medina.

Early in 625, the following year, Muslims assassinated the chief of the Nadīr. The killing was not a surprise: the chief had written poetry ridiculing Islam and insulting Muslim women. In Arab society, revenge was almost always taken for such an attack on a group's honor. Even so, his death probably made other Jews uneasy.

Then, on March 23, Muhammad and his followers lost a battle to the non-Muslim Arabs of Mecca at Mount Uhud. Once again Muhammad suspected treason, and this time he turned his attention to the Nadīr. Muhammad accused the tribe of plotting against his life and ordered its members to leave the city.

When none of its allies in Medina came to its aid, the tribe had no choice but to go into exile. Although members had to give up their lands and their weapons, they managed to keep their other possessions, and they left Medina in style—with heads held high and their wealth on display. The entire tribe—men, women, and children—left the city in a caravan of 600 camels. As their former neighbors gathered to watch, they marched through the heart of town to the music of pipes and timbrels (small drums or tambourines). The women were dressed in their finest clothes and had uncovered their faces to show off their beauty. Onlookers were impressed. Some Arabs wrote poetry in admiration of the tribe, especially its wealth and the beauty of its women.

Now only one large Jewish tribe, the Qurayza, remained in Medina. In 627, the Meccans and their Bedouin allies attacked the city once again. Although the Qurayza helped defend the city by supplying the tools to dig a deep trench around it, they remained in their forts and did not participate in the fighting. They did not openly aid the enemy, but from the Muslims' point of view, they had "sinned in their hearts."

As soon as the battle was won, Muhammad attacked the Qurayza. The tribe held out for 25 days. When all hope was gone, the Qurayza tried to surrender on the same terms as the Nadīr had, but this time Muhammad was not willing to compromise. He ordered the beheading of all adult males in the tribe and the enslavement of their wives and children. Their lands and other property were divided among Muhammad's Muslim followers.

The treatment of the Qurayza was not unusual at this time in history. Disloyalty was a crime not only in Arabian society but also in the Byzantine and Persian Empires. Almost everywhere, it was punished in ways that seem shocking today. But at the time, the beheading of more than 600 men added considerably to Muhammad's prestige. Admired or feared, he had become a powerful leader—one to be reckoned with.

In 629, Muhammad set out to conquer the oasis of Khaybar, the community where the Nadīr had found refuge among other Jews after being forced out of Medina. After more than a month of fierce fighting, the Jews surrendered. This time, Jews were allowed to remain on their lands and cultivate their fields as long as they paid a tribute, or tax, to the Muslims; the amount they had to pay was more than half of their harvest. However, members of the Nadīr tribe were not included in this agreement. Their men were slain, their wealth was confiscated, and their women and children were enslaved.

Muhammad used the agreement with the Jews of Khaybar as a model for pacts with Jews and Christians who controlled other oases. Once a group agreed to pay a tribute, the group was tolerated. That option was not open to other nonbelievers—particularly not to those who worshipped many gods. They had to convert to Islam or face death.

Muhammad's actions were consistent with the values of Arabian society. At that time and in that place, tribes and political factions constantly jockeyed for power. Everyone understood that the stakes were high and the winner took all. And in Medina, power seems to have been the crucial issue, rather than religious beliefs or cultural differences. The three tribes were targeted because they refused to accept Muhammad's political authority. Other Jewish tribes in Medina continued to live peacefully in the city.

Muhammad's treatment of minorities in Medina is important not because it was anti-Jewish or anti-Christian but because it established who was in charge of the community and on what conditions nonbelievers might continue to live in that community. Muslims were in charge and they alone determined the status of nonbelievers.

BUILDING AN ISLAMIC EMPIRE

Muhammad had wanted to bring his teachings to people throughout the world, but it was not until after his death that his followers were able to do so. Muhammad died in 632 after a brief illness. He left no clear instructions about who should be his successor, so the most urgent need was to choose someone to lead the community in his place. After a brief struggle for power, Muslim leaders agreed to make Abu Bakr the caliph, or successor, to Muhammad. He was a relative of Muhammad's as well as his closest friend and one of the first converts to Islam.

As one of his first acts, the new caliph sent out a small army of Arabs to build an Islamic empire. They invaded Palestine in 634. Many people expected Jews there to welcome the invaders. After all, the Byzantines were threatening to forcibly convert Jews to Christianity. But, though some Jews favored the new invaders, others tried to remain neutral and still others fought fiercely to protect their lands.

By 750, more than a century later, Muslims controlled much of the old Roman and Byzantine Empires well as parts of the Persian Empire. As they took over more and more territory, they had to figure out how to govern this new empire. They were a tiny minority in a huge area that included people who worshipped many gods, as well as Christians, Jews, and Zoroastrians. In dealing with people who worshipped many gods, the

Jewish Communities in the Muslim and Byzantine Empires (750 CE)

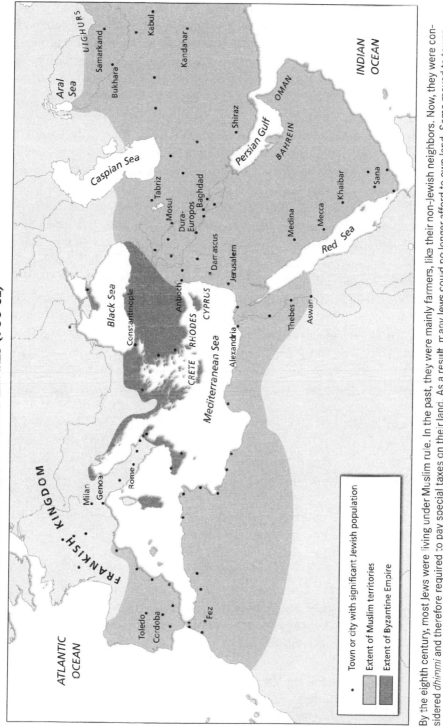

By the eighth century, most Jews were living under Muslim rule. In the past, they were mainly farmers, like their non-Jewish neighbors. Now, they were considered *dhimmi* and therefore required to pay special taxes on their land. As a result, many Jews could no longer afford to own land. Some moved to towns and cities, where they turned to trade or a craft to earn a living.

Muslims continued to call for conversion or death. But they dealt differently with Jews and Christians, with whom they had much in common. Members of all three religions worship one God, accept many of the same prophets, believe in life after death and judgment, and have similar ideas about the creation of the world. Muslims considered Jews and Christians not equals but *dhimmi*—people who belong to a tolerated religion.

Dhimmi had various rights and responsibilities, which were spelled out in an agreement often referred to as the Pact of Umar. It was a document of surrender supposedly sent by the Christians of Syria to the second caliph, Umar ibn al-Khattāb, or Umar I who ruled from 634 to 644. Many historians believe that the document was actually created by Muslims years later. They point out that the document is written in Arabic, a language Syrians at the time were unlikely to know. The document's authors also show a knowledge of the Qur'an—the teachings of Islam—that Christians in Syria were unlikely to have. Moreover, it is unheard of for a conquered people to be allowed to set the terms for its own surrender.

Nevertheless, the agreement—whether agreed to or imposed by force—reflects the status of the *dhimmi* under Muslim rule in the seventh century. The document states, in part:

> We shall keep our gates wide open for passersby and travelers.

> We shall provide three days' food and lodging to any Muslims who pass our way.

> We shall not shelter any spy in our churches or in our homes, nor shall we hide him from the Muslims.[6]

Such promises were important at a time when the Muslims were still establishing control over an area. Other promises are believed to have been added at a later time, including the following:

> We shall not build, in our cities or in their [neighborhood], any new monasteries, churches, hermitages, or monks' cells. We shall not restore, by night or by day, any of them that have fallen into ruin or which are located in the Muslims' quarters. . . .

> We shall not hold public religious ceremonies. We shall not seek to proselytize anyone. We shall not prevent any of our kin from embracing Islam if they so desire.

We shall show deference to the Muslims and shall rise from our seats when they wish to sit down.

We shall not seek to resemble the Muslims in any way with regard to their dress, as for example, with the . . . turban, sandals, or the parting the hair (in the Arab fashion). We shall not speak as they do, nor shall we adopt their [surnames].

We shall not ride on saddles.

We shall not wear swords or bear weapons of any kind, or ever carry them with us. . . .

Jews have been praying in the Ben Ezra Synagogue in Cairo since 882. When it was rebuilt in 1892, workers discovered a *geniza*, or storeroom, containing more than 250,000 fragments of scrolls, books, legal documents, and other works dating to the 800s and beyond.

We shall not display our crosses or our books anywhere in the Muslims' thoroughfares or in their marketplaces. We shall only beat our clappers in our churches very quietly. We shall not raise our voices when reciting the service in our churches nor when in the presence of Muslims. Neither shall we raise our voices in our funeral processions. . . . We shall not come near [the Muslims] with our funeral processions.

We shall not take any of the slaves that have been allotted to the Muslims.

We shall not build our homes higher than theirs.[7]

The agreement also contains clauses requiring that the *dhimmi* pay special taxes—a poll or head tax on every male over the age of 15 and/or a tax on land. These taxes were in addition to the ones that everyone in the empire was required to pay.

A letter attributed to one of the governors of the caliph Umar I offers some explanation of the underlying reasons for the Muslims' acceptance of this pact:

The Muslims of our day will eat [from the work of] these people as long as they live, and when we and they die, our sons will eat [from] their sons forever, as long as they remain, for they are slaves to the people of the religion of Islam as long as the religion of Islam shall prevail. Therefore, place a poll tax upon them and do not enslave them and do not let the Muslims oppress them or harm them or consume their property except as permitted, but faithfully observe the conditions which you have accorded to them and all that you have allowed to them.[8]

The pact views non-Muslims as people who have been given the opportunity to accept the truth but have willfully chosen to persist in erroneous beliefs. In accordance with this view, the government found ways not only to distinguish Muslims from nonbelievers but also to humiliate the *dhimmi* and constantly remind them of their inferiority.

The new rules affected everyone in the new empire. Christians who had once lived in the Byzantine Empire went from being members of the dominant religion to members of a humiliated minority. In general, they were allowed to practice their religion, follow the professions of their choice, and live their lives as they pleased. Yet no matter how high they rose or how much they blended into the society, they were never regarded as equals.

Perhaps to escape oppressive taxes and laws that labeled them as inferior, many Christians converted to Islam over the next 150 years. By the end of the eighth century, North Africa and southwest Asia, regions that had been predominantly Christian, had become Muslim.

Jews were also deeply affected by the changes. Approximately 90 percent of the world's Jews now lived under Muslim rule. Some converted to Islam, but most did not. Many found that the laws of the *dhimmi* gave them some measure of protection. Yet those same laws, along with others imposed by various Muslim rulers, also reinforced their second-class status and publicly humiliated them.

Jews, like Christians, were now a tolerated minority whose safety depended on the whim of a ruler. Before the Arab conquest, most Jews had been farmers. They, like other farmers in the empire, were hard hit by the taxes the Muslims imposed. But as *dhimmi*, Jews were required to pay extra taxes on their land as well as a poll tax. This additional burden overwhelmed many Jewish farmers, who now felt that they had no choice but to abandon their fields and move to cities and towns. By the end of the eighth century, the Jewish population in the Middle East was increasingly urban. Many now worked at a wide variety of trades. They were tanners, gold- and silversmiths, butchers, barbers, blacksmiths, dyers, and shoemakers. Some owned small shops, while others participated in the international trade the Arabs encouraged in their new empire. Trade was a valued occupation in Arabian society. But these were also years when a growing number of Jews began to move beyond the Mediterranean Sea to places in Europe that were still largely wilderness. Some were refugees from discrimination and even persecution, but most were immigrants eager to take advantage of the economic opportunities in the north.

---

[1] Sebeos, chapter 24, quoted in S. Safrai, "The Era of the Mishnah and Talmud (70–640)," in *A History of the Jewish People*, ed. H. H. Ben-Sasson, trans. George Weidenfeld and Nicolson Ltd., 9th ed. (Cambridge, MA: Harvard University Press, 1994), 362.

[2] "Muhammad's Ordinance for Medina," *Ibn Hishām, al-Sīra al-Nabawiyya* (Cairo, 1375/1955), 1:501–504, quoted in Norman A. Stillman, *The Jews of Arab Lands: A History and Source Book* (Philadelphia: Jewish Publication Society, 1979), 115–116.

[3] Ibid., 116.

[4] Ibid., 116–117.

[5] Ibid., 118.

[6] "The Pact of 'Umar," translated from al-Turtūshī, *Sirāj al-Mulūk* (Cairo, 1289/1872), 229–230, quoted in Stillman, *The Jews of Arab Lands*, 157–158.

[7] Ibid.

[8] Abū Yūsuf, *Kitāb al-Kharāj*, 3rd ed. (Cairo, 1382/1962–1963), 223–224, English translation in Bernard Lewis, *Islam*, 2:223–224, quoted in Bernard Lewis, *The Jews of Islam* (Princeton: Princeton University Press, 1984), 31.

4

Holy Wars and Antisemitism

(700s–1300)

At the end of the eleventh century, Muslim Turks threatened
Constantinople, the capital of the Byzantine Empire. Emperor Alexius
Comnenus, who was also the head of the Eastern or Greek Orthodox
Church, appealed to Pope Urban II for help. The pope, who headed the
Roman Catholic Church in the western part of the old Roman Empire,
called for a holy war. That holy war would later be called a crusade. It
was the first of several crusades. (The cross is the central symbol of the
Christian faith and the word *crusade* literally means "a war for the cross.")
Although the crusades did not stop the Turks from taking Constantinople,
they did have a profound impact on the way individuals and groups
throughout Europe, the Middle East, and beyond saw themselves and
others. Jews were deeply affected by the crusades, even though they
seemingly had nothing to do with the fight.

"US" AND "THEM" IN NORTHERN EUROPE

In the seventh century, only a few Jews lived in northern Europe. Many of
the earliest arrivals were former soldiers in the Roman armies or traders
who had followed those armies. By the eighth century, more Jews had
settled in the region. Many of them had come by way of the old Roman
trade routes. By 900, a growing number of Jewish families were living in
the valley of the Moselle River, in what is now France and Germany. And
by 1000, some were moving to the Rhineland—the valley of Germany's
Rhine River.

   The newcomers found themselves in a frontier society where war was
commonplace. As a result of repeated invasions by nomadic tribes from
other parts of Europe and central Asia, powerful men, each with an army
of warriors or knights loyal only to him, ruled much of the region. Each
kept the peace and protected the less powerful in his territory in exchange
for goods or services.

This system is known today as *feudalism*; it was based on personal relationships. Those relationships may have had their origins in the bonds between the invading warriors and their chiefs. As they settled into the territories they conquered, some chiefs became nobles who granted fiefs—estates—to their warriors in return for their service on the battlefield. These young men were known as *vassals*. The word comes from the Celtic word for "boy"; in a very real sense, early vassals were "the boys" who fought on behalf of their "chief."

In time the relationships among these warriors and chiefs created a society roughly arranged like a pyramid, with a king or an emperor at the top. Below him were his vassals—the most powerful nobles in the kingdom. Those nobles, in turn, had their own vassals, and so on down the line to the lowest vassals of all—warriors who had no land or soldiers of their own. One's rank in society depended on the value of the services provided. At the lowest level, serfs held the right to farm a few strips of land for themselves in return for their work on the lord's estate. At a much higher level, a duke held the right to the income of his large estate in return for providing the king with a certain number of warriors for 40 days each year.

Then, as now, titles and ranks could be somewhat misleading. A duke with a strong army could become more powerful than any king, and a peasant with a skill that was in high demand could maintain his independence in a world that was, increasingly, anything but free.

The only unifying force in northern Europe in the days of feudalism was the Roman Catholic Church, headed by the pope. The church struggled to unite Christians by keeping alive Roman laws and learning. Missionaries spread out across northern Europe to convert pagans and stamp out heresies. Although the church had members of all ranks, it was organized in much the way kingdoms were—with the pope at the top of the pyramid and bishops and abbots roughly equal to nobles and knights. In fact, they often came from the same families.

Many bishops owned large estates, had many vassals, and relied on serfs to work their land. These church leaders took part in the struggles for power that occurred often throughout northern Europe. A few even went to war themselves. Church leaders also helped kings and other rulers manage their affairs; they were able to read and write at a time when most people in Europe, including many kings, were illiterate.

How did Jews fit into this world? After all, they could not take an oath of loyalty to a great lord and become his vassals; to do so, they would have had to swear their loyalty on the relics of Christian saints, which meant at least partially accepting Christianity. And they certainly had not moved north to become serfs. They had settled in the north because they saw opportunities there for a better life.

Most Jews arrived in northern Europe in the eighth and ninth centuries. It was a time when the region's economy was beginning to recover from centuries of wars and invasions. Because Christians had had to concentrate for so long on protecting themselves from invaders, few of them had the skills, experience, or contacts to revive trade with countries along the Mediterranean Sea. For help, a number of rulers turned to Jewish merchants who had lived in the Mediterranean region for generations before making their way north. They were experienced in doing business with both Christians and Muslims.

These Jews had other advantages as well. Unlike most of their Christian neighbors—serfs, peasants, and even dukes—who were tied to a particular piece of land or even to a particular ruler, many Jews were free to move from place to place. Indeed, those who worked as traders needed to travel. They were also literate at a time when the vast majority of Europeans could neither read nor write. Many were also familiar with a new numbering system used in the Muslim world—the decimal system. It sounds like a small advantage until you think about the difficulties of adding, subtracting, multiplying, and dividing long columns of numbers using Roman numerals. Very few Christian merchants were familiar with this new way of working with numbers, because the church considered the decimal system a pagan device well into the 1400s.[1]

For Christians, the Jews' use of the new numbering system added to their differentness and strengthened the sense that they were outsiders. So did the fact that their business dealings were mainly with nobles rather than ordinary people. In a society in which hunger was a fact of life and money scarce, ordinary people could not possibly afford the exotic spices, jewels, or bolts of fancy cloth that many Jewish merchants brought to northern Europe.

Not every Jew, of course, was involved in buying and selling luxury goods. Most of the newcomers worked as dyers, shoemakers, blacksmiths, butchers, and harness makers. Others were scribes, winemakers, and physicians. Many did odd jobs. These Jews also aroused strong feelings. Their Christian neighbors saw them as rivals. Yet over the years, the two groups learned how to get along with one another. Christians and Jews swapped everyday goods and services in the marketplace. They also exchanged information, traded stories, and learned a little about one another's customs and beliefs. As neighbors, they shared many of the same problems and faced many of the same risks. Fires, floods, and a host of epidemics threatened both Christian and Jewish families. Records reveal that the two groups often fought side by side in defense of their town or city. Yet, although these experiences built trust, genuine friendships were rare.

Religious differences were often a barrier to close ties between Jews and Christians. The word *religion* comes from a Latin word meaning "to tie or bind together." People who share a religion are bound together by common beliefs, values, and customs. They form a community linked not only by a faith but also by a worldview. Although almost every religion teaches respect for individual differences, believers often see nonbelievers (or believers of other faiths and traditions) not only as misguided and blind to the truth but sometimes as devious, dangerous, or even treacherous.

Many Christians were particularly troubled by Jews' refusal to accept Jesus as their messiah. After all, Christians found what they understood to be predictions of Jesus's return to Earth throughout the Hebrew Scriptures (known to Christians as the Old Testament). Indeed, they viewed such Jewish prophets and leaders as Moses, Elijah, David, and Isaiah as individuals who foresaw the coming of Jesus centuries before his birth. Why, they wondered, did Jews interpret those passages differently and insist that the prophets were speaking about their own times rather than anticipating the coming of Jesus? Some Christians came to believe that Jews knew Christianity was the true religion but rejected it anyway. To these Christians, the idea that people would deny the truth was so outrageous that it could have only one explanation—Jews were in partnership with the devil.

Why, then, were Jews allowed to live among Christians? The answer dates back to the teachings of St. Augustine (see Chapter 2). He maintained that the church had a responsibility to keep Jews alive because of their connection to Jesus, who was a Jew. Augustine regarded Jews as a permanent reminder that Christianity had replaced Judaism as the true faith. He argued that the Jews' humiliation and loss of power showed what happens to those who reject God's truth.

Thus, for many Christians, showing contempt for Jews became a way of affirming their own faith. As early as the ninth century, Christians in a number of French towns had a custom of assaulting Jews at Easter, a time that recalled the crucifixion and accounts of Jewish responsibility for the execution of Jesus. For example, Christians in Chalon, a town in northern Burgundy, threw stones at their Jewish neighbors on Palm Sunday. Each year in Toulouse, religious leaders forced a Jew to stand in the town square and receive a slap in the face. One man was struck so hard that he died of a fractured skull. Most attacks, however, were far more restrained. The idea was to humiliate Jews—not to kill them or frighten them into leaving town.

Leaders of the Catholic Church were teaching two contradictory ideas—contempt for Jews and toleration of their right to practice their religion. If Jews and Christians seemed to be getting along too well, church leaders would thunder that Jews were an "accursed people in league with the devil." They also issued edicts making it a sin for a Christian to eat with a Jew, work for one, or visit a synagogue. Yet when congregants assaulted their Jewish neighbors, those same religious leaders would preach tolerance, following Augustine's belief that Jews should not be destroyed completely.

How did these opposing ideas affect Jewish life in northern Europe? Clues can be found in two documents. The first was written by an anonymous Jew who tells how his people came to Speyer, a city in the Rhineland, in 1084. It begins with these words:

> At the outset, when we came to establish our residence in Speyer—may its foundations never falter!—it was as a result of the fire that broke out in the city of Mainz. The city of Mainz was our city of origin and the residence of our ancestors, the ancient and revered community, praised above all communities in the empire. All the Jews' quarter and their street were burned, and we stood in great fear of the burghers. At the same time, Meir Cohen came from Worms, bearing a copy of Torat Cohanim [the part of the Hebrew Scriptures known in English as the book of Leviticus]. The burghers thought it was silver or gold and slew him. . . . We then decided to set forth from there and to settle wherever we might find a fortified city. . . . The bishop of Speyer [Bishop Rudiger] greeted us warmly, sending his ministers and soldiers after us. He gave us a place in the city and expressed his intention to build about us a strong wall to protect us from our enemies, to afford us fortification.[2]

According to the writer, he and other Jews "stood in great fear of the burghers." Burghers were citizens of a city or town. Not everyone who lived in a community could become a burgher. To do so, one had to be a Christian, own property, and have the ability to make a living as an artisan or a merchant. The burghers tended to see Jews as rivals, which is why Bishop Rudiger assumed that Jews would want to live apart from the burghers for their own safety. Notice, too, that Jews were free to move from one city to another. Many were traders whose skills and goods were portable. So if some of their neighbors were hostile—in this case, the burghers of Mainz—they could find another place to live.

The second document is a charter issued in 1087 by Bishop Rudiger of Speyer to the Jews who had settled in the city. A charter is a kind of contract between a ruler and a group of residents that spells out each party's rights and obligations. The bishop issued the charter because he was the town's ruler. As the first document indicates, he governed with the aid of his own warriors. The Speyer charter was the first issued to a Jewish community as a whole; earlier charters had been given to individuals or families. Bishop Rudiger wrote, in part:

1. *Those Jews whom I have gathered I placed outside the neighborhood and residential area of the other burghers. In order that [the Jews] not be easily disrupted by the insolence of the mob, I have encircled them with a wall.*

2. *The site of their residential area I have acquired properly—first the hill partially by purchase and partially by exchange; then the valley I received by gift of the heirs. I have given [the Jews] that area on the condition that they annually pay three and one-half pounds in Speyer currency for the shared use of the monks. [In other words, some of the tax money Jews were required to pay was used to support the monks under Bishop Rudiger's protection.]*

3. *I have accorded the free right of exchanging gold and silver and of buying and selling everything they use—both within their residential area and outside, beyond the gate down to the wharf and on the wharf itself. I have given them the same right throughout the entire city.*

4. *I have, moreover, given [the Jews] out of the land of the Church burial ground to be held in perpetuity.*

5. *I have also added that, if a Jew from elsewhere has quartered with them, he shall pay no toll.*

6. *Just as the mayor of the city serves among the burghers, so too shall the Jewish leader [pass judgment on] any quarrel which might arise among [the Jews] or against them. If he is unable to determine the issue, then the case shall come before the bishop of the town or his chamberlain [an official in charge of the bishop's household].*

7. *[The Jews] must discharge the responsibility of watch, guard, and fortification only in their own area. The responsibility of guarding they may discharge along with their servants.*

8. *[The Jews] may legally have nurses and servants from among our people.*

9. *[The Jews] may legally sell to Christians meat, which they consider unfit for themselves according to the sanctity of their law. Christians may legally buy such meats.*

In short, in order to achieve the height of kindness, I have granted them a legal status more generous than any the Jewish people have in any city of the German kingdom.

Lest one of my successors dare to deny this grant and concession and force them to a greater tax, claiming that the Jews themselves usurped this status and did not receive it from the bishop, I have given them this charter of aforesaid grant as proper testimony. In order that the meaning of this matter remains throughout the generations, I have strengthened it by signing it and by the imposition of my seal.[3]

The charter reflects the bishop's efforts to address the concerns of the Jews who settled in Speyer. He was aware that the burghers of Speyer, like the burghers of Mainz, viewed Jews with hostility, partly because they felt that Jews supported the bishops and other rulers at a time when the burghers and other townspeople were struggling to become more independent of those same rulers. These people saw the dependence of Jews on bishops and kings as proof that Jews were outsiders with special privileges.

Jews did support local rulers and relied on charters to guarantee their rights and define their responsibilities, because they understood how vulnerable they were as a small group of non-Christians in a Christian world. Indeed, just three years after Bishop Rudiger issued the Speyer charter, Jews there sought additional protection. They asked Henry IV, the Holy Roman emperor, to approve the terms of that charter. (Calling the area the emperor ruled the *Holy Roman Empire* was an attempt to promote unity through a name that recalled the old Roman Empire. It included much of present-day Germany as well as parts of France and Italy.) In 1090, Henry issued a document that affirmed the rights listed in the Speyer charter for all of his Jewish subjects. Just five years later, Pope Urban II called for a holy war against the Muslims, and everything changed. At the time, Muslims controlled many places there that were sacred to Christians, such as the Church of the Holy Sepulcher, which had been built over Jesus's burial place. For centuries, Christian pilgrims had been traveling to Jerusalem to pray there.

Urban II called on his followers to restore Christian holy places to the church. His audience included both secular and religious leaders.

A CALL TO ARMS

In November of 1095, hundreds of religious and political leaders gathered in a large open field near the old cathedral at Clermont, a town in France, to hear Pope Urban II. According to one account, he told the group:

> *Let none of your possessions detain you, no solicitude for your family affairs, since this land which you inhabit, shut in on all sides by the seas and surrounded by the mountain peaks [the Alps and the*

Pyrenees], is too narrow for your large population; nor does it abound in wealth; and it furnishes scarcely enough food for its cultivators. Hence it is that you murder one another, that you wage war, and that frequently you perish by mutual wounds. Let therefore hatred depart from among you, let your quarrels end, let wars cease, and let all dissensions and controversies slumber. Enter upon the road to the Holy Sepulcher [the tomb or burial place in Jerusalem where, according to Christian belief, Jesus lay between his death and his resurrection]; wrest that land [Jerusalem] from the wicked race [Muslims], and subject it to yourselves.[4]

In his passionate speech, the pope called upon Christians to take up arms and return Christian holy places in Jerusalem to the church.

The pope promised that the sins of those who took up the cross would be forgiven, and they would go directly to heaven when they died. As he ended his speech, the enthusiastic crowd called out, "Deus le volt!" ("God wills it!"). One man after another declared his willingness to fight a holy war against the so-called wicked race. The speech was one of many the pope would give in France in the months that followed. His audiences spread the word to relatives, neighbors, even strangers. Within a few months, tens of thousands of Christians—women, children, and men—were preparing for a holy war.

The Muslims had conquered Jerusalem and its holy sites in 638. Why did church leaders wait more than 450 years to call for a holy war? One reason was that invasions from the north and east had weakened the Roman church and much of Europe between 638 and 1000. In fact, Muslims were responsible for several of those invasions. By 732, they controlled Spain and were threatening France. That year, Abd-er Rahman, the Muslim governor of Spain, led an army across the western Pyrenees toward the Loire River in France. He and his men were defeated outside the city of Tours by Charles Martel, the ruler of the Franks (the people from whom France gets its name). That defeat ended Muslim expansion into western and northern Europe. But Christians in Europe were not yet strong enough to force the Muslims out of Spain, let alone invade the Holy Land and take control of Jerusalem.

By the end of the eleventh century, however, Europe was changing. The church was now more powerful and more willing to respond when Muslim rulers vowed to destroy Christian holy sites. Muslims were also threatening the Byzantine Empire. Months before the pope's speech at Clermont in November 1095, the Byzantine emperor Alexius Comnenus, who was also the head of the Eastern or Greek Orthodox Church, had asked Pope Urban II for soldiers to help defend Constantinople, his capital. By coming to his aid, Urban II hoped to expand the power and influence of the Roman church.

As Urban's speech suggests, he also wanted Christians in Europe to stop fighting among themselves and unite against a common enemy— in this case, Muslims. It was not a new idea. Since the 700s, Christian soldiers had been struggling to regain control of Spain. Christians had also fought Muslims in other places, including a number of cities along the Italian coast.

However, none of these earlier wars captured the imagination of Europeans the way the pope's call to arms in 1095 did. Urban was surprised by the enthusiasm. He had imagined that a few powerful rulers would send soldiers to fight in an army under the church's leadership. Several such armies were in fact organized, and they did conquer Jerusalem in 1099 and establish four Christian states in the region. However, the pope's speech also ignited a series of events that he neither expected nor wanted.

By the spring of 1096, hundreds of dukes, counts, barons, and knights were ready to join the crusade. They were motivated by religious zeal, a sense of adventure, and sometimes greed. The pope's call to arms also attracted tens of thousands of ordinary people. They had learned about the holy war from charismatic speakers who carried the pope's message across northern France through what is now Germany. One of the most famous was a preacher known only as Peter the Hermit. Throughout the spring of 1096, his words held audiences spellbound. His preaching inspired men, women, and even children of every social class to leave their homes and head for Jerusalem. The group Peter led consisted of about 10,000 knights, nobles, and foot soldiers as well as hundreds of ordinary people.

For the most part, these armies headed for the Middle East with little or no preparation. Instead of bringing supplies, many scavenged for food and other goods along the way. In a number of places, villagers and townspeople—both Christians and Jews—offered help in order to protect their communities from looting. Most, however, could barely feed their own families, let alone tens of thousands of hungry strangers. As a result, frequent raids on farms, villages, and towns were carried out along the way by the crusaders—as the warriors in this new holy war were called.

A number of rulers closed their borders. The Christian rulers of Hungary attacked crusaders who tried to pass through their territory. Although the crusade was at least in part a response to a call for help by the Byzantine emperor, even he was horrified by the huge, unruly armies that poured into his territory.

Many crusaders were eager to fight for their faith because of a reform movement in the Catholic Church in the eleventh century. It changed the way many Christians felt about their religion. As part of that movement, hundreds of churches were built in villages and towns throughout Europe, and in those churches, Christians came to a new understanding of their faith. Earlier, they had seen Jesus primarily as a distant figure whom they respected and viewed with awe—an all-powerful deity who had risen from death. Now many priests focused their teachings on Jesus's suffering and his dual role as a figure both human and divine. As a result, people in northern Europe came to view Jesus as a man who identified with the poor and the powerless, a man who died painfully on the cross at the hands of his enemy—and that enemy was, in their minds, "the Jews." It was at this time that the "deicide charge" took root in Christianity. A growing number of Christians now believed that Jews as a people were collectively guilty for the crucifixion of Jesus.

The church reinforced that belief. It was the theme of many statues and other art found in most churches. It was also expressed in the sermons and teachings not only of priests and bishops but also of charismatic speakers like Peter the Hermit. Not surprisingly, a number of crusaders and the pilgrims who accompanied them decided that it was "preposterous to set out on a long journey to kill God's enemies far away, while God's worst enemies, the Jews, are dwelling in ease close at hand."

In the fourth century, in ancient cities like Antioch and Alexandria, few Christians had paid much attention to preachers who claimed that "the Jews" had murdered Jesus. They lived among Jews and knew them as neighbors, relatives, and coworkers. As citizens of the Roman Empire, they also knew that it was Roman soldiers who had placed Jesus on the cross. However, in the eleventh century in northern Europe, most people knew little or nothing about Rome or its empire. Its history was, at best, a very distant memory.

A NEW KIND OF WAR

The Jews of France were the first to realize that this so-called holy war was something new and very dangerous to them and to other Jews. They listened to the fiery speeches and watched the armies gather. They also heard the cries for revenge on "God's enemies."

French Jews were no strangers to violence. Attacks were commonplace. Most were triggered by a local problem—an injustice or a dispute

Jewish Communities Attacked by Crusaders (1096–1149)

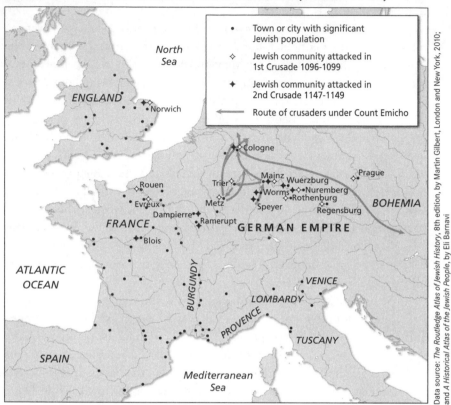

The map shows that most of the attacks on European Jews during the first and second crusades took place within the German Empire.

within a community. Still, once the matter was settled, calm returned and life continued as usual. But Jews in France now sensed that a different kind of violence was coming.

In December 1095, leaders of Jewish communities in France sent urgent letters to Jewish communities in the Rhineland. French Jews expressed fears for their own safety and warned that crusaders might soon be headed east. In the end, however, it was not the Jews of France but the Jews of Germany who were in grave danger. In 1095, France was divided into regions, each controlled by a powerful duke or count. These rulers had no intention of allowing any army to attack their villages and towns, and they were strong enough to keep order. In Germany, however, only the Holy Roman emperor had that much power, and he was in Italy when the crusaders set out on their journey. In the meantime, dozens of barons and knights put together their own armies and set out to fight "God's enemies."

One of those nobles was a landowner known as Count Emicho. In May and June of 1096, he and his followers systematically attacked Jewish communities in the Rhineland. In almost every community, they gave Jews a choice: conversion to Christianity or death. These crusaders insisted that forced conversions were the will of God. Not surprisingly, Jews had a different view. They believed that the choice before them was a supreme test of their commitment to God.

On the morning of May 3, 1096, a Saturday, Emicho led a surprise attack on the synagogue in Speyer. When he and his men burst into the building, they found it empty. Someone had warned the Jews. Outraged, the soldiers searched the town with the help of a number of burghers. In the end, they found and killed 11 Jews.

Where were the others? The current bishop, Johann, was determined to live up to the charter written by his predecessor, Bishop Rudiger. He used his own army to escort the Jews of Speyer to a safe place in the countryside. Then, after the crusaders left town, Bishop Johann tried and punished all of the burghers who had taken part in killing the 11 Jews. Justice prevailed in Speyer.

Jews in other cities were not as fortunate. After hearing what had happened in Speyer, Jews in Worms debated what to do. According to a chronicler, they could not agree on a plan of action. Some sought refuge with the bishop of Worms, while others remained in their homes. In the end, neither group survived. The first Jews to be assaulted were those who stayed home. The chronicler wrote:

> *[Enemies of the Jews] plotted craftily against them. They took a trampled corpse of theirs, that had been buried thirty days earlier, and carried it through the city, saying: "Behold what the Jews have done to our comrade. They took a gentile and boiled him in water. They then poured the water into our wells in order to kill us." When the crusaders and burghers heard this, they cried out and gathered— all who bore and unsheathed [a sword], from great to small—saying: "Behold, the time has come to avenge him who was crucified, whom their ancestors slew. Now let not a remnant or a residue escape; even an infant . . . in the cradle.* [5]

The mob killed almost every Jew who had chosen to remain in town. Two weeks later, Emicho turned his attention to those who had found refuge in the bishop's towers. As free men, Jews were allowed to have weapons, and many now used their swords and knives to defend themselves and their families. Their wives and children joined in the fight by hurling stones at their attackers. They were, however, hopelessly outnumbered.

By nightfall the battle was over. Many of the Jews who survived killed themselves and their children rather than allow the crusaders to do so. Jewish chroniclers would later refer to these acts as "the sanctification of the Name of God"—*Kiddush ha-Shem* in Hebrew. These Jews were seen as martyrs—individuals who had chosen to give up their lives rather than renounce their religion.

Next, Count Emicho turned his attention to Mainz, which was home to the largest Jewish community in the Rhineland. When the army reached the city, Mainz's burghers opened the gates. Once inside, the soldiers and the burghers headed for the archbishop's compound, where most Jews had found refuge. The Jews prepared to defend themselves, expecting support from the archbishop's knights. A chronicler later wrote:

> They [the Jews] all then drew near to the gate to do battle with the crusaders and with the burghers. . . . The enemy overcame them and captured the gate. The men of the archbishop, who had promised to assist, fled immediately, in order to turn them over to the enemy, for they are splintered reeds.[6]

The crusaders gave the Jews of Mainz the same choice they had offered Jews in the other communities: death or Christianity. Almost everyone chose death. Some simply waited for the crusaders to kill them. A few tried to escape, only to be captured and killed. Others—including women and children—took their own lives.

The crusaders then targeted the Jews who had hidden in the walled courtyard of a local ruler. Once they had been dealt with, soldiers went from house to house searching for any Jew who remained in the city. More than a thousand Jews were murdered that day. Emicho and his men then moved on to other cities and towns.

How do we know what happened? Men in the various crusader armies wrote eyewitness accounts that mention the attacks on Jews and Jewish resistance but provide few details. Most of the details have come from Jewish sources—particularly three chronicles that describe the events of the spring of 1096. In these accounts, the victims are the heroes. Many are mentioned by name, and their deeds are described at length. It is as if the authors wanted readers to know that this tragedy did not happen to nameless, faceless people but to real men, women, and children—individuals willing to fight for their religion and, if necessary, die for it.

For example, one chronicle tells of a young man named Simchah the *kohen*. (A *kohen* is a male member of the Jewish priestly class, a descendent of Moses's brother Aaron, according to Jewish tradition.) Crusaders surrounded Simchah in Worms, dragged him into a church, and demanded that he convert to Christianity on the spot or die. He promised to "fulfill their desire" but said he wanted to see the bishop first. Once in the bishop's chamber, Simchah pulled out a knife and attacked the crusaders. He killed three men before he himself was murdered.

In Mainz, David the *gabbai* (a synagogue official) used his last moments to confront the crusaders and their followers by publicly challenging their beliefs and defending his own. As he surely expected, his words enraged the mob and he and his family were promptly killed.

Jewish chroniclers praised the courage and religious devotion of Simchah, David and other Jews. They also honored those who had taken their own lives, even though Jews are permitted to do so only in the most extreme circumstances. To many European Jews in the eleventh century and later, these were the most extreme circumstances, and they called for the most extreme measures. What was said about Jews who were forced to convert to Christianity? A Jewish chronicler wrote of these converts:

> Now it is fitting to tell the praise of those forcibly converted. . . .
> They did not go to church except occasionally. Every time they went,
> they went out of great duress and fear. They went reluctantly. The
> gentiles themselves know that they had not converted wholeheart-
> edly, but only of fear of the crusaders, and that [the converts from
> Judaism] did not believe in [the Christians'] deity, but rather that
> they clung to the fear of the Lord and held fast to the sublime God,
> creator of heaven and earth. In the sight of the gentiles, they observed
> the [Christian] Sabbath properly and observed the Torah of the Lord
> secretly. Anyone who speaks ill of them insults the countenance of the
> Divine Presence.[7]

CRIMES AND PUNISHMENT

In time, Emicho and his army left the Rhineland and continued east on their journey to Jerusalem. However, they never reached the Holy Land. After they raided several villages in Hungary, local soldiers retaliated, killing almost everyone. Emicho managed to escape to Germany along with a few companions. A Christian chronicler said of Emicho's fall:

So the hand of the Lord is believed to have been against the pilgrims, who had sinned by excessive impurity . . . and who had slaughtered the exiled Jews through greed of money, rather than for the sake of God's justice, although the Jews were opposed to Christ. The Lord is a just judge and orders no one unwillingly, or under compulsion, to come under the yoke of the Catholic faith.[8]

Although other crusaders continued to attack Jews, by the fall of 1096 nearly all of the crusaders had moved on—some to Jerusalem and others back to their homes. In 1097, Henry IV returned to Germany from his lands in Italy. Almost immediately, he issued an edict allowing Jews who had been forced to convert to Christianity to return to Judaism. He also ordered that all Jewish property taken in the attacks be restored to its rightful owners.

Yet only the burghers in Speyer ever paid for their crimes. Neither Henry nor any other ruler brought to justice the vast majority of the people responsible for the attacks. Christians quickly learned that despite the words of kings and other rulers, there were no consequences for killing Jews.

Pope Urban II was also silent. In fact, the only recorded statement he made about the fate of the Jews was in response to the emperor's edict. The pope condemned Henry for allowing Jews who had been forcibly converted to return to Judaism, even though earlier in his papacy, he had written strong letters opposing forced conversions.

This new hostility toward Jews continued when the crusaders reached the Middle East. Before leaving France, Duke Godfrey of Bouillon, a leader of the first crusade, vowed to avenge the blood of Jesus by leaving "no member of the Jewish race alive." On July 8, 1099, he and his men reached the gates of Jerusalem. To avoid a war, the city's Muslim governor tried to make peace by offering to protect Christian pilgrims and worshippers in the city. Godfrey refused the offer and demanded unconditional surrender. After a week-long siege of the city, he and his men broke through the walls of Jerusalem and killed everyone they could find. The crusaders herded 6,000 Jews into a huge synagogue and then set fire to the building. They also murdered approximately 30,000 Muslims who had sought refuge in the al Aqsa Mosque (the second-oldest mosque; the oldest is in Medina).

THE CONSEQUENCES OF 1096

Violence triggered more violence. The holy wars that began in 1096 did not end in 1096 or even in 1099 with the fall of Jerusalem to the crusaders.

These wars—collectively known as the Crusades—continued for about 200 years. Each time Muslims won back a piece of land, the church would call for a new crusade. When the Crusades finally ended, Muslims were still in control of the Middle East, including Jerusalem and its holy sites. But these wars had a powerful effect on the way Jews, Christians, and Muslims viewed themselves and others.

Jews greet Henry VII soon after his coronation in 1312. The Jews are shown wearing oddly shaped hats. From the 1200s on, the Church insisted that all Jews wear clothing or head coverings that distinguished them from Christians.

Memories of the first crusade shaped Jewish communities throughout northern Europe. There had been very few Jewish martyrs before 1096; after 1096, there would be many. In the twelfth century, memorial ceremonies were held for these martyrs each year on the anniversary of the attack on Speyer. In synagogues throughout northern Europe, their names were read aloud, and the congregation then recited a new prayer, known in Hebrew as *Av ha-Rachamin* ("the merciful Father"), in memory of "the holy communities who offered their lives for the sanctification of the divine name." The prayer is still recited in synagogues today.

Jews were affected in other ways as well. Although the number of Jews living in northern Europe continued to grow and some Jews prospered, most were now more wary of their Christian neighbors. They had good reason to be guarded. In 1145, just 50 years after the first crusade, the call came for a second crusade. Once again, preachers sought to rouse Christians to begin the crusade by attacking Jews—the "enemy within."

That summer, fearing more violence, the archbishops of Mainz and Cologne sent urgent letters to Bernard of Clairvaux, an important religious scholar in France who led the call for a second crusade. Bernard responded with a letter that was widely circulated in Europe:

> The Jews are not to be persecuted, killed, or even put to flight. . . .
> The Jews are for us the living words of Scripture, for they remind
> us always of what our Lord suffered. They are dispersed all over the
> world so that by expiating their crime they may be everywhere the
> living witnesses of our redemption. . . . If the Jews are utterly wiped
> out, what will become of our hope for their promised salvation, their
> eventual conversion?[9]

Although Bernard was greatly respected, his letter had no significant impact. From the fall of 1146 through the spring of 1147, attacks on Jews in the Rhineland and northern France mounted. Unlike the attacks of 1096, these assaults were carried out not by crusader armies but by individuals or small groups of people who saw Jews as the enemy.

Bernard was outraged. He even traveled to the Rhineland to make the church's position as clear as possible. His impassioned speeches may have prevented attacks in some places, but in others his words only inflamed the mobs' fury. Other church leaders were not as supportive of Jews as they had once been. Peter the Venerable, the abbot of the monastery of Cluny, condemned tolerance toward Jews in a letter to the king of France. He did not favor killing Jews, but he thought it was all right to rob them.

In this way, the "ill-acquired" property of one "race of infidels" would help finance the war against the other "race of infidels"—the Muslims.

Jews were more vulnerable in the twelfth century than they had been in the eleventh century. Economic and social changes that improved life for Christians in Europe increased the vulnerability of Jews. In 1096, Jews had been mainly engaged in trade. The richest among them provided luxury goods to kings and other nobles. Christian merchants did most of their business locally and traded in products produced nearby—wool, timber, and grains. By the twelfth century, however, those local goods were finding markets in distant parts of Europe, Asia, and North Africa. As this trade grew, so did partnerships and contracts among Christian merchants.

By the end of the eleventh century, Jews were being squeezed out of international trade and into occupations forbidden to Jews, Christians, and Muslims—banking, money lending, and currency exchange. All three faiths regarded the idea of charging interest on a loan as usury, which was a sin. (Interest is the price a borrower pays for a loan. Today the word *usury* refers only to the practice of charging unfairly high interest rates for a loan.) Although some Jews tried to avoid money lending, increasingly it was the only way many could earn a living. Few other occupations were now open to them.

The process of turning Jews into money lenders was gradual; it took place more slowly in some places than in others. But nearly everywhere, it pushed Jews to the margins of society and led to the stereotype of the Jew as greedy and money-hungry. Because usury was prohibited under Jewish law, Christians also saw this new occupational shift as proof that Jews were unfaithful to the laws of the God they claimed to worship. Thus, having made it impossible for Jews to hold other jobs, many Christians now blamed Jews for charging interest on loans that many Christians were eager to secure.

As life became more precarious for Jews in Europe, Jews in many communities became the personal property of their protectors, with no rights except those they acquired by supplying nobles with money on demand. Nobles kept a tight rein on "their" Jews, whom they needed to help finance wars and build palaces, cathedrals, and roads. They expected Jews to pay special taxes or to lend them money at a very low rate of interest or with no interest at all. How could Jews survive if they did not receive a return on their investments? They could do so only by lending money to everyone else—merchants, farmers, artisans, and other borrowers—at very high interest rates. As a result, many Jews were caught in a trap from which they could not easily escape.

[1] Stephen E. Sachs, "New Math: The 'Countinghouse Theory' and the Medieval Revival of Arithmetic" (2000), http://www.stevesachs.com/papers/paper_90a.html; Paul Kriwaczek, Yiddish Civili*sation: The Rise and Fall of a Forgotten Nation* (New York: Vintage Books, 2005) 72–73.

[2] Quoted in Robert Chazan, *In the Year 1096: The First Crusade and the Jews* (Philadelphia: Jewish Publication Society, 1996), 6.

[3] Quoted in Robert Chazan, ed., *Church, State, and Jew in the Middle Ages* (West Orange: Behrman House, 1980), 58–59.

[4] Robert of Rheims, "The Speech of Urban" *Historia Hierosolymitana*, "The Jeresualem History," in RHC, *Occ.* III, trans. Munro, *Urban*, 5–8, quoted in Edward Peters, ed., *The First Crusade: "The Chronicle of Fulcher of Chartres" and Other Source Materials*, 2nd ed. (Philadelphia: University of Pennsylvania Press, 1998), 28.

[5] Quoted in Chazan, *In the Year 1096*, 31.

[6] Ibid., 31.

[7] Ibid., 78–79.

[8] Krey, *First Crusade: Accounts*, 56; Peters, *The First Crusade,* 104, quoted in Leonard B. Glick, *Abraham's Heirs: Jews and Christians in Medieval Europe* (Syracuse: Syracuse University Press, 1999), 102–103.

[9] Bernard of Clairvaux, *The Letters of St. Bernard of Clairvaux*, trans. Bruno James (Chicago: Henry Regnery, 1953), 462–63, quoted in Glick, *Abraham's Heirs*, 122.

5

The Power of a Lie

(1144–1300)

In the twelfth and thirteenth centuries in Europe, many people had a sense that disaster was just a step away. Life was precarious for rich and poor alike. It was a time when most babies died before their first birthday of diseases that are easily cured today. Few of those who survived their childhood lived much beyond their 30th birthday. In times of fear and anxiety, it is all too easy to blame "them"—the people who are not like "us"—for every tragedy, every hardship, and every loss.

During these years, Jews were under attack almost everywhere in Europe, not for who they were or even for what they believed but for what others *imagined* Jews were like and what they *imagined* Jews believed. Those imaginings led to myths that had horrific consequences for Jews then and in centuries to come. One of the most dangerous involved the accusation that Jews killed Christian children as part of their Passover ritual. This myth had its beginnings in an incident that took place in the twelfth century.

CHARGES OF RITUAL MURDER

On Good Friday in 1144, a forester stumbled upon the corpse of a young boy named William in a woods just outside of Norwich, England. According to a book written some years later by a monk and chronicler known as Thomas of Monmouth, "Becoming aware that [the boy] had been treated with unusual cruelty, [the forester] now began to suspect, from the manner of his treatment, that it was no Christian but in very truth a Jew who had ventured to slaughter an innocent child of this kind with such horrible barbarity."[1]

William's relatives agreed with the forester. His uncle angrily informed church authorities that "the Jews" had committed the murder because of their unrelenting hatred for Christians. He proclaimed, "I accuse the Jews, the enemies of the Christian name, as the perpetrators of this deed and the shedders of innocent blood." As proof, he described a dream his wife had had a few weeks earlier. In that dream, Jews attacked her in the marketplace and tore off one of her legs. The couple now interpreted the dream as a warning that she would lose a loved one because of the Jews.

Most people in Norwich in 1144 ignored these charges or attributed them to grief at the loss of a beloved child. After all, Jews had been living in the city for about 100 years without a single incident. Many in the town also realized that despite the accusation, there was no proof that a Jew was responsible for the boy's death. William was buried, and life in Norwich continued as usual until about 1149, when Thomas of Monmouth came to live in a monastery there.

Thomas quickly became obsessed with the murder. He was convinced that William was not a victim of random violence but a martyr who had died for his faith. He wrote a book about William's death, hoping to have the boy declared a saint. Thomas based his book on stories told by four people—two of whom he never met.

The first story was a deathbed confession by Aelward Ded, one of the richest men in Norwich. In 1149, Aelward told a priest that he had seen a Jew named Eleazar and another man walking with a horse early on the day William's body was discovered. On the horse was a huge sack. Curious about its contents, Aelward touched it and felt a human body. When the two men realized that Aelward knew their secret, he claimed, they fled into the woods with the sack.

Aelward told the priest that he had never told this story to a single person. But, he claimed, Eleazar and his companion had confessed the murder to the sheriff. They then bribed him to keep their secret and to force Aelward to do the same. Aelward spoke out only as he lay dying— three years after Eleazar's death in 1146 and the sheriff's own death shortly thereafter.

Thomas of Monmouth's second story came from William's aunt, who now came forward to say that William had come to see her on the day of his disappearance. With him that day was a cook who had offered the boy a job. Suspicious of the cook, the aunt asked her daughter to follow the pair when they left. The little girl told her that William and the cook entered Eleazar's house and that the door closed behind them. The girl died before Thomas came to Norwich, so he had only her mother's word for the story. Still, it appeared to connect Eleazar to the child.

The aunt's account revealed a gap in the complicated story that Thomas was weaving. What had happened to William between the time he supposedly entered Eleazar's house and the discovery of his body in the woods several days later? Once again, Thomas found a witness, this time a Christian woman who, in 1144, had worked for Eleazar as a servant. She claimed that on the day William disappeared, Eleazar had ordered her to bring him a pot of boiling water. When he carried the pot into another room, she peeked through a crack in the door to see what he did with it. She told Thomas that it was then that she saw a boy tied to a post.

Like Aelward, the woman had up to that point told no one what she had seen. According to Thomas, she was afraid she would lose her job. She also feared for her life, because she was "the only Christian living among so many Jews." This was an odd comment in a community that had no Jewish quarter; for the most part, Jews and Christians in Norwich lived side by side.

Thomas's most prized, and most amazing, testimony came from Theobold, a monk who was nowhere near Norwich in 1144. Theobold told Thomas that he had been born a Jew and had converted to Christianity because of William's martyrdom. He claimed that he and every other Jew in England in 1144 knew that a boy would be killed in Norwich on Good Friday. According to Theobold, prominent Jews gathered in Spain just before Passover each year to determine where a Christian child would be sacrificed. Jews who lived in the selected country drew lots to decide exactly where the crime would take place. In 1144, England was the country selected, and Norwich was the town.

Thomas never doubted Theobold's story, even though it required believing that thousands of people throughout England and the rest of Europe and the Middle East had kept, and continued to keep, a lifelong secret. It did not strike him as surprising that no one had ever revealed that secret—with the single exception of Theobold. Why would Jews risk their lives to commit such a murder? Theobold claimed that they did it to show their contempt for Christianity and to take revenge for their exile from their homeland.

Thomas added his own twist to Theobold's tale. He insisted that Jews did more than just kill their victims; they reenacted the crucifixion of Jesus. In his book, he described the scene as he imagined it:

> [The Jews] laid their blood-stained hands upon the innocent victim, and having lifted him from the ground and having fastened him upon the cross, they vied with one another in their efforts to make an end of him. . . . [I]n doing these things they were adding pang to pang and wound to wound, and yet were not able to satisfy their heartless cruelty and their inborn hatred of the Christian name, lo! after these many and great tortures, they inflicted a frightful wound in his left

side, reaching even to his heart, and as though to make an end of all
they extinguished his mortal life so far as it was in their power. And
since many streams of blood were running down from all parts of his
body, then, to stop the blood and to wash and close the wounds, they
poured boiling water over him.[2]

Accusations of ritual murder were not new. In the first century of the
Common Era, Apion, a Greek lawyer in Alexandria, Egypt, claimed that
once a year Jews kidnapped a Greek and fattened him up so that he could
be sacrificed to their deity. However, Apion never cited a specific example
of such a murder; he wrote in vague, general terms, and his accusation
was one of many wild charges that people from various ethnic groups at
that time made against others. A few generations later, the Romans would
make similar accusations against Christians. Once again, few people at
the time paid attention to such charges; they were seen as too outrageous
to be true.

In the twelfth century, however, accusations of ritual murder did
not seem so outrageous; instead, they seemed to confirm what many
people already believed about Jews and Judaism. When William died, the
Crusades had been going on for 50 years, and the speeches and sermons
that persuaded people to join the crusaders' armies blamed Jews as well
as Muslims for the "loss" of Jerusalem and for any attack on Christians or
their beliefs.

Changing attitudes toward Jews were reflected in images found in
churches. At a time when few people could read and write, churchgoers
"read" the story of Jesus's life and the founding of the Christian church in
stained-glass windows, murals, and altar paintings.

A popular image in many churches showed two women standing next
to the cross; one woman represented the church, and the other woman,
the synagogue. In the tenth and eleventh centuries, the two women looked
much the same, though the artists clearly favored the one who represented
the church. By the twelfth century, however, the synagogue was no longer
shown as an attractive woman who was simply unable to see the truth of
Christianity. Increasingly, she was portrayed as both blind and depraved—
a woman with ties to the devil. The shift in the image of the synagogue
mirrored the way Christians came to view real Jews in their communities,
while also reinforcing negative feelings about them.

We do not know for sure why Thomas of Monmouth put together the
web of false accusations about William's death or why the others involved
told lies about how the boy lost his life. Were they making themselves

Images that showed the church as superior to the synagogue appeared not only in sculptures, stained-glass windows, and tapestries but also in the artwork that adorned books and manuscripts.

feel important by sharing their fears and suspicions? Were they protecting someone else who might have killed William? Did they truly believe the stories they told, or did they make them up for reasons we will never know? Whatever motives these people had, the story that Thomas of Monmouth told about William's murder spread like wildfire.

By 1150, crowds of pilgrims were visiting William's tomb each year, and some were claiming that he performed miracles. Such claims inspired even more people to visit the boy's tomb in the hope of obtaining miracles of their own. The pilgrims who flocked to Norwich are proof of the success of Thomas's campaign to win sainthood for young William and fame for his own monastery. But the myth he created and spread had other long-term consequences. His invented tale further reinforced the image of Jews as evil and depraved—people who hated Christians so much that they would stop at nothing.

Thomas of Monmouth's accusations of ritual murder were not the last made against the Jews. In 1147, Christians in Würzburg, Germany, also accused Jews of murdering a Christian. In 1168, similar charges were made in Gloucester, England, and the same happened a few years later in Paris. By the end of the twelfth century, the lie had spread throughout Europe.

TRAGEDY IN BLOIS

The Jews of Blois, a town in France, were among those specifically accused of ritual murder. Their experience reveals the power of the myth Thomas of Monmouth created.

On a spring day in 1171, a Jewish tanner was walking along the banks of the Loire River. He was carrying a bundle of raw animal hides when he encountered the servant of a town official. As the two men passed one another, one of the skins dropped out of the tanner's bundle and fell into the river. The servant immediately assumed it was a corpse and ran to tell his master the news.

It seems that neither the servant's master nor any other Christian in town doubted the story, even though they had no evidence that any crime had been committed, let alone a ritual murder. After all, the tale was in keeping with what many already believed. The count of Blois also accepted the story as fact; he imprisoned all Jewish adults in the city and ordered their children baptized as Christians.

Blois was not, of course, the first place where a Jew was accused of ritual murder. It was, however, the first known place where Jews were punished for a crime that had not even occurred. Jewish leaders pointed out that there was absolutely no evidence of a crime; no one was missing and no body had been found. The count refused to reconsider his position. In exchange for a payment of 1,000 pounds, however—a fortune in those days—he did promise not to arrest Jews who lived in the area around the city.

On May 26, the Jews held in prison were given a choice: conversion or death. Eight or nine chose to be baptized. Most of the rest were herded into a hut and burned alive. When a few men managed to escape, the executioners killed them with swords and then pushed their bodies back into the fire. Almost all of the Jews of Blois—more than 30 men and women in all—died that day.

While little is known about the way Jews in most European cities reacted to news of an accusation of ritual murder, Blois is an exception. Historians have found several letters that Jews in neighboring towns wrote in 1171. The first were from Jews in Orléans, the city closest to Blois. After hearing two eyewitness accounts, they wrote letters to Jews in communities throughout northern France and what is now Germany. The letters described the events in Blois and asked for help in protecting Jews from similar libels. In Paris, a group of influential Jewish leaders persuaded King Louis VII to publicly condemn the actions of the count of Blois. In addition, Louis ordered his own officials to provide his Jewish subjects with better protection.

Jews also appealed to the count of Champagne, a brother of the count of Blois. The count of Champagne responded by saying publicly, "We find nowhere in Jewish law that it is permissible to kill a Christian." His statement was intended to deny the accusation that Judaism encourages the murder of Christians. When charges of ritual murder were made in the lands he ruled, he refused to act on those charges.

In the meantime, Jews continued to negotiate with the count of Blois. Although most of the Jews in Blois had been burned alive in May, a few remained in prison. A number of Jewish negotiators tried to win their release and secure permission for converts to return to Judaism. They worked mainly through another of the count's brothers, the bishop of Sens. Nathan ben Meshullam, one of the negotiators, wrote of those efforts:

> Yesterday I came before the bishop of Sens, to attempt to release those imprisoned by his brother, the wicked count, and those forcibly converted. I paid the bishop . . . 120 pounds, with a promise of 100 pounds for the count, for which I have already given guarantees. The count then signed an agreement to release the prisoners from confinement. Concerning the young people forcibly converted, he asked that they be permitted to return to [Judaism]. . . . He also signed an agreement that there would be no further groundless accusations.[3]

This letter reveals how the count was able to manipulate the situation to his own financial advantage. It also reveals how precarious life was for Jews. The best that the Jews of northern France could hope for was to save the lives of a handful of survivors in Blois and ask that nothing comparable happen again. They were unable to secure justice.

THE DEATH OF "LITTLE HUGH"

By the end of the twelfth century, Christians in eight cities had accused Jews of ritual murder—two each in England, France, and the German-speaking countries, and one each in Bohemia and Spain. By the end of the thirteenth century, the number of known accusations had more than tripled. And by the sixteenth century, such charges had spread south to what is now Italy and as far to the east as Poland and Hungary.

As accusations spread, so did the false belief that Jews routinely engaged in the practice of ritual murder. An accusation made repeatedly tends to be believed, no matter how illogical and false it is. Where there is smoke, people fear, there is fire.

In 1255, a five-year-old boy was found dead in a well in Lincoln, England. Many historians today believe that young Hugh accidentally fell into the well. But in 1255, Christians in Lincoln were absolutely certain that "the Jews" had murdered him and had then thrown his body into the well. Unlike officials in Norwich, those in Lincoln immediately charged an individual, a Jew known as Copin who lived nearby. They tortured him until he "confessed" to ritual murder, and they then arrested all the other Jews in the city.

This time, no king or emperor stepped in to save the Jewish community. Indeed, King Henry III traveled to Lincoln to order Copin's execution. Henry also imprisoned all of the other Jews in Lincoln in the Tower of London. Sources suggest that as many as 100 Jews were held there and at least 18 were hanged.

Like William of Norwich, young Hugh became a saint, and his story, like William's, was embellished with each telling. Eventually, one version claimed that the Jews had fattened the boy for ten days with milk and bread before murdering him. The murder itself was said to have mimicked the details of the Passion—a word that refers to the suffering of Jesus before the crucifixion. Hugh's story was later set to music; scholars have identified more than 21 versions of a ballad about his death. In the late 1300s, decades after the expulsion of the Jews from England, Geoffrey Chaucer, one of England's earliest poets, included Hugh's story in his *Canterbury Tales*. The cathedral in Lincoln contained a shrine to "Little St. Hugh" that was a tourist attraction for 700 years. In 1955, ten years after the Holocaust and in response to it, the plaque was removed. In its place is one with these words:

> *By the remains of the shrine of "Little St. Hugh": Trumped up stories of "ritual murders" of Christian boys by Jewish communities were common throughout Europe during the Middle Ages and even much later. These fictions cost many innocent Jews their lives. Lincoln had its own legend and the alleged victim was buried in the Cathedral in the year 1255. Such stories do not redound to the credit of Christendom, and so we pray: Lord, forgive what we have been, amend what we are, and direct what we shall be.*

BLOOD AND THE BLOOD LIBEL

Twenty years before Hugh's death in 1255, a new element had been added to charges of ritual murder against Jews. They were now accused of murdering Christian children for their blood. This accusation has become known as the "blood libel." Like other charges of ritual murder, the "blood libel" is a lie that has led to the death of countless Jews over the centuries.

In the thirteenth century, most people in northern Europe believed that blood had enormous power. Christians thought it was a source of strength, because it held the power of the soul. They used animal blood in medicines and in amulets, or charms, to ward off evil. Jews also thought blood had power. Because they thought that blood contained the spirit of living beings, Jews were forbidden to taste blood. Jewish dietary laws require great care in the preparation of meat to avoid the possibility of eating blood (as those who keep kosher are well aware). Animals are

BLOOD LIBELS (1144–1500)

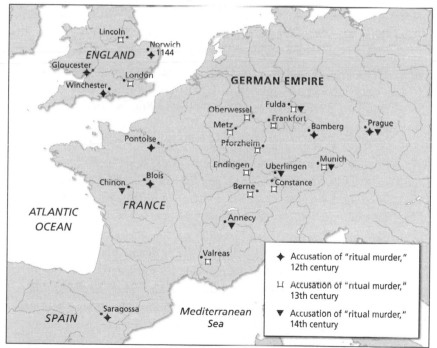

The map shows where in Europe Jews were accused of killing Christians for their blood for a period of approximately 300 years. Compare and contrast this map with the ones in Chapters 4 and 6. The three not only suggest the power of lies but also offer insight into the way lies spread over time and place.

slaughtered in such a way that most of the blood is drained rapidly. Whatever blood remains is removed by broiling or soaking and salting the meat. Even today, observant Jews are not permitted to eat so much as an egg that contains a blood spot. Jews who come into contact with blood have to purify themselves before carrying out their religious obligations.

Nevertheless, on Christmas Day in 1235, Jews in the town of Fulda in Germany were accused of murdering five children for their blood. The story begins when a miller and his wife, who lived just outside the town, returned from church to find their mill burned to the ground. The charred bodies of the couple's five sons lay in the ruins. They and their neighbors immediately accused "the Jews" of the crime. According to Christian chroniclers, "the Jews" had murdered the boys and had then drawn off their blood and placed it in waxed bags. What was the motive for such a horrendous crime? Some accounts give no explanation. Others suggest that "the Jews" needed the blood for medicinal or religious purposes.

Horrified by the "crime," townspeople placed the children's bodies in a cart and carried them to the emperor, Frederick II, as evidence of what "the Jews" had done. At a time when few people traveled more than a few miles from home in a lifetime, they walked more than 150 miles to the emperor's castle. At every stop along the way, they told their story.

Frederick did not know what to think; he had never heard of such a crime. So he sent messengers to other European rulers asking for advice. He also sent for recent converts to Christianity to help him determine the truth. In an edict issued in 1236, Frederick summarized what he had learned from his advisers:

> [It is] clear that it was not indicated in the Old Testament or in the New that Jews lust for the drinking of human blood. Rather, precisely the opposite, they guard against the intake of all blood, as we find expressly in the biblical book, which is called [Genesis in English], in the laws given by Moses, and in the Jewish decrees, which are called in Hebrew, "Talmud." We can surely assume that for those to whom even the blood of permitted animals is forbidden, the desire for human blood cannot exist, as a result of the horror of the matter, the prohibition of nature, and the common bond of the human species in which they also join Christians. Moreover, they would not expose to danger their substance and persons for that which they might have freely when taken from animals. By this sentence of the princes, we pronounce the Jews of the aforesaid place and the rest of the Jews of Germany completely absolved of this imputed crime. Therefore, we

decree . . . that no one, whether cleric or layman, proud or humble, whether under the pretext of preaching or otherwise, judges, lawyers, citizens, or others shall attack the aforesaid Jews individually or as a group a result of the aforesaid charge. Nor shall anyone cause them notoriety or harm in this regard. Let all know that, since a lord is honored through his servants, whosoever shows himself favorable and helpful to . . . the Jews will surely please us. However, whosoever presumes to contravene the edict of this present confirmation and of our absolution bears the offense of his majesty.[4]

Despite the emperor's order, the accusations continued. In March 1247, two Franciscans (members of a monastic order founded in about 1215) accused the Jews of Valréas, in France, of crucifying a Christian child and using his blood for ritual purposes. Several Jews in the town were tortured and many others were killed. The survivors appealed to Pope Innocent IV for help, and he condemned such accusations in strong language. So did his successor, Gregory X. In 1271, Gregory issued the following statement:

Since it happens occasionally that some Christians lose their Christian children, the Jews are accused by their enemies of secretly carrying off and killing these same Christian children and of making sacrifices of the heart and blood of these very children. It happens, too, that the parents of these children or some other Christian enemies of these Jews secretly hide these very children in order that they may be able to injure these Jews, and in order that they may be able to extort from them a certain amount of money by redeeming them from their straits. . . .

And most falsely do these Christians claim that the Jews have secretly and furtively carried away these children and killed them, and that the Jews offer sacrifice from the heart and the blood of these children, since their law in this matter precisely and expressly forbids Jews to sacrifice, eat, or drink the blood, or to eat the flesh of animals having claws. This has been demonstrated many times at our court by Jews converted to the Christian faith: nevertheless very many Jews are often seized and detained unjustly because of this.

We decree, therefore, that Christians need not be obeyed against Jews in a case or situation of this type, and we order that Jews seized under such a silly pretext be freed from imprisonment, and that they shall not be arrested henceforth on such a miserable pretext, unless— which we do not believe—they be caught in the commission of the crime. We decree that no Christian shall stir up anything new against them, but that they should be maintained in that status and position in which they were in the time of our predecessors, from antiquity till now.[5]

Gregory's statement suggests some of the reasons the accusations were readily believed. For one thing, life was difficult and dangerous for most people, and children were particularly vulnerable to accidents and illnesses. Grief-stricken parents may have wanted to blame someone for the death of their child, and by accusing "outsiders," they did not have to believe that God was responsible for their child's death. In addition, blaming an "outsider" meant that they themselves did not have to take responsibility for events like the fire in Fulda.

At a time when there were no newspapers and few books, and when most people could not read in any case, news arrived by way of travelers' stories and rumors. The more gruesome the story, the more interested people were (as they are today). And then, as now, rumors were almost always embellished in the retelling. There were generally no voices to be heard on the other side of the story. So, for example, by the time Frederick II issued his edict concerning the fire in Fulda, a year had passed, and the story was firmly embedded in people's minds.

Gregory mentions Christian enemies of Jews who falsely claimed that their children were dead in order to have Jews arrested and executed or to demand money from them before "finding" the children safe. Perhaps some of these Christians owed money to Jews and could not repay it; this might have seemed like an easy way to erase the debt. Others, influenced by those who preached against the Jews, doubtless believed they were acting as good Christians. For most Christians, the church was the major force in their lives and the only source of instruction and stories. It was also the main source of help in times of need and of medical care for the injured or ill. For such people, anyone who did not share their respect for and love of the church was easily suspected of terrible deeds.

Near the end of the thirteenth century, a new and even stranger accusation appeared—the desecration of the host. In many Christian churches, the central worship was—and is—the celebration of the Eucharist (a word that means "thanksgiving"). As part of the Eucharistic liturgy, unleavened bread and wine are blessed in remembrance of Jesus's words and actions at the Last Supper. According to the New Testament, at this Passover meal, Jesus blessed unleavened bread and wine and gave them to his disciples, saying, "This is my body. . . . This is my blood. Do this in remembrance of me." While there are different interpretations of what he might have meant by those words, many Christians believe they mean that Christ is truly present in the bread (the "host") and wine.

In the thirteenth century, however, a number of Christians came to believe that the host had magical powers. By 1290, some of these Christians were accusing Jews of desecrating the host. The rumor began in Paris. People whispered that a Jew had acquired a consecrated host (by theft or as security for a loan) in order to determine whether it had magical power. According to one version of the story, he stabbed it with a knife and then threw it into boiling water. The water immediately turned red with blood. According to rumors, after witnessing this miracle, the man and his family converted to Christianity.

The story spread from city to city and was widely believed. The pope even ordered a chapel built at the spot where the Parisian Jew had supposedly desecrated the host. It became a popular pilgrimage site. Despite the excitement, no one in Paris rioted or attacked Jews because of this story, perhaps because the story ended with the Jew's conversion. In other cities, however, particularly in what is now Germany, a charge of desecration was usually followed by riots in which many Jews were killed.

JEWS AND JUDAISM REDEFINED

With each new rumor, each new accusation, the way Christians thought about Jews became more and more distorted. Jews were increasingly seen as a powerful threat to Christianity, mainly because until the tenth century, Judaism was a faith that encouraged outsiders to convert. Even after Jews abandoned the practice of proselytizing, some Christians became Jews. The fear that many more Christians would do so was reflected in church laws.

For centuries, the church had declared that Jews were entitled to protection of their property and their person. They could not be forced to convert to Christianity, and their religious rituals were protected. These rights were balanced by limitations on what the church defined as "harmful" Jewish behavior. For example, Jews had to be in an inferior position in relation to Christians; therefore, they could not own Christian slaves or hold political positions that gave them authority over Christians.

The fear was that if Jews had power, they would use it to lure Christians away from their faith.

Those concerns can be seen in a bull issued in 1120 by Pope Calixtus II. (A bull is a formal proclamation issued by a pope. The word comes from the leaden *bulla*, or seal, that popes placed on legal documents.) The bull issued by Calixtus was addressed "to all the Christian Faithful." In it he declared that even though Jews remained "obstinately insistent" on keeping their beliefs, he was willing to protect their ancient rights, including the right to practice their faith, as long as they were "not guilty of plotting to subvert the Christian faith." Thus the pope maintained that his protection of Jews and their rights was conditional—that is, he would guard their rights provided that they did not challenge Christianity in any way.

Other popes issued similar statements. In 1205, for example, Innocent III stated that "Christian piety permits the Jews to dwell in the Christian midst." Yet he too warned that "Jews ought not be ungrateful to us, [repaying] Christian favor with [abuse] and intimacy with contempt."

In 1215, Innocent called together 400 bishops and hundreds of other religious and political leaders for the Fourth Lateran Council, an assembly that met in the Lateran Palace in Rome. The council issued 70 edicts in an effort to unite Christians and stamp out heresies, which were considered threats to the church. Five of the 70 edicts affected Jews or former Jews. Two addressed the cost of the loans Jews made to Christians. Charging interest for a loan was considered usury, a sin in the church. Another edict repeated a law that had been in effect for several hundred years: Jews were not to hold public office, "since this offers them a pretext to vent their wrath against Christians." Yet another edict dealt with Jews who converted to Christianity: church leaders were to keep those Jews from returning to Judaism. The final edict stated:

> *In some provinces a difference in dress distinguishes the Jews or Saracens [Muslims] from the Christians, but in certain others such a confusion has grown up that they cannot be distinguished by any difference. Thus it happens at times that through error Christians have relations with the women of Jews or [Muslims], and Jews and [Muslims] with Christian women. Therefore, that they may not, under pretext of error of this sort, excuse themselves in the future for the excesses of such prohibited intercourse, we decree that such Jews and [Muslims] of both sexes in every Christian province and at all times shall be marked off in the eyes of the public from other peoples through the character of their dress. . . .*

Moreover, during the last three days before Easter and especially on Good Friday, [Jews] shall not go forth in public at all, for the reason that some of them on these very days, as we hear, do not blush to go forth better dressed and are not afraid to mock the Christians who maintain the memory of the most holy Passion by wearing signs of mourning.

This, however, we forbid most severely, that any one should presume at all to break forth in insult to the Redeemer. And since we ought not to ignore any insult to Him who blotted out our disgraceful deeds, we command that such impudent fellows be checked by the secular princes by imposing [on] them proper punishment so that they shall not at all presume to blaspheme Him who was crucified for us.[6]

The first paragraph of the edict is similar to ones found in Muslim countries, because Christian authorities, like their Muslim counterparts, were concerned about "honest mistakes" in identifying the "other." And as in Muslim countries, the edict concerning clothing was not always enforced. A number of Jews quietly resisted the order, and a number of rulers quietly ignored their failure to obey. These rulers regarded Jews as their own subjects, and they did not want the pope to tell them how their subjects were to be treated. A few rulers pointed out that the requirement that all Jews wear a badge contradicted earlier bulls, which had said no change could be made in the customs of Jews.

Still, by the end of the thirteenth century, most European Jews were forced to wear badges or distinguishing clothing. The aim was to humiliate Jews by setting them apart from their neighbors. The effect was twofold: the image of Jews as a threat to Christians was reinforced, and as Jews became easier to identify, they were more vulnerable to attacks.

ATTACKS ON THE TALMUD

An even greater infringement on the traditional rights of Jews also had its start in the thirteenth century. The church began to attack the Talmud— the massive collection of Jewish laws and traditions compiled from about 200 to 600 CE. The first to denounce the Talmud was a former Jew named Nicholas Donin. Even before he converted to Christianity, he had rejected the Talmud as contrary to what he considered authentic Judaism—the Judaism of the Bible. The rabbis in La Rochelle, the French port city where he lived, excommunicated him for those beliefs in 1225. He then converted to Christianity and became a Franciscan friar.

WORMS

J U D E N.

A Jewish couple from Worms, a German city. The man has a badge sewn on his upper garment. Jews who failed to wear a badge were fined. In some places, all Jews also had to pay a special tax for the "right" to wear the badge.

In 1236, Donin presented Pope Gregory IX with a list of 35 charges against the Talmud and rabbinic Judaism—the form of Judaism practiced by most Jews since the first century of the Common Era. Donin told the pope that the Talmud was a work of heresy, as it contained lies and statements critical of Christians and Christianity. We do not know why Donin saw the Talmud as a threat to Christianity. Nor do we know why he thought the pope would care that Jews did not practice their faith in exactly the way their ancestors had.

What is known is that the pope waited three years to respond to Donin's charges. In June 1239, he sent Donin to the bishop of Paris with a copy of the charges and a request that the bishop pass them on to religious and political leaders in other parts of France. The letter contained an order to seize "all the books of Jews" in the leader's district on the first Saturday of Lent at a time when Jews gathered in their synagogues for prayer. A few weeks later, Gregory issued a second letter to the bishop of Paris directing that the books he had seized be burned.

King Louis IX of France decided to delay the book burnings. He first wanted to place the Talmud on trial. He asked Donin to serve as prosecutor and ordered the leading rabbi of Paris to answer Donin's charges. Another, more formal trial followed this public debate. The outcome was clear before either event took place: the Talmud was found "guilty," and the books were burned.

In June 1242, more than 24 wagonloads of books—about 10,000 volumes, each painstakingly created by hand—were destroyed in a public square in Paris. The fire burned for a day and a half. The book burning marked the beginning of a campaign against rabbinic Judaism, a campaign that was part of a larger war against heresies of all kinds. Jews tried desperately to persuade a new pope, Celestine IV, to change the ruling. Although he was willing, it was too late. The damage was done. In the years that followed, the Talmud would become the symbol of everything Christians feared about Jews and tried to suppress.

As a result of the "blood libel" and other lies, Christians in Europe in the thirteenth century and beyond increasingly saw Jews as a depraved and evil people. In many countries, Jews were now required to live apart from their neighbors and wear distinctive badges or clothes that alerted strangers to the "dangers" they posed. In times of war, plague, and other crises, those lies were used to blame "the Jews" for every misfortune.

---

[1] Quoted in Robert Chazan, *Medieval Stereotypes and Modern Antisemitism* (Berkeley: University of California Press, 1997), 64.

[2] Thomas of Monmouth, *The Life and Miracles of St. William of Norwich*, trans. and ed. Augustus Jessopp and Montague Rhodes James (Cambridge, UK: Cambridge University Press, 1896), 21–22.

[3] "The Letter of Nathan ben Rabbi Meshullam," quoted in Robert Chazan, ed., *Church, State, and Jew in the Middle Ages* (West Orange: Behrman House, 1980), 117.

[4] Emperor Frederick II, 1236, quoted in Chazan, ed., *Church, State, and Jew in the Middle Ages*, 125–126.

[5] "A Bull of Pope Gregory X," October 7, 1272, quoted in Jacob Rader Marcus, *The Jew in the Medieval World: A Source Book, 315–1791*, rev. ed. (Cincinnati: Hebrew Union College Press, 1999), 171–172.

[6] "That Jews Should be Distinguished from Christians in Dress," decree of the Fourth Lateran Council, November 1215, quoted in Marcus, *The Jew in the Medieval World*, 154–155.

6

Refugees from Intolerance

(1347–1492)

Throughout much of the history of Europe and the Middle East, religion shaped decisions about who belonged and who did not. Nonbelievers were often seen as outsiders and viewed with suspicion, fear, and sometimes hatred. In both Muslim and Christian lands during the 1300s and 1400s, Jews were considered outsiders no matter how long they and their families had lived in these regions. They were repeatedly told that they would be treated like everyone else if they accepted the religion of the majority. But many wondered whether this step would be enough to end discrimination and include them in the larger society.

THE BLACK DEATH

In October 1347, several trading ships from Genoa, Italy, pulled into the harbor at Messina in Sicily. Everyone aboard those ships was dead or dying of a mysterious plague. Europeans called it the Black Death, because victims had black swellings (each the size of an egg) on their bodies and black splotches on their skin. Today we know that bubonic plague is spread through the bites of fleas and lice that live on infected rats. But in 1347, people had no idea what caused the plague, how to treat it, or how to keep it from spreading.

In the countryside, an outbreak of plague usually lasted about six months and then faded away. In cities and other places where people lived in very crowded conditions—including monasteries and schools— the disease lasted much longer, often diminishing in the winter only to reappear in the spring. Jacob von Königshofen, a priest and historian, was a child during the years of the plague. He wrote of that time:

> *Death went from one end of the earth to the other, on that side and this side of the sea, and it was greater among the [Muslims] than among the Christians. In some lands everyone died so that no one was left. Ships were also found on the sea laden with wares; the crew*

THE SPREAD OF THE BLACK PLAGUE THROUGH EUROPE (1347–1351)

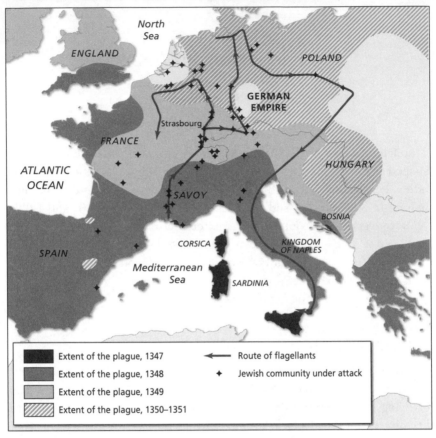

■ Extent of the plague, 1347	← Route of flagellants
■ Extent of the plague, 1348	✦ Jewish community under attack
▢ Extent of the plague, 1349	
▨ Extent of the plague, 1350–1351	

Notice the relationship between the route of the flagellants and the places where Jews were killed because people falsely believed that they were responsible for the plague.

> *had all died and no one guided the ship. The Bishop of Marseilles [in France] and priests and monks and more than half of all the people there died with them. In other kingdoms and cities so many people perished that it would be horrible to describe.*[1]

From ports like Messina, the plague spread through Europe, the Middle East, and North Africa. Between 1347 and 1351, the disease killed more than one out of every four people in those regions. Almost every family was affected. The rich died along with the poor, saints along with sinners. In Europe alone, some historians estimate the death toll at more than 20 million out of a population of approximately 80 million. No one knows the actual number, but so many people died that cemeteries were overflowing. At one point, Pope Clement VI sanctified the waters of the Rhone River in France so that bodies thrown into the river would be considered to have had a Christian burial.

Most people viewed the plague as an act of God, a kind of divine punishment. To avoid that punishment, Christians, Jews, and Muslims tried desperately to purify themselves through fasting and prayer. Ibn Battuta, a Muslim from Morocco who traveled through the Middle East in the fourteenth century, described the arrival of the plague in Damascus, Syria:

> [T]he people fasted for three successive days . . . then they assembled in the Great Mosque . . . until the place was filled to overflowing, and there they spent the Thursday night in prayers and litanies. After the dawn prayer next morning they all went out together on foot, holding Qurans in their hands. . . . The procession was joined by the entire population of the town, men and women, small and large; the Jews came with their Book of the Law and the Christians with their Gospel, all of them with their women and children.[2]

In Europe people also fasted and prayed, but they did not join together with those of other faiths. Instead, Christians increasingly blamed nonbelievers and heretics for the epidemic. Jews were the most common targets. Jacob von Königshofen wrote:

> In the matter of this plague the Jews throughout the world were reviled and accused in all lands of having caused it through the poison they are said to have put into the water and the wells—that is what they were accused of—and for this reason the Jews were burnt all the way from the Mediterranean [Sea] into Germany.[3]

Jews had been accused of poisoning wells long before the plague struck. Like the accusations of ritual murder, it was one of many myths fabricated about Jews in the fourteenth century. During the plague, those accusations were expanded to include lepers and Muslims as well as Jews. These outsiders supposedly boiled a mixture of frogs, spiders, lizards, consecrated hosts, and the hearts of Christians and then dried that mixture and ground it into a powder to drop into wells. Messengers supposedly transported the deadly powder to conspirators in cities and towns throughout Europe.

In September 1348, officials in Savoy, a town in southeastern France, became the first to formally accuse Jews of causing the plague by poisoning

In much of Europe, Christians blamed the Jews for the plague. In town after town, officials arrested Jewish residents and confiscated their property. The Jews were then burned at the stake.

wells. Every Jew in the town was arrested and his or her property confiscated. Officials tortured the prisoners until they confessed to their "crimes." After a trial based on those forced confessions, eleven Jews were burned alive.

As news of the murders spread, mobs in other cities and towns dragged Jews from their homes and threw them into bonfires. Pope Clement VI issued two bulls in an effort to stop the killing. He pointed out that people of all religions were dying from the disease. Jews were victims like everyone else; their death rate was about the same as that of Christians. But such arguments did nothing to ease the fears caused by the plague.

As the disease continued to spread north and east, a new Christian group, known as *flagellants*, suddenly appeared to fight the plague. Organized in bands of about 200 or more men, the flagellants traveled together for 33½ days before returning home. (The number reflects the traditional reckoning of Jesus's age at the time of the crucifixion—one day for each year.)

The flagellants recited prayers as they marched from city to city. When they approached a town, church bells rang to announce their arrival. Once in the town square, the men stripped to the waist and then whipped, or flagellated, themselves with heavy leather thongs tipped with metal studs. They were beating themselves to atone for the wickedness of the human race and to earn another chance from God. The flagellants believed that they alone not priests or bishops could save "all Christendom" from hell. Each tried to outdo the others in suffering, as townspeople looked on in amazement. Onlookers often sobbed and moaned as they recalled their own sins.

To join the group, a man had to confess his sins and agree to beat himself as the others did. He also had to vow not to bathe, shave, sleep in a bed, change his clothing, or have any contact with women during the length of his journey.

Many townspeople brought children to be healed by the flagellants; still others dipped cloth in the flagellants' blood and preserved it in the hope that it would protect their families from the plague. When priests tried to stop the marches, they were stoned. Many people were convinced that only the flagellants were pure enough to cast out evil spirits.

In every town the flagellants entered, they murdered Jews as the "poisoners of the wells." In Mainz, Germany, and in a few other places, Jews armed themselves in advance and fought back. Although they killed some of their attackers, they were hopelessly outnumbered by the crowds the flagellants attracted. Many Jews chose martyrdom. Like some Jews at the time of the first crusade (see Chapter 4), they killed themselves and their families in an act known as *Kiddush ha-Shem*, "the sanctification of the Name of God."

No one knows exactly how many Jewish communities were destroyed between 1347 and 1351 or how many Jews were murdered. According to some sources, mobs destroyed as many as 60 large Jewish communities and 150 smaller ones. A rabbi in Spain in the late 1300s estimated the number of Jews who died in these attacks in Europe to be 16,000 out of a total Jewish population of approximately 450,000.

Although the pope and other religious leaders condemned the murders, neither they nor political rulers were able to stop the flagellants until the plague began to decline. By 1350, some town councils were closing the gates of their cities to the flagellants. At about the same time, emperors and kings were warning that they would put to death anyone who took part in the movement. The groups began to disband and eventually disappeared, "vanishing as suddenly as they had come like night phantoms or mocking ghosts" as one chronicler wrote.

Elsewhere, in the Middle East and North Africa, millions of people also died as a result of the plague, but few there placed the blame on Jews—or on Christians. In these places, attacks on a minority group usually resulted from a local dispute or a culture clash, which rarely spread to other towns or regions. Why did Christians in Europe and Muslims in North Africa and the Middle East respond so differently to the plague?

One answer may lie in the difference between the way Christians and Muslims viewed nonbelievers in the fourteenth century. Muslims expected nonbelievers to obey the law, show respect for Islam, pay special taxes, and accept certain humiliations. As long as these requirements were met, they were left alone. Many Christians, however, saw the mere presence of non-believers as contaminating a community. They thought a community had to be united in a single faith to be acceptable to God. As a result, nonbelievers did not have to do anything to be considered a threat; the fact that they did not believe was reason enough to fear them and persecute them.

The Christian mobs in Europe were not carrying out a religious mandate. In fact, they were openly defying the pope and other religious leaders. They were also defying their own political leaders. For example, on February 9, 1349, the town council of Strasbourg, a city in present-day France, voted to protect local Jews from attack. That evening, the city's guilds overthrew the council and put a new one in its place. The new councilmen promptly ordered the arrest of all Jews. Jacob von Königshofen described what happened next:

> On Saturday—that was St. Valentine's Day—they burnt the Jews on a wooden platform in their cemetery. There were about two thousand people. Those who wanted to baptize themselves were spared. . . . Many small children were taken out of the fire and baptized against the will of their fathers and mothers. And everything that was owed to the Jews was cancelled, and the Jews had to surrender all pledges and notes that they had taken for debts. The council, however, took the cash that the Jews possessed and divided it among the workingmen proportionately. The money was indeed the thing that killed the Jews. If they had been poor and if the feudal lords had not been in debt to them, they would not have been burnt. After this wealth was divided among the artisans, some gave their share to the Cathedral or to the Church on the advice of their confessors.

> Thus were the Jews burnt at Strasbourg, and in the same year in all the cities of the Rhine. . . . In some towns they burnt the Jews after a trial, in others, without a trial. In some cities, the Jews themselves set fire to their own houses and cremated themselves.[4]

"THE MONEY WAS INDEED THE THING . . ."

Why did artisans and other workingmen in many cities feel differently about Jews than their city councils did? After all, they lived in the same place, shared the same religion, and feared the same plague.

The mobs were made up of people who were often deeply in debt. When they needed money for their businesses, family emergencies, or taxes, the only place they could get a loan was from a moneylender. And by the fourteenth century, in most European cities, that moneylender was almost always a Jew. Many Jews became moneylenders partly because many other occupations were closed to them and partly because Christians did not want to take on this "sin" themselves.

Then, as now, a lender and a borrower came to an agreement. The lender agreed to give the borrower a sum of money in exchange for the borrower's promise to repay the debt with interest. In most cases, the borrower also had to provide security for the loan—property or other assets that the lender could claim if the borrower failed to pay the debt. The item offered

A German farmer in the 1400s approaches a Jewish moneylender. The drawing is one of the very few to show Jews in a realistic manner.

as security had to be something of at least equal value to the loan itself—a piece of land, a building, a horse, a gemstone, or some other asset.

In many cities, including Strasbourg, Jewish moneylenders aroused hatred because they charged 30 percent to 50 percent interest or more for many loans. They felt that the high rates were justified because the risks were equally high. But such high rates infuriated many people, and Strasbourg's councilmen were not the first to give in to a mob by canceling all debts to Jewish lenders.

Despite the high interest rates, most people were able to pay their debts when times were good. However, when times were hard—as they often were in the fourteenth century—many borrowers lost everything they owned. They rarely blamed their losses on the drought that destroyed their crops, the wars that devastated much of Europe, the plague, or just bad luck. It was easier to direct their anger at the person who had loaned them the money and was now demanding repayment. The moneylender was not a big impersonal bank with hundreds of employees but a real person—someone the borrower knew by name and saw in the market or on the street. The loan was personal, and so was the anger when the moneylender asked for repayment with interest.

Although most moneylenders were Jews, most Jews were not money-lenders. To earn a living by lending money, you need to have money you can afford to risk, and most Jews did not. Why did those who did become moneylenders? Probably because they saw an opportunity to get ahead or make extra money. As trade in Europe expanded in the twelfth century, so did the demand for loans. As long as lenders could minimize their losses, they had the potential to earn large sums of money. (Of course, not all of them were successful.)

There was another reason some Jews became moneylenders around the end of the 1100s: they had few other ways of earning a living. Jews were no longer allowed to own land in many places, so they could not farm for a living. Only Christians could join guilds, so most crafts were closed to Jews. They could trade, but in many places their ability to compete was restricted. For instance, in some cities, they were allowed to sell goods only at certain hours. They also had to pay a special tax whenever they entered or left the market. Christians did not have such limitations.

City councils had protected Jews over the years because their members understood that borrowing was essential to the growth of their communities and their own businesses. Loans made it possible for cities to build roads and churches and to carry out other public projects. To some degree, then, a council's support for local Jews was a matter of self-interest—though standing up to an angry mob took courage, as it does today.

City councils got their power from a king or noble, and those rulers also needed money. Many of them not only borrowed from Jews but also taxed them heavily—far more heavily than they taxed their other subjects. When Jewish communities were established in Europe in the ninth and tenth centuries, Jews were free to move from place to place. By the fourteenth century, however, they were considered "serfs of the exchequer." In earlier centuries, that term had meant that Jews received the protection of a king or noble in exchange for paying taxes. Now Jews were increasingly considered the property of kings or nobles.

Jewish lenders, no matter how wealthy they might become, could lose everything at a ruler's whim. For example, in 1286, Rudolph I of Germany confiscated the possessions of Jews who were about to move out of his kingdom. Before they left, he declared that they were "serfs of the king's exchequer in their body and their possessions," and therefore their property belonged to him. In 1343, King Ludwig of Bavaria canceled the debts owed to Jews in Nuremburg by telling them, "You belong to us and the kingdom in your body and possessions and we are free to deal with you howsoever we wish."

As money lending became an increasingly risky business, Jews found themselves isolated. They could count on protection only when a ruler's interests matched their own and when that ruler was willing to risk the wrath of the mob. Most rulers were not willing to take such risks.

Why did Christians find it easy to hate Jews and to believe cruel lies about them? To people without money, it may have seemed as if Jewish moneylenders did no "real" work and yet were richer than their hardworking neighbors. And people who could not read or do arithmetic (an overwhelming majority of the population at that time) no doubt suspected that they were being cheated when the moneylender told them how much interest they owed. When a Jewish moneylender demanded repayment of money he had loaned, he may have seemed to be adding to the burdens of a family that was already in deep financial trouble. People who are deeply in debt sometimes see the money they owe as a sign of failure; they feel ashamed that they were unable to manage their affairs better. Such embarrassment or shame may have led Christian borrowers to blame the lender, and this was easier when that lender was an outsider. And because many believed that charging interest for a loan was a sin, their blame was particularly intense.

The church governed much of daily life in this period. The only book most people knew much about was the Bible. The church was their only source of help in times of flood or famine. The rules they lived by were said to be the word of God. From their perspective, Jews were seen both as outsiders who refused to participate in the spiritual life of the community and as wealthy misers who demanded impossible payments from hard-working people who could not afford to pay. Yet Christians needed to borrow money, and no one was willing to lend it to them without interest. When Jews were killed and their money and property confiscated, people might have felt guilty about the theft. However, if they could persuade themselves that the Jews deserved to be killed and robbed, there would be less to feel guilty about.

After the Black Death in the mid-1300s, the persecution of Jews intensified, and many Jews in Europe moved farther east. Some left because life at home had become too dangerous. Others headed east because they were forced from their homes. Increasingly, whenever a ruler decided that his debts were overwhelming or that he no longer needed the services Jews provided, he expelled them—no matter how long they and their families had lived in the country. In every instance, the ruler claimed their property and took charge of all money owed to them. Borrowers then had to pay their debts to the ruler instead of to the Jewish lenders.

SPAIN: AN EXCEPTION?

In contrast to much of northern Europe, where Jews faced persecution, Spain was a haven. From the eighth century onward, Jews there prospered under Muslim and, later, Christian rule. By the fifteen century, Spain had the largest Jewish population in the world. One out of every ten individuals in Spain was a Jew or of Jewish descent. Jews were prominent in trade, medicine, the arts, and even government. And yet in 1492, Spain expelled its entire Jewish population. The expulsion shows how precarious life was for outsiders, particularly Jews.

First, some background: By 715 CE, Muslims had conquered the entire Iberian Peninsula (Spain and Portugal). The newcomers treated the Iberian people they conquered, both Christians and Jews, as *dhimmi*—people who belonged to a tolerated religion—just as the Muslims in Syria did at about the same time (see Chapter 3). As *dhimmi*, Jews and Christians had rights, including the right to practice their religion and establish their own communities. In return, they had to obey Muslim laws, pay special taxes, and suffer discrimination and humiliation depending on the whim of a ruler.

Today, receiving *dhimmi* status does not sound like much of an accomplishment. In effect, the *dhimmi* were second-class citizens—separate from but definitely not equal to Muslims. But in the eighth century and later, *dhimmi* status was a step forward, particularly for Jews: most had more freedom in Muslim Spain than anywhere else in Europe. Jews there could own land and farm for a living. They could also become artisans, practice medicine, and buy and sell a variety of goods. Some worked as diplomats, advisers, and translators for the caliphs who then ruled Spain.

Christians were less satisfied with Muslim rule, and they fought from time to time to try to regain control of the peninsula. By the eleventh century, their fight had become a holy war. Slowly they made progress. By the beginning of the twelfth century, Spain was divided into small territories; most of the Christian kingdoms were in the north and the Muslim principalities in the south.

How Jews were treated in a particular place always depended on who was king or caliph. A ruler who was tolerant of Jews and other minorities might be followed by one who was greedy, cruel, or just weak. In the late twelfth century, the Almohades, a North African people who believed in an extreme form of Islam, overran much of Spain. Even though forced conversions were against Muslim law, the Almohades demanded that all *dhimmi* convert to Islam. Christians responded by fleeing north to kingdoms under Christian rule. Some Jews fled to the north, as well. Although the rulers of those kingdoms considered Jews "serfs of the exchequer" in much the way rulers did in other parts of Europe, they needed money and other aid from Jews and were therefore willing to give them considerable freedom. As a result, some Jews in Christian Spain provided supplies to the military, managed the financial affairs of various kingdoms, and even held high positions in government—occupations that were unthinkable in other parts of Europe. A few even fought in the *Reconquista*—the wars Christians waged to reconquer the Iberian Peninsula.

Many other Jews found refuge in more tolerant Muslim lands. Among them was the family of Moses Maimonides, one of the most extraordinary Jews of his or any other time. Maimonides was born in Cordoba in 1135. When the Almohades took control of the town in 1145, his parents and other Jews in the city were forced to convert to Islam. In order to become Jews again, they had to leave Cordoba. For ten years, the family moved from place to place in Spain before settling in Morocco, where young Maimonides studied science and medicine. In time he moved to Egypt, where he became a noted philosopher, a physician to the sultan of Egypt, and the leader of the Jewish community in Cairo. He was admired and revered by both Muslims and Jews.

Journeys like the one that the Maimonides family made became more and more common as the battle for control of Spain continued. By the thirteenth century, Christians ruled all of Spain except Grenada in the south, and Ferdinand III of Castile (who ruled his kingdom in northern Spain from 1230 to 1252) proudly declared himself "king of three religions." Yet even as he boasted of his toleration, there were signs of trouble. Many Christians resented the idea of Jews in high places. They complained that Jews were favored over Christians.

The preaching of two religious orders, the Dominicans and the Franciscans, reinforced distrust of Jews. Everywhere they traveled—and they spent most of their time traveling—these monks spread myths and lies about Jews. They claimed that Jews routinely committed ritual murder, desecrated the host (see Chapter 5), and poisoned wells. During the plague years in the fourteenth century, such stories led to massacres of Jews in Barcelona and other Spanish cities.

RIOTS AND CONVERSIONS

In 1378, a high-ranking Franciscan priest named Ferrán Martínez began a campaign against Jews in Castile. In sermon after sermon, he called on Christians to expel all Jews from Spain. Jewish leaders defended their community, reminding King Enrique II of their contributions to Spanish life. They also asked the king to denounce this priest. Although he was sympathetic, the king was in the midst of a political struggle of his own, trying desperately to hold on to his throne.

By 1390, Martínez was powerful enough to take advantage of the king's weakness. In December, Martínez ordered priests in his diocese to destroy all synagogues in their area. Then, early on the morning of June 4, 1391, he and his followers attacked the Jews of Seville, the capital of Castile. They murdered hundreds of Jews in their homes and countless more in the streets. Many Jewish women and children were captured and sold into slavery. A few Jews fled the country, but many converted to Christianity to escape death. According to one observer, "[In] the shortest time and with great speed, the tumult [in Seville] spread through all of Spain and even beyond the Pyrenees and to the islands of Majorca and Sardinia."

Martínez and his followers played a central role in the widening crisis. They moved through the countryside, murdering Jews wherever they went. Cordoba was their next target, then Toledo, where Jews were burned alive or drowned in the Tagus River. Again, hundreds of Jews converted to

Christianity to save themselves. By July, when the group reached Valencia in Aragon, that city's Jews had armed themselves in preparation for an attack. They won an early victory but were outnumbered by the growing mobs. Local officials were too fearful of the rioters to protect the Jews, even though the king had ordered them to do so.

Why did so many people join the mobs? Events in Barcelona offer some clues. When Martínez and his followers arrived there in early August, many Christians in the city joined in with them. Before the two groups made their first assault on the Jewish quarter, they burned the building that housed records of the debts Christians in Barcelona owed local Jews.

As in northern Europe, the rioters consisted mainly of workingmen and artisans who were deeply in debt to Jews. Unlike officials in northern Europe, those in Barcelona responded to the destruction by arresting the ringleaders. However, they were unable to prevent the rioters from storming the jail and freeing their leaders before continuing their attack on the city's Jews. As in other cities, thousands of Jews in Barcelona chose to convert rather than be slaughtered in the streets.

The rioting in many parts of Spain that began in June of 1391 did not end until August, and new violence broke out repeatedly between the fall of 1391 and 1420. In both Castile and Aragon, the violence was followed by increased pressure on Jews to convert. Jews were forced to attend sermons in which Christian preachers showed them the "errors" of their beliefs, and new laws were passed that segregated Jews from Christians, outlawed the Talmud and other rabbinic literature, and limited the occupations that were still open to Jews. As a result of the violence and the campaigns to convert them, large numbers of Spanish Jews did become Christians—most sources estimate the number to be more than 100,000.

For hundreds of years, Christians had been trying to convert the Jews, and now, for the first time, they had real success. Suddenly thousands of Jews had become Christians. Christians should have rejoiced, and many did. Yet within a generation or two, a growing number were uncomfortable with the changes that mass conversion had brought.

As baptized Christians, the *conversos* ("converted ones") were entitled to all the rights and privileges other Christians enjoyed, and they were quick to take advantage of this change in their status. As Christians, these former Jews entered new occupations even while some continued in traditionally "Jewish" ones like money lending and tax collecting. They held important posts in government and the church. They were a force in the arts as well as the marketplace. In short, the New Christians made the most of their economic and social opportunities.

One of the first signs of the growing resentment toward New Christians appeared in Toledo in 1449. The spark was an unpopular tax. When the king ordered *converso* tax collectors to enforce that tax, a riot broke out. Unwilling to challenge the king, the mob turned its anger not only on tax collectors but also on other *conversos*. They accused the New Christians of practicing Jewish customs and rituals. For the most part, these charges were false. Most *conversos* were sincere in their commitment to Christianity. By the mid-1400s, many came from families that had been Christian for two generations or more. They no longer had ties to Judaism.

Officials in Toledo and elsewhere responded to those charges not by defending *conversos* but by requiring "purity of blood" as proof of being a "true Christian." Because the *conversos* had "Jewish blood," they were considered "unworthy and unfit," and they were now segregated in much the way Jews were segregated. In a sense, officials in Toledo were saying that Jews were not just members of a religious group but were in fact members of a "race." Anyone can change religion, but a person cannot change his or her "blood." Purity-of-blood laws spread quickly throughout Christian Spain, even though the pope condemned them. He objected to them because they contradicted the idea that the church was "catholic," or universal.

Yet even as the pope denounced the laws, a number of popular monks and friars went a step further by linking *conversos* to Jews and Judaism. They accused the New Christians of being "false" Christians led astray by evil Jews who were guilty of blood rituals and devil worship. As a result, violent attacks on *conversos* increased.

King Ferdinand II and Queen Isabella created the Spanish Inquisition in 1480 primarily to deal with rumors of Judaizing by *conversos*. It was not the first inquisition in Europe or, indeed, in Spain. (The word originally meant an inquiry or investigation.) Pope Gregory IX had introduced the inquisition in France in 1231 as an organization within the church whose purpose was to root out heresies. The Spanish Inquisition had the same goal, but the government, rather than the church, was in charge. From the start, officials focused on the *conversos*.

What constituted Judaizing? Lighting candles on a Friday night, failure to attend church regularly, and even a dislike of pork were all considered signs of Judaizing. The inquisitors tortured one woman because she put fresh sheets on her bed on Friday, just before the Jewish Sabbath began.

How did the inquisitors uncover such behavior? Anyone could accuse another person of heresy. The defendants were never told who their accusers were or allowed to confront them in open court. The inquisitors also had the right to use torture to obtain evidence; this was standard procedure for all crimes at the time. Those convicted of heresy faced life in prison or death by burning at a public event known as an *auto-da-fé*—a Portuguese term that means "act of faith." The accusers were later rewarded for their actions by receiving part of the victim's estate (the government kept the rest). Historians estimate that by 1490, about 2,000 New Christians had been burned to death. Others died as a result of torture or were left to rot in prison. Many *conversos* decided to leave Spain during the years of the Inquisition. Some returned to Judaism, but many did not.

Even as the Spanish Inquisition took its toll on New Christians, new laws restricted the freedom of Jews in order to segregate them from Christians of both kinds. The laws were passed shortly after Ferdinand and Isabella united all of the kingdoms in Christian Spain under their rule. They were about to begin a final push to reunite the entire country by conquering Grenada, the last territory in Spain still ruled by Muslims. Much of the money needed for this war came from Jews; between 1482 and 1492, Jews paid a fortune in special taxes and forced "loans."

EXPULSION FROM SPAIN

On January 3, 1492, Ferdinand and Isabella defeated the last Muslim outpost in Grenada. Just three months later, on March 31, they issued an order addressed to the people of Spain, particularly the nation's Jews. It claimed that the presence of Jews had "resulted in great damage and detriment of our holy Catholic faith." Therefore, "after much deliberation," they "resolved that all Jews and Jewesses be ordered to leave our kingdoms, and that they never be allowed to return." Any Jew who remained in Spain after July of 1492 would "incur punishment by death and confiscation of all their belongings."

By accusing Jews of leading Christians astray, Ferdinand and Isabella gave their expulsion order a religious justification. Many historians believe that other forces were also at work; perhaps the most powerful was their desire for a strong central government in Spain based on Christianity.

Most Europeans at the end of the fifteenth century considered religious unity a good idea, but only Spain's rulers believed it was essential to building a strong nation. Spain's population, which included large

Jewish and Muslim communities, was more diverse than that of other European nations. Ferdinand and Isabella set out to eliminate these non-Christian communities. Jews were the first to be given the choice of exile or conversion. Once they were gone, attention turned to Muslims, who were offered a similar choice.

Yet even after the expulsion of both groups, concerns remained. Spaniards still looked at New Christians as outsiders. The laws requiring purity of blood remained on the books. And the Spanish Inquisition continued to root out people suspected of having "Judaizing" tendencies.

JEWS WITHOUT A HOME

Every Jew in Spain, no matter how rich or powerful, had been forced to leave the country in 1492. One of the most prominent was Isaac Abravanel, who had served as an adviser to Ferdinand and Isabella. Among other duties, he had helped them finance another kind of journey that took place in 1492—Christopher Columbus's voyage of discovery. Although Abravanel tried to persuade the king and queen to change their minds about expelling Jews, he was unsuccessful. He ended up in the Kingdom of Naples in what is now Italy. There, he wrote of the journey that ended more than 1,500 years of Jewish life in Spain:

> In the end there left, without strength, three hundred thousand people on foot, from the youngest to the oldest, all at one time, from all the provinces of the king, to wherever they were able to go. . . . Each pledged himself to God anew. Some went to Portugal and Navarre, which are close, but all they found were troubles and darkness, looting, starvation and pestilence. Some traveled through the perilous ocean, and here, too, God's hand was against them, and many were seized and sold as slaves, while many others drowned in the sea. Others again, were burned alive, as the ships on which they were traveling were engulfed by flames.

> In the end, all suffered: some by the sword and some by captivity and some by disease, until but a few remained of the many. . . . I, too, chose the way of the sea, and I arrived in the famed Naples, a city whose kings are merciful.[5]

The task of finding a new home was complicated by the fact that Spain was not the only country that had expelled its Jews. Jews were also

In this drawing, the artist imagines that King Philip Augustus personally expelled the Jews from France in 1182.

forced out of regions that today make up the following countries: France in 1182, 1306, and 1394; England in 1290; Germany in 1348 and 1498; Hungary in 1349 and 1360; and Lithuania in 1445 and 1495.

Jews were expelled from some places more than once. After a few years, they were sometimes allowed to return to a city, a region, or even a country for a specific amount of time.

Where did Jews go? Those expelled from England, France, and the various German states headed for Eastern Europe. Some Jews from Spain, Portugal, and, in the sixteenth century, parts of Italy also settled in Poland and other parts of Eastern Europe, but most went to places closer to Spain—including many Muslim countries.

Moving from one country to another is never easy. For Jews, it was particularly difficult. Jewish families needed permission to settle in a new country and enough money to make a fresh start. Although Christians saw all Jews as rich, and some were, the vast majority barely eked out a living, and moving was even more expensive then than it is today. Of course, the more money a family had, the better its chances of finding a new home. Rulers routinely expected large cash payments before they allowed Jews to move into or out of their countries.

For example, the vast majority of the Jews who left Spain in 1492 went to Portugal. King John II made them pay for the privilege of settling in his kingdom. He charged each individual for the right to stay in the country for eight months. When that time was up, the person had to go elsewhere or convert to Christianity. Wealthier Jews paid even more money for the right to settle permanently in the country. However, just five years later, John's successor expelled these and all other Jews from the country. Why? He wanted to marry the daughter of Isabella and Ferdinand. She and her parents would not agree to the marriage unless Portugal was free of Jews.

Only a few places allowed Jews to settle openly and in large numbers. Among them were Italy, particularly the Papal States (territories controlled by the pope), and Poland in Eastern Europe. The rulers of the Ottoman Empire, which would soon stretch from Eastern Europe across the Middle East through North Africa, also welcomed Jews. According to a popular story at the time, Sultan Bayezid II said of Ferdinand's expulsion of the Jews, "How can you call such a king wise and intelligent? He is making his country poorer and enriching my kingdom."

By the middle of the 1500s, the sultan had made Constantinople (now Istanbul, in Turkey), the capital of his empire. It was soon home to about 50,000 Jews. Thousands more found homes in other parts of the empire, including what is now Israel.

A particular group of *conversos* made a different journey in 1492. One of them kept a diary. His Christian name was Luis de Torres. He converted the day before his ship left shore—mainly so that he could make the journey. He wrote:

> *The fateful day, the day of our expulsion from Spain, was [the ninth of Av] on the Jewish calendar in the year 5252/1492. That day marked the tragedy of the destruction of both holy temples many centuries before, and now, one more tragic event was added to that mournful day. Three hundred thousand people, half the amount that were redeemed from Egyptian slavery, descended to the Mediterranean shore, searching for passage to a new land, to a land where they could openly practice Judaism. I was among them.*

> *However, I was not a refugee; I had been commissioned to join Christopher Columbus's voyage of discovery. I agreed to accompany him because I hoped that if we found Jewish brethren, I would be able to live my life in peace and in freedom. Don Rodriguez, his uncle Don Gabriel Sanchez, Alonso de Loquir, Rodrigo de Triana,*

Chon Kabrera, Doctor Briena and Doctor Marco, all agreed with my reasoning and joined, but except for Rodrigo, they sailed on the other ships. We were a large group of conversos *(Morranos), living in perpetual fear of the Inquisition, hoping that we would find a way out of the precarious situation we were in. . . .*

Columbus thought that when he would reach China and the Far East, he would locate the exiled Jews from the Ten Lost Tribes, and he wanted me [with a knowledge of Hebrew] to be able to communicate with them.[6]

DeTorres's skill as a translator was never tested on the voyage—because Columbus never found the Ten Lost Tribes. However, he did unknowingly stumble upon two continents new to Europeans that would, in time, provide a refuge for many Jews.

---

[1] Jacob von Königshofen, "The Cremation of Strasbourg Jewry St. Valentine's Day," February 14, 1349, quoted in Jacob Rader Marcus, ed., *The Jew in the Medieval World: A Source Book, 315–1791*, rev. ed (Cincinnati: Hebrew Union College Press, 1999), 51–52.

[2] H. A. R. Gibb, trans. and ed., *Ibn Battuta: Travels in Asia and Africa*, (London: Broadway House, 1929), 69.

[3] Königshofen, "The Cremation of Strasbourg Jewry," quoted in Marcus, ed., *The Jew in the Medieval World*, 52.

[4] Ibid., 53.

[5] Isaac Abravanel, *Commentary to the Prophets*, quoted and trans. in Benjamin Blech, *Eyewitness to Jewish History* (Hoboken: John Wiley & Sons, 2004), 148.

[6] "The Diary of Luis De Torres" in the *Los Angeles Jewish Times*, December 24, 1999, quoted in Blech, *Eyewitness to Jewish History*, 149–150.

7

In Search of Toleration

(1500–1635)

In 1500, Christian beliefs and traditions shaped daily life throughout western Europe. Almost everywhere, church bells marked the hours and called the faithful to prayer. Conformity was the rule in a world that valued obedience and considered toleration a dangerous idea.

The word *toleration* has many meanings. It can refer to respect for and recognition of the beliefs of others. But it can also mean the act of enduring something or someone unpleasant. And sometimes it means simply allowing the presence of others without actively opposing them. Most Christians in Europe in 1500 considered toleration morally wrong. They were convinced that the very presence of nonbelievers in a community threatened that community's welfare.

Yet within just a few decades, the religious unity of western Europe would be shattered. And as a result of that shattering, a chain of events would be set into motion that eventually led both to horrific acts of violence and to the shaky beginnings of religious coexistence and even toleration. Although much of the drama of those years centered on Christianity, the key events that marked the sixteenth century had a profound impact on Jews. According to an old Jewish saying, "When the earth shakes, we feel it." The earth shook in the 1500s and early 1600s, for Jews as well as for Christians.

NEW OUTLOOKS

Despite outward appearances, life in western Europe in 1500 was very different from what it had been even 50 years earlier. Some of those changes were the result of voyages of discovery, like the one Christopher Columbus began in 1492. Other changes arose from a less dramatic but equally profound event. In 1440, a German goldsmith named Johannes Gutenberg invented the printing press in Europe. Before his invention, books had been handwritten, a single copy could take months, even years, to complete. By 1500, 236 cities and towns in Europe had their own print shops. At a time when the continent's total population was approximately 70 million, most of whom could neither read nor write, an estimated 20 million books were now in print.[1]

That explosion of knowledge encouraged the growth of a movement known as *humanism*. It is not an easy term to define. Humanism has had different meanings at different times and in different places. Still, almost everywhere in sixteenth-century Europe, humanism centered on a rediscovery of the great writers of ancient Greece and Rome—writers who reflected on human endeavors and achievements. For centuries, their works had been kept alive by Muslim scholars. Now they were rediscovered by Christians who found the ideas of these writers extremely relevant to their lives.

Hundreds of Christian scholars now studied ancient Greek and Latin so that they could read Aristotle, Virgil, and Ovid in the languages in which these great thinkers had written. The enthusiasm of such scholars changed education. Many universities no longer focused almost entirely on religious studies. Students now explored the liberal arts—including the literature, music, and art of the ancient world.

Today the word *humanist* is often used to describe those who focus on worldly concerns and reject religion and religious authority. In the 1500s, however, almost all humanists were devout Christians who saw no contradiction between their interest in humankind and their religious beliefs. Indeed, their interest in the ancient world led them to reread religious books with a new eye so that they could correct errors in translation and interpretation.

Humanism had begun in Florence, Italy, about 20 years before the invention of the printing press. Many scholars there were astonished at how freely people in ancient Greece and Rome had debated ideas and challenged popular beliefs with logic and reason. They and humanists in other parts of Europe tried to revive that spirit of inquiry. They focused on descriptions recorded by witnesses to an event, as opposed to accounts written later by those who were not present.

For centuries, Christian scholars had relied on such secondary sources for information to shape their understanding of their religion. Now a few began to critically examine primary sources, including early versions of the Bible, to deepen their insights. This new approach to reading religious texts changed the way many scholars viewed their world and altered their ideas about difference.

THE BATTLE OF THE PAMPHLETS

Many scholars now believed that they could study Jewish texts and still remain true to Christianity. Today that idea does not seem very radical. But in sixteenth-century Europe, it was revolutionary. Most Christians still believed that Hebrew books were so dangerous that they had to be destroyed. Among such Christians was a recent convert from Judaism named Johannes Pfefferkorn. In 1509, Pfefferkorn, with the help of Dominican friars at the University of Cologne in present-day Germany, persuaded Maximilian I, the Holy Roman emperor, to confiscate and burn all Jewish books, with the exception of the Hebrew Scriptures, "since by these means [Jews] grow more firmly planted in their faithlessness."

After Jews asked the emperor to reconsider his stand, Maximilian turned to Johannes Reuchlin, a Christian scholar and humanist, for advice. Reuchlin recommended preserving Hebrew books, because they might help Christian scholars in "deriving proof of our Christian faith." He scorned those who wanted to destroy Jewish books even though they had never read one: "If someone wished to write against the mathematicians and was himself ignorant in simple arithmetic or mathematics, he would be made a laughingstock."

Reuchlin also questioned whether Christians had the right to burn Jewish books. In his view, both Jews and Christians were "citizens of the Holy Roman Empire, we Christians by virtue of the Emperor's choice by electors, the Jews through their submission [to the emperor] and their public profession [of loyalty]."[2] Still, even though he regarded Jews as "legal equals" living "under one civil law and one civil peace," Reuchlin, as a faithful Christian, insisted that unless Jews showed "signs of improvement"—for example, by no longer charging interest for loans—they could and should be exiled.

Reuchlin's argument was a complicated mixture of toleration and prejudice, but it persuaded Maximilian. The emperor ordered the books returned to their owners. Josel of Rosheim, a rabbi who served as an advocate for Jews in their dealings with the Holy Roman Empire, described the decision as a "double miracle": first, the books were returned unharmed, and second, they had been saved by a Christian.

Enraged by Reuchlin's success, Pfefferkorn and his supporters published pamphlets attacking Reuchlin. Reuchlin and his supporters replied with pamphlets of their own. In one, Reuchlin claimed that Pfefferkorn was wrong to insist that "Divine Law forbids our holding [everyday contact] with Jews; this is not true. Every Christian must go to law with them, buy from them. . . . It is allowed to converse with and learn from them, as St. Jerome . . . did. And lastly, a Christian should love a Jew as his neighbor; for all is founded on the law."[3] It was an amazing statement at a time and in a place in which most Christians saw Jews as evil and dangerous. Not surprisingly, the statement stirred up further controversy.

Before long, dozens of pamphlets had been printed, as each side in the debate attacked the other with passion and often venom. The battle of the pamphlets raged wherever scholars gathered. Those at the universities of Mainz, Cologne, Erfurt, Heidelberg, and Paris sided with Pfefferkorn; they remained faithful to the traditional policies of the church. Reuchlin's supporters saw themselves as "fosterers of the arts and of the study of humanity." Unlike Pfefferkorn's supporters, they were not gathered at one university or even a group of nearby schools but were scattered among the faculty at universities throughout Europe.

In 1514, the Dominican friars at the University of Cologne tried to end the controversy by charging Reuchlin with the crime of "Judaizing." They wanted to put him on trial before an inquisition in Cologne. Fearful that he wouldn't get a fair hearing in a city where the Dominicans had great influence, Reuchlin asked Pope Leo X to transfer the trial to another city. Leo agreed; he referred the matter to the bishop of Speyer, who ruled in Reuchlin's favor in 1516.

But the controversy was not over. Reuchlin's enemies asked the pope to overturn the bishop's decision. In 1520, Leo found Reuchlin guilty and condemned him to silence. He could no longer participate in public debates or discussions. Reuchlin died two years later.

A RELIGIOUS REVOLUTION

In 1517, as the controversy still raged, Martin Luther, a young professor of theology at the University of Wittenberg in Germany, nailed a list of 95 theses, or arguments, to his church door. This was what scholars traditionally did when they wanted to spark a debate: they posted their ideas in a public place. The issue Luther wanted to discuss was the pope's sale of indulgences— cancellations of part or all of the penance due for a person's sins. Leo X needed money for the renovation of St. Peter's cathedral in Rome. He had hired Raphael, one of the most famous artists of his time, to enlarge the church and make it grander. Leo planned to raise the funds he needed for the church by selling more indulgences.

Many Christians were outraged by the pope's actions. Some resented the idea of raising large sums of money to beautify a church in Rome rather than those in their own cities and towns. Others were troubled by the idea of selling a cancellation of God's punishment.

Luther was among those who wanted to end such practices. He thought that the sale of indulgences turned God's forgiveness into an object that could be bought and sold rather than a divine gift to those who sincerely repented. Thus he saw the sale as contrary to the spirit and teaching of the Bible, which for him and his followers was the ultimate religious authority. Indeed, he would later translate the Bible into German so that ordinary people could read it or, if they could not read, at least hear it and understand the meaning of the words. Luther believed that Christians did not need a priest to interpret the Bible or to speak directly with God on their behalf. They could do so themselves.

Luther was not the first Christian to call for reforms in the church. About a hundred years earlier, Jan Hus, a priest from Prague in what is now the Czech Republic, had expressed similar beliefs; in 1415, he was burned as a heretic. Some historians believe that Luther might have suffered a similar fate had the printing press not been invented. By 1520, more than 500,000 copies of his works had been printed and sold—an amazing number at a time when most Europeans still could not read. Because Luther's ideas were so widely known and discussed, the pope and other religious leaders were reluctant to deal with him the way their predecessors had dealt with Hus and earlier heretics.

Still, in 1520, Leo X issued a bull condemning Luther's books and speeches as heresy. Before the order went into effect, however, the pope offered Luther an opportunity to recant—that is, to take back his words. Luther responded by burning the paper on which the bull was printed. He was excommunicated in January 1521.

Emperor Charles V, the new head of the Holy Roman Empire, also saw Luther as a serious threat. Charles was particularly troubled by Luther's insistence that Christians be guided solely by their understanding of the Bible rather than by papal laws. After all, if Christians could ignore the orders of a pope, they could also ignore those of an emperor.

Charles had been chosen as Holy Roman emperor in 1519 at the age of nineteen, after the death of his grandfather Maximilian I. Charles knew very little about the lands he now ruled. He had spent nearly all of his life in Belgium, the Netherlands, and Spain—lands he inherited from his other grandparents, King Ferdinand and Queen Isabella of Spain. But Charles was very much aware of Luther's popularity.

In 1521, Charles invited Luther to meet with his diet in the city of Worms. In the Holy Roman Empire, a diet was an assembly of the powerful princes who had elected, or chosen, the emperor. At the assembly, Charles and the electors urged Luther to recant his teachings. Luther asked for time to think. The next day he appeared before the princes and made a long speech in which he tried to explain his beliefs, only to be interrupted by the young emperor, who asked him to directly answer the question: Will you recant? Luther replied, "Unless I am convinced by the testimony of Scripture or by clear reason, I cannot and will not recant anything, for it is neither safe nor honest to act against one's conscience."

The diet declared Luther an outlaw, which meant that no one could offer him help. Even owning his books was now a crime. The declaration did not stop Luther from writing, nor did it reduce his popularity— mainly because Prince John Frederick, the elector of Saxony and one of Luther's strongest supporters, chose to ignore the diet's declaration by hiding Luther and his followers from the authorities. Frederick knew he would not be punished; even Charles was reluctant to challenge such a powerful prince.

LUTHER AND THE JEWS

At first Jews paid little attention to what they saw as a quarrel among Christians. Then, in 1523, Luther published a pamphlet entitled "That Jesus Christ Was Born a Jew." It was a response to attacks on his ideas. In the essay, he condemned the way the church treated Jews:

> [I]f I had been a Jew and had seen such idiots and blockheads ruling and teaching the Christian religion, I would sooner have become a [pig] than a Christian. . . .

> I would advise and beg everybody to deal kindly with the Jews and to instruct them in the Scriptures; in such a case we could expect them to come over to us. If, however, we use brute force and slander them, saying that they need the blood of Christians to get rid of their stench and I know not what other nonsense of that kind, and treat them like dogs, what good can we expect of them? . . . Finally, how can we expect them to improve if we forbid them to work among us and to have social intercourse with us, and so force them into usury?

> If we wish to make them better, we must deal with them not according to the law of the pope but according to the law of Christian charity. We must receive them kindly and allow them to compete with us in

earning a livelihood, so that they may have a good reason to be with us and among us and an opportunity to witness Christian life and doctrine; and if some remain obstinate, what of it? Not every one of us is a good Christian.[1]

Many readers, including some Jews, were surprised by the final lines of the essay, which seemed to show an astonishing degree of religious toleration. Perhaps that's why some Christians used the essay as "proof" that Luther was a "Judaizer"—a Christian who is attracted to Jewish beliefs and practices. But a more careful reading suggests that Luther seemed to regard Jews in much the way Christians did at the time of the first crusade in 1096. Like them, he saw the conversion of the Jews as the ultimate goal. He, too, viewed "toleration" as little more than enduring the presence of Jews until they became Christians.

But Luther's ideas about Jews were not exactly the same as those of the crusaders. The crusaders tended to regard Jews as an evil people who had murdered their Lord—an act that required revenge. Luther's view was more complicated. An early hymn often attributed to Luther contains the following stanza:

Our heinous crime and weighty sin
Nailed Jesus to the cross, God's true Son.
Therefore, we should not in bitterness scold
You, poor Judas, or the Jewish host.
The guilt is our own.[5]

These words express the idea that Jesus died to redeem all people from their sins and therefore that all people are responsible for his death. The idea of Christians assuming any guilt for the crucifixion would not have been accepted by the crusaders.

Many German peasants were inspired by Luther's teachings about the importance of liberty, of following one's conscience, and of reason. Some applied his ideas to their own lives. Others turned to the Bible for inspiration. Increasingly, both groups used their newly discovered understanding to challenge the basic unfairness that defined their relationship with princes and other nobles. A chronicler at the time wrote "Calling upon the Gospel as their justification, the common folk rose against their lords in protest against the injustices, taxes, burdens, and the general oppression under which they were forced to live."[6] The peasants did not realize that when Luther wrote about freedom, he was talking about spiritual freedom, not political or social liberty. And he certainly did not want to overturn the structure of society, which he believed was ordained by God.

In fact, Luther was outraged by this revolt. He felt that the rebels had misunderstood his ideas and misread the Gospels. Like many people both then and now, he feared the violence often associated with protests and rebellions. In 1524, as an uprising began in southwestern Germany, he published a pamphlet called "Against the Murdering Hordes of Peasants," in which he urged German princes to "strike, throttle and crush" the rebels. He went on, "Let everyone who can smite, slay and stab, secretly or openly, remembering that nothing is more poisonous, hurtful, or devilish than a rebel."

Jews listened to the arguments and watched the violence spread farther and farther north with concern. In times of war or political upheaval, Jews had often been falsely accused of ritual murders, kidnappings, and desecrations of the host (see Chapter 5). There were 49 accusations of ritual murder alone in the 1400s and 1500s, and more than half of them occurred in German-speaking lands.[7] Many Jews feared that this new violence would only add fuel to a smoldering fire. As the conflict grew, a number of Jewish communities asked a *shtadlan*, or advocate, to "keep his eyes open in special care of the community." The man they chose was Rabbi Joseph ben Gershon, popularly known as Josel of Rosheim.

Josel had a reputation as a man who could get things done. He also understood how precarious life was for Jews in the Holy Roman Empire. In 1470, three of his uncles had been killed after being falsely charged with ritual murder. In 1514, Josel himself and several other Jews were falsely accused of desecrating the host. They were held in prison for several months before they were able to establish their innocence.

Josel's job as *shtadlan* required not only knowledge of Judaism and Christianity but also skill as a writer and speaker. As early as 1507, Josel had successfully argued for the right of Jews to have free access to all the markets in the Holy Roman Empire by reminding the authorities of the concept of *civibus Romanis* (Roman citizenship). Perhaps his most important quality, however, was his knack for making friends.

In 1525, rebellious peasants in Alsace (then a part of Germany) turned their anger on the Jews and wanted to drive them from Rosheim and other Alsatian towns. Two of Luther's followers tried but failed to change their minds. Yet somehow Josel succeeded where they had failed. He convinced the peasants to leave the Jews in peace.[8] How did Josel persuade the leaders of this peasant group to even meet with him, let alone to consider a change in plans? One of the rebel leaders was Ittel Jörg. He, like Josel,

Josel of Rosheim as a representative of "the Jews" is shown with a "golden calf." In the Bible, when Moses returns after receiving the Ten Commandments on Mount Sinai, he is so outraged to find Jews worshipping a golden calf that he breaks the two tablets.

was from Rosheim, so Josel may have appealed to him as a neighbor or even a friend. No one knows exactly what their relationship was, but Josel was able to convince Jörg and the others to talk with him. Although they were unable to keep most of their promises, the peasants did not attack the Jews of Rosheim.

IN SEARCH OF COMPROMISES

At a time when every state had an official religion, religious divisions and political struggles for power were often closely linked. Even after the German princes had ruthlessly put down the peasants' revolt, the conflict between Catholics and Luther's followers continued. Now, however, it was the princes who took the lead in the growing division between the two. In 1526, a Lutheran majority in the diet passed a law allowing each prince to decide whether his state church would be Roman Catholic or Lutheran.

The electors hoped the compromise would end the conflict. But three years later, Catholics held a majority in the diet and overturned the compromise that allowed the princes to decide whether their state church would remain Catholic. In a show of solidarity, Lutheran reformers, now in the minority, issued a *protestatio* (Latin for "protestation") to affirm their beliefs: this is how they came to be known as "Protestants" (and how the reforms they championed became known as the "Protestant Reformation"). The following year, the split between Catholics and Protestants widened. At the Diet of Augsburg in 1530, the Protestants presented a formal statement of their beliefs to the emperor, and the Catholics responded with a refutation.

To complicate matters, the Holy Roman Empire itself was at the time increasingly vulnerable to attack. In the east, the threat came from the Ottoman Empire, which had overrun Hungary in 1529 and then laid siege to Vienna, the capital of what is now Austria. In the west, the danger came from France and England. To keep his empire from being divided among his enemies, Charles realized that he would have to make concessions within its borders. He hoped that the assembly at Augsburg would lead to such compromises.

Among the leaders who attended the diet was Josel of Rosheim. He held meetings there with rabbis and Jewish merchants and businessmen. The group hoped to ease tensions with Christians by formally endorsing a code of conduct that would guide their financial dealings with their neighbors. Josel presented the code to the princes at Augsburg. He told the gathering that in return, he and other Jews would like to live in the empire without fear of expulsion. They also wished to be free to travel and trade without restrictions, and they wanted protection from false accusations. He asked for these concessions "because we, too, are human beings, created by the Almighty, to live on earth with you."[9]

Although Josel appealed to a common humanity, the princes did not take his speech to heart. They were too busy preparing for civil war. Only Charles seemed willing to listen.

At the diet in Augsburg, Josel showed Charles a copy of the charter Emperor Frederick Barbarossa had issued in 1157. It renewed "for all time" the privileges Henry IV had granted to Jews just before the first crusade in 1096 (see Chapter 4). Those privileges included the freedom of Jews to travel safely and worship openly in their synagogues throughout the empire. After reading the document, Charles declared it was binding, and he renewed it a few years later.

The emperor also ruled that Jews could not be brought to trial on trumped-up charges of kidnapping or ritual murder. Anyone who imprisoned a Jew on a charge not authorized by the emperor would be fined, and the fine would double if the Jew was found innocent. In addition, the emperor allowed Jews to raise interest rates on loans, since Jews had to pay higher taxes than their neighbors.

TAKING SIDES

As the conflict between Catholics and Protestants intensified, Jews had to choose sides. It is impossible to remain a bystander in a war fought in your backyard. Yet neither side was particularly sympathetic to the plight of Jews. Luther was primarily interested in converting them. Charles, although he had renewed their charter, was not only the Holy Roman emperor but also king of Spain and Portugal. In those countries, he had supported the expulsion of Jews and the Inquisition—he even established an inquisition in Mexico, Peru, and Spain's other American colonies. Yet in the end, Josel and many other Jews decided to support Charles because of his willingness to protect their rights in exchange for their help and loyalty.

By 1537, a disappointed Luther became convinced that most Jews had no intention of converting to Christianity. If conversion was not a possibility, Luther believed there was no reason to tolerate the Jews. He therefore persuaded one of his strongest supporters—the prince of Saxony—to expel Jews from his territory. They could no longer live in, engage in business in, or even pass through Saxony. Aware of the prince's close relationship with Luther, Josel tried to meet with Luther to discuss the expulsion order. Luther refused to see him. In response to a letter from Josel, Luther urged him to convert and then added, "I would willingly do my best for your people but I will not contribute to your [Jewish] obstinacy by my own kind actions. You must find another intermediary with my good lord."

Josel did find another intermediary—a Lutheran scholar from Alsace. In 1537, Wolfgang Capito wrote the letter of introduction to the prince that Josel needed. When he met with the prince, Josel managed to persuade him to cancel the order of expulsion. But at Luther's request, the order was later reinstated.

In the years that followed, Josel tried repeatedly to meet with Luther but was turned away. Then, in 1542, just three years before Luther's death, the reformer published a new essay, "Concerning the Jews and Their Lies." In it, Luther asked what Christians should "do with this damned, rejected race of Jews." His answer:

First, their synagogues or churches should be set on fire, and whatever does not burn up should be covered or spread over with dirt so that no one may ever be able to see a cinder or stone of it. . . .

Secondly, their homes should likewise be broken down and destroyed. For they perpetrate the same things there that they do in their synagogues. . . .

Thirdly, they should be deprived of their prayer-books and Talmud in which such idolatry, lies, cursing, and blasphemy are taught. . . .

Fourthly, their rabbis must be forbidden under threat of death to teach any more. . . .

Fifthly . . . traveling privileges should be absolutely forbidden to the Jews. . . . Let them stay at home. . . .

Sixthly, they ought to be stopped from usury. All their cash and valuables of silver and gold ought to be taken from them and put aside for safe keeping. . . .

Seventhly, let the young and strong Jews and Jewesses be given the flail, the ax, the hoe, the spade, the distaff, and spindle, and let them earn their bread . . . as is enjoined upon Adam's children. . . .

If, however, we are afraid that they might harm us personally, or our wives, children, servants, cattle, etc., when they serve us or work for us . . . then let us apply the same cleverness [expulsion] as the other nations, such as France, Spain, Bohemia, etc., and settle with them for that which they have extorted usuriously from us, and after having divided it up fairly let us drive them out of the country for all time.[10]

After reading the essay, Josel decided to create a pamphlet that would refute Luther's charges. To do so, he needed the permission of a prince or even members of a city council. (Nowhere in Europe in the 1500s were people—including Luther—free to publish or even speak in public without permission from a local or national government.) In 1542, no council was willing to grant Josel the right to publish a pamphlet. The best he could do was to persuade the Strasbourg city council to ban Luther's book in their city.

Two years later, in 1544, Luther stirred up more controversy with a sermon entitled "Admonition against the Jews." It repeated old libels against Jews, including false accusations of ritual murder, poisoning of wells, and black magic. The sermon conflicted with the earlier essay in which Luther expressed outrage at "blood libels" and other attempts to slander the Jews (page 118).

Josel and other Jewish leaders found this new sermon particularly worrisome, because a number of Protestant rulers, including the princes of Saxony and Hesse, used Luther's writings to guide their decisions. Indeed, those writings would continue to shape opinions long after Luther's death. In the 1930s and 1940s—nearly 400 years after they were written—Adolf Hitler and his Nazi Party would quote them as "proof" of how evil and dangerous "the Jews" were.

Over the years, a number of Lutherans and other Protestants have tried to explain the viciousness of Luther's attacks not only on Jews but also on Catholics, Muslims, and even some Protestants. Some scholars think his attacks may reflect a fear that his reforms had failed to bring about the changes he had envisioned. Based on a careful examination of Luther's writings during the last years of his life, other scholars think he came to believe that he was living at the "end of days" (see Chapter 2) and that the need for sinners to repent was more urgent than ever. In their view, Luther increasingly saw himself as a prophet whose voice was not being heard. Still others maintained that Luther seemed to regard the actions of Jews, Catholics, Muslims, and even some Protestants as part of a satanic conspiracy. His language may have reflected his sense of urgency as well as his outrage and frustration.

SPEAKING OUT

Luther believed that individuals ought to follow their consciences. As he had told Charles, "It is neither safe nor honest to act against one's conscience." Many of his followers agreed—even though following their consciences sometimes meant criticizing Luther himself. One of those critics was Andreas Osiander, a Lutheran from Nuremberg. In 1543, he wrote to a Jewish humanist in Italy expressing his dismay at Luther's essays on Jews. Osiander expressed those same views in a letter to Luther. After Luther's death, Osiander's words were used as evidence of his "unreliability" because he had failed to stand with Luther on the matter of toleration of the Jews.

In 1529, Osiander had received a letter from a nobleman asking whether Jews committed ritual murder. Osiander replied with a long essay that stated, in part, "I have not been able to find, to think of, or to hear anything which could have moved me to believe such suspicion and accusation. Rather, I have found, on the contrary, . . . that injustice has been done to the Jews in this matter."[11] To support that conclusion, Osiander offered 20 reasons why ritual murder charges were based on lies rather than reality. He noted, for example, that Jews lived in places where there were no Christians. If Jews really needed Christian blood for religious purposes, how, he wondered, were they able to practice their religion in those lands?

Osiander argued that to imprison, torture, or execute Jews on charges that they stood against "God's Word, Nature, and Human Reason" was to do the work of the devil, "the Father of Lies." Osiander's essay was made public in 1540, after several Jews found a copy of it and decided to have it printed without securing permission in advance. They planned to use it to defend Jews accused of ritual murder in the town of Sappenfeld.

Jews also searched for other allies in their efforts to promote toleration. Those allies included not only Osiander but also Philipp Melanchthon, a grandnephew of Reuchlin and one of Luther's closest advisers. In 1539, Protestant electors at a meeting in Frankfurt were debating whether to expel Jews from their territories. In an emotional speech, Melanchthon changed the direction of the debate by describing an incident that took place in Berlin in 1510. At the time, he was a young priest. Just before the execution of 38 Jews convicted of desecrating the host, their accuser confessed to Melanchthon that he had lied.

The young priest immediately rushed to his bishop to ask for permission to inform Duke Joachim of Brandenburg of the confession so that he could stop the execution. His request was denied. Instead the bishop ordered Melanchthon to remain silent even as the 38 Jews were murdered. Now, 29 years later, he was finally able to openly tell what had happened. In the audience was Duke Joachim, who heard the story for the first time.

Josel of Rosheim was also in the audience. He recalled that as a result of the speech, the dukes gave up plans to expel the Jews—and all of them with the exception of the prince of Saxony kept their word.

CATHOLIC RESPONSES

In 1520, soon after Martin Luther set fire to the papal bull that condemned him and his books, he had called for a special council to reform the Catholic Church. Two years later, the electors of the Holy Roman Empire made a similar appeal to the pope; they had the support of Emperor Charles V, who thought such a council might help reunite the church and end the Protestant Reformation. Both appeals were ignored.

By the 1540s, however, the pope could no longer ignore calls for reform. The Reformation had grown well beyond the heresy of Luther and a few other preachers; it now divided one country after another. In 1545, just one year before Luther's death, Pope Paul III called for a church assembly in Trent in what is now Italy (it was then a free city in the Holy Roman Empire). Most Protestants refused to attend; they no longer saw themselves as part of the Catholic Church or subject to the pope's laws. The few who did come were not allowed to vote.

Nevertheless, the council, which met on and off between 1545 and 1563, called for important reforms—reforms that eliminated many of the abuses that had disturbed Luther and other Christians. The group also tried to define exactly what Catholics believed and set new, tougher regulations for the training of priests.

The council did not pay much attention to Jews; its emphasis was on heresy within the church. But Jews were the focus of at least one statement. In reply to the question of who killed Jesus, Catholic leaders at the Council of Trent wrote in 1551:

> *In the guilt of the crucifixion are involved all those who frequently fell into sin; for as our sins consigned Christ to death on the cross, most certainly those who wallow in sin and iniquity themselves crucify again the Son of God. This guilt seems more enormous in us than in the Jews since, according to the testimony of the apostle, if they had known it they would never have crucified the Lord of glory; while, we, on the contrary, professing to know him yet denying him by our actions, seem in some sort to lay violent hands on him.* [12]

In other words, the church was saying that Jesus was crucified for the sins of all people, especially Christians, and not just because of the sins of "the Jews." If this understanding of the crucifixion had been widely preached and taught, history—particularly the history of antisemitism—might have taken a different course; the Protestant hymn quoted earlier in this chapter expressed much the same idea, and it might have come to be broadly echoed. But at the time, the myth of Jews as "Christ killers" was very powerful, and it continued to inform the way both Catholics and Protestants viewed Jews. Indeed, few people knew of the statement made at the Council of Trent until 1965, when the Catholic Church once again considered reform.

THE FIGHT AGAINST HERESY

Even as the Council of Trent debated a variety of reforms, the pope and other church leaders were trying to stamp out every form of heresy, and they directed their efforts not only at Protestants but also at *conversos* and Jews. Some regarded *conversos* as a particular threat to Christianity. All Jews who had converted to Christianity—not just the ones forcibly baptized in Spain and Portugal—were viewed with suspicion. Even humanists referred to Pfefferkorn as a "baptized Jew" rather than as a full-fledged Christian. For example, Erasmus, the most famous humanist of his day, said of Pfefferkorn, "If one were to operate on him, six hundred Jews would spring out."

In 1547, the archbishop of Toledo in Spain protested when Pope Paul III appointed a priest who came from a Jewish family to serve in Toledo's cathedral. The archbishop claimed that the priest had "impure blood" (see Chapter 6). Paul backed down and named someone else to the post. His concession encouraged the archbishop to go even further: later that year, he issued the Statute of Toledo. It stated that no one of "Jewish blood" could ever hold office in the cathedral. The Spanish Inquisition then applied the archbishop's ruling to other positions as well—including those at some universities, religious orders, guilds, and city governments. Paul III denounced this statute, which contradicted the idea that the church was universal, or open to all. But by the mid-1550s, the statute was increasingly seen as part of the church's war on heresy.

A new Catholic religious order known as the Society of Jesus, or the Jesuits, was central to that continuing war. Founded in 1540 by Ignatius Loyola, the Society of Jesus established hundreds of colleges and seminaries throughout Europe and soon carried Christianity to India, Japan, China, Africa, and the Americas. Like several other religious orders, the Jesuits required that their members provide genealogical charts to prove that there were no Jews among their ancestors. These regulations remained in force until 1946.

The weapons used by the Jesuits and others in the war against heresy included not only education but also the inquisition, which became in 1542 the Vatican's final court of appeal in heresy trials. Seven years later, the church issued its first "Index of Forbidden Books"—a list of books church leaders believed would contaminate or corrupt the morals of Roman Catholics. That list would eventually include works not only by religious scholars but also by scientists, such as Galileo and Copernicus. Their heresy? They used logic and mathematics to conclude that the earth revolved around the sun—at a time when the church taught that the sun revolved around the earth.

PAUL IV AND THE JEWS

By the 1550s, popes were not as willing to protect Jews as they had been earlier. In August 1553, a Franciscan friar who converted to Judaism was burned at the stake in Rome. A few months later, Julius III, who served as pope from 1550 to 1555, declared that the Talmud was disrespectful to Christians and ordered it burned. Book burnings took place in Rome, Bologna, Florence, Venice, and other cities in Italy. In 1555 the church had a new pope, Paul IV, and he was even more determined to end all heresies than earlier popes had been.

Almost immediately, Paul issued a bull in which he stated:

> *It is absurd and inconvenient that the Jews, who through their own fault were condemned by God to eternal slavery, can . . . show such ingratitude towards Christians and affront them by asking for their mercy. [They] have become so bold as to not only live amongst Christians but near their churches without any distinctive clothing.*[15]

He therefore ordered that Jews in Rome and the Papal States wear special clothing and be confined to ghettos.

For hundreds of years, Jews, like other ethnic groups, had tended to live together. There were Jewish quarters in Alexandria in the early days of the Roman Empire and in both Muslim and Christian cities in Europe and the Middle East in later centuries. But these were not ghettos; they were places where many Jews—but by no means all—chose to live. A ghetto was a place where Jews were required to live by law. The first ghetto was built in Venice in 1516. (The word in Italian means "foundry"; the Venetian ghetto was located near a foundry.)

About 40 years later, Jews in Rome were also required to live in a ghetto. If they owned property, they had to sell it to Christians. They could not employ Christian servants. They also had to wear distinctive clothing (yellow hats for men and yellow scarves for women). They could leave the ghetto during the day but had to return by sunset. The ghetto gates were locked from sundown to sunrise. Those gates were installed and guarded by Christians, but the Jewish community had to pay the cost through a special tax.

Paul IV also turned his attention to *conversos*. In the past, popes had allowed Jews who had been forced to convert to Christianity in Spain or

THE GROWTH OF GHETTOS (1215–1570)

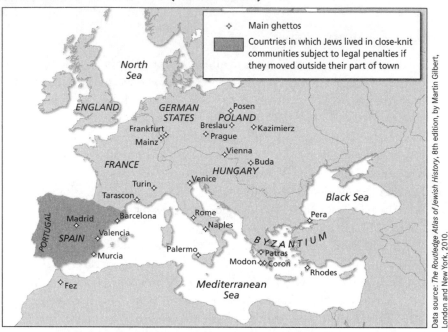

By the 1500s many Jews in European cities and towns were required to live in a ghetto–
a street, neighborhood, or section of town set aside for Jews. Many ghettos were surrounded
by walls and could be entered only through a gate guarded by Christians. The result was a
segregated society but not an isolated one. Many Jewish men worked beyond the ghetto
but had to return to it at the end of each day.

Portugal to return to Judaism if they chose. But this pope insisted that
conversos everywhere must remain Christian. He sent officials to carry out
the order. In Ancona, a papal state on the Adriatic Sea, the arrival of the
pope's representative set off a firestorm. Since 1492, the year Jews were
expelled from Spain, the city had been a refuge for Christians of Jewish
descent.

Almost immediately, the papal representative imprisoned about
a hundred *conversos* in Ancona—all from Jewish families of Spanish
descent—and confiscated their property. Although they were officially
Christians, they considered themselves Jews. When they appealed to
the authorities for help, they reminded officials that earlier popes had
allowed them to return to Judaism because they had been forced to
become Christians. When their appeals went unheard, a group of about
30 prisoners bribed the pope's representative to look the other way while
they fled to more friendly territories—the dukedoms or duchies of Urbino
and Ferrara.

Word of the events in Ancona quickly spread through Europe and the Middle East. The news reached Istanbul in the autumn of 1555. Among the first to hear it was Doña Gracia Mendes Nasi, a wealthy Jewish widow. With her nephew's help, she bought and sold such goods as wool, grain, pepper, and textiles throughout Europe and Asia. Doña Gracia's parents were *conversos* who had been forcibly converted to Christianity in Portugal. As an adult, Doña Gracia had traveled through Europe seeking a safe haven and eventually found one in the Ottoman Empire, where she converted to Judaism.

The prisoners in Ancona were not strangers to Doña Gracia. She and her family had helped some of them escape from Portugal. Others worked for her company. She immediately arranged a meeting in Istanbul with Suleiman, the sultan of the Ottoman Empire. She pointed out that some of the prisoners had lived in the Ottoman Empire and were therefore entitled to his protection. She also noted that much of the property the pope had confiscated belonged to companies owned by her family and other Jews currently living in the Ottoman Empire. Suleiman promised to help, and he kept his word. He sent a deputy to Ancona to demand the release of all prisoners under Ottoman protection.

Officials in Ancona wanted to help the sultan; his empire was one of the city's main trading partners. So they sent an agent to explain to the pope that much of the confiscated property belonged not only to Jews in the Ottoman Empire but also to non-Jewish merchants. They noted that ships that once docked in Ancona were now heading for other ports, depriving the city and the pope of earnings from their trade. And they told the pope of their fears that traders from Ancona and other Papal States were now at risk when they tried to do business in the Ottoman Empire. The pope ignored their pleas.

Doña Gracia did not give up. She continued to apply pressure by meeting with the French ambassador. At her request, he brought the pope a letter written by Suleiman. It stated in part:

> *When you shall have received my Divine and Imperial Seal, which will be presented to you, you must know that certain persons of the race of the Jews have informed my Elevated and Sublime [Court] that, whereas certain subjects and tributaries of Ours have gone to your territories to [trade], and especially to Ancona, their goods and property have been seized on your instructions. This is in particular to the prejudice of Our Treasury, to the amount of 400,000 ducats, over and above the damage done to Our subjects, who have been*

A bronze medallion of Doña Gracia Mendes Nasi.

ruined and cannot pay their obligations to Our said Treasury. . . . We therefore request Your Holiness, that by virtue of this Our universal and illustrious Seal . . . you will be pleased to liberate our above-mentioned . . . subjects, with all the property which they had and owned, in order that they may be able to satisfy their debts. . . . By so doing, you will give Us occasion to treat in friendly fashion your subjects and the other Christians who traffic in these parts.[14]

The letter was dated March 9, 1556. It reached Italy at the end of April. By then, the first group of prisoners had been burned in Ancona. The pope did not reply to the letter until June 1. He agreed, as a personal favor to a fellow ruler, to release any remaining prisoners who were the sultan's subjects and return their property. He also agreed to release property that belonged to Doña Gracia's agents as a friendly gesture. But on the central issue, he stood firm: New Christians who returned to Judaism had to pay the consequences. On June 6, more prisoners were killed, and a week later the last three were murdered.

From Suleiman's point of view, the incident was over. He had done what he could, and it was too late to do more; the victims were dead. But from the *conversos'* point of view, the incident was not over. Some *conversos* who had fled Ancona wanted all merchants to boycott the port and go to Pesaro, the main port in the duchy of Urbino, instead. They had the support of the duke of Urbino, who defied the pope's demand that the duke return all *conversos* to Ancona. But it was impossible for a handful of refugees to organize a boycott without help.

Judah Faraj, one of the refugees, sailed to the Ottoman Empire with a letter describing the *conversos'* plight. His first stop was Salonika in what is now Greece. Jewish merchants there agreed to support the boycott. Next he traveled to Constantinople, where he met with Doña Gracia and her nephew. She immediately called a meeting so that Faraj could tell his story to the city's rabbis and other community leaders. They too agreed to boycott Ancona for the next eight months—until Passover in the spring of 1557. During that period, all goods that would have been shipped to Ancona were sent to Pesaro.

Doña Gracia transferred all of her business to Pesaro; she also wrote to prominent Jews throughout the Ottoman Empire asking them to join the boycott. Ancona soon felt the results of her efforts. Some merchants went bankrupt. Goods that could not be shipped piled up in warehouses and on the wharves. Jews as well as Christians were harmed by the boycott. On the other hand, *conversos* in Pesaro rejoiced. It was an amazing moment— for the first time in history, a group of Jews, Christians, and Muslims had joined together to express outrage at an injustice.

In the end, however, the boycott failed. Carrying out a boycott is difficult even with today's instant communications; in the 1550s, it was almost impossible—partly because people's goals differ. In the end, their internal quarrels sabotaged the effort. But the idea of the boycott offered hope at a time when things looked hopeless for many Jews in western Europe. It also revealed the power of a commitment to working together.

Before long, the port of Ancona was busy again. The town now had its own ghetto. Its purpose, like those in other Italian cities, was not to punish Jews but to lead them to conversion.

OTHER REFORMS AND REFORMERS

Even before the boycott of Ancona was organized, the conflict between Protestants and Catholics had grown more and more deadly. Compromises no longer worked. In 1552, Charles V had become so disillusioned that he retired to a monastery and turned over the throne of the Holy Roman Empire to his brother Ferdinand. Ferdinand did not reach an agreement with the Protestant princes until 1555. That agreement allowed each prince to decide which church would be the official, or state, church in his domain. In reaching that agreement, the Holy Roman Empire acknowledged that there might be more than one source of religious authority and more than one recognized church within the empire. It was a step toward toleration in the sense of allowing the presence of others without actively opposing them.

The divisions that shook the Holy Roman Empire affected other countries as well. People everywhere were making up their own minds about religious questions, and some were forming their own churches. Although many Christians in what are now Germany and Scandinavia remained Lutherans, other leaders were emerging who did not necessarily share all of Luther's views.

Among those leaders was John Calvin, a French lawyer who had become a Protestant in the 1530s. Forced to flee France because of his beliefs, Calvin settled in Geneva, Switzerland, where he established a theocracy—a state governed by the godly, in this case Calvinists. In time, Calvin's ideas became popular in the Netherlands, Scotland, and even France, as well as Switzerland. These were places where few Jews lived; most had been expelled generations earlier.

As quarrels among Catholics, Lutherans, Calvinists, and other Protestant sects intensified, they led to a series of wars that devastated much of the continent for nearly 100 years—from 1550 to 1648. These were more than religious wars; they were also struggles for political domination of the Holy Roman Empire. Each group seemed incapable of tolerating, let alone living with, the others. Each was convinced it was waging a war against heresy. As the fighting continued, villages were burned, towns were looted, and men, women, and children were murdered. There seemed no end to the violence. Hundreds of thousands of people were forced into exile.

Calvinists in particular experienced persecution and exile. These refugees were finding it increasingly difficult to interpret Jewish misfortunes as an expression of God's wrath. Some now identified with the Israelites of the Hebrew Scriptures and began to imagine a covenant with God that included both Christians and Jews. Their views spread by way of France and the Netherlands to England and Scotland and eventually to North America.

In 1556, the Netherlands, one of the most Protestant regions of Europe, was under the rule of the Catholic king of Spain. When he organized an inquisition, the Dutch revolted and a religious war began. When it finally ended, the southern provinces (present-day Belgium) remained under Spanish rule, and the north (the present kingdom of the Netherlands, which included both Holland and Zeeland) considered itself a Protestant country, even though it was home to many Catholics. With the independence of the northern provinces came public clamor for a new right: the right to follow one's own religious beliefs regardless of anyone else's views.

For the first time, ordinary people had the right to freedom of conscience. Hundreds of refugees flocked to the new country—including many Jews. But those Jews had few rights until 1657, when the government of the United Netherlands took a stand similar to the one the Ottoman Empire took in 1556: it demanded that other nations recognize Dutch Jews as citizens of the Netherlands and treat them accordingly. In doing so, the government was also taking the first steps toward toleration in the modern sense of the word by acknowledging the rights and beliefs of others. It was a toleration that probably grew in part from weariness with war and a strong sense that persecution was bad for business.

In the Netherlands, toleration was a decision made by rulers; it was not a God-given right. Only a few people in the 1600s believed it was such a right. Among them was an English minister named Roger Williams who immigrated to Britain's North American colonies in 1631. In a book published in England, he called the alliance of church and state "a bloody tenent of persecution." He believed that when the "wall of separation" between the "Garden of the Church" and the "Wilderness of the World" breaks down, the only way to set things right is to rebuild that wall.[15] In 1635, Williams was banished from the Massachusetts Bay Colony for having such "erroneous and very dangerous" opinions.

To Williams, who later founded the colony of Rhode Island, "mere toleration" was not enough. He advocated total "freedom of conscience" and insisted that it be extended to all. He believed that Christianity would flourish only under a government that had the courage to guarantee liberty for "diverse and contrary consciences." It was a lonely position to take in the 1600s, but his stand would gain more support in the 1700s and beyond.

In 1790, George Washington, the first president of the United States, wrote a letter to a Jewish congregation in Newport, Rhode Island. In that letter he described the new nation as giving "bigotry no sanction" and "persecution no assistance." A growing number of Jews and non-Jews welcomed those words. They considered a government willing to protect all of its citizens their best protection. But to many others, toleration remained a dangerous idea.

1 Fernand Braudel, *Civilization & Capitalism, 15th–18th Century*, vol. 1, *The Structures of Everyday Life: The Limits of the Possible*, trans. Siân Reynolds, (New York: Harper & Row, 1979), 400.

2 Johannes Reuchlin, quoted in Paul Kriwaczek, *Yiddish Civilisation: The Rise and Fall of a Forgotten Nation* (New York: Vintage Books, 2005), 166.

3 In Heinrich Graetz, *Geschichte der Juden* (Leipzig, 1873), 4:447–448, quoted in Edward H. Flannery, *The Anguish of the Jews: Twenty-Three Centuries of Antisemitism*, rev. ed. (New York: Stimulus, 1999), 151.

4 Martin Luther, "That Jesus Christ Was Born a Jew," *Luther's Works* (Philadelphia: Muehlenberg and Fortress, and St. Louis: Concordia, 1955-86), 45:199–229, quoted in Jacob Rader Marcus, ed., *The Jew in the Medieval World: A Source Book, 315–1791*, rev. ed. (Cincinnati: Hebrew Union College Press, 1999), 186–187.

5 Martin Luther, "Concerning the Jews and Their Lies," 1543, quoted in Heiko A. Oberman, *The Roots of Anti-Semitism: In the Age of Renaissance and Reformation*, trans. James I. Porter (Philadelphia: Fortress Press, 1984), 124.

6 Sebastian Franck, *Chronik, Geschichte und Zeitbuch aller Sachen und Handlungen*, 1531, quoted in Kriwaczek, *Yiddish Civilisation*, 169.

7 R. Po-chia Hsia, *The Myth of Ritual Murder: Jews and Magic in Reformation Germany* (New Haven: Yale University Press, 1988), 3.

8 I. Kracauer, "Rabbi Joselmann De Rosheym,"*Revue des Études Juives* (Paris) 16 (1888), in Kriwaczek, *Yiddish Civilisation*, 170.

9 Quoted in Abba Eban, *Heritage: Civilization and the Jews* (New York: Summit Books, 1984), 201.

10 Martin Luther, "Concerning the Jews and Their Lies," *Luther's Works*, 45:199–229, quoted in Marcus, ed., *The Jew in the Medieval World*, 187–189.

11 Andreas Osiander, *Andreas Osianders Schrift über die Blutbeschuldigung* (Berlin, 1903), Moritz Stern, ed., 6–7, quoted in Hsia, *The Myth of Ritual Murder*, 137.

12 "The Council of Trent," quoted in William Nicholls, *Christian Antisemitism: A History of Hate* (Lanham, MD: Rowman & Littlefield, 1993), 267.

13 Paul IV, *Cum nimis absurdum*, Papal Bill, July 14, 1555.

14 Sultan Suleiman to Pope Paul IV, 9 March 1556, in *Lettre di Principi*, ed. Girolama Ruscelli (Venice, 1581), 1:177–8, quoted in Cecil Roth, *Doña Gracia of the House of Nasi*, 2nd ed. (Philadelphia: Jewish Publication Society, 1977), 151–152.

15 Roger Williams, *The Bloudy Tenent of Persecution* (1644).

8

Safe Havens?: Poland and the Ottoman Empire

(1200s–1666)

At a time when much of western Europe was in the midst of religious wars, the rulers of Poland and the Ottoman Empire offered many minorities a safe haven. In both places, rulers actively encouraged outsiders of different backgrounds to settle in their territory. Jews were among the thousands who piled their belongings onto ships, ox-drawn wagons, or handcarts and made their way to a new land. Some of those people

THE MIGRATION OF JEWS TO POLAND AND THE OTTOMAN EMPIRE (1200s–1500s)

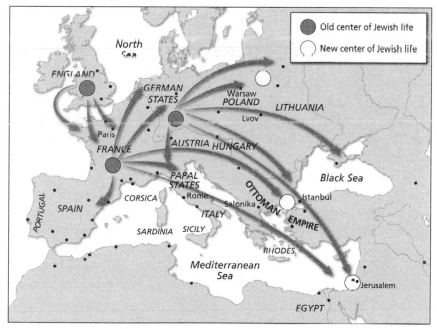

In the thirteenth century, the centers of Jewish life in Europe were mainly in the west. By 1500, those centers had shifted to the east–to Poland and the Ottoman Empire. That shift was the direct result of 200 years of expulsions and an increasingly violent antisemitism in the west.

were fleeing persecution, war, and famine; others were attracted to the possibility of a better life in a more welcoming place.

TOWARD TOLERATION IN POLAND

Poland's leaders were the first to recruit outsiders. Their efforts began in the 1200s, when Poland was a land ravaged by the repeated invasions of Tartars, Mongols, and other nomadic tribes from central Asia. The invaders had devastated the countryside and destroyed villages and towns. Poland needed to rebuild, but at the time few Poles had the skills, tools, or freedom needed to revive the economy. So Polish kings and princes recruited artisans, merchants, bankers, and builders from other countries by offering them more freedom and independence than they had in their native lands.

Many responded enthusiastically. Most of the new arrivals came from other parts of Europe, particularly cities in what is now Germany. They received special charters that allowed them to live under their own laws and customs. Krakow, Lublin, Lwow, and Brest were a few of the cities in Poland that operated under these charters in the thirteenth century and later.

Like immigrants throughout history, the newcomers arrived with more than knowledge, skills, and experience; they also came with attitudes, values, and heartfelt beliefs. Those beliefs included the notion that competition was evil. Many believed that the amount of wealth in the world was fixed; it could not be increased or decreased. They claimed, therefore, that a competitor could succeed only by stealing their business and their livelihood. The newcomers were not the only ones to regard their rivals as potential thieves. Many Poles held similar views.

As a result, both newcomers and established merchants and artisans tried to eliminate competition by denying their rivals the right to buy and sell goods or even to live in a particular city or town. Both focused on religious minorities—Jews, Muslims, and even Christians who belonged to the Armenian and Greek Orthodox Churches. (Most people in Poland were Roman Catholic.) For the most part, rulers in other parts of Europe had supported such efforts to thwart competition, but Polish rulers in the 1200s did not.

Poland was not a united country in the thirteenth century. It was divided into dozens of principalities and duchies. Each had its own laws and its own ruler. And as in other parts of Europe, nearly all of these regions limited the rights and privileges of citizenship in a city or town to burghers—Christian merchants and artisans who owned property in a city or town. Nevertheless, Poland's rulers had no interest in limiting the rights of Jews and other minorities in order to satisfy the burghers. Some rulers protected minorities out of a sense of simple fairness. One king justified a decree that gave Jews and non-Jews equal trading rights by noting that Jews "pay the same taxes and carry the same burdens as non-Jews."[1] Others were frank about their need for the goods and services Jews provided. Jews in Poland helped establish trade with other countries, lent money to build roads and ports, and found ways to turn salt mines, forests, and other resources into flourishing industries.

Poland's rulers also saw their support of Jews as a way of balancing and sometimes curbing the growing power of the burghers. Kings and other nobles had little interest in allowing anyone to monopolize the sale of horses, spices, iron, or other goods. After all, competition tends to keep prices down—and nobles were consumers as well as rulers.

In 1264, one of these rulers—Prince Boleslaw of Great Poland and Kalisz—issued a charter that placed Jews directly under his rule rather than under the laws and restrictions of whatever city they happened to live in. Their right to settle in a place came directly from the prince. Like charters issued in western Europe in the eleventh and twelfth centuries, the one issued by Boleslaw defined his obligations toward Jews. In exchange for their taxes, he agreed to provide them with his personal protection. Anyone who attacked a Jew not only faced the usual punishment for the crime but also had to pay an additional fine to the royal treasury.

Many of the rights and privileges provided in this new charter were similar to those Jews had once had in other parts of Europe. These included the right to own and inherit property; engage in lawful trade; travel within the borders of the country without paying a special tax or duty; determine who will be welcomed into one's home (no one could demand hospitality without the host's consent); remain a Jew (Christians could not force Jews to convert); and live under Jewish law (if there was a dispute between a Jew and a Christian, each party had the right to argue its case according to its own laws).

Important differences also existed. Boleslaw's charter granted Jews four privileges that they had not had in charters granted in other places:

1. In keeping with papal decrees, Jews were not to be accused of using Christian blood "because their law prohibits the use of any blood." Unlike papal decrees, however, this provision called for a specific punishment for making a false accusation: a Christian

who made such a charge was to suffer the same punishment a Jew would receive if the accusation were true.

2. Jews could receive a horse as security for a loan only during the daylight hours. (This provision was meant to protect Jews against accusations that they had accepted stolen horses as pledges. Stolen horses were more likely to be transferred at night than during the day.)

3. A Jew could be accused of cheating on a loan only if the accusation was supported by the prince or his local representative.

4. A Christian who failed to help a Jew who was attacked at night was required to pay a fine.

This new Polish charter was unique in another way as well. It obligated Jews to defend their king or prince in battle. So Jews, like their Christian neighbors, formed battalions and even turned their synagogues into fortresses in times of war.

In the thirteenth century, kings and princes were not the only lawmakers in Poland. Nobles also issued charters for Jews who lived on their lands, and so did the Polish Roman Catholic Church. Although these charters varied from place to place and time to time, most regarded Jews as a free people. By contrast, in other parts of Europe, rulers had abandoned the old charters; they now considered Jews their personal property and therefore believed that they had a right to rob or expel them whenever they chose to do so.

RESPONSES TO TOLERATION

While Polish kings and nobles were convinced that Jews and other minorities enriched their country, Polish merchants and artisans regarded toleration as harmful, and they were not alone. Many church leaders shared that view. They feared that charters like the one Boleslaw issued would blur the line between Christianity and Judaism. In their opinion, Poland needed laws that strengthened the country's Christian identity.

In 1267, just three years after Boleslaw granted Jews their first charter, church leaders from all over Europe gathered for a synod, or council, in Breslau. There they demanded that Christians and Jews live in separate areas divided by a moat, so that "Christians should not be affected by the superstitions and bad morals of the Jews while living among them."[2] They ordered Christians to no longer eat with Jews, share the same bathhouses, or even dance at Jewish weddings. The priests also wanted Jews to wear special hats so that they could easily be distinguished from Christians.

Most of these church leaders came from countries in western and central Europe where such restrictions were already in place. So they were surprised to discover that Poland's rulers vigorously opposed these measures. Kings wanted to encourage Jewish settlement, not drive Jews out of the country. Indeed, in the 1300s, King Casimir III confirmed the privileges granted to Jews in earlier charters and extended them to the entire country, including newly acquired territories in the east.

Church leaders did not accept defeat, and by the mid-1300s, they were making some headway with the help of burghers and other townspeople. Although records are incomplete, historians have documented 19 attacks on Jews in Poland between 1340 and 1500, ranging from mob violence to expulsion from various cities or provinces. With the exception of two incidents at the end of the 1400s, almost all of the attacks occurred in three cities in western Poland—Krakow, Poznan, and Warsaw.

No accusation or cause was given for 6 of the 19 attacks (Krakow in 1423; Poznan in 1434; Bochnia, near Krakow, in 1445; Warsaw in 1483 and 1498; and Lithuania in 1495). At least five were based on old myths. In Krakow and Kalisz in 1348 and 1349, Jews were falsely accused of causing the Black Death—the terrible plague that wiped out more than a quarter of Europe's population in the mid-1300s (see Chapter 6). In 1367, Christians in Poznan accused Jews of ritual murder, and similar accusations were made in Krakow in 1407. In 1399, Jews in Poznan were also accused of desecrating the host (see Chapter 5). Other attacks on Jews were prompted by the sermons of Giovanni Capistrano, a monk who represented the pope (Krakow in 1454 and Warsaw in 1455); crusaders traveling south to fight the Turks (Krakow in 1463 and 1498–1500 and Lwow in 1498–1500); and false accusations of arson (Poznan in 1447 and 1464 and Krakow 1477 and 1494–1495).

A closer look at one of these incidents—the violence that resulted from the preaching of Giovanni Capistrano in 1454—shows how church leaders were able to arouse anti-Jewish feelings. Zbigniew Olesnicki, the archbishop of Krakow, had invited Capistrano, an Italian monk, to speak in his city. The archbishop was furious with Casimir IV, because earlier that year the king had reaffirmed the privileges his father had granted Jews. The archbishop wrote the king an angry letter, denouncing him for protecting the Jews "to the injury and insult of the holy faith." He went on to warn:

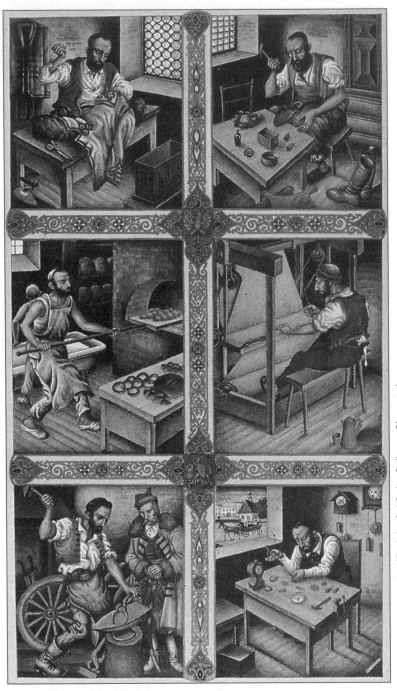

In the early twentieth century, an artist recalled the variety of crafts and trades Jews traditionally carried out in Poland.

Do not imagine that in matters touching the Christian religion you are at liberty to pass any law you please. No one is great and strong enough to put down all opposition to himself when the interests of the faith are at stake. I therefore beg and implore your Royal Majesty to revoke the aforementioned privileges and liberties. Prove that you are a Catholic sovereign, and remove all occasion for disgracing your name and for worse offenses that are likely to follow.[3]

When the king ignored the letter, the archbishop appealed to Capistrano for help. Capistrano was a charismatic speaker with a reputation for encouraging violence against Jews. Although Jews tried desperately to persuade the king to keep the preacher out of Krakow, their efforts failed. And Capistrano lived up to their worst fears. In sermon after sermon, he denounced Jews as ritual murderers and desecrators of the host, and he demanded that the king revoke the "godless" privileges he had given the Jews. Capistrano warned the king that if he continued to favor Jews, he would suffer the torments of hell and bring misfortune to his country.

At first, Casimir stood firm. Then, in September 1454, the Polish army lost a battle against German knights on its northwest border. The archbishop immediately blamed the loss on the king's neglect of the church and his protection of Jews. In November, despite frantic appeals from the Jews of Krakow, Casimir revoked their charter, which he now described as "equally opposed to Divine right and earthly laws." Years later, Casimir's sons would restore the old charter held by the Jews of Krakow. Yet they too had to give in to public pressure from time to time.

Most of the 19 known anti-Jewish incidents in Poland between 1340 and 1500 took place in the 1300s. The rest occurred in the 1400s, and the violence expanded to new cities and towns over the next 300 years.[4] On average, two known acts of violence against Jews occurred every 25 years between 1340 and 1500. Over the next 300 years, a significant attack took place in Poland approximately every other year.

The violence was not evenly spread across the country. Almost all of it occurred in western Poland, where most Jews lived. Just 40 cities and towns were involved, even though Jews lived throughout the country. And three cities—Poznan, Krakow, and Lwow—accounted for about half of all reported incidents.

Why did violence increase over the years? The answer is complicated. Some historians point to economics. In the sixteenth century, almost any major event—fire, war, famine, or plague—could destroy a city's economy, disrupt trade routes, or wipe out the supply of or demand for particular goods or services. In addition, in the 1500s, a decline in the market for many Polish goods and a rise in immigration heightened tensions among various groups in the country.

Poland's population also became more diverse during those years. Only 40 percent of the people living in Poland were Poles. (The name comes from the Polani, one of the Slavic tribes that settled the region.) The shift in population was due in part to expansion; by the end of the sixteenth century, Poland included Lithuania, the Ukraine, and other non-Polish territories. The increase in immigration also had an effect. At the beginning of the sixteenth century, there were about 30,000 Jews in Poland—less than one percent of the population. By the mid-1600s, according to some historians, the country had about 500,000 Jews—nearly five percent of the population at that time. As their numbers increased, Jews became more visible, and they were therefore, perhaps, an easier target for those seeking someone to blame for Poland's economic problems.

Other historians point to religious factors. During the 1500s, a number of Catholics in Poland had begun to identify themselves as Lutherans, Calvinists, and followers of other Protestant movements. As in western Europe, church leaders in Poland were determined to protect Catholicism and tended to blame Jews for this new "heresy."

Still other scholars point to political causes—primarily a sharp rise in the power of the nobles and a decline in the power of Poland's kings. Kings were now elected by nobles and therefore had to keep a closer watch on public opinion. They were no longer strong enough to enforce unpopular edicts.

By the late 1500s, a number of Polish kings had granted more than 20 cities the privilege of "not tolerating Jews"—that is, the right to exclude Jews from their community. In a few of these cities, including Krakow, Jews simply moved just beyond the city limits and then traveled to their jobs in the city each day. In others, they were able to stay by promising not to engage in certain economic activities, especially money lending and banking. In a few places, Jews responded by seeking the privilege of "not tolerating Christians"—that is, the right to exclude Christians from their community. They won that privilege in Kazimir (a city built by Jews expelled from Krakow) in 1568, in Poznan in 1633, and in various towns in Lithuania in 1641.

JEWISH SELF-DEFENSE

Despite the increase in violence against Jews in the sixteenth century, most continued to see Poland as a haven. Rabbi Moses Isserles, one of the outstanding Jewish scholars of his time, lived in Krakow in the mid-1500s. In a letter to a former student, he wrote, "In this country [Poland] there is no fierce hatred of us as in Germany. May it so continue until the advent of the Messiah." He even urged the young man to move to Poland, telling him, "You will be better off in this country . . . you have here peace of mind."[5]

Rabbi Isserles was not naïve. He and other Jews were fully aware of the dangers they faced in Poland. More than any other minority in the country, they understood that their rights had to be defended. They took nothing for granted. Jews negotiated for improvements in their charters, bargained for privileges, and demanded interventions by kings or nobles in times of trouble. Whenever the authorities failed to respond, Jews took steps to protect themselves. Some hired armed men—Jews and non-Jews alike—to guard their homes and businesses. Others armed themselves with swords and other weapons. Still others sought allies.

One of the first things Jews did when they moved to a new town or city was to join a *kehillah* or establish one if they were the first Jews to settle there. A *kehillah* was the central Jewish organization in a community, and it had a variety of responsibilities. Perhaps most important, the leaders of the *kehillah* spoke to authorities on behalf of members. In 1407, for example, when Jews in Krakow were falsely accused of killing a Christian child for his blood, it was the city's *kehillah* that turned to the king for help by reminding him of the terms of the charter he had signed. He responded by closing the entire city: no one was allowed to leave until those who had made the false charges were sent to prison. Would the king have enforced the charter if Jews had not spoken up? No one can say for sure. What we do know is that law enforcement in those days was haphazard at best, and without an outcry, justice was rarely done.

A *kehillah* also acted as a government for Jews within a city or town. It kept order and settled disputes among Jews according to Jewish law. In some places, it was responsible for cleaning the streets and removing the garbage in the Jewish quarter. In addition, the *kehillah* arranged funerals, maintained a cemetery, provided children with religious training, and operated a ritual bath, a kosher slaughterhouse, and even a hospital (in those days hospitals sheltered travelers as well as sick people). The *kehillah* also helped needy individuals and families.

Kings and nobles also valued these organizations, because they provided an efficient way of collecting taxes. In fact, most rulers required that Jews set up a *kehillah* in their town in order to speed up and simplify tax payments. At first government officials appointed the leaders of almost every *kehillah*. By the 1500s, however, Jews were choosing their own leaders and deciding who qualified for membership.

A *kehillah* was by no means a democracy. The organization was governed by a minority—the most prosperous men in the community and therefore the ones who paid the most taxes. (Women had no communal rights.) The poor, who made up the majority in every community, had no say in the way the *kehillah* was run. Nevertheless, both the rich and the poor understood the importance of a united voice and some measure of security in an insecure world.

By the 1500s, many Jewish leaders realized that working with their counterparts in neighboring communities would enhance that united voice. They began to organize regional associations and, later, a national one. The kingdom of Poland consisted of four provinces; in 1569, a fifth province was added when the Grand Dukes of Lithuania and their descendants became the kings of Poland. Each of the five provinces had its own association of *kehillot* (the plural of *kehillah*). From time to time, the leaders of these groups gathered at annual trading fairs to settle disputes and discuss common concerns.

Some of these leaders were noted rabbis and scholars. In making decisions in disputes that were brought to them, they used a code of Jewish law known as *Shulhan Arukh*. (The words literally mean "set table.") The *Shulhan Arukh* is a list of laws compiled by Joseph Karo, a Jewish scholar who, after being exiled from Spain in 1492, settled in Safed, a city in what is now Israel. In creating this code of laws, he drew mainly on Sephardic and Middle Eastern traditions. (The word *Sephardic* refers to the Jewish culture that developed in Spain and other lands along the Mediterranean Sea.) Later in the century, Rabbi Isserles added Ashkenazi customs and practices to the code. (The term *Ashkenazi* refers to the Jewish culture that developed in northern and, later, eastern Europe.)

The *kehillot* helped Jews in Poland protect their rights and privileges by insisting that rulers honor their promises. For example, in the 1500s, Jewish leaders in the Polish town of Kowel confronted the general who ruled the town after he ignored the terms of the community's charter. He responded to their protests by throwing them into a dungeon filled with water and then demanding that the *kehillah* pay a ransom for their release. Outraged, the Jews of Kowel turned to the king of Poland for help. After hearing both sides of the story, the king ordered the general to release the Jewish prisoners and fulfill the terms of the *kehillah*'s charter. The general obeyed.

Kehillot also fought for the rights of their members in the courts. Many Jews believed it was essential to bring every perpetrator of a crime against Jews to trial. If the victims or their families could not afford a lawyer, the *kehillah* provided the money to pay for one. Rabbis said that even in cases in which the perpetrators were unlikely to be punished, Jews were still obligated to insist on a trial "in order that it should become known that Jewish blood is not free for all."

CATASTROPHE IN THE EAST

In the sixteenth century, as life was becoming more difficult for Jews in western Poland, a new frontier was opening in the east. As Poland expanded its borders, many Polish nobles acquired large estates in the new territories. Those nobles relied on Jews for help in managing their estates and supervising the work of the peasants. In the 1560s, about 4,000 Jews lived in the Ukraine. By the 1640s, historians estimate, more than 50,000 Jews made their homes in 115 separate communities there; some historians place the number of Jews at more than 100,000.

Jews in western Poland lived mainly in cities and towns. In the east, however, Jews lived mainly in rural areas as a result of a new economic system that evolved there—the *arenda*. *Arenda* is a Polish word for a complicated leasing arrangement in which a noble leases the right to manage an estate or group of estates to an individual or a family. As the following agreement suggests, leaseholders were more than administrators:

> We do hereby lease to the worthy Master Abraham, son of Samuel, our estates, villages, and towns, and the monetary payments that come from the tax on grain, beehives, fishponds, lakes, and places of beaver hunting, on meadows, on forests, and on threshing floors.
>
> We also give him the authority to judge and sentence all our subjects, to punish by monetary fines or by sentence of death those who are guilty or who disobey.[6]

Abraham and other such leaseholders had political as well as economic power. They served, for example, as both police officers and judges for hundreds and sometimes thousands of peasants whose religion and culture differed from their own and from that of the nobles for whom they worked.

Leaseholders did not receive a salary for their work. Instead the nobles allowed them to keep some of the taxes they collected. A leaseholder could also earn money by subleasing some of his work. Job seekers paid for the right to open an inn or a tavern, collect taxes, or work as a carpenter or blacksmith. Although many Polish nobles and some Jewish leaseholders like Abraham grew rich from these arrangements, most people earned barely enough to feed their families. In the Ukraine, for example, an estimated 25 percent of the Jewish population at this time was living on charity.

Nathan Hanover, a Jewish scholar who lived in the Ukraine in the 1600s, described the consequences of this new system in which Polish Roman Catholic nobles and Jewish leaseholders governed Greek Orthodox Ukrainians:

> [King Sigismund III] was a kind and upright man. He loved justice and loved [the Jewish people]. In his days the religion of the Pope gained strength in the Kingdom of Poland. Formerly most of the dukes and ruling nobility [in the Ukraine] adhered to the Greek Orthodox faith, thus the followers of both faiths were treated with equal regard. King Sigismund, however, raised the status of the Catholic dukes and princes above those of the Ukrainians, so that most of the latter abandoned their Greek Orthodox faith and embraced Catholicism. And the masses that followed the Greek Orthodox Church became gradually impoverished. They were looked upon as lowly and inferior beings and became the slaves and the handmaids of the Polish people and of the Jews. . . . The nobles levied upon them heavy taxes, and some even resorted to cruelty and torture with the intent of persuading them to accept Catholicism. So wretched and lowly had they become that all classes of people, even the lowliest among them, became their overlords.[7]

In the spring of 1648, a Ukrainian named Bohdan Chmielnicki led an uprising, uniting those peasants against their Catholic Polish rulers and the "unbelieving" Jews with words such as these: "You know the wrongs done us by the Poles and Jews, their leaseholders and beloved factors, the oppressions, the evil deeds, and the impoverishment, you know and you remember."[8] Chmielnicki was a nobleman and a Cossack. The Cossacks were a Slavic people who lived in the Ukraine and organized themselves into semi-military bands to guard their land and their freedom. They viewed both the Poles and the Jews as invaders and were determined to oust them from the area.

Chmielnicki and his followers did not distinguish between the small number of wealthy Jewish leaseholders and the many thousands of Jews who eked out a living in the Ukraine. Both were attacked with fury. So

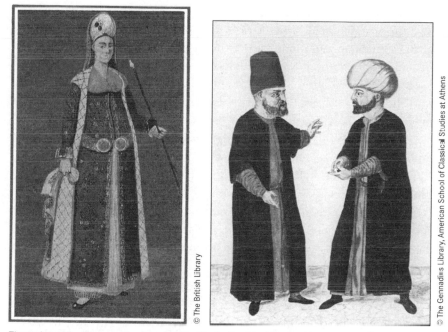

Throughout the Ottoman Empire, clothing (including headdresses) indicated a person's religious affiliation and status in society. The woman in the first image is a wealthy Jew. In the second image, the man on the left is a doctor, and the one on the right is a merchant.

were Polish nobles and Catholic priests. According to some sources, more than one-fourth of all the Jews in Poland were killed in the attacks, and countless others were left homeless.

Although the uprising was quickly put down, violence continued as one country after another along the Polish borders took advantage of Poland's growing weakness. Little by little, over years of turmoil, its land was divided among its neighbors. As Poland disappeared, so did the charters that had once protected Jews. Only one haven still remained for them—the Ottoman Empire.

JEWS IN THE OTTOMAN EMPIRE

In the eleventh century, nomadic tribes in what is now Turkey had converted to Islam. Among those tribes were the Ottoman Turks, named after their leader Othman. By the thirteenth century, they were settling just south of the Bosporus Strait. By the mid-fifteenth century, the Turks had created a huge empire that included much of the old Byzantine and Arab Empires. The turning point had come in 1453, when Sultan Mehmet II, then ruler of the Ottomans, captured Constantinople, the Byzantine capital and the historic center of the Eastern Orthodox Church, and renamed it Istanbul. By the 1500s, he and other Ottoman sultans had expanded the empire until it stretched from the Balkans north to Hungary in Europe, across most of southwest Asia, and as far west as Algeria in North Africa.

In the 1500s, most of the world's Jews still lived in the Middle East and North Africa—some in the old Arab Empire and others, known as Romaniotes, in the old Byzantine Empire. (Romaniotes are Jews who speak Greek and have Greek-sounding names. Their families had lived under Byzantine rule for more than a thousand years.) In the 1500s and beyond, these Jews were joined by newcomers escaping persecution in Europe. Like Poland in earlier centuries, the Ottoman Empire in the 1500s actively recruited immigrants—particularly wealthy Jews from Spain, Portugal, Italy, and other parts of Europe. Like Poland, the Ottoman Empire needed skilled workers to expand the economy and increase international trade. The sultan even sent ships to transport Jews who were being forced from Spain. These Jews brought with them relatively new technologies such as forging steel and printing.

Some historians estimate that by the 1530s, as many as 50,000 Jews were living in Istanbul. Salonika, in what is now Greece, was home to about 20,000 Jews; it was the only city in the world in which the majority of the population was Jewish. Its harbor was even closed on Saturdays, the Jewish Sabbath.

In 1550, when the few Jews who still lived in Provence in southern France were threatened with expulsion, they sent representatives to the Ottoman Empire to find out whether it really was a good place for Jews to live. Their representatives were astonished: "We have no words to record the enlargement and deliverance that has been achieved by the Jews in this place."[9] They were impressed because the Ottomans permitted Jews to freely practice their religion, follow almost any occupation, and own property without restrictions. In return, the Ottomans expected absolute loyalty and the payment of a personal tax imposed only on Jews, Christians, and other religious minorities.

As in other Muslim empires, the Ottomans allowed each religious minority to organize its own community. And like Jews in Poland, those in the Ottoman Empire established *kehillot*. The Ottomans also encouraged Jews to participate in the larger society and in nearly every aspect of the economy. The very rich bought and sold goods in London and Amsterdam and sent agents to trade in Hungary, Poland, and Russia. Some speculated by buying and then selling huge amounts of coffee, sugar, and indigo. As a result, the port of Salonika became a key stop for traders traveling between the Mediterranean countries and central Europe.

However, most Jews in Salonika and other Ottoman cities and towns were neither wealthy nor international traders. Most worked as tax collectors, tanners, carpenters, weavers, shopkeepers, gold- and silversmiths, or in one of countless other occupations. A French diplomat who visited in the 1550s was surprised at how varied their jobs were and the extent of their influence. He was particularly impressed at the size of the Jewish printing industry and the skill of Jewish engravers, artists, and writers.[10]

IN THE INTEREST OF THE EMPIRE

As in Poland, the reality of life in the Ottoman Empire was more complicated than the Jews from Provence or the French diplomat realized. Like Poland, the Ottoman Empire had an official religion— in this case, Islam. Sultans and other rulers firmly believed that "Islam is exalted, and nothing is exalted above it." That meant that people of tolerated faiths—*dhimmi*— faced restrictions.

The special taxes Jews and other minorities were required to pay were just one of those restrictions. Some government jobs were open only to Muslims. And the sultan, like his counterparts in Europe, often required that Jews and other minorities wear special clothing, hats, or even shoes to set them apart from Muslims. Muslims wore green, while Jews were required to wear yellow and Christians had to wear blue. Jewish physicians, who were much admired by many sultans, were the exception to this rule; they were required to wear tall red hats. The Ottomans considered it important to know immediately what a person's place was in society.

The sultans ruled with an iron fist. They expected their subjects— Muslims, Christians, and Jews alike—to serve the interests of the empire. If the sultan decided that he needed more merchants in Istanbul, he could order merchants in another part of the empire to move there. That is what happened in 1453, just after the Ottomans conquered the city. Thousands of Christian Greeks, most of them merchants, fled. So the sultan ordered Jewish merchants removed from smaller cities and towns in other parts of the empire and resettled in Istanbul. They took over businesses abandoned by the Christians.

Soon after the Ottomans conquered the island of Cyprus in 1571, a similar transfer of people took place. The sultan sent Turkish peasants to live on the island so that its rural population would include Turkish Muslims as well as Greek Christians. At about the same time, the sultan ordered Turkish nomads who raised sheep, horses, and other livestock to move to Cyprus so that the supply of animals used for food and transportation would remain in Muslim hands. A few years later, he ordered Jews from Safed to Cyprus. He did not want just any Jews; he insisted that the Muslim governor of Safed send "1,000 rich and prosperous Jews . . . with their property and effects and with their families." In his order, the sultan warned the governor that he would be punished if he substituted poor Jews for rich ones.

In fact, the Jews of Safed never left home. With the help of friends in Istanbul, they managed to get the order cancelled. No one knows exactly how they convinced the sultan, but documents indicate that he informed the governor of Cyprus of a change in plans. When the governor complained, he was allowed to intercept a group of Jews from Salonika who were being relocated to Safed and bring them to Cyprus instead. Reports of similar transfers occurred well into the 1600s throughout Ottoman-controlled territories.

Why, then, did many Jews regard the Ottoman Empire as a great place to live? The answer lies in what they saw as the alternative. In the mid-1400s, an Ottoman Jew wrote to fellow Jews in Europe:

> I, Isaac Zarfati . . . proclaim to you that Turkey is a land wherein nothing is lacking, and where, if you will, all shall yet be well with you. The way to the Holy Land lies open to you through Turkey. Is it not better for you to live under Muslims than under Christians? Here every man may dwell at peace under his own vine and fig tree. Here you are allowed to wear the most precious garments. In Christendom, on the contrary, you dare not even venture to clothe your children in red or in blue, according to our taste, without exposing them to the insult of being beaten black and blue, or kicked green and red, and therefore are ye condemned to go about meanly clad in sad-colored raiment [garments].[11]

Why did Isaac Zarfati claim that Jews could dress as they pleased? Surely he knew that Jews and Christians could wear only certain colors. He probably did, but when times were good—and times were very good in the 1400s and 1500s—those rules were rarely enforced. It was only in tough times that sultans and governors made sure every restriction on minorities was obeyed.

PROTECTING JEWS

In the 1500s and early 1600s, the sultans regarded Jews as an asset; they were more than willing to relax the enforcement of laws and, if need be, to protect Jews from harm. They were less supportive of Christians, who had similar skills but were suspected of being sympathetic to the Christian kingdoms of Europe—which were enemies of the Ottoman Empire.

Protection was considered a privilege, not a right. In 1556, when Suleiman wrote a letter to the pope demanding the release of all *conversos* living under the protection of the Ottoman Empire but working in Ancona, (see Chapter 7), he did not make his case on humanitarian or religious grounds. Instead, he argued that the seizure of their goods and property was "to the prejudice of Our Treasury, to the amount of 400,000 ducats, over and above the damage done to Our subjects, who have been ruined and cannot pay their obligations to Our said Treasury." And he demanded the release of Ottoman Jews so that "they may be able to satisfy their debts."

Suleiman ended by warning that if his subjects were not treated well, the pope could expect that Christians would not be treated in a "friendly fashion" in the Ottoman Empire. The pope released the Ottoman Jews even though the others were killed.

Suleiman and other sultans were not as quick to protect Jews within the empire. In 1530, for example, when Ottoman Jews were accused of ritual murder for the first time, no one came to their aid. The accusers were Armenian Christians in the town of Amasya, east of Ankara in present-day Turkey. An Armenian child was missing, and Christians in the town claimed that "the Jews" had killed him. They attacked dozens of homes, killing men, women, and children before order was restored. At their urging, the local governor, a Muslim, arrested a rabbi and several other Jewish leaders. Under torture, the men "confessed" to the crime and were hanged. A few days later, the boy whose murder had sparked the violence showed up alive and unharmed.

A few years later, there was another accusation of ritual murder, this time in Tokat, an inland city not far from the Black Sea. After Greek Christians responded to the charge by destroying a Jewish neighborhood and killing dozens of Jews, Moses Hamon, a powerful Jew, demanded that the sultan intervene. Hamon, who was Suleiman's physician, persuaded the sultan to issue a *firman*, or imperial decree. It denounced the charges as false and barred local officials from taking criminal action against Jews in such cases. In the future, any charge of ritual murder would have to be brought before the sultan and his advisers. Although the *firman* was not a lasting solution, it did prevent further violence for a time.

When Suleiman died in 1566, his son Selim II became sultan. Like his father, Selim II had a Jewish physician, Joseph Hamon (Moses's son). Although Joseph Hamon had less influence than his father, he managed to renew the *firman* outlawing false charges of ritual murder. And when the sultan's advisers debated whether to renew the right of Jews to live in Salonika, it was Hamon who spoke on the Jews' behalf.

By the 1600s, the Ottoman Empire was declining, as it lost territory to Russia and to rebellions in various parts of the empire. The decline came at a time when the military and financial power of European countries like England and France were on the rise. As the influence of these countries expanded, so did the power of Christians in the Ottoman Empire. They had many advantages over Jews—including the fact that a number of European traders preferred to do business with other Christians. The Levant Company in England, which conducted trade between Europe and the Middle East, is a good example. It banned Jews both as members in England and as interpreters and guides in the Ottoman Empire.

As Jews were squeezed out of prominent positions in government and trade in the Ottoman Empire, restrictions on them increased, though persecution and violence were rare. When there were attacks, they were almost always a result of rivalries among *dhimmi* communities. Still, in the 1600s, many Ottoman Jews, like Jews in Poland, were praying for someone to save them.

A FALSE MESSIAH

In 1665, a number of Jews in Poland, the Ottoman Empire, and other parts of the world believed that their prayers were about to be answered. Shabtai Zvi, a Jewish mystic from a well-to-do Sephardic family in Smyrna (a city in the Ottoman Empire), declared that redemption was at hand and that he was the long-awaited Messiah. Despite the doubt and disapproval of many rabbis, thousands of Jews were overjoyed at his message. As he traveled through the Ottoman Empire in both Europe and Asia, the mystic gained more and more followers not only within the empire but also in Poland—where many Jews were still reeling from both the massacres in the Ukraine in 1648 and the political and economic upheaval that followed.

As Shabtai Zvi traveled from city to city, officials in Istanbul began to take notice, especially after some of his followers announced that they would honor his name instead of the sultan's at Friday night services in their synagogues. Then, in September, Nathan of Gaza, a young scholar who was Shabtai Zvi's most devoted follower, sent a letter to Jews in Europe and Asia announcing that the Day of Judgment was at hand. The news spread quickly. Many Jews prayed and then paraded through the streets shouting Shabtai Zvi's name. In places as far away as Germany, Jews prepared for the event. In her memoir, a Jewish woman known as Glueckel of Hameln recalled the excitement of those days:

> *Many sold their houses and land and all of their possessions, for any day they hoped to be redeemed. My good father-in-law left his home in Hameln, abandoned his house and lands and all his goodly furniture. . . . He sent on to us in Hamburg two enormous casks packed with linens and peas, beans, dried meats, shredded prunes, and . . . every manner of food that could be kept. For the old man expected to sail any moment from Hamburg to the Holy Land. . . . For three years the casks stood ready, and all this while my father-in-law awaited the signal to depart. But the Most High pleased otherwise.*[12]

Many Jews did not wait. As 1666 began, thousands headed toward Palestine, taking part in what they believed was the long-awaited "ingathering of the exiles." But it was not to be.

Ottoman officials saw Shabtai Zvi as the leader of a possible uprising. Throughout history, government officials have found messianic movements disquieting. They shake up the established order and challenge long-held traditions. The Ottomans were no exception. They arrested Shabtai Zvi and brought him to Istanbul in chains. Amazingly, he was not killed; he was locked in a cell and allowed to have visitors. All the while, he continued to promise new miracles. Then, in September, he was brought before the sultan's court and forced to choose between Islam and death. He chose Islam.

Many Jews were shocked. They had expected Shabtai Zvi to follow the tradition of *Kiddush ha-Shem*—the sanctification of the name of God—by choosing martyrdom. His followers were crushed; some felt ashamed that they had been taken in by his message. Sill others clung to the idea that it was all a tragic misunderstanding. But in fact, the dream had turned into a nightmare. It took Jews throughout Europe and particularly the Ottoman Empire decades to recover, and for many, life was never the same again.

[1] Quoted in Bernard D. Weinryb, *The Jews of Poland: A Social and Economic History of the Jewish Community in Poland from 1100–1800* (Philadelphia: Jewish Publication Society, 1972), 124.

[2] Quoted in Weinryb, *The Jews of Poland*, 26.

[3] Zbignyev Oleshnitzki to Casimir IV, May 1454, quoted in S. M. Dubnow, *History of the Jews in Russia and Poland*, vol. 1, *From the Beginning until the Death of Alexander I (1825)*, trans. I. Friedlaender (Philadelphia: Jewish Publication Society, 1916), 62.

[4] Weinryb, *The Jews of Poland*, 152–153.

[5] Solomon Luria, *Yam Shel Shlomo*, Baba Batra 10:21, quoted in Weinryb, *The Jews of Poland*, 166.

[6] Quoted in Abba Eban, *Heritage: Civilization and the Jews* (New York: Summit Books, 1984), 212.

[7] Nathan Hanover, *Abyss of Despair (Yeven Metzulah)*, trans. by Abraham J. Mesch (New Brunswick: Transaction Books, 1983), 27–28.

[8] Quoted in Lucy S. Dawidowicz, *The Golden Tradition: Jewish Life and Thought in Eastern Europe* (New York: Schocken Books, 1967), 10.

[9] Quoted in Cecil Roth, *Doña Gracia of the House of Nasi*, 2nd ed. (Philadelphia: Jewish Publication Society, 1977), 90.

[10] Allan Levine, *Scattered Among the Peoples: The Jewish Diaspora in Twelve Portraits* (Woodstock, NY: Overlook Duckworth, 2003), 85.

[11] Heinrich Graetz, *Geschichte der Juden* (Leipzig, 1875), 8:423–425, in Franz Kobler, ed., *Letters of Jews Through the Ages* (London, 1953), 1:282–285, quoted in Bernard Lewis, *The Jews of Islam* (Princeton: Princeton University Press, 1984), 136.

[12] *The Memoirs of Glückel of Hameln*, trans. Marvin Lowenthal (New York: Schocken Books, 1989), 46–47.

9

The Age of Enlightenment and the Reaction

(1600s–1848)

*There is no such thing as a Christian commonwealth. . . . [N]either
Pagan nor [Muslim], nor Jew, ought to be excluded from the civil
rights of the commonwealth because of his religion.*
John Locke, England, 1689

*All religions are equal and good, if only the people that practice them
are honest people; and if Turks and heathens came and wanted to live
here in this country, we would build them mosques and churches.*
Frederick II, king of Prussia, 1740

*Men are born, and always continue, free and equal in respect of their
rights.*
Declaration of the Rights of Man and Citizen, France, 1789

These three quotations reflect a dramatic change in the way a growing
number of Europeans thought about ethnic and religious differences.
John Locke was an English philosopher whose ideas influenced both the
American and French revolutions. Frederick II was the king of Prussia,
the most powerful German state in the 1700s; and the Declaration of the
Rights of Man and Citizen expressed the ideals of the French Revolution.

By the early 1700s, a growing number of educated Europeans had
come to believe that they were living in a new age. They saw it as a time
when scientific knowledge was replacing old superstitions and when
progress was valued more than tradition. Not everyone welcomed those
changes. In an essay written in 1784, Immanuel Kant, a German philosopher, expressed his belief that these people, too, would eventually come
to accept the changes.

*As matters now stand, a great deal is still lacking in order for men as
a whole to . . . apply [reason] confidently to religious issues. But we
do have clear indications that the way is now being opened for men*

to proceed freely in this direction and that the obstacles to general
enlightenment . . . are gradually diminishing. In this regard, this age
is the age of enlightenment.[1]

According to Kant, the motto of this new era, which came to be known as the Enlightenment, was "Dare to know!"—*Sapere aude!* in Latin. He described the movement's leaders as those who dared to "reject the authority of tradition, and to think and inquire." Modern science grew out of that daring. So did many personal journeys. One of the most remarkable was taken by a young Jew from a poor family in the Prussian town of Dessau. His name was Moses Mendelssohn, and his story reveals the opportunities that opened for some European Jews during this time of change.

Mendelssohn's story also reveals that "enlightenment" is not easily achieved. In a world that valued equality and liberty, one group could exclude another only by demonstrating a "natural difference." In other words, discrimination had to be justified by "scientific" evidence showing that human nature differs according to age, gender, and "race." Until the 1700s, the word *race* was widely used to refer to a people, a tribe, or a nation. By the end of the century, however, it described a distinct group of human beings with inherited physical traits and moral qualities that set them apart from other "races." The beginnings of that notion can also be detected in Mendelssohn's story.

MENDELSSOHN AND THE ENLIGHTENMENT

In 1742, at the age of 14, Moses Mendelssohn left Dessau to continue his Hebrew studies in Berlin. He walked the entire way—about 100 miles— even though he was small for his age and frail. He had a hump on his back (probably due to rickets, a childhood disease caused by a lack of vitamin D).

When Mendelssohn reached the outskirts of Berlin, he was directed to a special gate that Jews were required to use. It was the same gate that farmers used to bring pigs and cattle into the city. The gatekeeper probably asked Mendelssohn what had brought him to Berlin and how long he expected to stay. The gatekeeper was not being nosy; he was just doing his job. Jews needed permission to enter the city for even a few days. They also had to pay a special tax whenever they entered or left the city.

Mendelssohn had come to the city because he was interested not only in religious learning but also in secular studies. He wanted to know more about the world. So, with money earned from copying sacred texts and

© akz-images

A portrait of Moses Mendelssohn.

tutoring, he bought books about philosophy, literature, and mathematics. To read those books, he taught himself English, French, Latin, and even German. Like most young Jews at that time, Mendelssohn had a limited knowledge of the German language. At home, he spoke only Yiddish— the everyday language of the Jews of northern and central Europe in the 1700s. Yiddish is an early form of German, even though about 20 percent of its vocabulary consists of Hebrew and Aramaic words.

At another time in history, a bright boy like Mendelssohn might have learned German at school, but by the 1700s, Jewish education in Germany had become increasingly narrow and focused almost entirely on religious texts. Secular learning was frowned upon. So Mendelssohn studied on his own. In time, he met others who shared his passion for education. These new friends included Catholics, Protestants, and freethinkers as well as Jews.

One of Mendelssohn's closest friends was Gotthold Ephraim Lessing, the son of a Lutheran minister. He was a freethinker who often expressed his ideas in the plays he wrote. It was Lessing who encouraged Mendelssohn to publish his own thoughts and ideas. In time,

Mendelssohn's books on philosophy and literature were hailed throughout Europe. He was described as "exceptional"—an "un-Jewish Jew," one of a kind, a genius. As Mendelssohn's fame grew, government officials allowed him to live outside the ghetto and travel freely without paying a tax required of other Jews. Mendelssohn's admirers persuaded officials to exempt him from many other restrictions on Jews, but they never challenged the basic unfairness of those restrictions.

Mendelssohn was keenly aware of the difference between the respect he received and the disdain shown to other Jews. In a letter to a Benedictine monk, he expressed his frustration: "Throughout this so-called tolerant land I feel hemmed in; my life is so restricted on all sides by genuine intolerance."[2] Yet he continued to believe that much of that prejudice would eventually disappear if young Jews combined their religious training with secular studies. It was a controversial idea at a time when many Jews feared that secular learning would lead to the loss of their culture, customs, and traditions. Mendelssohn disagreed. He insisted that it was possible to be both a Jew and a German.

To encourage young people to learn the German language, Mendelssohn and Naphtali Herz Wessely, the son of a privileged Jew from Hamburg, wrote a German translation of the Hebrew Scriptures that included a running commentary on the text. The translation and the commentary were written in Hebrew characters so that Jews could readily read them. Both men were aware that Martin Luther's translation of the Christian Bible into German had inspired many Christians to learn how to read and write their language (see Chapter 7). The two men hoped their project would have a similar effect on Jews. The translation was completed in 1783 and was a success. Within a few years, most Jewish families who considered themselves modern owned the four-volume work.

Many young Jewish men—and a few young women—responded enthusiastically to the idea of broadening their education. But they quickly found that knowledge of German culture could take a Jew only so far. German Christians accepted a mere handful of geniuses and privileged Jews—enough to pride themselves on their "enlightenment" without confronting their prejudices.

Even the great thinkers of the Enlightenment, with their commitment to reason, failed to recognize the ways they stereotyped others. For example, the French philosopher Voltaire believed that Jews were "ignorant and barbarous people who have long united the most sordid avarice with the most detestable superstition and the most invincible hatred for every people by whom they are tolerated and enriched."[3] The power of stereotypes like those Voltaire expressed helps to explain why the ghetto gates were slow to open. It may also explain why many of those prejudices have survived for so long.

Hannah Arendt, a twentieth-century thinker who, like Mendelssohn, described herself as a German and a Jew, retold this popular story from the early 1700s. A noble scolded a Jew for his pride, pointing out that Jews had "no princes among them and no part in government." Referring to the dependence of many nobles on Jewish bankers and merchants, the Jew replied, "We have no princes, but we govern them." The noble thoughtfully argued, "But this means happiness only for a few. The people considered a [separate nation within a nation] is hunted everywhere, has no self-government, is subject to foreign rule, has no power and no dignity, and wanders all over the world, a stranger everywhere."[4] For Arendt, the story showed that education and wealth were not enough to pull down the walls of the ghettos; Jews would need political rights, as well.

GERMANY: IN SEARCH OF "USEFUL JEWS"

In the 1600s, a century before Moses Mendelssohn arrived in Berlin, Europe was in the midst of an economic revolution. It was a time when world trade expanded and money became increasingly central to everyday

On the shooting target from the eighteenth century, a Jewish peddler's head serves as the bull's-eye.

life. Even a few generations earlier, ordinary people bartered for goods and services they could not produce themselves. By the early 1600s, however, they had more opportunities to earn money, and with enough gold, even serfs could buy freedom and land. Money was also the key to power for rulers eager to finance lavish courts and large armies, so they were always on the lookout for newcomers willing and able to expand trade and build industry.

Frederick I of Prussia was one such ruler. In 1669, a group of Jews who had recently been expelled from Vienna asked him for permission to settle in Berlin because "the earth and the entire world, which, after all, God created for all humans, appears to be shutting us out."[5] Their plea was written in the language of reason and a common humanity; Frederick responded with a business deal. He offered the 50 richest Jews permission to live in Berlin in exchange for a payment of 2,000 thaler apiece, a huge sum in those days (roughly $90,000 per person in today's dollars). They were also required to develop industry in Prussia. Other Jewish refugees were not welcome; Frederick had no interest in poor Jews.

The Jews who settled in Berlin in 1669, like most Jews in Prussia and other German states, lived under a bewildering number of laws that applied only to them. Those laws, written centuries earlier, determined where Jews could live, what clothing they could wear, and on which streets they could walk. Until 1710, they also had to wear a yellow patch on their clothes to distinguish them from Germans. By then Frederick William was king, and he, like his father, saw Jews mainly in terms of their economic value. That year he announced that any Jew who paid him 8,000 thaler could remove the yellow patch.

In 1715, Frederick William sold Jews in Berlin the right to build a synagogue. He required, however, that its floor be laid several feet below street level so that the synagogue would be lower than neighboring buildings. In 1722, he decreed that Jews could marry only if they purchased from him a certain number of wild boars. The king knew that Jews were not permitted to eat pork; the law was a way of showing his contempt even as he extorted money from them. It was a malicious and expensive "joke" at Jews' expense.

In 1740, Frederick II became king of Prussia. Unlike his father and grandfather, he considered himself "enlightened." Although he, like them, ruled with a heavy hand, he established the first code of laws in Germany, eliminated the use of torture, and reduced corruption in the courts. He also enacted laws designed to protect most religious minorities, but the only Jews he was willing to tolerate were the wealthiest. He encouraged them to develop ironworks, silk factories, and other new industries, and they more than fulfilled his expectations. During his reign, those Jews created 37 of the 46 new enterprises in Prussia.

Those privileged Jews were known as *court Jews* (because of their relationship with the king). Many were very rich, and some had rights that were almost equal to those of Christians. The vast majority of Jews, however, had few rights and at best just barely made a living. Historians estimate that about 10 percent were homeless. They could not live in Berlin or other German cities unless a privileged Jew was willing to support them. For example, when Mendelssohn came to Berlin as a student, he tutored the son of a court Jew, which is why he had a certificate of residence. When the son no longer needed help, Mendelssohn could have been expelled from Berlin. He was able to stay because that court Jew hired him as a bookkeeper. When Mendelssohn later became a privileged Jew, his wife and children were allowed to live in Berlin only because of his status. If he died, they could be expelled. The same was true of the wives and children of other privileged Jews.

What happened to those who were expelled? Some had enough money to purchase a residence permit in another town. Others had relatives willing to shelter them. Those who lacked money or connections had no choice, as a Christian observer wrote in 1783, but to "roam through life as beggars or be rogues." For the most part, the homeless traveled through the countryside in large ragtag groups—townspeople described them as "horde[s] of wretched creatures . . . with their children, carrying their entire possessions on their backs."[6] They were truly outcasts.

These rootless Jews inspired a new stereotype. In 1781, Johann David Michaelis, a professor of Bible studies at the University of Goettingen, insisted that half of the criminal gangs in Germany were made up of Jews. Since Jews accounted for just a twenty-fifth of the population, the professor reasoned that Jewish criminality must be 25 times higher than Christian criminality. Such statements led many Christians to conclude that almost every Jew was a criminal.

Michaelis expressed his ideas in response to an essay by a Christian legal scholar, Wilhelm von Dohm. Von Dohm had called for equal rights for Jews in Germany even though he, too, believed that the Jews "may be more morally corrupt than other nations; that they are guilty of a proportionately greater number of crimes than Christians; that their character in general inclines more toward usury and fraud in commerce, that their religious prejudice is more antisocial and clannish." Why, then, did he favor equal rights for Jews?

*Everything the Jews are blamed for is caused by the political condi-
tions under which they now live, and any other group of men, under
such conditions, would be guilty of identical errors. . . .*

*If, therefore, those prejudices today prevent the Jew from being a good
citizen, a social human being, if he feels antipathy and hatred against
the Christian, if he feels himself in his dealings with him not so much
bound by his moral code, then all this is our doing.*[7]

Moses Mendelssohn did not entirely agree with the arguments on
either side of the debate, but he was particularly disturbed by Michaelis's
views. In 1793, he wrote:

*[Sir] Michaelis does not seem to know any other vice besides fraud
and roguery. I think, however, that where the wickedness of a people
is to be evaluated one should not entirely overlook murderers, robbers,
traitors, arsonists, adulterers, whores, killers of infants, etc.*

*But even if one were to judge [a people's] wickedness only by the
quantity of thieves and receivers of stolen goods among them, this
number should not be viewed in terms of that people's proportion of
the entire population. The comparison should rather be made between
traders and [peddlers] among the Jews on the one hand, and among
other peoples on the other. I am sure that such a comparison would
yield very different proportions. . . . This is aside from the fact that the
Jew is forced to take up such a calling, while the others could have
become field marshals or ministers. They freely chose their profession,
be it trader, [peddler], seller of mouse traps . . . or vendor of curios.*

*It is true that quite a number of Jewish [peddlers] deal in stolen
goods; but few of them are outright thieves, and those, mostly, are
people without refuge or sanctuary anywhere on earth. As soon as
they have made some fortune they acquire a patent of protection from
their territorial prince and change their profession. This is public
knowledge; when I was younger I personally met a number of [Jews]
who were esteemed in my native country after they had elsewhere
made enough dubious money to purchase a patent of protection. This
injustice is directly created by that fine policy which denies the poor
Jews protection and residence, but receives with open arms those very
same Jews as soon as they have "thieved their way to wealth."*[8]

Frederick II ignored the debate. Prussia did not grant citizenship to Jews until 1812—long after his death. Von Dohm's ideas made more of an impression in other parts of Europe, including Austria.

TOLERATION IN AUSTRIA

In 1782, soon after von Dohm's essay was published, the emperor of Austria, Joseph II, issued an "Edict of Tolerance." Its goal was "to make the Jewish nation useful and serviceable to the State, mainly through better education and enlightenment of its youth as well as by directing them to the sciences, the arts, and the crafts." The document made it clear that Jews would be "tolerated" only in proportion to their "usefulness." They even had to pay a special tax for their "protected" status. To keep down the number of "tolerated" Jews, the king allowed Jews to pass whatever wealth they had accumulated to only one son.

The edict also stated that Jews were no longer to be regarded as a separate people or nation. They were no longer to be governed by *kehillot*—communal organizations with some governmental authority as well as religious and economic rights (see Chapter 8). That change meant that Jews no longer had an official organization that could speak in their name. Other edicts aimed at assimilating Jews into Austrian society had similar drawbacks.

These documents did offer Jews some benefits. They no longer had to live in ghettos or wear special clothing. They also had more freedom in choosing an occupation and a place to live. In addition, some discriminatory taxes were abolished. Jews also had more freedom of movement. They no longer had to stay indoors during Christian holidays, and the men no longer had to wear beards.

Although many Jews welcomed these changes, many others saw the edict as an attempt to undermine Judaism as a religion and Jews as a people. After all, the *kehillot* gave Jews a defined role and a measure of security in a society that regarded them with hostility. A number of rabbis and other Jewish leaders also pointed out that the changes did nothing to end prejudice or discrimination. Indeed, after Joseph's death in 1790, many of the old restrictions were revived, and *kehillot* were still not allowed. Jewish efforts to keep those communal organizations gave new life to the old stereotype of Jews as "clannish," even though Jews have always adapted to the customs and laws of the country in which they live. The story of English Jews is an example of how adaptable they could be.

ENGLAND'S JEWS: HIDDEN IN PLAIN SIGHT

Unlike Germany or Austria, England in 1600 had a very small Jewish population—a few hundred in a population of approximately five million. Jews had been expelled from England in 1290, but in the 1600s, a few Sephardic Jews entered the country by claiming they were Catholics. They settled mainly in London and other cities.

By the mid-1600s, there was talk of readmitting Jews to England. The idea caused a sensation. The country at that time was divided along religious lines. The official church was the Anglican Church, or Church of England, but not everyone was satisfied with it. Some wanted England to be a Catholic country again. Others accepted many of the teachings of the Church of England but did not approve of some practices. Because they wanted to "purify" the church, they were known as Puritans. Disagreements among these groups had led to civil war and the overthrow of the monarchy: in 1649, a republic was established under the leadership of Oliver Cromwell, a Puritan.

In 1654, Menasseh ben Israel, one of Amsterdam's leading rabbis, sent Cromwell a petition asking that Jews be allowed to settle in England. The rabbi did not ask for a charter or contract like those Jews had in other places. Instead he asked that Jews be allowed to live "with the same equalness and conveniences that your . . . born subjects do enjoy." In other words, he wanted Jews to have rights equal to those of other people in England—including the right of citizenship.

Cromwell was not a tolerant man, and he had little use for Anglicans and even less for Catholics. Yet he seemed eager to admit Jews to England. Why? He believed that Jewish merchants were responsible for at least some of the prosperity the Netherlands enjoyed, and he hoped they would have a similar effect on England.

Cromwell's interest in Jews sparked hundreds of new rumors. Some claimed that Jews were about to buy St. Paul's Cathedral in London and turn it into a synagogue. Others insisted that Jews had no interest in the cathedral but were planning to buy entire towns and force out Christians. Still others maintained that Jews were going to take over the great libraries of the universities at Oxford and Cambridge. Merchants and artisans feared "unfair competition" from Jews. And some Protestant leaders were convinced that Jews were coming to England solely to convert Christians.

To avoid a political battle, Cromwell invited 25 of England's leading legal and religious scholars to a conference. He wanted their support for a law permitting Jewish immigration. The scholars told him that he did not need a new law that would allow Jews to settle in England. The order of expulsion in 1290 applied only to Jews living in England at that time; it did not include Jews born centuries later. So Jews could legally settle in England if they wished to do so. Nevertheless, the group made it clear that they opposed the idea. When Cromwell realized how hostile they were, he abruptly ended the meeting and never brought up the idea in public again.

Two years later, in 1656, England went to war against Spain. That war presented a problem for Jewish families living in London as "Spanish Catholics." They were now considered "enemy aliens," and Cromwell's government had the right to arrest them and seize their belongings. They decided that it was time to declare themselves as Jews. They sent Cromwell two petitions—one asking for the release of a Jew who had been arrested as an enemy alien and the other for permission to gather for prayer and buy land for a cemetery.

Cromwell and his advisers held two meetings on the matter. At the first, they ordered the release of the Jew who had been imprisoned as an enemy alien. At the other meeting, they may have granted the second petition. The minutes of that meeting disappeared centuries ago, so no one knows exactly what was decided. Nevertheless, shortly after it took place, Jews purchased land for a cemetery and ordered a Torah scroll from Amsterdam. The scroll arrived along with a cantor (a person who leads a Jewish congregation in prayer). In the months that followed, Jews rented a house for use as a synagogue. They were not likely to have taken these steps if they did not have permission to do so.

The way Cromwell responded to the question of whether to permit Jewish immigration had consequences. Those who opposed the idea had no reason to speak out or try to sway public opinion, because no one was now suggesting that the country open its doors to Jews. On the other hand, Jews already living in England were free to settle wherever they pleased and openly practice their religion—England had no laws that denied them those rights.

Cromwell's republic did not last long. When the monarchy was restored in 1660, the new king, Charles II, continued Cromwell's policy toward Jews, even though Protestant merchants (who did not want competition from Jews) repeatedly asked him to reissue the expulsion decree of 1290. Charles and his advisers stated many times that Jews were free to live and trade in England as long as they did so quietly. Like Cromwell, Charles and his successors believed that Jews were economically useful, and they were therefore willing to tolerate them.

In the years that followed, Jewish immigration grew. The new arrivals were Ashkenazi Jews from eastern Europe. Like Sephardic Jews, the newcomers had no charter, nor did they ask for one. Like everyone else in the nation, they were taxed as individuals and judged as individuals in English courts. In many ways, England was home to the first modern Jewish community in the world.

By the 1700s, a number of Jews were English citizens simply because they had been born in England. The only restrictions these Jews encountered were laws and customs that favored Anglicans over not only Jews but also Catholics and even other Protestants. Little by little, however, many of these restrictions were overturned—sometimes by new laws, but more often by legal decisions based on existing laws and traditions.

The way Jews won the right to testify in court is a good example of the process. According to English law, a witness had to take an oath "on the true faith of a Christian." As early as 1667, however, English courts were interpreting that law in a way that allowed Jews to take their oath on the Hebrew Scriptures rather than the New Testament. When that practice was challenged in court in 1744, Sir John Willes, the lord chief justice, ruled that to refuse to allow the oath (and therefore the testimony of a particular witness) was "contrary not only to the [Christian Bible] but to common sense and common humanity." He argued that denying Jews the right to testify in court was "a little mean, narrow notion," because it assumed "that no one but a Christian could be an honest man."[9]

That ruling marked an important improvement in the status of Jews under English law. It did not, however, mark an end to bigotry, as the fight over a naturalization law a decade later reveals. Any foreigner living in England could become a naturalized citizen, although few bothered to do so—the process was long, complicated, and expensive. Applicants were also required to take a Christian oath of loyalty. As a result, no Jew could become a naturalized citizen.

In 1753, a few foreign-born Jews asked Parliament to change the law. They pointed out that it was unfair. Not only did other immigrants have the right to become citizens but so did Jews who lived in British colonies; in 1740, Parliament had passed a law allowing them to become naturalized citizens after seven years without taking the Christian oath. Parliament responded by passing the Naturalization Act, a similar law for foreign Jews in England.

Although both houses of Parliament approved the law by a large margin, angry calls for its repeal came from all parts of English society— merchants and farmers, rich men and poor, highly skilled artisans and unskilled workers, clergymen and freethinkers. Mobs paraded through the streets of London carrying signs that read, "No Jews, No Naturalization Bill, Old England and Christianity Forever!"

Some opponents of the law revived old myths about Jews committing ritual murders and poisoning wells. Others claimed that Britain would soon be swamped by unscrupulous traders and greedy moneylenders who would use their ill-gotten gains to acquire farmland and large houses. Because the right to vote was based on ownership of property, these people insisted that Jews would soon control Parliament. At times, the wild rumors led to acts of violence. Within six months Parliament had repealed the law, and almost overnight the campaign against "the Jews" came to an end.

Why did a law that would have affected only a handful of individuals cause so much turmoil? If the English were so antisemitic, why didn't they place restrictions on Jews born in England? One answer to these questions lies in the fact that 1754 was an election year. The Tories, members of England's conservative political party, used antisemitism to bring down the Whigs, members of the more liberal party that controlled Parliament at the time. But the Tories' strategy would not have worked if it had not touched a nerve. Although most people in England had never met a Jew, many regarded "the Jews" as different and strange—outsiders who were not like them. And almost everyone was familiar with the old stereotypes and myths about Jews.

The English were also hostile for another reason. In 1700, about a thousand Jews lived in England—a country with a population of about 5.5 million. By 1800, England was home to more than 20,000 Jews. By the mid-1700s, people were becoming aware of that dramatic rise in immigration, and it aroused strong feelings. One Tory opponent of the Naturalization Act claimed that the bill would naturalize "hordes" of foreign Jews. In his opinion, those Jews could never become part of the English nation.[10]

The newcomers aroused fear for yet another reason as well. Unlike the wealthy Jewish merchants who had settled in London in the early 1600s, many of the Jews who came to England during the 1700s were poor. They also tended to be young, and few had much education. Most found work on the fringes of society—peddling trinkets, doing odd jobs, or selling secondhand goods. Newspapers and magazines portrayed them as suspicious, shifty, and cunning. In the 1700s, criminals were identified by name if they were Christian and by name and religion if they were Jews. John Toland, a philosopher who was born in Ireland but lived in England, observed:

So strong is the force of prejudice that I know a person, no fool in other instances, who labored to persuade, contrary to the evidence of his own eye and my eyes . . . that every Jew in the world had one eye [that was remarkably smaller] than the other, which silly notion he took from the mob. Others will gravely tell you, that [Jews] may be distinguished by a peculiar sort of smell, that they have a mark of blood on one shoulder, and they cannot spit to any distance.[11]

Yet as long as no one stirred up those prejudices, Jews in England had more rights and freedom than Jews in almost any European country in the 1700s. They were also more assimilated than Jews in other countries. And it was the question of assimilation that took center stage as the French considered the status of Jews in their country in the late 1700s.

THE FRENCH REVOLUTION AND THE JEWS

Like England, France had expelled its Jews centuries earlier—most recently in 1394. Nevertheless, in the 1700s, more than 40,000 Jews lived in France (which had a population of about 28 million). Most of these Jews lived in two areas: Alsace and Lorraine, in the northeastern part of the country, and Bordeaux, Bayonne, and neighboring towns in southwestern France. The southwest was a region that France had acquired over the years from various popes and foreign kings.

The approximately 5,000 Jews who lived in the southwest were Sephardic Jews. A much larger group—about 35,000 Ashkenazi Jews—lived in Alsace and Lorraine, which France had acquired from Germany in the 1600s.

The two groups of Jews were not treated alike. In many ways France was still a feudal country, with a king and thousands of wealthy nobles at the top and millions of peasant farmers at the bottom. As a result, every Jewish community had its own charter that defined its particular rights and responsibilities. Charters for Jews in southern France generally allowed more freedom than did charters granted in the north. Sephardic Jews were rarely confined to ghettos, and a wider variety of occupations was open to them. In contrast, Jews in Alsace and Lorraine lived much the way they had when the region was still part of Germany. Most were very poor and earned their living as peddlers or pawnbrokers.

In the late 1700s, King Louis XVI paid little attention to either group of Jews. He was more focused on the fact that France was deeply in debt.

To find a solution, in May of 1789, Louis brought together representatives of the three estates, or social classes, in France—nobles, clergy, and commoners. He hoped they would help him deal with the nation's financial problems. Instead the delegates put into motion a series of changes that reduced the king's power and, eventually, led to his overthrow. By summer, representatives from local assemblies throughout France had formed the National Assembly. Its aim was to eliminate the privileges enjoyed by the king and his nobles. Its members also began work on a constitution that would set out the basic principles and laws of a new government. It was inspired by the Constitution of the United States, new at that time, and the ideals of the Enlightenment.

Even before this constitution was written, the National Assembly issued the Declaration of the Rights of Man and Citizen. It stated that all men "are born and remain free and equal in rights." The document also said, "No person shall be molested for his opinions, even such as are religious, provided that the manifestation of these opinions does not disturb the public order established by the law."

The Declaration raised important questions: Were women included? Did the document include non-Catholics? The assembly largely ignored the first question, but the second became the focus of heated debate. Three years earlier, a royal commission had proposed that the king grant equal citizenship to Protestants. The king did not object. However, when the commission recommended citizenship for Jews, he vetoed the idea. Now the French National Assembly debated whether to overrule the king and make Jews eligible for citizenship. The count of Clermont-Tonnerre told the deputies:

> *The Jews should be denied everything as a nation, but granted everything as individuals. They must be citizens. . . . It is intolerable that the Jews should become a separate political formation or class in the country. Every one of them must individually become a citizen; if they do not want to do this, they must inform us and we shall then be compelled to expel them. The existence of a nation within a nation is unacceptable in our country.[12]*

Some of the ideas in the count's statement echo those of many German scholars. He, too, insisted that Jews assimilate or face expulsion. The bishop of Nancy, a city in Lorraine, responded to the count. Although the bishop acknowledged that "the Jews certainly have grievances which require redress," he wondered if France was obliged to "admit into the family a tribe that is a stranger to oneself."[13] In other words, he was doubtful that Jews were capable of assimilation.

Even as the assembly debated whether to grant equal rights to Jews, anti-Jewish riots were taking place in Alsace. The leaders were local farmers who were in debt to Jewish moneylenders. In October 1789, the growing violence prompted the National Assembly to invite six prominent Jews from Alsace and Lorraine to Paris to discuss their situation. Berr Isaac Cerfberr, the owner of a tobacco company, headed the group. He asked the lawmakers to remove some restrictions that forced Jewish lenders to charge borrowers high interest rates. For example, many taxes applied only to Jews. Alsace farmers sent their own representatives to Paris to protest "Jewish usury."

In the end, the National Assembly reaffirmed equal rights for Protestants but ignored the issue of rights for Jews. When Sephardic Jews in the southwest heard the news, they protested vigorously. As a result, the National Assembly voted on January 28, 1790, more than a year later, to give equal rights to Jews—but only to Sephardic Jews.

Now it was the Ashkenazi Jews who were outraged. They decided to take action. Aware that power was shifting from the National Assembly to the Paris Commune—a city government that was led by middle-class and working-class citizens—Ashkenazi Jews decided to plead their case that all Jews deserved the rights of citizenship before the Commune. On January 29, 1791, the six men who had been chosen as their representatives wore their National Guard uniforms to emphasize their loyalty to the state. Members of the Commune were impressed and voted to approve their petition.

Even though the Paris Commune supported the petition, the National Assembly moved slowly. In April, it placed Jews and their property under "protection of the law." In July, it ended all taxes that applied solely to Jews. Finally, on September 27, the assembly granted all Jews in France the right of citizenship. However, Jews had to give up their right to be governed by a *kehillah* and judged in rabbinical courts. Jewish representatives tried to persuade the delegates to allow a special exemption for the rabbinical courts but were not successful.

In a letter to the Jews of Alsace and Lorraine, Cerfberr urged that they fulfill their duties as citizens "guided only by a true patriotism and by the general good of the nation." Jews did, in fact, volunteer in large numbers for the National Guard and the army. Some also contributed money to revolutionary militias. And Jews suffered along with their Catholic and Protestant neighbors when the revolution turned against all religions in 1793. Synagogues and churches alike were looted and then closed.

Other aspects of Jewish life did not change much. For example, many in France expected Jews to give up peddling or money lending now that more occupations were open to them. In fact, very few did so. After all, why would someone who is successful at one trade abandon it for another for which he is less qualified? But many French Christians looked at that decision from a different perspective. They saw the failure of Jews to change occupations as proof that being a Jew was an obstacle to French citizenship. Although neither peddling nor money lending was illegal, such occupations were considered shady, even dishonest.

REACTIONS AND DOUBTS

In 1799, Napoleon Bonaparte took power in France, and in 1804 he proclaimed himself emperor. Within six years, he directly or indirectly controlled Spain, the Netherlands, Switzerland, western Germany, northeastern Italy, the Kingdom of Naples, and the Grand Duchy of Warsaw (all that was left of Poland).

Every time the French army took over a new country, Napoleon called on that country's people to "break their chains." For most Europeans, that meant an end to privileges and rigid social rules based on class. For Jews, it meant the end of the ghettos. When the French army entered Ancona in what is now Italy (see Chapter 7), Jewish soldiers led the march. Entering the ghetto, they tore off the yellow badges worn by Jews in the city and offered them tricolor rosettes, symbols of the French Revolution.

Despite the patriotism of these and other Jews in France, Napoleon continued to question their loyalty. Therefore, when French farmers in Alsace complained of usury, he decided to take action not against individual Jews who charged high interest rates but against Jews as a group or community. In May 1806, he signed a decree suspending for one year all loan repayments to Jewish lenders in Alsace. At the same time, he called for an assembly of 80 Jewish "notables." They were to answer such questions as "In the eyes of Jews, are Frenchmen considered as their brethren?" and "Do Jews born in France, and treated by the laws as French citizens, consider France their country? Are they bound to defend it?"

The Assembly of Jewish Notables expressed its loyalty to France. The group reminded the emperor that Jewish soldiers had fought bravely in the French army against Jewish soldiers in the English army. Soon after Napoleon received their written responses, he called for a Great Sanhedrin, a modern version of the ancient Jewish high court. It would

An 1802 poster entitled "A wise government protects all religions." It shows Napoleon Bonaparte proclaiming freedom of worship to all Frenchmen, including Jews.

include representatives from the Assembly of Jewish Notables and rabbis from various parts of France's empire.

The emperor asked the Sanhedrin to confirm the answers given by the assembly. He also ordered them to condemn "Jewish money lending." The group assured him that Jews were as patriotic as anyone else in France. Nevertheless, they encouraged Jews to participate in a wider variety of professions and occupations and, with some reluctance, condemned money lending at high rates of interest.

On March 17, 1808, Napoleon signed three decrees. One declared Judaism a "state-recognized religion." The second organized Jewish institutions into a *consistoire*, or consistory, a religious governing body similar to the one the government created for Protestants. Modeled after the organization of the Roman Catholic Church, the Consistoire Central des Israelites (Central Consistory of French Jews) was based in Paris and headed by a chief rabbi and a council of laymen from each of the nation's regional *consistoires*.

In theory, Napoleon was treating Jews in much the way he treated Roman Catholics and Protestants. There were, however, important distinctions. The French government used tax money to pay the expenses of Protestant and Catholic religious institutions but not Jewish ones. Instead, Jews had to pay special taxes to support synagogues and schools in addition to the taxes they and everyone else paid in support of Christian institutions. Jewish organizations were also expected to ensure the "good behavior" of the nation's Jews. They were required to reprimand Jews who engaged in usury and other "antisocial behavior." They were also supposed to promote patriotism and encourage young Jews to join the army. No other religious group had similar requirements.

The third decree, known among Jews as the "Infamous Decree," imposed restrictions on Jewish moneylenders, shopkeepers, and dealers in secondhand goods. They had to have government permits, and only a limited number would be issued. These laws were to remain in effect for ten years in the hope that by then, Jews would be assimilated. In fact, by the time the laws expired, the emperor had been defeated on the battlefield, and France once again had a king.

GERMAN NATIONALISM AND GERMAN JEWS

As Napoleon built his empire, he unknowingly promoted nationalism. Between 1799 and 1815, England, Russia, Austria, and the various German states fought a series of wars against France. During those wars, many people in the German states began to think of themselves as Germans rather than as Prussians, Bavarians, or members of some other state. Before long, they were debating what it meant to be a German—and who belonged in Germany and who did not. In 1819, that debate turned violent.

That year, a professor at the University of Wurzburg in Bavaria urged an end to discrimination against Jews. His outraged students physically

A contemporary drawing of the *Hep! Hep!* riots in Frankfurt am Main in 1819. Notice that both men and women participated in the violence.

attacked him and then took to the streets, where they were joined by local shopkeepers, artisans, and other workers. For several days the mob ran through the city, destroying Jewish homes and businesses and shouting, "*Hep! Hep!* Death to all Jews!" The letters *h*, *e*, and *p* together form an acronym for the Latin phrase *Hieroslyma est perdita*—"Jerusalem is lost." This was believed to have been the battle cry of the crusaders who had attacked Jews as they made their way to the Holy Land more than 500 years earlier (see Chapter 4).

When the *Hep! Hep!* riots in Wurzburg finally ended, two people were dead and more than 20 were wounded. By then the violence had spread to other parts of Bavaria and, from there, to other German states. One Christian wrote that he felt as if he had stepped back in time and the year was 1419 rather than 1819.

Most Germans did not join the rioters. Instead they locked their doors and shut their windows to keep out the noise. In only a few cities did ordinary citizens try to help the victims. In Heidelberg, a city in southwestern Germany, two professors and their students contained the mob until the police arrived. They even placed a few people under "citizen's arrest."

Soon after soldiers came to restore order in Karlsruhe, a city in Baden near the French border, anonymous flyers blanketed the city. They were written in response to an earlier flyer that had called for the massacre of Jews. The new message read, "Emperors, kings, dukes, beggars, Catholics, and Jews are all human and as such our equals." To emphasize that idea, the grand-duke of Baden showed his solidarity with the city's Jews by spending the night at the home of a prominent Jew. The gesture helped restore calm to the city.

The riots stopped as suddenly as they began. No one ever took responsibility for the violence. But many Jews noted that for at least a decade before the riots, a number of professors had been preaching a form of nationalism that imagined the Germans as a "pure" people or "race" struggling for freedom from "the Jews," whom they saw as a "race" of dangerous outsiders. Jakob Friedrich Fries, a professor at the University of Heidelberg, insisted that "the Jews" were so great a threat that they ought to be exterminated "root and branch." After the riots, some people accused Fries of sparking the violence. He denied the charge, claiming that he had "only" called for the extermination "root and branch" of Judaism, not of Jews.

Fries and those who shared his views romanticized their history by picturing their ancestors as heroic, self-reliant, brave, and loyal. It was a vision of the past that appealed to many young Germans, humiliated by losses to France. These German nationalists did not believe that Jews could ever be "true Germans." They saw Jews as "a race apart." Others insisted that Jews could become Germans if they were "properly" educated and converted to Christianity.

Many Jews questioned the sincerity of such views. During the Napoleonic wars, Jews had joined their German neighbors in fighting the French. In Prussia alone, 71 Jewish soldiers had earned the Iron Cross, a medal given for bravery in battle. Jewish women had volunteered to work in hospitals, raise funds for the war, and organize aid for needy soldiers and their families. Despite such patriotism, once Napoleon had been defeated, one German state after another revoked the rights Jews had received under French rule. Prussia's minister of justice justified the move by noting that the Jews' "temporary bravery did not preclude a lower degree of morality."[14]

In Mendelssohn's day, Germans were only willing to accept Jews they considered geniuses or Jews who were exceptional. By the early 1800s, even Jews who were geniuses found it almost impossible to win acceptance. During these years, there was no repetition of the *Hep! Hep!* riots.

Instead, in small ways and large, Jews were made to feel they did not belong. Assimilation did not turn Jews into Germans, nor did conversion— as Heinrich Heine, one of Germany's greatest writers, discovered.

Unlike Mendelssohn, Heine grew up in an assimilated Jewish family. He thought of himself as more of a German than a Jew. Indeed, many Germans believed that his poems and essays expressed not only their own innermost feelings but also the soul of the German people. Prince Metternich of Austria, one of the most powerful men in Europe, once said that Heine's poems were so beautiful that he wept while reading them.[15] Some of the world's greatest composers, including Richard Wagner, Robert Schumann, and Johannes Brahms, set those poems to music. And yet in 1831, Eduard Meyer, a German historian, wrote of Heine and other Jewish converts:

> Baptized or not, it's all the same. We don't hate the religion of the Jews but the many hateful characteristics of these Asiatics, among them their so frequent impudence and presumption, their immorality and frivolity, their noisy behavior, and their so frequently base approach to life. . . . They belong to no people, no State, no community; they rove about the world as adventurers, sniffing around . . . and they stay where they find lots of opportunity for speculation. Where things go quietly and in accordance with the law, there they find it uncomfortable.[16]

In other words, Heine was not a "true German," and conversion could not alter his "race." A growing number of Germans—particularly German leaders—shared that view. They were uncomfortable with Heine's sharp criticism of German society, even though other critical German writers (including Kant, Lessing, and Johann Wolfgang von Goethe) were forgiven for their views. After all, they were "Germans," and, according to Meyer, Heine was not. In 1831, Prussian leaders posted warrants for Heine's arrest at every border crossing. Heine went into exile. He lived in Paris for the rest of his life but continued to define himself as a "German poet." In 1844, Heine addressed his critics in the introduction to A Winter's Tale:

> Plant the black-red-gold flag on the height of German thought, make it a standard of a free humanity and I will give my heart's blood for it. Calm yourselves! I love the fatherland as much as you do. Because of that love, I spent thirteen years in exile, and because of this love I return to exile perhaps forever.[17]

Heine was not the only Jew to demand acceptance as both a German and a Jew. One of the most prominent was Gabriel Riesser of Hamburg. At a time when only a few Jews were permitted to study at a university, he earned a doctorate degree in law from the University of Heidelberg. Although Riesser graduated in 1826 with the highest honors, he quickly discovered that no German was willing to hire a Jew as a lawyer or a professor of law.

In 1831, Riesser wrote an article demanding equal rights for Jews as a matter of "honor and justice." Heinrich Paulus, a professor of languages and theology at the University of Heidelberg, responded to Riesser by arguing that Jews were "Ausländer"—foreigners incapable of understanding the German soul.[18] Riesser replied, "Whoever disputes my claim to this my German fatherland disputes my right to my own thoughts, my feelings, my language—the very air I breathe. Therefore I must defend myself against him as I would against a murderer."[19]

Riesser took pride in being both a German and a Jew at a time when the word *Jew* was considered so offensive that many Jews preferred to think of themselves as "Germans of the Israelite or Mosaic persuasion."[20] Riesser saw no contradiction between his religion and his right to German citizenship. He argued:

> *There is only one baptism that can initiate one into a nationality and that is the baptism of the blood in the common struggle for a fatherland and for freedom. "Your blood was mixed with ours on the battlefield," this was that cry which put an end to the last feeble stirrings of intolerance and antipathy in France. The German Jews also have earned this valid claim to nationality. . . . They have fought both as conscripts and volunteers in proportionate numbers within the ranks of the German forces.*[21]

Riesser challenged discriminatory laws on a regular basis. He made a point of going to cafés where Jews were not welcome. If he did not get served, he sued the owners and sometimes won. His uncompromising stand served as a model for other young Jewish activists. As Jews, they sought equal rights, and as Germans, they struggled to unite their country and make it more democratic.

In 1848, Riesser and other Jewish activists joined their Christian counterparts in a revolution that rocked much of Europe, including Germany. Their goal was democracy and unification of Germany. In February, an assembly in Baden called for a bill of rights. Assemblies in other German states supported that demand. The idea was so popular that many rulers felt that they had no choice but to accept it. By March, a number of German states had formed governments that favored both democracy and a united Germany. Even Friedrich Wilhelm IV of Prussia gave in to many of the rebels' demands.

Riesser played an active role in these events. He was one of nine Jews elected to a National German Parliament in Frankfurt; he also served as a vice president. Among the first acts of the parliament was a proclamation that stated: "Every German has full freedom of conscience. Nobody shall be forced to disclose his religious creed." The document also stated that "enjoyment of civil or political rights shall be neither conditioned nor limited by [disclosure of one's religion.]"

At one point in their deliberations, a number of delegates called for a law that would correct "the peculiar condition of the Israelitisch race." Riesser and the other Jewish delegates objected, insisting that Jews were not a separate "race" but "Germans of the Jewish faith." The other

CIVIC EQUALITY FOR EUROPEAN JEWS (1789–1918)

Data source: *The Routledge Atlas of Jewish History*, 8th edition, by Martin Gilbert, London and New York, 2010; and *A Historical Atlas of the Jewish People*, by Eli Barnavi

The map shows the year in which Jews achieved full political and legal rights in various European nations. In places like Russia, the Ottoman Empire, and Spain, Jews had few rights until well into the twentieth century.

lawmakers disagreed and passed the bill into law. Yet even as the delegates were planning for a united Germany under a democratic government, the mood in Europe was changing—particularly the mood of the educated and well-to-do. Within a few months, most of Europe's kings and princes, including those in Germany, had regained their power, and the old order was restored. Still, not all of the gains made in 1848 were lost.

In 1859, Riesser, the man who was not allowed to practice law because he was a Jew, became the first Jew to serve as a judge. He died in 1863, however, so he did not live to see the unification of Germany in 1871 or the emancipation of the Jews soon after. Changes are rarely easy, and many take more than a lifetime to achieve.

The "age of enlightenment" ended some of the isolation, discrimination, and humiliation Jews had experienced in earlier times in Europe. Jews now had more freedom than in the past. Yet these changes did not end antisemitism. Instead this new age, with its emerging nationalism, promoted dangerous new stereotypes that would haunt Jews in years to come. They were increasingly seen as a hostile "nation within a nation"—one whose loyalty was almost always in question.

[1] Immanuel Kant, "An Answer to the Question: What Is the Enlightenment?" (1784), quoted in Vincent G. Potter, ed., *Readings in Epistemology from Aquinas, Bacon, Galileo, Descartes, Locke, Berkeley, Hume, Kant*, 2nd rev. ed. (New York: Fordham University Press, 1993), 226.

[2] Mendelssohn, *Gesammelte Schriften*, 5:566, quoted in Amos Elon, *The Pity of It All: A Portrait of the German-Jewish Epoch, 1743–1933* (New York: Picador, 2002), 63.

[3] Voltaire, "Juifs," *Dictionnaire Philosophique in Oeuvres Complètes de Voltaire* (Paris, 1785) 56:152, quoted in Robert S. Wistrich, *Antisemitism: The Longest Hatred* (New York: Schocken Books, 1991), 45.

[4] Johann Jacob Schudt, *Jüdishche Merkwürdigkeiten* (Frankfurt: 1715–1717), 1:19, quoted in Hannah Arendt, *The Origins of Totalitarianism* (San Diego: Harvest, 1976), 63.

[5] H. Spiel, *Fanny von Arnstein, oder die Emanzipation* (Vienna, 1975), quoted in Elon, *The Pity of It All*, 14.

[6] H. Heuback, ed., *Jüdisches Leben in Frankfurt, Materialen*, vol. 1, 1462–1796 (Frankfurt, 1988), 88–89, quoted in Elon, *The Pity of It All*, 29.

[7] Christian Wilhelm von Dohn, "Concerning the Amelioration of the Civil Status of the Jews" in Ellis Rivkin, ed., *Readings in Modern Jewish History*, trans. Helen Lederer (Cincinnati: Hebrew Union College-Jewish Institute of Religion, 1957), 5–7, 9–22, 50–71, quoted in Paul R. Mendes-Flohr and Jehuda Reinharz, eds., *The Jew in the Modern World: A Documentary History*, 2nd ed. (New York: Oxford University Press, 1995), 31.

[8] Moses Mendelssohn, "Anmerkung zu des Ritters Michaelis Beurtheilung des ersten Theils von Dohm, ueber die buergerliche Verbesserung der Juden" (1783), in *Moses Mendelssohns gesammelte Schriften*, G. B. Mendelssohn, ed. (Leipzig, 1843), vol. 3, 365–67, trans. J. Hessing, quoted in Mendes-Flohr and Reinharz, eds., *The Jew in the Modern World*, 48.

[9] Omichund v. Barker, 23 February 1774, *Cases argued and determined in the Court of Common Pleas. Reports of Chief Justice Willes, 1737–60*, ed. C. Durnford, 538–54, in M. C. N. Salbstein, *The Emancipation of the Jews in Britain: The Question of the Admission of the Jews to Parliament* (East Brunswick, 1982), 46–7, quoted in David Vital, *A People Apart: The Jews in Europe, 1789–1939* (New York: Oxford University Press, 1999), 40.

[10] Bernard Glassman, *Protean Prejudice: Anti-Semitism in England's Age of Reason* (Atlanta: Scholars Press, 1998), 185.

[11] Abraham Cohen, *An Anglo-Jewish Scrapbook, 1600–1840: The Jew Through English Eyes*, 324, quoted in Glassman, *Protean Prejudice*, 177.

[12] Achille-Edmond Halphen, Recueil des Lois, Décrets, ordonnances, avis du conseil d'état, *Arrêtés et Règlements concernant les Israélites depuis la Révolution de 1789* (Paris, 1851), 184–189, trans. J. Rubin, quoted in Mendes-Flohr and Reinharz, eds., *The Jew in the Modern World*, 115.

[13] Ibid., 115

[14] *Leo Baeck Institute Yearbook* (1964) 9:211, quoted in Elon, *The Pity of It All*, 108.

[15] Yigal Lossin, *Heine: His Double Life* (New York: Schocken Books, 2000).

[16] Quoted in Gordon A. Craig, *The Germans* (New York: Meridian, 1991), 135.

[17] Ibid., 136.

[18] Quoted in Howard M. Sachar, *A History of the Jews in the Modern World* (New York: Vintage Books, 2005), 81.

[19] Gabriel Riesser, *Gesammelte Schriften*, (Frankfurt, 1867–68), 2:679, quoted in Elon, *The Pity of It All*, 177.

[20] Quoted in Sachar, *A History of the Jews in the Modern World*, 81.

[21] Gabriel Riesser, *Gesammelte Schriften*, Das Comite der Reisser-Stiftung, ed. Z. Isler (Leipzig, 1867), 2:131, 133, 150, 152, 183ff, trans. M. Gerber and P. Mendes-Flohr, quoted in Mendes-Flohr and Reinharz, eds., *The Jew in the Modern World*, 145.

10

Antisemitism in an Age of Nationalism

(1840–1878)

On the evening of February 5, 1840, a monk known as Father Thomas and his servant, Ibrahim Amara, disappeared without a trace in Damascus, Syria. Within weeks, Christians in the city were accusing Jews of murdering the two men. Newspapers around the world carried the story. In March, the editor of a Paris newspaper proclaimed, "Rightly or wrongly, the Jews . . . have the terrifying and inconceivable reputation of sacrificing a Christian on their Passover and distributing the blood to their coreligionists in the region."[1] "And all of this is happening in 1840," wrote the editor of another paper, horrified at the idea of ritual murder in his own time.

A contemporary drawing of Father Thomas and his servant.

How did a disappearance become a possible murder and then a "ritual murder"? Why were people who lived thousands of miles from Damascus so interested in the story? How do Jews or any other people combat a lie about "terrifying and inconceivable" crimes—particularly when such a lie erupts at a time when most people like to think of themselves as modern, even "enlightened"?

Many people in the 1800s believed that they had cast off the prejudices of earlier times. Indeed, some devoted their lives to undoing the great injustices of earlier, less enlightened eras. One western European nation after another granted Jews their rights as citizens. In 1861, Russia freed its serfs; four years later, the United States abolished slavery; and in 1876, reluctantly and under great pressure, the Ottoman Empire granted non-Muslims civic equality (which was, however, later revoked).

And yet despite such progress, discrimination and persecution persisted throughout the 1800s. Instead of turning to reason and science to challenge old myths and misinformation, many people used reason and science to justify their prejudices. In the early 1800s, Frederick Douglass, an African American who fought slavery, explained:

> It is the province of prejudice to blind; and scientific writers, not less than others, write to please, as well as to instruct, and even unconsciously . . . sometimes sacrifice what is true to what is popular. Fashion is not confined to dress; but extends to philosophy as well— and it is fashionable now in our land to exaggerate the differences between the [African American] and the European.[2]

It was also fashionable to exaggerate differences between the Jew and the European. When the disappearance of Father Thomas and his servant led to charges of ritual murder against prominent Jews in Damascus, a number of educated people in Europe and the Middle East readily believed the accusation—not because they saw Jews as a threat to Christianity or Islam but because they saw Jews as a separate and dangerous "race." Their responses reveal much about the way individuals and groups adapt the myths and stereotypes of earlier times to current events. The Damascus affair also reveals the impact of nationalism and racism on antisemitism.

MURDER IN DAMASCUS?

In 1840, about 100,000 people lived in Damascus, the capital of Syria. To Europeans, its crowded markets and narrow streets gave it an air of remoteness and mystery. To people in the Middle East and North Africa, it was a center of trade where camel caravans stopped on their way to Baghdad in the east or Beirut to the north. Although Damascus was mainly a Muslim city, it was also home to about 12,000 Christians of various denominations and about 5,000 Jews. Each group lived in its own quarter, but people of all faiths mingled in the markets, and some knew one another socially as well. Both Christians and Jews had a long history in the city, dating back more than 18 centuries.

In 1840, the Ottoman Empire was not as powerful as it had been in earlier times; Syria, for example, was under Egyptian rule, even though it was officially part of the Ottoman Empire. In 1831, Muhammad Ali, the viceroy of Egypt, had driven the Ottomans out of Syria and made his adopted son, Sherif Pasha, governor-general. But that victory did not end the dispute over the territory.

That dispute between Egypt and the Ottoman Empire attracted attention in several European nations whose leaders were eager to expand their economic and political influence in the region. Throughout the 1800s, these nations competed for colonies, markets, and influence. France, which had occupied Algeria since 1830, hoped to gain additional territory in North Africa and the Middle East; its leaders supported Egypt and Muhammad Ali. Therefore Austria and Britain backed the Ottoman sultan as a way of preventing French expansion.

To make things more confusing, a few people in Syria in 1840 were not under the protection of the Ottomans or the Egyptians. Among them was Father Thomas. Even though he had lived in Damascus for more than 30 years, he and other Catholic missionaries in the region were under French protection. As European influence in the Middle East increased, France and other European nations had placed a number of people in Syria under their protection. The sultan had recognized their right to do so in various treaties; so had Muhammad Ali. Like Father Thomas, most of these people had been born in Europe but now lived in the region; a few had been born in Syria but had business dealings with various European nations.

Soon after Father Thomas disappeared, the monks notified the Count de Ratti-Menton, the French consul in Syria. Three weeks later, Ratti-Menton sent a report to his superiors that emphasized the victim's connections to France:

> *An appalling drama has just stained the city of Damascus in blood.*
> *The fact that the principal victim had direct ties to the [French]*

consulate; that he occupied a position that was both public and consecrated; that those who played the primary role in this scene of murder enjoy a [high] social position; and above all, that their actions were inspired by an anti-human idea, all conjoin to justify the length and detail of what I am about to report.

On the afternoon of the 5th of this month, Father Thomas, a . . . missionary and chaplain of the French Capuchin monastery at Damascus, left in the direction of the Jewish quarter in order to put up a notice on the door of one of the synagogues about an auction for the benefit of a poor European family. He was due on the following day, the 6th, to have dinner with the other members of the religious orders at Dr. Massari's where he failed to appear. His absence was rendered the more unusual by the fact that he was not at the monastery at the usual time for the celebration of the mass and also by the simultaneous disappearance of his only domestic servant. However, this could initially be explained by the supposition that Father Thomas had gone to one of the neighboring villages in order to vaccinate some of the children there.

Informed of what had happened, I went to the monastery where the street was full of Christians from all the different sects who were shouting that Father Thomas had been slain by the Jews.[3]

On Friday, February 7, Ratti-Menton reported the disappearance to the Egyptian governor-general, Sherif Pasha, and asked his permission to lead police in a search of the Jewish quarter, which was believed to be the last place the two men had been seen. As a result of that search, Ratti-Menton brought a barber named Solomon Halek to the French consulate for questioning. Halek was singled out because the notice Father Thomas had taken to the Jewish quarter hung on a wall near his shop. Still, after three days of interrogation, the barber continued to insist that he knew nothing. Describing Halek's refusal to talk as "obstinate silence," Ratti-Menton claimed that he had no choice but to turn the man over to Sherif Pasha.

The French consul knew exactly what would happen next. Even though France and other western European nations had outlawed torture as a "barbarous practice"—one that too often resulted in false admissions of guilt—torture was routine in the Ottoman Empire. After beatings so brutal that he was unable to sit, Halek "confessed." He told the authorities that Thomas had been brought to the home of a Jewish businessman. There, several Jews, including a rabbi, had bound the monk and then slit his throat. The account continued:

> [The Jews] collected the blood in a large silver bowl, because it was to serve for their [Passover] holiday. They stripped the dead friar of his vestments . . . took his body to another room, cut it to pieces, and crushed its bones with an iron grinder. They put everything into a big coffee sack and threw it into a ditch. Then they poured the blood into bottles, which they gave to the rabbi.[4]

This was the same "blood libel" that had been used against Jews throughout Europe and the Middle East for more than 600 years (see Chapter 5).

Sherif Pasha and Ratti-Menton kept written records of their dealings with every witness and every suspect. They quoted the barber as saying, "Go to the important people in the quarter and they will settle everything."[5] As a result, seven of the richest and most respected Jews in the city were arrested. They too "confessed" after torture so brutal that two of them died. The authorities then searched for evidence but found nothing. Rather than reconsider the theories about the supposed crime, Sherif Pasha took hostages—60 boys ranging in age from 5 to 11—in the hope that their frightened parents would "talk."

Ratti-Menton claimed that at first he had been skeptical that "the Jews" "employ human blood in the celebration of their religious mysteries," but with "the mounting evidence," he overcame his doubts (see Chapter 5). What was that evidence? Essentially, it consisted of little more than a few forced confessions and the discovery of a handful of possibly human bones in a sewer in the Jewish quarter.

Early in the investigation, a young Jew named Isaac Yavo reluctantly told the chief rabbi of Damascus that he had seen Father Thomas and his servant in another part of the city on the night of February 5. He had even spoken to them. Knowing that the authorities firmly believed that the Jews they had in custody were guilty of murder, the rabbi tried to make sure that Yavo would be safe if he testified. Ratti-Menton assured the rabbi that no honest witness had anything to fear. As a result, Yavo agreed to tell his story.

The French questioned Yavo for three days and then turned him over to Sherif Pasha for "further interrogation." Pasha later issued a statement explaining what happened next. It was summarized in this report to the French government:

As the place where this young man stated that he had seen the monk is situated in the west of the town while the Jewish quarter is in the east, he [Sherif Pasha] realized that [Yavo] was therefore lying; he asked [the young man] whether he had not been coached by anybody, but he denied it. He was then flogged; he confessed nothing and was taken to the prison where he died.[6]

Yavo's death was a turning point for many Jews in Damascus. They now understood that the authorities were interested only in "evidence" that would "prove" Jews had committed a ritual murder. Several events over the next few weeks confirmed that conclusion. The authorities quickly arrested five more men—this time for the murder of Father Thomas's servant. Once again, the men charged were among the most prominent Jews in the city, including the chief rabbi. These new prisoners were also subjected to torture; one man died, bringing the death toll to four. But this time two men—the chief rabbi and Moses Salonicli, a merchant—refused to confess to crimes they had not committed.

Charges of ritual murder against Jews were not unusual in the Middle East. Throughout the early nineteenth century, Christians in the Ottoman Empire had accused Jews of ritual murder—in Aleppo in 1810, Beirut in 1824, Antioch in 1826, Hama in 1829, Tripoli in 1834, and Jerusalem in 1838, to name a few. The Ottoman authorities had not punished Jews in any of these cases.

This time was different, because the libelous accusation had the backing of not only the French consul but also nearly every European and American diplomat in the region. The American vice-consul stationed in Beirut claimed in a letter to the U.S. secretary of state that "a most barbarous secret for a long time suspected in the Jewish nation . . . at last came to light in the city of Damascus, that of serving themselves of Christian blood in their unleavened bread at Easter, a secret which in these 1840 years must have made many unfortunate victims."[7]

Casper Merlato, the Austrian consul, warned Jews under his protection that "the secret guarded by the Jewish nation would serve no purpose and would only prove prejudicial to the innocent." He also congratulated Sherif Pasha on the "zeal and vigor" with which he was conducting the case.[8]

Why were Europeans so certain Jews were responsible? Were they blinded by old stereotypes and myths? Were they motivated by economic and social competition between Christians and Jews in a city where both were vulnerable minorities? Or were they taking advantage of a local dispute in order to advance their national interests? There are no clear answers. We only know that they were united in their thinking until one European had second thoughts.

Within days of declaring his support for Sherif Pasha, the Austrian consul challenged the entire investigation. Merlato reconsidered his stand in March, soon after the authorities accused more Jews of murdering Father Thomas's servant. Among them was Isaac Picciotto, a young Jewish merchant under Austria's protection. As soon as Picciotto was named a suspect, Merlato told the French consul and Sherif Pasha that he would be tried under Austrian law.

Without waiting for a reply, Merlato and his staff began questioning Picciotto, and they quickly discovered that he had a solid alibi. On the evening of February 5, Picciotto and his wife had attended a party in the Christian quarter. The host, an employee of the British East India Company, confirmed the alibi. Other people also recalled seeing Picciotto and his wife that evening. Yet in spite of this strong alibi, Ratti-Menton and Sherif Pasha continued to insist that Picciotto was guilty.

After much negotiation, Merlato allowed Ratti-Menton and Sherif Pasha to question Picciotto. But unlike the other prisoners, Picciotto never faced his interrogators alone. He was always accompanied by an Austrian official, who was there solely to ensure that he was not mistreated. The consul was making it clear to everyone involved in the case that Austria would do everything possible to protect Picciotto's rights.

Like Ratti-Menton, Merlato reported the interrogations to his superior, Anton von Laurin, the Austrian consul-general in Alexandria, Egypt. He emphasized that the case against the prisoners was based entirely on forced confessions. There was no evidence to support the idea that the two men were dead, let alone murder victims. Merlato asked von Laurin to transfer the case to Egypt "to prevent not only a subject of our empire, but any European whosoever, from being handed over . . . to the horrors of this infamous judicial inquisition."[9]

Von Laurin was one of the few diplomats in the Middle East who did not believe that Jews engaged in ritual murder. When Merlato changed his mind about the case, von Laurin supported the consul's new stand. He also asked Muhammad Ali to intervene. To add weight to the request, he persuaded other European diplomats in Alexandria to support the call for a new investigation. Only the French refused.

The increasingly uncompromising stand taken by the Austrian diplomats placed Sherif Pasha in a difficult situation. The only way he could get a confession from Picciotto was to use torture. But to do so in defiance of a powerful European nation would be dangerous to him and to his father, Muhammad Ali. At a time when European rulers were competing for colonies, many were willing to use any excuse to attack a weaker country. So even though Sherif Pasha bombarded Merlato with complaints, he made no effort to torture Picciotto or take him into his own custody. At the same time, Sherif Pasha slowed the pace of the interrogations and released the children he had been holding hostage. It was becoming clear to him that the fate of his prisoners would be decided in Egypt, not Syria.

As the case was winding down in Damascus, however, it took on new urgency elsewhere. As the story spread through the Middle East, anger against Jews grew in many other cities. A Jew in Beirut wrote in March, "[W]e can hardly leave our homes. Everybody, great and small alike, attacks us and forces their way into our houses. We are utterly abased."[10] Tensions were also high in Alexandria, Constantinople, Jerusalem, and the island of Rhodes.

Indeed, Christians in Rhodes had charged Jews with another ritual murder at around the same time. On February 17, a young Greek Orthodox boy had failed to return home from an errand. The next day his mother appealed to the authorities for help. When the boy was still missing after a few days, the European consuls put pressure on the local government to solve the case. The agitation increased when news of the Damascus affair reached Rhodes.

THE POWER OF PUBLICITY

In the 1840s, news traveled slowly—the first telegraph line was not built until 1844, and the telephone was not invented until the 1870s. Using the fastest transportation available, it took about 20 days for a letter from Syria to reach Paris or Vienna. As a result, most Europeans were unaware of the events unfolding in Damascus until early March when a steady stream of letters arrived from a variety of sources. Frantic Jews in the Middle East wrote to relatives, friends, and anyone who could possibly help. Letters also came from European diplomats, businessmen, missionaries, and travelers.

Anton von Laurin, the Austrian consul-general in Alexandria, sent one of those letters to James Rothschild, a member of one of the richest and most influential Jewish families in the 1800s. James's father, Mayer Rothschild, had made his fortune buying and selling antique coins and medals in the Frankfurt ghetto in what is now Germany. Later he branched out into money lending and investment banking. In time, his sons joined the business. Each set up a branch in a major European city: Amschel, the oldest, remained in Frankfurt, Nathan settled in London, Solomon in Vienna, James in Paris, and Karl in Naples. During the Napoleonic wars, the brothers had increased the family's wealth by lending money to governments and transporting gold and other precious metals across enemy lines for the British, Prussian, and Austrian armies.

The letter von Laurin sent to James Rothschild detailed everything he knew about the Damascus affair. It was not the only letter Rothschild and his brothers received. Jews in Istanbul and Jerusalem, Christian missionaries, heads of Jewish charities in Syria, and many others also pleaded with the brothers to intervene. In 1840, there was nowhere else to turn for help.

Although many people believed that the Rothschild family had enormous power, the brothers were acutely aware of the limits of their influence. Antisemitism affected all Jews, including the very rich. For example, the emperor of Austria made Solomon Rothschild an honorary citizen and awarded him the title of baron in recognition of his contributions to the empire. Yet, as a Jew, Solomon could only be an "honorary citizen," not a real one. He and his family lived in a hotel, because no Jew—not even one with the title of baron—could buy a house in Vienna. That right was reserved for Christians.

A few days after sending his first letter to James Rothschild, Anton von Laurin sent a second letter, informing Rothschild that the situation was getting worse and urging that he go to the newspapers with the story, because they would "raise a cry of horror."[11]

Von Laurin had no way of knowing that the story was already headline news in Europe. And most of the early newspaper accounts supported the French consul and Sherif Pasha. These papers spoke of the "barbarity of the Jews," denounced the "horror of the crime," and expressed outrage at "human sacrifices." Why were European editors so certain that "the Jews" were guilty of such terrible crimes? No newspaper in the 1840s had a single reporter in any foreign country. The press got its information from Europeans in the area—in this case, in Damascus and nearby cities.

Some Jews responded to the sensational stories with indignant letters to the editor. One of those letters was written at the request of James Rothschild, based on information from von Laurin and others in the region. The author was Adolphe Crémieux, the vice president of the Central Consistory of French Jews (see Chapter 9). His letter changed the way the Damascus affair was treated in the French press.

Crémieux claimed that he spoke, "in the name of your Jewish fellow-citizens whom your report has shocked; in the name of all the Jews throughout the world who will protest *en masse*; and in the name of the Damascus Jews over whom at this very moment the sword of death may be poised."[12] He began by questioning the assumptions made by the authorities in Damascus. Why would a few wealthy Jews plotting a horrendous crime have let a stranger—Solomon Halek, the barber—in on their scheme? How likely was it that murderers eager to escape detection would dispose of "the bones" of their victim near their own homes? And finally, why would Jews be collecting blood for Passover two months early?

On the issue of ritual murder, Crémieux pointed out that Jewish law does not permit Jews to eat eggs that have a blood spot. How likely was it, he asked, that such a religion would allow the use of blood to make unleavened bread?

Although the letter did not stop talk of ritual murder, it did change the tone of the newspaper stories. One paper backed off, declaring, "We had not intended to be understood as guaranteeing the truth of this accusation." In other words, that paper and others like it had printed whatever information they received without questioning its truth or its logic.

The Rothschilds and other Jewish leaders also met privately with heads of government and religious leaders. Their success varied. The Austrian and British governments were eager to help, mainly because it was in their interest to do so. Both saw the affair as an opportunity to embarrass France. Some Jews tried to persuade Pope Gregory XVI to speak out, but he chose to remain silent and banned all public discussion of the affair in Rome. When asked for permission to reprint statements made by earlier popes condemning Christians who accused Jews of ritual murder (see Chapter 5), the pope refused.

Adolphe Thiers, the French prime minister, was also silent. In an effort to force him to speak, Benoît Fould, the only Jew in the Chamber of Deputies, gave a speech on June 2 in which he charged:

> *The disappearance of the [monk] became an occasion for deliberate religious persecution. The consul of France incites to torture: at a time when the French nation offers an example not only of equality before the law, but of religious equality, it is a Frenchman who instigates exceptional [police] measures, who has recourse to torture, who upholds arbitrary measures [and] the executioners of the Pasha.*[13]

In response, Thiers declared, "The more [Ratti-Menton and his colleagues] are attacked by foreign agents, the firmer will be my support for them, above all when they are attacked by the interested parties [such as Britain and Austria]." The deputies applauded.

Nevertheless, as people around the world followed the debate, public opinion began to shift. On July 8, at a meeting in London, Christian clergymen and members of Britain's Parliament joined others in England in protesting the tortures and the charges of ritual murder. Similar rallies took place in Paris, New York City, and Philadelphia. U.S. President Martin Van Buren sent letters to the U.S. consul in Alexandria and the U.S. ambassador to the Ottoman Empire, asking them to help Jews in Damascus. American diplomats throughout the region, including the vice-consul in Beirut, quickly adjusted their stand on the case.

MISSION TO THE MIDDLE EAST

By early summer, Jewish leaders in Paris and London were planning a trip to Egypt to try to resolve the crisis. Adolphe Crémieux and Moses

BLOOD LIBELS (1800–1914)

The false claim that Jews murdered Christians for "their blood" did not end with the Enlightenment. It continued throughout the nineteenth century and well into the twentieth.

Montefiore, the president of the Board of Deputies of British Jews, headed the mission. Montefiore was an Orthodox Jew whose activism was rooted in his religious beliefs. Crémieux was a secular Jew—one who is not observant but who identifies with Jews as a people. His activism grew out of his strong commitment to the values of the French Revolution—*liberté, egalité,* and *fraternité* (liberty, equality, and fraternity, or brotherhood).

The two men left for Egypt on July 18, 1840, after learning that the viceroy of Egypt, Muhammad Ali, was going to open a new investigation into the Damascus affair. Crémieux and Montefiore hoped that he would give them permission to question witnesses and collect evidence in support of the defendants. By the time they reached Alexandria, however, the situation had changed dramatically: The French consul-general had persuaded Muhammad Ali to abandon the idea of reopening the case.

To further complicate the situation, Egypt was now on the brink of a war with the Ottoman Empire and its four European allies—Austria, Britain, Russia, and Prussia. Just a few days after Crémieux and Montefiore reached Alexandria, the five governments gave Muhammad Ali an ultimatum: give up Syria and other conquered territories within 30 days or risk a war.

Although this ultimatum had nothing to do with the Damascus affair, it made it more difficult for Crémieux and Montefiore to meet with Muhammad Ali. As a result, they decided to alter their strategy. Instead of insisting on a new investigation, they urged Muhammad Ali to free the prisoners and issue a royal decree declaring the accusation that Jews commit ritual murder is false and slanderous.

Until August 26, Muhammad Ali refused to take action. That day, he learned that the British had sunk several Egyptian supply ships in the Mediterranean Sea and were preparing to land on the beaches of Lebanon. The British were aiding the Ottomans, and the two were willing to use any means to get the Egyptians out of Syria—including attacks on unarmed ships and innocent civilians. Muhammad Ali was now convinced that unless he acted quickly, he could lose everything, including Egypt. On August 28, he gave up his claim to Syria without consulting his ally, France. The French were also not consulted about a second concession—this time, one regarding the outcome of the Damascus affair. How that decision came about sounds incredible, but it appears to be a true story.

Muhammad Ali had called his two private physicians—both Christians, one French and the other Italian—to the palace early on the morning of August 28 to remove a painful boil from his buttocks. As they lanced the boil, one of the doctors remarked that the viceroy would need all his strength to deal with the political threats he was facing, and surely the voice of six million Jews raised in his favor would be of great importance. (At the time, it was widely believed that there were six million Jews in the world.) To the surprise of the two men, Muhammad Ali agreed, saying that he would free the Jewish prisoners immediately. The tactic used by the two doctors had worked partly because Muhammad Ali, like many other people, agreed with their exaggerated view of "Jewish power."

As soon as the physicians finished their work, they told Crémieux the news. Over the next few days, Crémieux and Montefiore tried once again to persuade the viceroy to issue a decree declaring that Jews do not engage in ritual murder. Muhammad Ali turned them down, saying that even though he did not believe that Jews killed Christians for their blood, he had no interest in issuing a public statement.

Montefiore was determined to get a decree—if not from the viceroy of Egypt, then from the sultan of the Ottoman Empire. So he stopped in Istanbul before heading home. The sultan, who had already dismissed charges of ritual murder against Jews in Rhodes, agreed. He announced that after examining Jewish beliefs and religious books, he had concluded that accusations of ritual murder made against Jews were "pure slander."

OUTCOMES AND LEGACIES

On September 6, news of the viceroy's decision reached Damascus. The next day, Merlato, the Austrian consul, sent a letter to Crémieux:

> *Yesterday was the happiest day of my life. All the prisoners . . . were set at liberty and sent to their homes. . . . The joyful liberated men before returning . . . to their enraptured families proceeded to the [synagogue] where in unison with an immense multitude they . . . prayed for peace and every blessing upon Muhammad Ali and all their other powerful benefactors.*[14]

Jews around the world also rejoiced. They greeted Montefiore and Crémieux as heroes wherever they traveled. Jews were proud of themselves as well. Never before had so many Jews in so many countries worked together to shape public opinion on an issue. Many also took pride in the fact that a large number of Christians had actively supported the Jews of Damascus, and a few, like Merlato and von Laurin, had shown courage in their defense of Jews.

But not everyone was pleased with the outcome. Thiers, France's prime minister, along with many French citizens, continued to support Ratti-Menton. *Univers*, a conservative Catholic newspaper, proclaimed that "Judaism has reappeared as a power, as a nationality . . . and, as such, it has held all of Christianity in check." After asking "Who can now say how far their aspirations will extend?" the editors turned their attention to the Rothschild family. "On [King] David's throne, once it is restored, there will sit that financial dynasty which all Europe recognizes and to which all of Europe submits; its inauguration will surely provide a scene . . . most worthy of the [corrupt] century in which we are living."[15]

These French writers attributed great power to Jews in general, and to the Rothschilds in particular, at a time when Jews were powerless almost everywhere. As the twentieth-century philosopher Hannah Arendt noted,

> *Where . . . was there better proof . . . than in this one family, the Rothschilds, nationals of five different countries, prominent every-where, in close cooperation with at least three different governments (French, Austrian, British) . . . ? No propaganda could have created a symbol more effective for political purposes than the reality itself.*[16]

In other words, the power of a few wealthy and prominent Jews was seen as proof of the power of all Jews even though that power did not really exist.

THE LIMITS OF PUBLICITY'S POWER

During the Damascus affair, Jews discovered the power of publicity in fighting prejudice and discrimination. They were successful in shaping public opinion in part because many people in the early 1800s shared their belief in universal human rights. They were also successful because modern rulers—even dictators like Muhammad Ali—could not afford to completely ignore public opinion at home or abroad. In 1858, however, an incident in what is now Italy revealed that public opinion does not always prevail.

Early on the morning of June 24, papal guards in Bologna came to the home of a Jewish couple, Salomone David Mortara and his wife, and demanded their six-year-old son Edgardo. To the parents' horror, the guards had a written order, signed by Father Pier Gaetano Feletti, a local priest, to take the child. At the time, Italy was divided into territories, some of which were ruled by other countries and some by the pope. Bologna was located in a papal state.

Convinced that a terrible error had been made, Mortara raced to Feletti's home, only to learn that it was no mistake. Five years earlier, when Edgardo was ill, a Christian servant of the family had secretly baptized the baby by sprinkling water on his head and saying a prayer. The woman later left her job without telling anyone what she had done. In time, however, the woman spoke to friends about the baptism, and the information eventually reached Feletti.

In the view of the Catholic Church in the 1800s, once a child has been baptized, even if it was done without the parents' knowledge or consent, the child is a Christian. And under papal laws, Jewish parents could not rear a Christian child, even if he was their own. Frantic efforts to release the boy failed. He had been taken with the approval of the secretary of state at the Vatican, Cardinal Giacomo Antonelli, who proudly told Edgardo's father that his son was already "joyously wearing the cross" and attending mass.

Edgardo was not the first child the church had taken from Jewish parents in the 1800s, but his parents were the first to publicize their case. And like the Damascus affair, the story made headlines. In almost every western European city, Christians and Jews protested "the heartless abduction of a small child." They were outraged that a child could be taken from loving parents for any reason.

Several government leaders, including the emperor of France, found the story so troubling that they quietly tried to persuade Pope Pius IX to release the boy. He refused. Moses Montefiore tried to arrange a meeting with the pope to discuss the matter, only to be told there was nothing to discuss. The church saw no reason to respond to public opinion about a matter of faith. This time, publicity only hardened the church's stand.

Italy won its independence as a united nation in 1870—12 years after Edgardo's abduction. During the fight for independence, the pope lost all of his territory in Italy except for the Vatican itself. Pius blamed those losses on his refusal to release Edgardo. The pope was painfully aware that most Italians, regardless of their faith, identified with the Mortaras. Yet Pius continued to believe that he had done the right thing. He was convinced that the baptism had saved the child's soul and was therefore justified. Pius also felt threatened by the changes that were taking place in Italy and was convinced that bending the rules even slightly would endanger the traditions he valued and the beliefs he had vowed to uphold.

Soon after the independent Kingdom of Italy was formed, Jews became citizens in the new nation, entitled to the full protection of the law. Almost immediately, the authorities informed the Mortaras that their son was now free to rejoin his family. But by then it was too late: the boy was 18 and studying to become a priest.

IN DEFENSE OF JEWS

The Damascus affair and the Mortara case had shown how precarious it was to be outside a government's universe of obligation—the circle of individuals and groups toward whom the government has obligations, whose rights are respected, and in whose name justice is sought. In May 1860, Adolphe Crémieux and other French Jewish leaders held a meeting in Paris to create a new organization known as the Universal Israelite Alliance. They explained why Jews needed such a group:

> [A]ll other important faiths are represented in the world by nations— embodied, that is to say, in governments that have a special interest and an official to represent and speak for them. Ours alone is without this important advantage; it corresponds neither to a state nor to a society nor again to a specific territory; it is no more than a rallying- cry for scattered individuals—the very people whom it is therefore essential to bring together.[17]

Those who joined the alliance were mainly secular Jews who had come to believe that they must unite in response to a growing nationalism, which tended to treat Jews as permanent outsiders—a people beyond any nation's universe of obligation. The early successes of the alliance eventually led to the founding of parallel organizations in other nations— the Anglo-Jewish Association in Britain in 1871, the Israelite Alliance in Vienna in 1873, the *Hilfsverein der Deutschen Juden* in Berlin in 1901, and the American Jewish Committee in New York in 1906. These groups often worked together or at least coordinated their efforts.

The French alliance relied on three main tools to protect Jews: education, publicity, and diplomacy. On his first trip to the Middle East during the Damascus affair, Crémieux had been appalled at the lack of educational opportunities for Jews in the region. After meeting with Jewish leaders in Alexandria, he offered to raise money for a school. Under his leadership, the alliance expanded that idea by building a network of schools in North Africa, the Middle East, and eastern Europe to provide secular education and voca- tional training for both girls and boys. Those schools helped thousands of young Jews from poor families learn a trade or profession.

The French alliance also fought discrimination and prejudice through a combination of publicity and diplomacy. In earlier times, even large-scale massacres had gone unnoticed by most of the world. Now the alliance set out to document acts of violence against Jews. Frantic letters like the ones Jews wrote during the Damascus affair now went to a dedicated staff with the resources needed to take action.

How successful were such efforts? The late 1800s were a time of realpolitik. The word had been coined earlier in the century to describe Austrian efforts to keep the peace by balancing the influence of Europe's great empires—Britain, France, Germany, Austria, and Russia—so that no single power would have the upper hand. Leaders of the French alliance and similar Jewish groups in other nations were increasingly aware that they must take into account not only a growing nationalism in eastern Europe but also the competing interests of the great powers.

In 1858, for example, the provinces of Wallachia and Moldavia in southeastern Europe broke away from the Ottoman Empire and formed a country later known as Romania. Like people in other newly independent countries in the 1800s, the Romanians wanted the great powers to accept

© Alliance israélite universelle (Paris)

The Universal Israelite Alliance supported schools for poor Jewish girls as well as for boys in the Ottoman Empire and eastern Europe. The students shown in the photograph are learning a valuable trade dressmaking.

and acknowledge their independence. At a meeting in Paris, representatives of the five powers prepared a treaty that recognized the new nation. At the urging of a number of Jews, that treaty included an important condition: legal equality for all Moldavians and Wallachians. The condition was an attempt to make Jews citizens. The leaders of the new nation signed the treaty but avoided granting Jews citizenship by declaring that they were not, and never could be, Moldavians or Wallachians.

As discrimination against Jews continued in Romania, Emperor Louis Napoleon of France protested. So did Otto von Bismarck of Prussia, the chancellor of a newly united Germany. Romanian leaders ignored them. They also ignored efforts by various Jewish groups to secure at least some rights for Romanian Jews.

Then, in 1877, Russia defeated the Ottoman Empire in one of the many wars of the nineteenth century. Afterward, several countries in southeastern Europe declared their independence from Ottoman rule; others, like Romania, expanded their borders. These new nation-states asked their more powerful neighbors to recognize the change in their status. In 1878, diplomats from France, Germany, Britain, Austria, Russia, and other nations gathered in Berlin to prepare a treaty that would set the conditions for such recognition. Members of various Jewish groups saw the Congress of Berlin as an opportunity to protect Jews in an expanded Romania. Although they had no official standing at the Congress, they could state their case through intermediaries or in written statements.

These lobbying efforts were carefully coordinated, and they succeeded beyond expectation. The delegates to the Congress of Berlin tried to make it clear that citizenship could not be limited to people of a particular religion or culture. The new treaty stated:

> In Romania the distinctions of religion, creed, or confession cannot be brought up against anyone as a motive of exclusion and incapacity, as regards the enjoyment of civil and political rights, admission to public employment and honors, or exercise of different professions or industry. The freedom and open practice of all religions shall be assured to all citizens of the Romanian state, and also to foreigners.[18]

The French ambassador boasted that in defending the Jewish cause at the congress, delegates had "defended the cause of justice, humanity, and civilization." Jews throughout Europe celebrated. A group in Romania sent Crémieux a telegram: "Hallelujah! We are free. God be praised! Glory to you, noble and illustrious champions of our cause, glory to the Alliance!"

But the tone was very different in Romania's parliament, where Jews were seen not as fellow citizens but as aliens who did not share in Romanian culture. One deputy declared, "I have the courage to say from this rostrum, that I shall never agree to the Jews of Romania, *en masse*, enjoying political rights." He added, "If it turns out that injustice goes as far as Europe demanding any such a thing, the Powers will have first to pass over my body rather than get me to join in the murder of my country."[19]

Romania refused to sign the treaty. After 18 months of debates, negotiations, and arguments, the nation's deputies offered a compromise—a slightly improved version of the 1858 treaty they had signed but had ignored ever since. It allowed a few Jews to become citizens. Austria, Italy, France, Britain, and Germany all agreed to the compromise, despite frantic efforts by Jews and Jewish organizations fearful that this new treaty would provide no more protection than the one signed in 1858.

Why did the great powers back down? Some historians point out that the treaty process was a long one and that most nations had other priorities and interests. Perhaps they felt that they had done all they could and it was time to move on. Regardless of their motives, the decision to accept the compromise had consequences.

By the end of the 1800s, only a handful of Romania's 250,000 Jews were citizens, and even they experienced constant persecution and discrimination. In 1891, for example, the government evicted all Jewish children from state schools and then blocked the French alliance's attempts to open schools for Jewish students. Whenever elections were held, the government would inflame public opinion by announcing a policy of "repression" against "the Jews." Before long, thugs would roam Jewish neighborhoods, attacking people, looting stores, and setting fires. By the turn of the twentieth century, tens of thousands of Romanian Jews were leaving the country. Between 1881 and 1914, about 74,000 poured into the United States—a little over 28 percent of Romania's total Jewish population in the late 1800s.

OLD MYTHS IN MODERN DRESS

Western Jews had defended the rights of Romanian Jews with determination, passion, and skill. In the end, however, they were unable to provide Romanian Jews with even a small measure of safety and security. Yet to some Europeans, the fact that Jews had tried to influence the Congress of Berlin was proof that Jews had a world government that threatened the

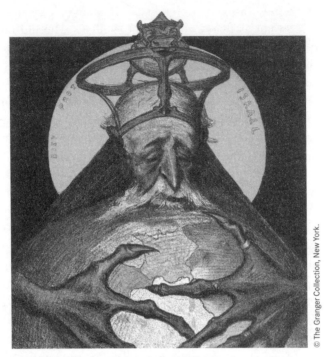

In this French cartoon, James Rothschild is shown controlling the world. Notice that the crown on his head includes a golden calf. Note, too, that his hands look more like claws than the hands of a man.

citizens of every country. Wilhelm Marr, a German journalist who believed in that myth, tried to document the power of European Jews in an 1878 pamphlet entitled "The Victory of Judaism over Germandom." He wrote:

> *There is no stopping them. . . .*
> *German culture has proved itself ineffective and powerless against this foreign power. This is a fact; a brutal [inescapable] fact. State, Church, Catholicism, Protestantism, Creed and Dogma, all are brought low before the Jewish tribunal, that is, the [irreverent] daily press [which the Jews control].*
>
> *The Jews were late in their assault on Germany, but once they started there was no stopping them.*
>
> *Gambetta, Simon and Crémieux were the dictators of France in 1870–1871. . . .*

Poor, Judaized France!
In England, the Semite Disraeli [Prime Minister Benjamin Disraeli],
a German hater . . . , holds in his vest pocket the key to war and peace
in the Orient [the East].

Who derived the real benefit at the Congress of Berlin from the
spilled blood of the Orient? Jewry. The Alliance Israélite Universelle
[French Universal Israelite Alliance] was first in line. [Romania] was
forced to open officially its doors and gates to destructive Semitism.
Jewry did not yet dare to make the same demand of Russia. But, this
demand, too, will soon come.[20]

The pamphlet was widely read even though it was filled with errors.
Jews did not control the press in any country. Although Crémieux was
a Jew, he was not a dictator or a head of state; he did serve as France's
minister of justice in 1870. Leon Gambetta, the president of the French
Chamber of Deputies in 1879, and Jules Francois Simon, a minister of
education in 1870, were not dictators either. Nor were they Jews; both men
were Christians. "The Jews" have never controlled France, even though a
few individual Jews have held important government positions.

As for England, Marr referred to Prime Minister Benjamin Disraeli, a
member of the Anglican Church, as a "Semite" because Disraeli was born
to Jewish parents. To Marr and a growing number of other Europeans,
all Jews, regardless of their religious beliefs, belonged to the "Semitic
race." In the 1800s, many European and American scientists believed that
humankind was divided into "races," one of which was the "Semitic race."*

Marr viewed Jews as more than just members of a distinct "race":
in his view, theirs was a dangerous and alien race. He used the word
antisemitism to describe his opposition to Jews. He also founded the
League of Antisemites in Berlin in 1879 to combat the threat he imagined
Jews posed. The group tried to turn antisemitism into a popular political
movement. Although it never attracted many members, another political
party founded a year earlier by Adolf Stoecker—the Christian Socialist
Worker's Party—had more success.

At first Stoecker's party focused more on the social effects of industrial-
ization and the need for German society to rededicate itself to Christianity
and return to Germanic rule in law and business. Antisemitism was a

---

* The word *Semitic* does not actually refer to a group of people but to a group of languages traditionally
spoken in the Middle East and parts of Africa. Semitic languages include Amharic, a language spoken in
Ethiopia, as well as Hebrew and Arabic.

relatively minor theme. The party gained in popularity only after it began to emphasize an antisemitic agenda. Stoecker and other members demanded that German Jews renounce their supposed dream of ruling Germany and called on the government to limit the number of Jews allowed in certain professions and universities. Like Marr, Stoecker and his followers were convinced that Jews belonged to a separate and dangerous "race." And they claimed that modern "science" justified discrimination against Jews.

By the end of the century, antisemitism had found a home almost everywhere in Europe and beyond. Every country interpreted racist ideas a little differently. In Germany, Ernst Haeckel, a biologist, popularized the idea by combining it with romantic notions about the German *Volk*, or people. In a book called *Riddles of the Universe*, he divided humankind into "races" and ranked them. Not surprisingly, "Aryans"—the mythical ancestors of the German people—were at the top of his list.

Scientists who tried to show that more differences existed within a so-called "race" than between one "race" and another were ignored. In the late 1800s, for example, the German Anthropological Society conducted a study to determine whether there were racial differences between Jewish and Aryan children. After studying nearly seven million students, the society concluded that the two groups were more alike than different. Historian George Mosse said of the study:

> *This survey should have ended controversies about the existence of pure Aryans and Jews. However, it seems to have had surprisingly small impact. The idea of race had been infused with myths, stereotypes, and subjectivities long ago, and a scientific survey could change little. The ideal of pure, superior races and the concept of a racial enemy solved too many pressing problems to be easily discarded. The survey itself was unintelligible to the uneducated part of the population. For them, Haeckel's* Riddles of the Universe *was a better answer to their problems.*[21]

So the myth that Jews belonged to a distinct and inferior race continued to grow throughout Europe. That myth gave individuals and governments a new excuse for discrimination and persecution. It was based not on ethnicity or religion (although the myth was sometimes expressed in religious and cultural terms) but on "race."

1 *Presse*, March 20, 1840, quoted in Ronald Florence, *Blood Libel: The Damascus Affair of 1840* (New York: Other Press, 2006), 114.

2 Philip S. Foner, ed., *The Life and Writings of Frederick Douglass*, vol. 2 (New York: International Publishers, 1950), 298.

3 Ratti-Menton to Soult, 29 February 1840, no. 16, Ministère des Relations Extérieures Archives: Affaires Étrangères, Turquie: Affaires Diverses (Assassinat du Père Thomas), quoted in Jonathan Frankel, *The Damascus Affair: "Ritual Murder," Politics, and the Jews in 1840* (Cambridge, UK: Cambridge University Press, 1997), 20.

4 Quoted in Howard M. Sachar, *A History of the Jews in the Modern World* (New York: Vintage Books, 2005), 82. Also quoted in David I. Kertzer, *The Popes Against the Jews: The Vatican's Role in the Rise of Modern Anti-Semitism* (New York: Alfred A. Knopf, 2001), 87.

5 Interrogation of el-Telli, 2 August 1980, Ministère des Relations Extérieures Archives: Affaires Étrangères, Turquie: Affaires Diverses (Assassinat du Père Thomas), 713–714, quoted in Frankel, *The Damascus Affair*, 39.

6 Ministère des Relations Extérieures Archives: Affaires Étrangères, Turquie: Affaires Diverses (Assassinat du Père Thomas), 510–511, quoted in Frankel, *The Damascus Affair*, 37.

7 Chasseaud to Forsyth, 24 March 1840, no. 12, State Department archives, National Archives (Washington, DC), microfilm, quoted in Frankel, *The Damascus Affair*, 67.

8 Achille Laurent, *Relation Historique*, 2:286–287, 289, quoted in Frankel, *The Damascus Affair*, 53.

9 Merlato to Laurin, 23 March 1840, "Affaire des Juifs de Damas," *Journal des Débats*, quoted in Frankel, *The Damascus Affair*, 97.

10 Alfandari to Lehren, 15 March 1840, "Persécution Excercée contra les Juifs en Orient," *Archives Israélites de France*, 215, quoted in Frankel, *The Damascus Affair*, 67.

11 Laurin to J. Rothschild, 5 April 1840, in Colber, Österreich und die Damaskusaffaire, 16–17, quoted in Frankel, *The Damascus Affair*, 104.

12 "Affaire des Juifs de Damas," *Gazette des Tribunaux*, April 8, 1840, quoted in Frankel, *The Damascus Affair*, 112. Emphasis added.

13 *Le Moniteur Universel*, June 3, 1840, quoted in David Vital, *A People Apart: The Jews in Europe, 1789–1939* (New York: Oxford University Press, 1999), 240.

14 Merlato to Crémieux, 7 September 1840, quoted in Frankel, *The Damascus Affair*, 360.

15 "Affaire de Damas," *Univers*, October 8, 1840, quoted in Frankel, *The Damascus Affair*, 367.

16 Hannah Arendt, quoted in Sachar, *A History of the Jews in the Modern World*, 107–108.

17 "Manifeste de juillet 1860," André Chouraqui, *L'Alliance Israélite Universelle et la renaissance juive contemporaine* (Paris, 1965), 3:411, quoted in Vital, *A People Apart*, 485–86.

18 In F. Stern, *Gold and Iron: Bismark, Bleichroder and the Building of the German Empire* (London, 1977), 378, quoted in Michael Graetz "Jewry in the Modern Period," in *Assimilation and Community: The Jews in Nineteenth-Century Europe*, ed. Jonathan Frankel and Steven J. Zipperstein (Cambridge, UK: Cambridge University Press, 1992), 171.

19 *Monitorul Oficial*, 24 February 1879, in Iancu, *Les Juifs en Roumanie*, 165, quoted in Vital, *A People Apart*, 503.

20 Wilhelm Marr, *Der Sieg des Judenthums ueber das Germanenthum vom nicht confessionellen Standpunkt ausbetrachtet* (Bern: Rudolph Costenoble, 1879), 30–35, trans. Paul Mendes-Flohr and Jehuda Reinharz, quoted in Mendes-Flohr and Reinharz, eds., *The Jew in the Modern World: A Documentary History*, 2nd ed. (New York: Oxford University Press, 1995), 331–332.

21 George L. Mosse, *Toward the Final Solution: A History of European Racism* (New York: Howard Fertig, 1978), 92.

11

Antisemitism in France and Russia:

"The Snake ... Crept out of the Marshes"

(1880–1905)

"Now different times began, new songs were heard. The snake that had not dared to show its face in the daylight now crept out of the marshes. Antisemitism broke out." With these words, Pauline Wengeroff, a Jew who lived in the Russian Empire, described a sharp rise in antisemitism in the late 1800s.

This new burst of antisemitism came at a time when the Industrial Revolution was altering life almost everywhere. The revolution had begun in England in the late 1700s with the invention of machines powered by steam. That invention set off a chain reaction, with each new innovation leading to thousands of others. By the late 1800s, inexpensive machine-made products could be found in almost every country, as improvements in transportation connected even remote places to the rest of the world. These changes created new kinds of jobs, while many older occupations became obsolete.

The Industrial Revolution changed more than the way goods were made and distributed; it also altered the way societies were organized. More people left the countryside to find work in the many factories that sprang up in large cities. Changes also took place in governments. By the 1880s, after more than a century of revolutions, even the most absolute rulers were aware of the power of public opinion and the dangers of unrest in the streets.

As with any major change, some people benefited from the various revolutions, while others lost everything. Those who suffered losses were often very angry and looking for someone to blame for the disturbing changes in their lives. In Europe, some revived old stereotypes of "the Jews" as exploiters of the poor and usurers who get rich from the financial misfortunes of others. These stereotypes were increasingly intertwined with the myth that Jews were an "evil race" bent on dominating the world.

That combination proved to be a disaster for Jews not only in autocracies like Russia but also in democracies like France.

FRANCE: ANTISEMITISM IN A DEMOCRACY

Although Jews in the late 1800s were a tiny minority in France—about 75,000 out of a total population of 39 million—they participated fully in the life of the nation. They could be found not only in business but also in the arts, government, education, law, medicine, and the military. Many Jews were fiercely loyal to France. When Germany annexed Alsace and Lorraine in 1871, about one-third of Alsatian Jews chose to relocate to other parts of France rather than remain in their homes and become German citizens.

There were, however, disquieting signs in the late 1800s that antisemitism was alive and well in France. In 1886, a Frenchman named Édouard Drumont wrote a book entitled *La France Juive* (Jewish France). This two-volume collection of antisemitic rumors, myths, and insinuations was an attempt to "prove" that Jews were "peculiar" and "so very different from all other beings." In Drumont's view, that "peculiarity" endangered France. He claimed that whenever Jews rose in power or wealth, the nation fell. His argument was based on the assumption that Jews could never be "real" citizens, because they would never act in the best interests of France.

Drumont's book was not the first antisemitic book published in France, but it was the first to become a bestseller. During its first year in print, 100,000 copies were sold. It was reprinted 200 times over a period of 25 years.

Like Wilhelm Marr, the German journalist who coined the term *antisemitism* in 1878 (see Chapter 10), Drumont insisted that he was not opposed to Judaism but only to "the Semitic race." To warn his fellow citizens of the "danger," he founded a newspaper known as *Le Parole Libre* (*The Free Word*) in 1892. It repeatedly claimed that France was in the clutches of corrupt and unscrupulous Jews, many of whom were in the military. In issue after issue, the paper came very close to accusing Jewish officers of treason. Several of those articles were written by the Marquis de Morès, a wealthy antisemite.

Most Jews in France ignored the attacks, believing that it was best to remain silent. But Captain Armand Mayer, one of the Jews that de Morès libeled, was so outraged by the accusations that he challenged the marquis to a duel. De Morès, a veteran of many such duels, accepted the challenge and killed Mayer in their confrontation.

People throughout the country were outraged. They bombarded the newspaper with complaints about the accusations and demanded apologies for its libel of a respected officer. Backing down, Drumont and de Morès issued a statement expressing regret at the death of "such an honorable man."

Thousands attended Mayer's funeral. The rabbi who conducted the service spoke of the army as a "magnificent example of toleration." He saw the outpouring of sympathy for Mayer as an expression of "the unifying force of French opinion" in support of nondiscrimination and decency.[1] Yet just two years later, in 1894, a similar accusation would rock not only the French Jewish community but also the French army and the government it served. Public opinion was changing.

THE DREYFUS CASE: MORE THAN A TRIAL

In 1894, a French worker discovered a document while cleaning the German embassy in Paris. She immediately turned it over to French military intelligence officers. The document was a *bordereau*, or memo, that listed the French military secrets that the author was willing to sell to Germany. After reading it, the officers concluded that the traitor had to be a member of the general staff of the army or to have access to its files and to those of the Ministry of War. Through a process of elimination, they narrowed down their suspects to a few officers. They then decided that the traitor was Captain Alfred Dreyfus, an officer on the general staff and the first Jew to hold such a position.

Charging a military officer with treason has far-reaching consequences. Before arresting Dreyfus, the intelligence officers informed the minister of war and the chief of the general staff. Those officials, in turn, told the French president and the prime minister. After some discussion, they all agreed that Dreyfus was the traitor.

Today the evidence seems flimsy for such a serious accusation, particularly against a man with an excellent military record and no apparent motive. As a child, Dreyfus had dreamed of becoming an officer in the French army; he had worked his entire life to make that dream a reality. Although he was not particularly popular with fellow officers, he earned regular promotions and had the support of his immediate superiors. He was widely considered a man who played by the rules—not someone who took chances or cut corners. Dreyfus was also a wealthy man; his father was an industrialist and his father-in-law a diamond merchant, so it was unlikely that he would have sold military secrets because he needed the money. In addition, he was a French patriot, one of the many Alsatian Jews who had moved to Paris to avoid losing French citizenship after Germany annexed Alsace and Lorraine. Why would such a man betray his country?

In 1894, Dreyfus did not think he was accused of treason because he was a Jew. He believed that the accusation was simply a terrible mistake. After all, at the time, the French army had about 300 Jewish officers, including 10 generals. Also within its ranks were many Protestants and a large number of men who considered themselves freethinkers. But even if antisemitism had not been a factor in Dreyfus's arrest, it played a powerful role in everything that happened after that arrest.

Dreyfus was taken into custody on the morning of October 15, 1894. At first the government did not even tell him what crime he had been accused of, nor was he allowed to communicate with his wife or anyone else in his family. When his wife was later informed of the charges against him, she was told to remain silent. If the details of the case were known, she was told, they might set off a war with Germany. She informed no one, but someone in the army did.

On November 1, Drumont's newspaper became the first to publish the story, denouncing Dreyfus as a "Judas," the disciple who betrayed Jesus to his enemies. The paper also falsely claimed that Dreyfus had confessed to the crime and that the army had absolute proof of his guilt. The reporting in other papers was less sensational, but all assumed that Dreyfus was guilty. In fact, in November 1894, most people in France, including most Jews, were convinced of Dreyfus's guilt. Why were they so certain? Just before the trial began, General Auguste Mercier, the minister of war and the nation's highest military officer, announced that Dreyfus was guilty beyond a doubt. No one except Dreyfus's family and friends had reason to question his word.

Yet by all accounts, the defense presented a strong case at the trial, and many began to think Dreyfus might be acquitted. Then, suddenly, two prominent men stepped forward with dramatic evidence of Dreyfus's guilt.

One was Hubert Henry, the intelligence officer who had headed the investigation. Toward the end of the trial, when the prosecution recalled him to the stand, he made a startling statement: a highly reliable "secret informant" had confirmed Dreyfus's guilt. Henry refused to identify the informant or provide information about him. To do so, he claimed, would endanger the informant and might lead to war with Germany. So the prosecutor asked Henry to swear on his honor that Dreyfus was a spy. He immediately raised his arm, looked deliberately at a painting of Jesus on the wall, and swore that his statement was correct. His "total sincerity" impressed almost everyone in the courtroom.

On the last day of the trial, General Mercier himself offered new evidence. He sent the judges a sealed dossier that pointed to Dreyfus as the spy. The defense attorney was not allowed to see it, even though French law gives a defendant and his attorney the right to examine all evidence. The judges chose to ignore that law, because the general told them that revealing the contents of the file could endanger French intelligence officers.

After reading the file, the seven judges unanimously found Dreyfus guilty of treason. He was sentenced to degradation and then deportation and imprisonment for life on Devil's Island off the coast of South America.

The French army had a special ceremony for degrading officers who had committed crimes. In the courtyard of the nation's chief military academy, before approximately 4,000 French soldiers and a large crowd of reporters and invited guests, a senior officer announced, "Alfred Dreyfus, you are unworthy to bear arms. In the name of the French people we degrade you!" Then the officer cut off Dreyfus's badges, insignia, even the buttons on his jacket, and broke his sword in half. The prisoner was then marched around the courtyard as his fellow soldiers watched in silence. But Dreyfus was not silent. He shouted over and over that they were degrading an innocent man.

A huge crowd had gathered outside the gates of the academy. When they heard Dreyfus shouting, they responded by chanting, "Death to Dreyfus! Death to the Jew!" During the trial, neither the prosecutors nor the judges had referred to Dreyfus as a Jew. Yet the mob clearly considered his religion, or perhaps his "race," relevant. So did the press. One reporter wrote, "I need no one to tell me why Dreyfus committed treason. . . . That Dreyfus was capable of treason, I conclude from his race."

As soon as the trial ended, Dreyfus's family, particularly his brother Mathieu, searched for evidence that would prove Alfred's innocence. Mathieu was reluctant to work publicly, fearing his efforts might stir antisemitic feelings. But he quickly learned that everything he and his family did was misinterpreted. When he tried to meet with public officials, he was accused of bribery; when he looked for new evidence, he was accused of searching for a "patsy"—another officer who could be blamed for Dreyfus's treason. At last, in 1896, the family's luck began to change. Two unconnected events brought the case back into the headlines and turned it into an "affair"—the kind of incident that seizes the public's imagination and causes widespread excitement and mass demonstrations.

Surtout! Ne parlons pas de l'affaire Dreyfus!
("No talking about the Dreyfus Affair!")

. . . Ils en ont parlé.
("They talked about it.")

Few in France were indifferent to the Dreyfus Affair. A cartoonist highlights the strong emotions that divided the nation by showing a family dinner before and after a discussion of the affair.

Early in 1896, Colonel Georges Picquart became head of French military intelligence. He soon discovered that the Germans were still receiving French military secrets, even though the supposed traitor, Dreyfus, was thousands of miles away. Picquart began to investigate, and his suspicions soon centered on a single man—Walsin Esterhazy, a French officer known as a gambler and scam artist. Picquart quickly became convinced that Esterhazy was guilty.

Picquart was an unlikely champion of justice for a Jew. He was a conservative Catholic from Alsace who worried about being "tricked" by the "devious" Dreyfus family. As a result, he refused to meet with members of the family. He also feared damage to his own career. Yet in the end, his report identified Esterhazy as the spy.

Picquart's superiors refused to accept it. They did not want to admit that they might have made a mistake. One is said to have asked, "What does it matter to you if this Jew stays on Devil's Island?" Still others claimed that even if Esterhazy was guilty, his guilt did not mean that Dreyfus was innocent.

To keep Picquart quiet, the army sent him to a post in North Africa. Before he left, he wrote a letter that spelled out his reasons for believing that Esterhazy was guilty; he told his lawyer that if he died while in North Africa, the letter should be given to the president of France. Some historians think that the lawyer leaked the information in the letter to a member of the parliament.

As rumors about Esterhazy began to circulate, a number of people said that "the Jews" had found their "patsy." They also whispered that Jews had paid Picquart to say Dreyfus was innocent. In the end, Picquart's superiors decided to stop the rumors by putting Esterhazy on trial; they believed that the case against him was so weak that there was not much risk in doing so. They were right. On January 10, 1898, his court-martial ended with a verdict of "not guilty." When he left the courtroom, he was greeted with cheers.

On January 13, 1898, just three days after the trial, France's most famous novelist, Emile Zola, wrote a letter to the president of France. It was published in a newspaper under a huge headline that read *"J'Accuse!"* ("I Accuse!"). Zola accused the government and the army of conspiring to convict Dreyfus. Zola claimed that at the trial, powerful officials had covered up the truth. That day the newspaper sold more than 200,000 copies in Paris alone.

The government responded by suing Zola for libel. He had no proof to support his charges and was quickly found guilty. Nevertheless, his trial heightened interest in the case. Like Picquart, Zola had little interest in defending Jews. Many of his novels contain characters that are little more than crude antisemitic stereotypes. Why did he speak out? Perhaps because, just as Drumont feared a "Jewish conspiracy," Zola feared a military conspiracy led by "fanatic Catholics."

Whatever his motives, Zola's accusations and the government's response pulled thousands of people into the controversy. Those who disagreed with Zola's conclusions took to the streets, where they attacked Jewish businesses, synagogues, and homes—including the Dreyfus residence. There were anti-Jewish riots in about 70 cities.

The violence in the streets troubled many people on both sides of the issue, and some decided it was time to take a stand. They called for a new trial for Dreyfus in the hope that it would settle the matter once and for all. Charles Chanoine, the new minister of war, reopened the investigation in order to quiet the uproar. The new chief investigator, Louis Cuignet, quickly discovered that Hubert Henry, who had testified so powerfully at Dreyfus's trial, had forged evidence and lied to the court. Although

Many saw the Dreyfus Affair as a conspiracy organized by Jews to betray France.

Cuignet considered Henry a friend, he brought his findings to the minister of war. Zola turned out to be right: there had been a military conspiracy against Dreyfus.

Chanoine made Cuignet's findings public and ordered Henry's arrest. Before he could be questioned, Henry committed suicide and promptly became a folk hero. Thousands were convinced that the "Jewish syndicate" had murdered him. Some of Dreyfus's supporters also thought Henry had been murdered, but they believed it had been ordered by the military general staff because he knew too much.

As the French argued about Henry's death, Esterhazy fled to England and then confessed that he had written the original memo listing military secrets for sale to the Germans. He claimed that the general staff had ordered him to create the document as part of a secret counter-espionage plan. Once again, however, many insisted that "the Jews" had paid Esterhazy to say this.

In August of 1899, five years after his conviction, Dreyfus was retried and, to the surprise of many, once again convicted. But strangely, the day after his second conviction, he was pardoned. When a government issues a pardon, it does not say that the person who was convicted of a crime is innocent; it simply forgives the crime and cancels the punishment. The courts did not declare Dreyfus innocent until 1906—12 years after his first conviction. Only then was he reinstated as a captain in the army. He and his son Pierre would later fight in the French army during the First World War.

The Dreyfus Affair, as it came to be known, changed the way many Jews in western Europe saw themselves and others. In 1894, Theodore Herzl, then a reporter for an Austrian newspaper, covered the ceremony in which Dreyfus was degraded. Although Herzl recognized the power of antisemitism long before the Dreyfus Affair, this event strengthened his views. In 1896, he wrote:

> *The Jewish Question still exists. It would be foolish to deny it. It exists wherever Jews live in perceptible numbers. Where it does not yet exist, it will be brought by Jews in the course of their migrations. We naturally move to those places where we are not persecuted, and there our presence soon produces persecution. This is true in every country, and will remain true even in those most highly civilized— France itself is no exception—till the Jewish Question finds a solution on a political basis.*[2]

Herzl proposed a solution: the establishment of a Jewish state. He believed that Jews must have their own country.

RUSSIA: "BEYOND THE PALE"

Although the rising antisemitism in democratic France in the late 1800s stunned many people, few were surprised to learn that it was also increasing in Russia. After all, Russian tsars had long used their almost unlimited power against Jews. For centuries, they had refused to permit Jews to live in Russia or even to visit there. In 1772, Russia then joined Austria and Prussia in a takeover of Poland and the first division of its land and people (two more partitions followed). Russia gained about nine million Roman Catholic and nearly one million Jewish subjects.

The Eastern Orthodox, or Byzantine, Church was Russia's official church—and as "defenders of the Orthodox faith," the tsars of Russia did not want to open their country to Jews. In the end, however, the tsar at the time of the division decided that Jews could remain in the formerly Polish parts of the empire but could not settle or work in the heart of Russia.

The area to which the Jews were confined was known as the Pale of Settlement. A *pale* is an enclosed space; it can also be a fence or a pole that marks a boundary. The Pale of Settlement was made up of 25 provinces in western Russia, from the Baltic Sea in the north to the Black Sea in the south. It was never home only to Jews—they made up only about 9 percent of the total population in the Pale. Other residents included Poles, Ukrainians, Germans, Belorussians, Lithuanians, Turks, and Russians.

Over the years, the boundaries of the Pale shifted occasionally, but the idea of confining Jewish settlement to a limited area remained unchanged. Yet even as the tsars tried to keep Jews apart from "real" Russians, they also supported a seemingly opposite policy—assimilation. The idea was to turn Jews into Russians by converting them to the Russian Orthodox faith. Once they had all converted, there would be no need for a Pale of Settlement.

The first step was to open the Russian army to Jews. In 1825, Tsar Nicholas I issued a decree stating that all Jewish men were now subject to a military draft when they reached the age of 18 and that they would be required to serve for 25 years. According to a memo the tsar sent his generals, "The chief benefit to be derived from the drafting of Jews is the certainty that it will move them most effectively to change their religion."[3] When Nicholas discovered that very few Jewish soldiers were converting to Christianity, he issued a new order. Now the army would conscript 12-year-old Jewish boys and give them six years of "special training" to prepare them for military life at age 18.

Jewish parents tried desperately to keep their sons out of the army. Wealthy Jews were allowed to purchase substitutes to serve in their sons' places. The substitutes were Jews from poor families. Every Jewish community had to provide a certain number of 12-year-old recruits; if a community could not meet its quota, boys as young as 8 or 10 were forced into the army to make up the required number.

In 1835, Alexander Herzen, a Russian writer, saw a group of these very young Jewish draftees at a train station several hundred miles from Moscow. He asked who the children were and where they were being taken. An officer told him that they were "cursed little Jew boys of eight or nine years old." He went on to say that half would die before they reached their destination. Herzen asked if there had been an epidemic. The officer replied:

> *"No, not epidemics, but they just die like flies. A Jew boy, you know, is such a frail, weakly creature, like a skinned cat; he is not used to tramping in the mud for ten hours a day and eating biscuit—then again, being among strangers, no father nor mother nor petting; well, they cough and cough until they cough themselves into their graves. And I ask you, what use is it to [the authorities]? What can they do with little boys?"*

Herzen watched the soldiers round up the boys. He noted:

> *They brought the children and formed them into regular ranks: it was one of the most awful sights I have ever seen, those poor, poor children! Boys of twelve or thirteen might somehow have survived it, but [not] little fellows of eight and ten. . . .*

> *Pale, exhausted, with frightened faces, they stood in thick, clumsy, soldiers' overcoats with stand-up collars, fixing helpless, pitiful eyes on the garrison soldiers who were roughly getting them into ranks. The white lips, the blue rings under their eyes bore witness to fever or chill. And these sick children, without care or kindness, exposed to the icy wind that blows unobstructed from the Arctic Ocean, were going to their graves.*[4]

Once in camp, the boys were pressured to convert and punished if they tried to practice Judaism in any way. After months of beatings, harassment, and even jail sentences, about two-thirds of the boys became Christians. Nicholas also tried to convert Jewish children who were still at home by opening special state schools designed to teach them Russian culture and the Russian Orthodox religion. Not surprisingly, most Jewish parents refused to let their children attend.

Nicholas also encouraged the assimilation of "useful Jews" (those few with money or with skills that were in short supply) by permitting them to live in Moscow, St. Petersburg, and other Russian cities. The millions of other Jews whom he considered "useless" remained in the crowded Pale, where jobs were hard to find.

By 1855, the year Nicholas died, many Russians were calling for economic and political reforms. Jews were not the only vulnerable group in Russia, and many other minorities were also threatened. In response to the discontent, Alexander II, the new tsar, announced plans to modernize

Russia and provide "education, equal justice, tolerance, and humaneness" for every citizen. Almost immediately, he relaxed censorship laws and eased restrictions on foreign travel. Universities were opened to students from all parts of Russian society, the poor as well as the rich. Alexander reduced the length of military service from 25 years to 6—even less for those who attended high school or college—and he abolished the military preparation program for young Jewish boys.

In March 1861, Alexander freed Russia's 47 million serfs and announced that all Russian citizens were equal before the law. In fact, however, the serfs were not as free as Alexander claimed, nor were all Russian citizens truly equal before the law. Nevertheless, the proclamation marked a step forward for everyone except Jews. Even though many Jews still hoped that he would eventually expand their rights, Alexander privately told officials that he expected Jews to "earn" their civil rights through "moral improvement." To the tsar, "moral improvement" meant conversion to the Russian Orthodox Church. To his surprise, some Russians disagreed. An editorial in a newspaper published by the Ministry of War declared:

> *Let us be worthy of our age. Let us abandon the childish habit of presenting the Jews in our literary works as [ridiculous and disreputable] creatures. On the contrary, remembering the causes that brought them to such a state, . . . [let] us offer them a place among us, let us use their energy, readiness of wit, and skill as a new means for satisfying the growing needs of our people.*[5]

Such statements reflected a belief that Jews would make a positive contribution to Russia if they had more freedom. Although Alexander had no intention of granting Jews equal rights, he did increase the number of Jewish businessmen who could live and work outside the Pale. He granted similar privileges to Jewish artisans, university graduates, and veterans of the army. He had hoped these Jews would energize the economy and encourage investment by Jews in other countries. They fulfilled his expectations. With the help of foreign Jews, they opened factories, founded banks, and helped build more than 75 percent of the nation's railroads.

The success of these Jews inspired tens of thousands of young people in the Pale to enroll not only in secular schools run by various Jewish groups but also in government-sponsored schools for Jewish students— the same schools Jews had shunned during Nicholas's reign. Now fewer parents objected, mainly because young men who attended government-sponsored schools could avoid army service. In the 1860s, a new law opened the Russian state school system to Jewish students, and the government-run schools for Jews gradually disappeared. Young Jews, like their non-Jewish neighbors, were attracted to state schools because graduates were eligible for government employment as well as for a variety of commercial and professional careers in the heart of Russia.

Despite such successes, or perhaps because of those successes, antisemitism intensified throughout Russia in the 1870s. Many Russians believed that Jews were becoming too powerful and had too many privileges. Articles in Russian newspapers reinforced that view by warning of the danger Jews posed to Russia. They claimed that the presence of Jewish students in state schools would lead to Jewish domination of such professions as law, engineering, medicine, and architecture—occupations that had once been open only to Russians.

Other publications held Jews responsible for the revolutionary movement that was arising in Russia as well as the evils associated with both socialism and capitalism. Socialism, which was popular with many young revolutionaries, is an economic system in which the means of production and distribution are publicly owned and controlled. Capitalism, on the other hand, is an economic system in which the means of production and distribution are privately owned. In the real world, there has never been a purely capitalist economy or a purely socialist one. Most economic systems contain elements of both but lean a little more to one than to the other. It is illogical to think that "the Jews" could have been advocates of both these systems, since they are opposites of one another. But antisemites had no difficulty in claiming that both were being advocated as part of a Jewish plot to control Russia. Hatred has never been logical.

Jews and non-Jews who tried to use facts and logic to counter antisemitic remarks were ignored. One writer provided statistics showing that non-Jews in the Pale of Settlement were better off economically than those who lived outside it. A government study conducted in the late 1880s confirmed his findings. Although no one disputed the facts, this information did not change the widespread belief that Jews were a "mass of usurers and hucksters of dubious honesty, who will enrich themselves by exploiting gullible Russians."[6]

Many Russians also held Jews responsible for Russia's foreign policy failures. They were particularly outraged by British Prime Minister Benjamin Disraeli. At the Congress of Berlin in 1878 (see Chapter 10), he had supported equal rights for Jews in countries that Russia had recently freed from Ottoman rule. The Russian press pointed to Disraeli's Jewish ancestry and suggested that he wanted to take personal revenge on Russia for denying civil rights to Jews. The attacks were so vicious that Jews in one town in the Pale published a declaration in a Moscow newspaper stating that they had nothing in common with Disraeli and were loyal to Russia.[7]

This kind of antisemitism was not new anywhere in Europe, and in ordinary times, it might have blown over. But an unexpected event on March 1, 1881, changed everything. Pauline Wengeroff described it as the day "on which the sun that had risen over Jewish life in the 1850s was suddenly extinguished."[8] Alexander II was shot to death on the banks of the Moika Canal in St. Petersburg.

"LIVING ON TOP OF A VOLCANO"

Some Jews compared the days immediately following Alexander's assassination to "living on top of a volcano." Rumors spread like wildfire. Many of these rumors claimed that the new tsar, Alexander III, had ordered Russians to attack Jews and that anyone who failed to do so would be punished severely. Why would he or anyone else blame Jews for the tsar's death? The revolutionary group responsible for the assassination included a Jewish woman named Gessia Gelfman. Although she was tried and convicted along with her non-Jewish comrades, the rumors maintained that only by "beating the Jews" would Alexander III be able to avenge his father's death. Even though the tsar denied the rumor, many people insisted that he really did want them to beat the Jews. They were convinced that he issued a denial to quiet foreigners.

The violence began on April 15, 1881, in Elizavetgrad (now Kirovograd). The rioting quickly spread to other parts of the Ukraine and much of southern Russia. On April 26, 1881, it reached Kiev, the Ukrainian capital. A witness described the first day of rioting:

> At twelve o'clock at noon, the air echoed with wild shouts, whistling, jeering, hooting, and laughing. An enormous crowd of young boys, artisans, and laborers was marching. The entire street was jammed with the barefoot brigade. The destruction of the Jewish homes began. Windowpanes and doors began to fly about, and shortly thereafter the mob, having gained access to the houses and stores, began to throw upon the streets absolutely everything that fell into their hands. Clouds of feathers began to whirl in the air. The sound of broken windowpanes and frames, the crying, shouting, and despair on the

POGROMS IN THE PALE OF SETTLEMENT

Between 1791 and 1917, the Pale of Settlement was the only part of the Russian Empire where Jews could legally live. The Pale, which included parts of present-day Poland, Lithuania, Belorussia, Ukraine, and Moldavia, was home to 95 percent of all Jews in Russia. In fact, more Jews were concentrated there than in any other region in the world.

one hand, and the terrible yelling and jeering on the other, completed the picture. . . . Shortly afterwards the mob threw itself upon the Jewish synagogue, which, despite its strong bars, locks and shutters, was wrecked in a moment. One should have seen the fury with which the riff-raff fell upon the [Torah] scrolls, of which there were many in the synagogue. The scrolls were torn to shreds, trampled in the dirt, and destroyed with incredible passion.[9]

Not every Jewish community experienced violence, but all of them were deeply affected by it. As Pauline Wengeroff wrote, "The new word, launched in the 1880s, was pogrom."[10] The term *pogrom* comes from the Russian word for "thunder"—the sound heard just after lightning strikes, signaling the storm to come. Now the word came to refer to an organized, and sometimes officially encouraged, massacre. Wengeroff described its effect on her, her family, and other Jews:

In the city of Minsk the mood was dark. Business slowed down, the Jews left their stores, they hurried through the streets uneasily, casting suspicious glances about them. They were on guard. In case of a pogrom, they were ready to fight desperately. The air was charged; an explosion was expected any moment. The Jewish market women who came into my home, filled with fear and horror, told of the rough threats made against them by the farmers who brought their wares to market twice a week, speaking openly of an imminent attack and of the imminent murder of all Jews. My husband, too, brought such news from the bank, and the children brought it home from school. . . .

The Jews of Minsk armed for battle. Their homes became fortresses, everyone according to his way, whatever was possible for him. One might provide himself with strong clubs called drongi. *Another might be mixing sand and tobacco to be thrown into the eyes of attackers. Boys as young as eight, girls as young as ten, took part in these terrible preparations and were courageous and unafraid in the streets. . . .*

Nobody felt safe, even in his own house. The Christian servants, who had worked for us for some time, suddenly became impolite and impertinent so that we were forced to protect ourselves in our own home. After the servants had gone to bed every evening, I took all the knives and hammers out of the kitchen and locked them up in a cupboard in my bedroom. I put up a barricade, secretly, in front of the door, consisting of kitchen benches, chairs, a ladder, and other pieces of furniture. I smiled a little as I did this, for I didn't believe for a minute that in the case of a pogrom we would be able to save ourselves in this way. But I built this barricade over and over again, got up first every morning to take it down and put everything back into place, so that the servants would not notice our fear.[11]

As the pogroms spread from town to town, Count Nikolai P. Ignatiev, the minister of the interior, called for an investigation to determine who was responsible for the violence. He claimed it would show that Jews were to blame because of the "Jewish exploitation of the peasants." Jews were outraged. Moses Leib Lilienblum was one of the most influential Jewish writers of the time. When he learned about Ignatiev's comments, he wrote what became one of the first calls for Jews to establish a homeland in Palestine:

They write: "One should collect and assemble the data about those Jewish activities which harm the natives." We, then, are not native. During the pogroms, a native woman, ragged and drunk, danced in the streets, joyously shouting, "This is our country, this is our country." Can we say the same, even without dancing in the streets, without being drunk? Yes, we are aliens, not only here but in all of Europe, for it is not our fatherland. Now I understand the word "antisemitism." This is the secret of our affliction in exile. Even in Alexandria [Egypt], in the time of the Second Temple, and in all the lands of our dispersion, we were aliens, unwanted guests. We were aliens in Europe, when religion flourished because of our religion; now when nationalism reigns, we are aliens because of our origin. . . .

Our future is fearful, without a spark of hope or a ray of light—slaves, aliens, strangers, forever. Yet why should we be aliens in alien countries if the land of our fathers has not yet been forgotten and remains vacant? It can absorb our people! We must cease to be aliens and return to our fatherland. We must buy land there, little by little, becoming rooted there, like other people who live in the land of their fathers. We are

As a result of the pogroms, many Jews in Russia made plans to emigrate. As the image on the postcard suggests, hundreds of thousands headed west to Germany, France, Britain, and the United States.

being uprooted from the land of our residence, the gates are open for us to leave. We are, in fact, fleeing. Why, then, flee to America and be alien there, too, instead of to the land of our fathers?[12]

Lilienblum and others wanted to settle in Palestine, the traditional homeland of the Jewish people. They called themselves Zionists (after the name of the hill where the Temple once stood in Jerusalem) and organized groups like *Hibbat Zion* (Lovers of Zion) and BILU, an acronym based on a verse from the Biblical book of Isaiah (*Beit Ya'akov Lekhu Ve-nelkha*—"Let the house of Jacob go").

Over the years, some have criticized Lilienblum for suggesting that Palestine was "vacant." At the time, it was home to about 450,000 Muslims and Christians and about 24,000 Jews. Lilienblum was aware that the land was occupied; he was simply describing it as a place that could absorb many more people. If he had seen the land as having no people, he would not have urged his fellow Zionists to buy land—which many of them did.

In the years immediately after the pogroms, about 35,000 Jews answered Lilienblum's call and left Russia for Palestine. But thousands more emigrated to North America and western Europe. Between 1880 and 1914, more than two million Russian Jews settled in the United States.

COURAGE AT HOME, OUTRAGE ABROAD

Jews in Russia had few ways to resist in the 1880s. Poorly armed civilians were no match for a mob supported by police battalions and an army. A few Jews decided that their best hope was to let the world know exactly what was happening. A small group of Orthodox Jews in Russian Lithuania formed a secret society to do exactly that. Although members of the group lived in the northern province of Kovno and the pogroms were farther south, they managed to collect hundreds of bits of information. Little by little, they put the pieces together. The group's leader, Rabbi Yischak Elhanan Spektor, then wrote a letter summarizing their findings. He sent it to prominent Jews in other countries, asking them to make the story known.

The letter sent to England was addressed to Baron Nathaniel Rothschild. He immediately turned it over to the *Times* of London. A reporter used the information to write two articles, which appeared on January 11 and 13, 1882. The beginning of the first article suggests the power of the story the rabbi wanted told:

Men ruthlessly murdered, tender married women the prey of a brutal lust that has also caused their death, and young girls violated in the sight of their relatives by soldiers who should have been the guardians of their honor, these have been the deeds with which the population of southern Russia has been stained since last April."[13]

In the paragraphs that followed, the reporter listed the names of towns in which pogroms had taken place, exactly what crimes had been committed, and the number of victims. Wherever possible, he used the victims' names and provided details that would allow readers to picture them as real people. Readers were not told simply that "a child" was thrown from a window; they were told that the child thrown was the three-year-old son of Mordichai Wienarsky. They read not merely that a house was burned to the ground but that it was the house of the Preskoff family in Kitzkis. And they learned that the father of that family and two of his children died in the fire. The authors used that same attention to detail in identifying the perpetrators.

The articles ended with a call to action by the editors of the *Times*. "It is the lesson taught by all experience that the only solution of the Jewish Question is the granting of full equality. . . . The Russian Jewish question may . . . be summed up in the words: Are three and a half millions of human beings to perish because they are Jews."[14]

The articles in the *Times* prompted demonstrations in support of Russian Jews. The largest was held in London on February 1, 1882. The leader of the Catholic Church in England condemned not only the violence but also the degrading laws that had harassed Jews throughout Europe for centuries. The demonstrators passed a resolution condemning the pogroms as an "offense to Christian civilization" and expressing the hope that "Her Majesty's government [of Great Britain] may be able, when an opportunity arises, to exercise a friendly influence with the Russian government in accordance with the spirit of the preceding resolution."[15]

Prime Minister William Gladstone acknowledged the horror of the pogroms but refused to send the resolutions or even petitions signed by British Jews to the Russian government. He also refused to respond to the United States' request that the American and British governments jointly approach the Russians.

Why was Gladstone unwilling to speak out? He may have been following standard diplomatic procedure: one nation is not supposed to interfere in the internal affairs of another. However, Britain and other nations had interfered in the internal affairs of a number of nations from time to time throughout the 1800s. Some historians think that Gladstone revealed his reason for remaining silent when he asked the House of Commons to avoid a public discussion of the pogroms because it was "more likely to harm than to help the Jewish population." He told them that he would prefer to rely on private, unofficial contacts to express England's feelings on the matter.

Gladstone's comments suggest that the Russian government was threatening to harm Jews if other countries intervened. A statement that appeared in a Russian government journal supports that idea: "Any attempt on the part of another government to intercede on behalf of the Jewish people can only have the result of calling forth the resentment of the lower classes and thereby affect unfavorably the condition of Russian Jews."[16]

Despite Britain's silence, other nations did send messages and petitions to Russia. And demonstrations took place in many countries, including the United States, France, Spain, and Italy. The tsar ignored this disapproval.

DISAPPROVAL AT HOME

Foreigners were not the only people outraged by the pogroms. Many Russians, including some antisemites, were also deeply disturbed. They believed that the government's policies were hurting Russia's economy. On May 30, 1881, not long after the pogroms began, one of these Russians, an important textile manufacturer in Moscow, sent a letter to Ignatiev, the minister of the interior, outlining some of the economic problems he was having as a result of the violence. He usually sold his cloth to Jewish merchants in the Ukraine, but now they were unable to work, and some could not pay their bills. If these problems continued, he and other textile manufacturers would be forced to make less cloth and to lay off workers in central Russia. He urged the government to take action.

That letter was just the beginning. In May of the following year, representatives of 50 Moscow businesses presented a petition to the Ministry of Finance that described how the pogroms were harming their businesses. They said that merchants in the southern provinces owed them tens of millions of rubles, and they feared that if the debt was not paid, the entire economy would be affected.

Independent observers—diplomats from Austria-Hungary—confirmed the manufacturers' fears. They reported that in areas where there were pogroms, it was nearly impossible for peasants or ordinary workers to borrow money. Jewish lenders refused to make loans because they knew those loans would never be repaid. As a result, train stations in central

Russia were jammed with peasants looking for work. There was also a rise in unemployment beyond the Pale of Settlement, including in cities like Moscow and St. Petersburg.

The pogroms also worried government officials. When Ignatiev, the minister of the interior, offered a plan to help the peasants by expelling Jews from all rural areas in the Pale of Settlement, many of his colleagues were critical. The minister of finance claimed that the plan would outrage Jews around the world and therefore make it impossible for Russia to borrow money abroad. He also pointed out that if Jews were expelled from rural areas, Christians would suffer as well as Jews. The strong trade networks that had developed in the south involved people of all religions, and what harmed one group would surely harm the others. And, he added, if Jews were expelled from the countryside, they would move to urban areas, placing an enormous burden on the towns and cities.

Other ministers spoke of the "sufferings of tens of thousands of individuals, although they may be Jews."[17] They called on Ignatiev to stop the antisemitic slurs that stirred hatred. The chairman of the Committee of Ministers feared that the behavior of the police would spread: "Today they bait and rob the Jews. Tomorrow they will turn on the so-called *kulaks* [rich peasants]. . . . Then merchants and landowners will take their turn under the gun."[18]

Such statements from other government officials forced Ignatiev to make compromises. As a result, on May 3, 1882, Tsar Alexander III issued "temporary rules" that would govern the lives of Jews in the Pale of Settlement for the next 35 years, until 1917. Overall, the new rules did not help Jews, although they did reduce the violence. Pauline Wengeroff described their impact:

> *Restrictions were piled upon restrictions, and these continue more or less to this day, with no end in sight. The areas where Jews were allowed to live were more and more restricted. St. Petersburg and other Russian cities were forbidden to them; only certain categories of Jews—for example, merchants . . . who paid very dearly for the right, and who had earned an academic diploma in Russia—were permitted to remain.*
>
> *Academic education itself was made harder and harder to get. Only a very small number of Jews were admitted to the high schools. Of the few who managed to graduate from high school, only a few would be admitted to the university. Inevitably there was corruption among*

both Jews and Russians. Jews used any means they could think of to enable their children to enter high schools and universities, to circumvent the brutal ordinances. . . .

Finally, when after unimaginable effort the parents had succeeded in bringing their Jewish boy to the point of taking the exam, even if he passed it at the head of his year, there was no certainty that he would get in, even into the high school. Once again, it was the question of the quota. How many Jewish students would be admitted depended on how many non-Jews were studying. By the time it came to admission to the university, many Jews were left behind.

The choice of a profession for a young Jew in Russia was not determined by his inclination or his abilities, nor by his parents' plans for him, but simply and solely by coincidence, which would admit some and cut off others, for no other reason than they were Jews. And as in school, so it was in further life. The atmosphere surrounding the Jews became dark and threatening. They were scorned and ridiculed, even by the lowest levels of society, and persecuted.[19]

NEW POGROMS AND NEW RESPONSES

As a result of the "temporary rules," Russia had only ten relatively isolated pogroms between June 1882 and 1903. Each was triggered by local conditions; none of them set off a chain reaction the way the 1881 pogrom in Elizavetgrad had. But there were disquieting signs. The tsar and his key advisers increasingly used antisemitism to win popular support. They financed anti-Jewish newspapers and journals, as well as "patriotic" organizations that regarded Jews as the enemy. In 1894, Alexander III died, and the new tsar, Nicholas II, continued his father's policies.

As more and more Russians gave up any hope of reform, some joined revolutionary groups that had little in common except a strong opposition to tsarist rule. To try to turn attention away from himself, the tsar decided to unite the Russian people against a common enemy—"the Jews." His agents began to organize pogroms and revive the old blood libels. In 1903, just before Easter in Kishinev, then the capital of Bessarabia (Moldavia today), a government-supported newspaper charged that "the Jews" had killed a Christian child so that they could use his blood in the matzos they baked for Passover (see Chapter 5). A government-backed patriotic society

Western newspapers reported the fury of the mob that attacked the Jews of Kishinev at Easter, 1903. The photograph shows just a few of the many Jews injured by a mob fueled with religious passion and patriotic zeal.

known as the "Black Hundreds" took to the streets to demand justice. Within hours, a pogrom was under way.

But revolutionary groups in Russia were quick to point out that this pogrom had been planned by the government from start to finish. A rebel then in exile reported, "It has been learned that there were about 12,000 troops in Kishinev at the time, against 200 to 300 active rioters and house-breakers. And, as soon as the Government chose to proclaim martial law, after two days of delay, all disorders instantly stopped. The *New York Times* confirmed those claims:

> *The anti-Jewish riots in Kishinev, Bessarabia, are worse than the censor will permit to publish. There was a well laid-out plan for the general massacre of Jews on the day following the Russian Easter. The mob was led by priests, and the general cry, "Kill the Jews," was taken up all over the city. . . . The dead number 120 and the injured about 500. . . . Babes were literally torn to pieces by the frenzied and bloodthirsty mob. The local police made no attempt to [halt] the reign of terror. At sunset the streets were piled with corpses and*

wounded. Those who could make their escape fled in terror, and the city is now practically deserted of Jews.[20]*

Young Russian Jews, angered by reports from Kishinev, decided it was time to fight back. When violence spread to the city of Homel, in what is now Belarus, they armed themselves to defend their families. The authorities responded by arresting them, as the rioting continued under police protection. In the end, however, even pogroms could not stop change from reaching Russia. In 1905, after a disastrous defeat in a war with Japan, the tsar was forced to make changes that reduced his power. In February, he agreed to organize an advisory council, or *duma*. He and his followers tried unsuccessfully to deprive Jews of the right to vote, on the grounds that they were not full citizens. By October 17, the tsar was forced to issue a manifesto guaranteeing the basic freedoms of all Russian citizens—including Jews.

Once again, the government organized massive demonstrations to protest the changes. Those demonstrations quickly turned into riots directed against the Jews. An investigation by the *duma* later revealed that leaflets urging violence were printed at police headquarters and financed by the tsar himself.

The uprising ended in 1907 with the tsar still in control. Before long, he mounted a new campaign against the Jews. As part of the campaign against the Jews, the Russian secret police created a forgery known as *The Protocols of the Elders of Zion*. It was said to be "proof" that Jews were plotting to take over the world. Like other myths about "the Jews," it would quickly spread to countries around the world in the early 1900s.

---

* The actual number of Jews killed during the Kishinev pogrom was about 50, not the 120 originally reported by the *New York Times*.

[1] Michael Marrus, *The Politics of Assimilation: The French Community at the Time of the Dreyfus Affair* (Oxford, 1971), 197-201, quoted in Albert S. Lindemann, *The Jew Accused: Three Anti-Semitic Affairs (Dreyfus, Beilis, Frank), 1894-1915* (Cambridge, UK: Cambridge University Press, 1991), 92.

[2] Theodor Herzl, "A Solution of the Jewish Question," *The Jewish Chronicle*, January 17, 1896, 12-13, quoted in Paul Mendes-Flohr and Jehuda Reinharz, eds., *The Jew in the Modern World: A Documentary History*, 2nd ed. (New York: Oxford University Press, 1995), 534.

[3] In Salo W. Baron, *The Russian Jew Under Tsars and Soviets* (New York: Macmillan, 1964), 29, quoted in Allan Levine, *Scattered Among the Peoples: The Jewish Diaspora in Twelve Portraits* (Woodstock, NY: Overlook Duckworth, 2003), 207.

[4] Alexander Herzen, *My Past and Thoughts: The Memoirs of Alexander Herzen*, trans. Constance Garnett, rev. Humphrey Higgins, 1968 (Berkeley: University of California Press, 1982), 169-170.

[5] *Russki Invalid*, 1858, quoted in Howard M. Sachar, *A History of the Jews in the Modern World* (New York: Vintage Books, 2005), 184.

[6] Orshanskii, *Evrei v Rossii* 71-72, quoted in Stephen M. Berk, *Year of Crisis, Year of Hope: Russian Jewry and the Pogroms of 1881-1882* (Westport: Greenwood Press, 1985), 48.

[7] Berk, *Year of Crisis, Year of Hope*, 49.

[8] Pauline Wengeroff, *Rememberings: The World of a Russian-Jewish Woman in the Nineteenth Century*, trans. Henny Wenkart (Bethesda: University Press of Maryland, 2000), 221.

[9] *Razsvet* (St. Petersburg), 19, May 8, 1881, 741-742, quoted in Berk, *Year of Crisis, Year of Hope*, 35-36.

[10] Wengeroff, *Rememberings*, 223. Original emphasis.

[11] Ibid., 224-225. Original emphasis.

[12] Moses Leib Lilienblum to J. L. Gordon, *Derekh Teshuva*, quoted in Lucy S. Dawidowicz, ed., *The Golden Tradition: Jewish Life and Thought in Eastern Europe* (New York: Schocken Books, 1967), 128-129.

[13] The articles in *The Times* were republished in *Persecution of the Jews in Russia 1881* (London: Spottiswoode, 1882), quoted in Berk, *Year of Crisis, Year of Hope*, 66-67.

[14] Ibid.

[15] *Supplement to the Jewish Chronicle*, February 3, 1882, 3, quoted in Berk, *Year of Crisis, Year of Hope*, 68.

[16] *Nedel'naia khronika voskhoda*, 7 (February 1882): 163-164, quoted in Berk, *Year of Crisis, Year of Hope*, 69.

[17] Iu. Gessen, "Graf N. P. Ignatiev i 'Vremennyia pravila' o evreiakh 3 Maia 1882 goda," *Pravo* 3 (1908):16/9, quoted in Berk, *Year of Crisis, Year of Hope*, 72-73.

[18] Peter A. Zaionchkovsky, *The Russian Autocracy in Crisis, 1878-1882*, trans. Gary Hamburg (Gulf Breeze, FL: Academic International Press, 1979), 265, quoted in Berk, *Year of Crisis, Year of Hope*, 73.

[19] Wengeroff, *Rememberings*, 222-223.

[20] "Jewish Massacre Denounced," *New York Times*, April 28, 1903.

12

Lies, Stereotypes, and Antisemitism in an Age of War and Revolution

(1914–1920s)

Between 1903 and 1905, more than 3,000 antisemitic pamphlets, books, and articles were published in Russia alone. One of those works was *The Protocols of the Elders of Zion*, which supposedly contained the minutes of a secret meeting of Jewish leaders—the so-called "Elders of Zion." At that meeting, according to the *Protocols*, the "Elders" plotted to take over the world.

In 1905, few people had paid much attention to the document, but after World War I, it became a worldwide sensation. Many believed that it explained seemingly "unexplainable" events—wars, economic crises, revolutions, epidemics. The idea of a Jewish conspiracy had been around for centuries, but the *Protocols* gave that belief new life, and it remained rooted in popular culture long after it was exposed as a hoax in the early 1920s. For many people, World War I and the earthshaking events that followed it confirmed the authenticity of the document, no matter what evidence was offered to the contrary.

QUESTIONS OF LOYALTY IN WARTIME

World War I was sparked not by a Jewish conspiracy but by an assassination in Sarajevo, the capital of Bosnia. On June 28, 1914, a Bosnian Serb who belonged to an extreme nationalist group killed Archduke Franz Ferdinand, the heir to the throne of Austria-Hungary, an empire that controlled much of central Europe. Just two months later, the world was engulfed in a war that lasted four years, was fought on three continents, and ultimately involved 30 nations. On one side were the Central Powers—Austria-Hungary, Germany, and the Ottoman Empire, and the countries that supported them. On the other side were the Allies—Serbia, Russia, France, and Britain, and the countries that supported them. More than 19 million people were killed during the fighting; about half of them were civilians.

Winston Churchill, who later became prime minister of Britain, described the terrible nature of this "world war":

> All the horrors of all the ages were brought together, and not only armies but whole populations were thrust into the midst of them. The mighty educated States involved conceived—not without reason— that their very existence was at stake. Neither peoples nor rulers drew the line at any deed which they thought could help them win. . . . Every outrage against humanity or international law was repaid by reprisals—often of a greater scale and of longer duration. No truce or parley mitigated the strife of the armies. The wounded died between the lines: the dead moldered into the soil. Merchant ships and neutral ships and hospital ships were sunk on the seas and all on board left to their fate, or killed as they swam. Every effort was made to starve whole nations into submission without regard to age or sex.[1]

EUROPE AT WAR (1914–1918)

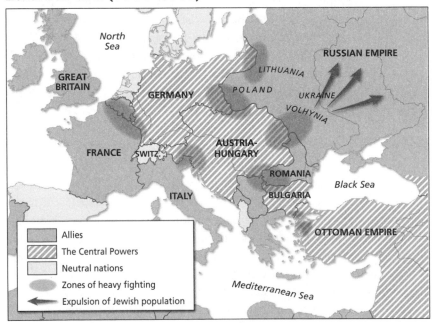

The areas of heavy fighting during World War I in Europe, particularly in the east, were areas where most Jews lived. Many were caught in the crossfire.

Approximately 400,000 Jews served in the armies of the Central Powers, including 300,000 who fought for Austria-Hungary. Among these fighting for the Allies were 300,000 Jews in the Russian military and 4,000–5,000 in the American armed forces.

When people are engaged in such a war, their search for enemies focuses not only on the foreign armies outside their country's borders but also on enemies—real and imagined—within those borders. During World War I, a number of rulers, generals, and ordinary citizens accused vulnerable minorities in their own countries of treason and disloyalty. In the Ottoman Empire, Christian Armenians were the primary victims. In much of eastern Europe—particularly Russia—Jews were the target. They were seen as disloyal, even though more than 300,000 Jews fought, often with distinction, in the Russian army. In fact, Jews fought in every army involved in the conflict; for example, 100,000 served in the German army.

Accusations of disloyalty have consequences, particularly in a war zone, and according to the American Jewish Committee, "one-half of the Jewish population of the world was trapped in a corner of eastern Europe that is absolutely shut off from all neutral lands and from the sea."[2] The American Jewish Committee had been founded in 1906 by American Jews who wanted to protect Jews in Russia from the pogroms (see Chapter 11). Now, ten years later, they feared for the safety of Jews throughout eastern and central Europe.

The war in Europe was being fought on two fronts, or lines of battle. On the western front, which stretched from Belgium to Switzerland, the two sides were mired in trench warfare, each determined to exhaust the other. Neither was strong enough to win a decisive victory. On the eastern front, however, large stretches of land shifted back and forth from one side to the other.

Early in the war, the Russians won control of much of the Austrian province of Galicia and then bombarded the German state of East Prussia. But as the war progressed, the Germans prevailed. In a battle fought near the city of Tannenberg in August 1914, Germans nearly destroyed the Russian army. To exploit their victory, the Germans went on the offensive. Within two months, they controlled the northwestern part of Russian Poland and parts of Lithuania and the Ukraine. As the Russians retreated, they set fire to homes, farms, and businesses. Millions of people—Jews and Christians alike—were left homeless.

In the eyes of the Russian government, not all of those homeless civilians were loyal. During the war, a Jewish playwright and journalist who called himself S. Ansky traveled through the small towns, or shtetels, that dotted the Pale of Settlement and Russian-controlled Galicia to organize aid to Jewish communities there and investigate accusations that Jews were spying for the Germans. He summarized his findings:

> At first, the slanderers did their work quietly and furtively. But soon they took off their masks and accused the Jews openly. . . .
>
> From the generals down to the lowest ensign, the officers knew how the czar, his family, the general staff, and [the commanders] felt about Jews; and so they worked to outdo one another in their antisemitism. The conscripts were less negative but hearing the venom of their superiors and reading about Jewish treason day after day they too came to suspect and hate Jews. . . .
>
> Every commander and every colonel who made a mistake had found a way to justify his crime, his incompetence, his carelessness. He could make everything kosher by blaming his failures on a Jewish spy. The officers, who accepted lies against Jews without question or investigation, were quick to settle accounts with the accused. . . .
>
> The persecution reached mammoth proportions. . . . When the Russian army passed through many towns and villages, especially when there were Cossacks [members of the army's elite cavalry], bloody pogroms took place. The soldiers torched and demolished whole neighborhoods, looted the Jewish homes and shops, killed

dozens of people for no reason, took revenge on the rest, inflicted the worst humiliation on them, raped women, injured children. . . . A Russian officer talked about seeing Cossacks "playing" with a Jewish two-year-old: one of them tossed the child aloft, and the others caught him on their swords. After that, it was easy to believe the German newspapers when they wrote that the Cossacks hacked off people's arms and legs and buried victims alive. . . .

On the assumption that every Jew was a spy, [the Russian government] began by expelling Jews from the towns closest to the front: at first it was just individuals, then whole communities. In many places Jews and ethnic Germans were deported together. This process spread farther and farther with each passing day. Ultimately all the Jews—a total of over two hundred thousand—were deported from Kovno and Grodno provinces.[3]

At a meeting in St. Petersburg, N. B. Shcherbatov, the Russian minister of the interior, confirmed the charges made by Ansky and other Jews. He told fellow officials that even though "one does not like to say this," military officers were attributing to Jews "imaginary actions of sabotage against the Russian forces" so that they could hold the Jews "responsible for [the army's] own failure and defeat at the front."[4] Another official noted that the Jews "are being chased out of the [eastern front] with whips and accused . . . of helping the enemy"—with no attempt to distinguish the guilty from the innocent. He feared that when these refugees arrived in new areas, they would be in a "revolutionary mood."[5]

By late summer of 1915, the Russian army had uprooted more than 600,000 Jews. A non-Jewish deputy in Russia's parliament described their removal from the province of Radom:

The entire population was driven out within a few hours during the night. . . . Old men, invalids and paralytics had to be carried in people's arms because there were no vehicles. The police . . . treated the Jewish refugees precisely like criminals. At one station, for instance, the Jewish Commission of Homel was not even allowed to approach the trains to render aid to the refugees or to give them food and water. In one case, a train which was conveying the victims was completely sealed and when finally opened most of the inmates were found half-dead, sixteen down with scarlet fever and one with typhus.[6]

Thousands of Jewish families were displaced during World War I. Some were forced out by the fighting, but many more were expelled from their homes because the Russians saw them as potential traitors.

Soldiers who "catch" toddlers on their swords and police officers who force "old men, invalids, and paralytics" from their homes are not protecting their country from treason. Rather, they are seeing Jews as stereotypes, not as human beings. A stereotype is more than a label or judgment about an individual based on the real or imagined characteristics of a group. Stereotypes dehumanize people by reducing them to categories; in this case, officials treated babies and paralytics as traitors despite all evidence and logic.

Similar stereotypes shaped the irrational decisions of the tsar, his ministers, and top generals. For example, by 1916, Russian soldiers experienced shortages of food, fuel, ammunition, and other necessities, partly because the government was using freight trains and supply wagons to remove thousands of Jewish civilians from cities and towns in western Russia and resettle them farther east.

Although the Council of Ministers expressed no regret for the expulsions or the pogroms, its members did worry about their impact on Russia's ability to borrow money abroad. The stereotype of the "rich Jewish banker" encouraged the ministers to exaggerate Jewish wealth and influence. In 1915, Jacob Schiff, a German-Jewish American banker, had refused to help the Allies secure a large loan if even "one cent of the proceeds" went to the Russian government. Russian officials saw his action as proof of a "Jewish plot" to overthrow the tsar. But, despite the power attributed to Schiff, the Allies easily found other bankers willing to lend them the money they needed. Although some of those bankers were Jews, the vast majority of them were Christians.

THE POWER OF OLD MYTHS IN A MODERN WORLD

The Russian ministers who saw evidence everywhere of an "international Jewish conspiracy" were not alone. A number of British, French, German, Austrian, and other European officials also routinely exaggerated the power of Jews—particularly American Jews.

Throughout 1915 and 1916, the United States did not take sides in the war, despite the efforts of the Allies and the Central Powers to win the nation's support. Both believed that American Jews could tip the decision to one side or the other. Why were they so convinced that about three million Jews (most of whom were penniless immigrants) in a nation that was home to more than 88 million people had so much power?[7] That belief was based in part on the old myth that Jews controlled the world's wealth. It was also influenced by the vigor with which Jews defended one another. Every time a group of Jews protested an injustice or helped a poverty-stricken Jewish community at home or abroad, some non-Jews saw those efforts as evidence of an international conspiracy and concluded that Jews were loyal only to one another and not to the countries they lived in.

David Lloyd George, who became Britain's prime minister in 1916, was among those who believed that "the Jews" had enormous power. He was also convinced that 1917 would be the critical year in the war and that the Allies must make a tremendous effort to ensure their victory— especially after Russia was rocked by a revolution in the spring. He later wrote that he had faced two major problems that year: how to convince the new government in Russia to continue fighting the war and how to persuade the Americans to join the Allies. "In the solution of these two problems," he noted, "public opinion in Russia and America played a great part, and we [believed] . . . that in both countries the friendliness or hostility of the Jewish race might make a considerable difference."[8]

The Ottoman Empire, which controlled Palestine and other parts of the Middle East, was an ally of Germany and Austria-Hungary. Early in the war, the Ottoman governor of Palestine had feared that Arab and Jewish nationalists there would side with the Allies. So he arrested some of them and banished about 6,000 of the 85,000 Jewish settlers in the province. Many of them found refuge in British-controlled Egypt.

Almost everyone the governor deported was a Russian Jew. In his view, all Russian Jews were enemy aliens, even though many of them considered themselves refugees from Russian persecution. He ordered their newspapers, schools, banks, and political offices closed. When David Ben-Gurion and other Zionist leaders protested, they too were exiled.

That policy persuaded some Zionists and Arab nationalists to help the Allies. In 1916, the British offered to aid the Hashemites, a powerful Arab family, in creating an independent Arab kingdom in exchange for their military support for the Allies. Zionists were interested in a similar arrangement. They wanted the British to recognize the rights of the Jewish people in Palestine. To show their commitment to the Allies, a group of young Jews organized a Jewish legion that fought on behalf of the British. About one-third were from Palestine (including many Russian Jews, some of whom had been expelled by the Ottomans earlier in the war); another third came from the United States. The rest were from various countries, including Britain, Canada, and Argentina.[9]

On November 2, 1917, Arthur James Balfour, the British foreign secretary, issued a declaration that stated, in part: "His Majesty's Government view with favor the establishment in Palestine of a national home for the Jewish people, and will use their best endeavors to facilitate the achievement of this object." To many antisemites, the Balfour Declaration, as it became known, was "proof" that "the Jews" controlled Britain. To Lloyd George, Balfour, and other government leaders, it was a rational decision that, they believed, would result in strong support for the Allies.

In nations that were already committed to the Allies' cause, most Jews celebrated the announcement. But some were wary; they thought the declaration suggested that Jews were more loyal to other Jews than to the countries they lived in. And it did not change the way most German and Austrian Jews viewed the war—they remained loyal to their countries.

The Central Powers shared the British government's view of Jews as a "united race," and therefore they saw the Balfour Declaration as a powerful piece of propaganda for the Allies; they believed it would prompt Jewish bankers to lend more money to the Allies. To minimize the effects of the declaration, Ottoman officials ended restrictions on Jewish immigration to Palestine. And in January 1918, when the Germans approved their own plan to create an autonomous Jewish settlement in Palestine, the Ottomans reluctantly agreed.

Although the Balfour Declaration would have important long-term effects, it had no impact on the two problems that British Prime Minister Lloyd George struggled with in 1917. As he had hoped, the United States did declare war in April 1917—but the decision could not be attributed to Jewish influence because it occurred about seven months before the Balfour Declaration was issued. In addition, by November 1917, a second revolution was under way in Russia. Not only had the tsar been overthrown but now Russia's first democratic government had been replaced as well. Russia's newest government, led by a Communist group known as the Bolsheviks, officially withdrew from the war and signed a peace treaty with the Germans. In spite of Lloyd George's hopes, Jewish public opinion had no effect on that decision, either.

Thanks to that treaty, Germany was able to transfer thousands of soldiers from the eastern front to battlefields in the west. There they faced a new opponent, the United States. By June 1918, American troops were arriving in France at the rate of 250,000 a month. By fall, the Americans were helping the Allies push the Germans back. On November 1, they crashed through the center of the German line. It was then only a matter of days until Germany surrendered and the war was finally over.

REVOLUTIONS AND CIVIL WARS

As World War I was coming to an end, Jewish civilians in eastern Europe found that the dangers they faced were intensifying rather than diminishing. Three of the great empires that had controlled eastern and central Europe and western Asia had begun to break apart during the war. Russia, Austria-Hungary, and the Ottoman Empire were each home to dozens of ethnic groups who were determined to take advantage of the collapse. As these groups jockeyed for power and independence, revolutions and civil wars broke out almost everywhere. And almost everywhere, Jews were caught in the middle.

Soon after the Bolsheviks gained control in Russia in 1917, they gave the country both a new name—the Union of Soviet Socialist Republics (USSR, or the Soviet Union)—and a Communist government based on the ideas of Karl Marx, a German philosopher who lived from 1818 to 1883. Marx believed that the struggle between workers and manufacturers and other industrialists would end only when workers owned all land and other resources not as individuals but as a community. In his view, only then would everyone be equal.

Because of his belief in communal, or shared, ownership of land and other resources, the system Marx envisioned became known as Communism. It was a radical form of socialism based on the idea of taking from each person according to his or her ability and giving to each according to his or her needs. This meant that a communist government "took" work and other contributions from its citizens and "gave" them support based on their needs rather than on their status in society, efforts, education, or talent. Marx also advocated a dictatorship of the proletariat (the workers), or rule by the majority class in society. Such rule would be a step toward a new classless society.

V. I. Lenin, the leader of the Bolsheviks, agreed with most of Marx's ideas, but he quickly realized that the real world did not always match Marx's theories. Almost as soon as the Communists took power, they found themselves at war with the White Army, which was made up mainly of Russians who hoped to restore the deposed tsar to power. The White Army had the support of Britain and the Allies, now that the Bolshevik government in Russia had made its own peace agreement with Germany. The Bolsheviks also faced opposition from nationalist groups who wanted their own independent countries and from bands of outlaws who simply saw an opportunity to acquire wealth and power amid the confusion. As a result, in some parts of the old Russian Empire, no one was in control.

The situation was particularly treacherous in the Ukraine. Like other ethnic groups in the old Russian Empire, Ukrainians wanted independence. As a result, the Bolsheviks' Red Army there faced not only the White Army, but also gangs of bandits and thugs, and a newly organized Ukrainian national army. With the exception of the Communists, these armies all targeted Jews, in the belief that in doing so they were attacking Bolsheviks. To them, all Jews were Communists and all Communists were Jews.

In fact, most Jews were not Communists, although some Jews did belong to the Communist Party and a few held high positions in the party. Many Russians believed Jews were all Communists because Karl Marx was of Jewish descent. Perhaps the best known Jew in the Russian Communist party was Leon Trotsky, who organized and led the Red Army. Like Marx and other Communists, he had no interest in Judaism or any other religion, and he rejected any connection to Jews as a people. Nevertheless, non-Jews in Russia viewed him and other Communists of Jewish descent as Jews and increasingly regarded Communism as a Jewish creation, even though the vast majority of Communists were non-Jews.

About 60 pogroms against Jews took place in the Ukraine in November and December 1917, and attacks continued off and on for another two years. One of the most horrific took place in February 1919 in the town of Proskurov, about 175 miles south of Kiev. At the time, the town was ruled by an independent Ukrainian government known as the Directory. Early on the morning of February 15, local Communists, including a number of Ukrainians and Jews, tried to regain control of the city by attacking a rail yard where Directory soldiers were encamped. The Ukrainian officer in charge was a man known only as Semosenko. Within a few hours, he and his men had put down the uprising and killed those responsible.

Later that day, Semosenko, who apparently believed that all Jews were Communists, decided to take revenge for the attack by slaughtering all the Jews in the town. He warned his officers that their men were not to loot or steal; they were simply to kill every Jew in Proskurov. He explained that the attack was a matter of honor.

One Ukrainian officer refused to participate in the massacre; he would not allow his men to kill unarmed civilians. The officer and the soldiers under his command were promptly sent out of town. Everyone else obeyed. The men marched through the center of town in battle formation, with the band in front. They then "dispersed into the side streets which were all inhabited by Jews only."[10]

It was the Sabbath, and most Jews knew nothing about the early-morning uprising against the Directory or its outcome. They went to synagogue as usual and then returned home for their Sabbath meal. They learned of the attack only when soldiers burst into their houses, unsheathed swords, and "calmly proceeded to massacre the inhabitants without regard to age or sex. They killed alike old men, women, children, and even infants in arms."[11]

Among the dead was a local Catholic priest who begged the soldiers to stop. He was killed at the door to his own church. A town councilor begged Semosenko to stop the killing but was ignored. So the councilor sent a telegraph to Semosenko's commander, who immediately ordered an end to the massacre. Only then did the slaughter stop. As soon as the soldiers heard a prearranged signal, "they fell in at the place previously appointed, and, in orderly ranks, as on a campaign, singing regimental songs, marched to their camp behind the [train] station."[12] In three hours, they had killed 1,200 infants, children, women, and men.

Before leaving town, Semosenko issued a proclamation blaming the Jews for the massacre and warning that he would return if they dared to cause trouble again. He and his troops then headed for a nearby town, where they carried out yet another pogrom.

Despite atrocities like this one, Ukrainian officials insisted that they were not hostile to Jews. But their words did not keep Ukrainian nationalist troops from continuing to target Jews. When a survivor of one massacre protested that neither he nor his neighbors were Communists, he was told, "We aren't after Communists; we are after Jews."[13] Once again, neither truth nor logic was a match for deep-seated beliefs.

THE *PROTOCOLS* AND THE WHITE ARMY

The White Army also participated in pogroms in the territories under its control, and, by late summer of 1919, these forces had taken the lead in attacking Jews. John Ernest Hodgson, a British journalist who traveled with White Army troops, explained why:

> *The officers and the men of the army laid practically all the blame for their country's troubles on the Hebrew. They held that the whole [catastrophe] had been engineered by some great and mysterious secret society of international Jews who, in the pay and at the orders of Germany, had seized the psychological moment and snatched the reins of government.[14]*

Those ideas (except for the part about the secret society being in the pay of Germany) came straight from *The Protocols of the Elders of Zion*. The *Protocols* had disappeared from view during the world war, but the brutal murder of Tsar Nicholas II, his wife Alexandra, and their five children at the hands of the Bolsheviks in July 1918 had turned new attention to the document. A week after the killing, White Army soldiers found a copy of the *Protocols* among Alexandra's possessions. They also discovered that she had drawn a swastika on one wall. For the tsar's supporters, the two discoveries had great meaning.

Historians have found letters suggesting that Alexandra's copy of the *Protocols* was probably not a treasured possession but rather a gift she received just before she was taken into custody. Her letters also indicate that she regarded the swastika as a good luck symbol, as many people did at the time. The symbol, which is at least 3,000 years old, had been used in countries around the world to signify life, power, strength, or good fortune. But in the early 1900s, the symbol had begun to take on a new meaning in Germany. Some Germans now regarded it as a sign of the purity of "Germanic blood" and the struggle of "the Aryans" against "the Jews." That view of the swastika, as a symbol of a fight against "the Jews," was also popular among some of the tsar's supporters. They now imagined that the book and the swastika were signs from the tsarina that the White Army was engaged in an epic battle against the evil Red Army, controlled by "the Jews."

The news that the tsarina had owned a copy of the *Protocols* spread quickly through the army. Before long, many officers and ordinary soldiers were convinced that the fact that she had carried the book with her was proof that it was true. However, as early 1905, the tsar, and possibly the tsarina, knew that the *Protocols* was a hoax. Not long after the tsar first read the document, he had been told that it was a forgery created by his own secret police. He immediately halted plans for mass distribution. "One cannot defend a pure cause," he wrote, "by dirty methods."[15] But despite his stand, the *Protocols* had remained in print and spread throughout the Russian Empire.

Did the leaders of the White Army know the work was a forgery? Some clearly did. They had held high positions in the secret police and in the tsar's army. But most of the men who served in the White Army probably believed it was true because it seemed to provide an explanation for the terrible things that had happened to Russia over the past ten years. Hodgson writes that among the White Russians, the idea of a Jewish world conspiracy became "an obsession of such terrible bitterness and insistency as to lead them into making statements of the most wild and fantastic character."[16]

Statistics reveal that as a result of that "fierce and unreasoning hatred," more than 2,000 pogroms took place in eastern Europe between 1917 and 1921. About 75,000 Jews were killed, many more were injured, and at least half a million were left homeless.

PROTECTING MINORITIES

During World War I, Jews throughout the world had tried to help their fellow Jews in Europe. After the war, their aid continued and even expanded. Jewish organizations set up soup kitchens, created clinics, and built orphanages in Poland, Hungary, and other eastern and central European countries. They also gathered information about attacks on Jews, particularly in Poland and other newly independent nations in the region. Many were eager to find a way to protect Jews from further violence.

As the war ended in November 1918, Louis Marshall, a prominent American lawyer and a founder of the American Jewish Committee, sent a series of memos to U.S. President Woodrow Wilson. He argued that the Allies should require newly formed nations in the region to accept a treaty guaranteeing the rights of all minorities in exchange for international recognition. It was not a new idea. In 1878, Jews in the West had tried to protect Romanian Jews with a similar treaty at the Congress of Berlin (see Chapter 10). The Romanian government signed the pact but refused to enforce key provisions, and the major powers were unwilling to require it to do so.

In 1878, the major powers had not been fully convinced of the need to protect minorities. After the war, however, they had a better understanding of why it was essential to do so. In 1919, even as world leaders gathered in Paris to write the treaties that would officially end the war, much of eastern Europe was still engulfed in violence. That violence exposed the dangers that Jews and other minorities faced in a region where every newly independent nation had sizeable minority populations. If those populations were not guaranteed political and social equality, the fighting was almost certain to continue.

In a speech to Congress in January 1918, President Wilson had listed 14 points he considered essential to a lasting peace. Many of them dealt with the "frustrated nationalism" that he believed had been responsible for the world war. Therefore he supported the division of the old multinational empires into independent nations. In Wilson's view, his 14th point was the most important. It called for a league of nations to keep the peace and guarantee the independence of "great and small States alike." In a speech delivered to a joint session of Congress on January 8, 1918, Wilson claimed that all 14 points were based on a single principle:

> It is the principle of justice to all peoples and nationalities, and their right to live on equal terms of liberty and safety with one another, whether they be strong or weak. Unless this principle be made its foundation, no part of the structure of international justice can stand.

In 1919, almost every minority group in Europe, including many Jewish groups, understood the importance of that principle, which is why each sent a delegation to the peace conference in Paris. They demanded not only civil rights but also "self-determination"—the right to maintain their own languages and to govern themselves.

Some Jews in the West were troubled by the calls for self-determination. They believed that demands for "national rights" could backfire. Henry Morgenthau, a Jew who had served as the U.S. ambassador to the Ottoman Empire, shared that view. He argued:

> *under this plan, a Jew in Poland or Romania, for example, would soon face conflicting duties, and . . . any American who advocated such a conflict of allegiance for the Jews of central Europe would perhaps expose the Jews in America to the suspicion of harbouring a similar desire.*[17]

Joseph Tenenbaum, a Jew who grew up in Poland, disagreed:

> *"Why does not America grant the Jews minority rights?" was the common question raised by most of the peace envoys. The answer was: Because America, the great melting pot, does not preach nationalism. There is no such thing as group rights in America, because fundamentally there is no such thing as national group domination.*[18]

Such arguments convinced Louis Marshall. He insisted:

> *[W]e must be careful not to permit ourselves to judge what is most desirable for the people who live in Eastern Europe by the standards which prevail on Fifth Avenue [in New York City] or in the States of Maine or Ohio, where a different horizon from that which prevails in Poland, Galicia, Ukraine, or Lithuania bounds one's vision.*[19]

That argument led to the Minorities Treaty, which granted civil, religious, and political rights to all citizens of a state. The word *citizen* now applied to anyone who was born or "habitually" lived in that state. The treaty also guaranteed every minority group the right to freely use its own language in trade, in court, and in primary schools in places where that group had a sizeable population. In addition, taxes and other public funds were to be used to support not only the schools, religious institutions, and charities of the majority but also those of minorities. To receive international recognition, a new state had to sign the Minorities Treaty and include the rights it guaranteed in its national constitution. The new League of Nations would be responsible for enforcing those treaties.

Most newly independent states objected to the treaty, arguing that it infringed on their right to govern without outside interference. On May

31, 1919, delegations from Poland, Romania, Hungary, Serbia, and Greece protested the treaty at the peace conference. Austria, Bulgaria, and Turkey also voiced objections. The Allies stood firm, however, and one new nation after another signed a version of the treaty. In the end, though, they did not enforce it for long—and the League of Nations lacked the power to force them to do so.

The only new nation that did not protest the Minorities Treaty was Czechoslovakia. Although many Czechs resented the document, their president, Thomas Masaryk, vigorously defended it. When asked why, he replied, "How can the suppressed nations deny the Jews that which they demand for themselves?"

Although the Allies established new states in eastern and central Europe, they did not even consider doing the same in other parts of the world. Much of Asia and Africa remained under European rule. The British and the French divided up the old Ottoman Empire, ignoring the promises they had made to Arab nationalists and Zionists during the war. The British now controlled Palestine and Iraq, and the French ruled Syria and Lebanon. The Zionists did make one important gain: the text of the Balfour Declaration was included in the mandate that the League of Nations gave to Britain in Palestine, over Arab objections. The league defined a mandate as a territory held in trust by a European nation until that nation gave the territory its independence.

THE *PROTOCOLS* REACH THE WEST AND BEYOND

The new Soviet Union was one of the few nations that did not attend the peace conference. It had made peace with Germany before the war's end. Moreover, Russia's former allies now regarded it as an outlaw state. Many people feared that the Bolsheviks were exporting Communism. Some allies actively supported the White Russians in their efforts to stop Communism. In the end, however, the White Russians were defeated. By 1920, the civil war was largely over, and the Communists had won.

As White Russians fled the Soviet Union, they brought the *Protocols of the Elders of Zion* with them. To many of them and to a growing number of people in other countries, the *Protocols* seemed to explain the losses and anxieties of the modern world.

In 1920, Eyre & Spottiswood, a respected British publisher, produced the first English edition of the *Protocols of the Elders of Zion*. Many people in Britain were intrigued by the document. The editors of the *Times* of London asked:

Despite the exposé published by the *Times* of London, *The Protocols of the Elders of Zion* was a publishing sensation in the 1920s and 1930s. The book could be found in countries around the world, including Japan, Mexico, and Syria.

What are these "Protocols"? Are they authentic? If so, what malevolent assembly concocted these plans, and gloated over their exposition? Are they a forgery? If so, whence comes the uncanny note of prophecy, prophecy in parts fulfilled, in parts far gone in the way of fulfillment? [20]

In August 1921, the *Times* answered those questions by exposing the *Protocols* as a fraud. The newspaper showed how the original author of the document had copied fictional works to create the *Protocols*. One of those works was an 1868 novel by Hermann Goedsche, a German antisemite. The novel contains a chapter describing a secret meeting of the "Elders of Zion" at midnight in the oldest Jewish cemetery in Prague. In this chapter, as the men gather to plot the enslavement of non-Jews, two Christians hidden among the tombstones eavesdrop. One of them summarizes how "the Jews" intend to undermine Christian nations.

To concentrate in their hands all the capital of the nations of all lands; to secure possession of all the land, railroads, mines, houses; to be at the head of all organizations, to occupy the highest governmental posts, to paralyze commerce and industry everywhere, to seize the press, to direct legislation, public opinion and national movements—and all for the purpose of subjugating all nations on earth to their power! [21]

As a result of the exposé by the *Times*, Eyre & Spottiswood stopped publishing the *Protocols*, and many newspapers no longer gave it publicity. But neither action hurt its popularity. A group known only as the Britons now published its own edition. The preface claimed that the *Times* exposé proved nothing:

Of course, Jews say the Protocols are a forgery. But the Great War was no forgery; the fate of Russia is no forgery; and these were predicted by the Learned Elders as long ago as 1901. The Great War was no German war—it was a Jew war. It was plotted by Jews, and was waged by Jewry on the Stock Exchanges of the world. The generals and admirals were all controlled by Jewry. [22]

By 1922, translations of the *Protocols* had also appeared in Germany, France, and Poland. The Polish edition appeared at a time when many Poles, including leaders of the Roman Catholic Church in Poland, believed the nation was about to be attacked by the Red Army. Two cardinals, two archbishops, and three bishops—all influenced by the *Protocols*—sent out a "cry for help" that was read in churches around the world. It said, in part:

> *The real object of Bolshevism is world-conquest. The race which has the leadership of Bolshevism in its hands, has already in the past subjugated the whole world by means of gold and the banks, and now, driven by the everlasting imperialistic greed which flows in its veins is already aiming at the final subjugation of the nations under the yoke of its rule.* [23]

The first sentence is true; the Bolsheviks were plotting "world conquest," but their leaders were not Jews. Jews did not control Russia's Communist government or the world's banks.

Translations also appeared in Denmark, Finland, Greece, Hungary, Italy, Romania, Spain, and a number of South American countries. White Russian exiles in Siberia carried the document to Japan, where it was published in 1924. The patriarch of Jerusalem (the head of the Eastern Orthodox Church in Palestine) urged his followers to buy the Arabic translation in 1925. And almost everywhere, the false statements contained in the book had seeped into the general culture; exposés of the forgery made little difference. After all, who could deny the wars, the revolutions, and the economic disasters that had taken place in the early 1900s? All had supposedly been prophesied in the *Protocols*.

THE *PROTOCOLS* IN THE UNITED STATES

In the United States, the strongest supporter of the *Protocols* was none other than Henry Ford, the manufacturer of the first affordable automobile. In 1919, he began publishing a weekly newspaper called the *Dearborn Independent*. He gave away copies of the paper to customers and sold subscriptions through his car dealerships.

In 1920, a Russian émigré gave Ford a copy of the *Protocols*. Like many others, Ford never doubted its authenticity. He immediately serialized the *Protocols* in his newspaper and printed articles that supported its claims. Those articles promised to reveal "The Scope of Jewish Dictatorship in the United States," "Jewish Degradation of American Baseball," and "The International Jew—The World's Foremost Problem." In 1922, he turned those articles into a book that sold more than a half-million copies.

American Jews tried repeatedly to show Ford that the book was a forgery. When he ignored them, many expressed their disapproval by refusing to buy Ford cars. So did some non-Jews. But few American Jewish leaders supported the boycott. Most thought they had a better chance of persuading Ford to reconsider his views in private meetings. When he refused to see them, they created a public-relations campaign to educate Americans about Jews and Judaism.

That campaign had the support of a number of prominent Catholic and Protestant leaders, who expressed their confidence in the "patriotism and good citizenship" of "our Jewish brethren." In addition, 119 prominent Americans, including President Woodrow Wilson and former president William Howard Taft, signed a letter in January, 1921 condemning anti-semitism. "We believe it should not be left to men and women of the Jewish faith to fight this evil," the letter said, "but that it is in a very special sense the duty of citizens who are not Jews by ancestry or faith."[24]

None of these efforts seemed to affect the popularity of the *Protocols* or Ford's newspaper. Every week, he received money and letters of appreciation from fans for his "exposé" of Jewish conspiracy. Then, in 1924, the *Dearborn Independent* ran a series of articles attacking Aaron Sapiro,

Political cartoonists made fun of the tactics Henry Ford used to fight the million-dollar defamation lawsuit that Aaron Sapiro filed against him.

a Chicago attorney for the National Council of the Farmers' Cooperative Marketing Association. Ford accused Sapiro of being part of a "conspiracy of Jewish bankers who seek to control the food market of the world." (According to the *Protocols*, Jews wanted control of the world's food supply as a step toward global domination.) Against the advice of family and friends, Sapiro hired a lawyer, who filed a one-million-dollar defamation lawsuit against Ford. (Libel and slander are two forms of defamation. Libel is published defamation, and slander is spoken.) Ford hired a team of lawyers and an army of detectives to defend himself.

The proceedings ended in a mistrial after a reporter interviewed a juror before the case was decided. As the second trial unfolded, it became increasingly clear that Ford was going to lose the lawsuit, because he had no proof of his charges against Sapiro. At that point, he contacted Louis Marshall and U.S. congressman Nathan Perlman. He told them that he had been wrong to attack Sapiro and other Jews and wanted to make amends. The two men suggested a public apology and an end to Ford's antisemitic campaign. Ford agreed.

Although some people praised Ford's change of heart, others were unconvinced. There were five antisemitic organizations in the United States before 1932. Between 1932 and 1940, there were over 120 groups. Many of them relied on the articles and books Ford had published in the 1920s to support their attacks on the Jews.

Among the antisemites who acknowledged their debt to Ford was Father Charles Coughlin, a Detroit-based Catholic priest. At the height of his popularity in the 1930s, his radio show reached more than three million homes across the nation. He also published *Social Justice*, a magazine with a circulation of about one million. When it reprinted the *Protocols*, Coughlin wrote, "Yes, the Jews have always claimed that the *Protocols* were forgeries, but I prefer the words of Henry Ford, who said, 'The best test of the truth of *The Protocols* is in the fact that up to the present minute they have been carried out.'" Coughlin added, "Mr. Ford did retract his accusations against the Jews. But neither Mr. Ford nor I retract the statement that many of the events predicted in the *Protocols* have come to pass."[25]

Those "predicted" events included World War I, the Russian Revolution, the Balfour Declaration, and the Minorities Treaty. They were not actually predicted in the *Protocols*, but the document uses such vague language that it could be interpreted as "proof" of almost any event.

THE DOORS CLOSE

Even before Ford published the *Protocols*, antisemitism was on the rise in the United States. Some of the antagonism has been linked to the fact that in the early 1900s, about a million immigrants entered the United States each year. Unlike earlier arrivals, most of them were Catholics or Jews from eastern and southern Europe.

Much of the new anti-Jewish feeling was visible but not as conspicuous as the antisemitism in Europe. Nevertheless, American Jews experienced some discrimination almost everywhere they turned. Many colleges, private clubs, and civic organizations limited the number of Jews they would accept, while others excluded all Jews from membership. Employers routinely asked for the "nationality" of job applicants or indicated in their ads that only gentiles (non-Jews) need apply. Even large corporations that were willing to hire Jews for low-level jobs excluded Jews from executive positions or limited their number. Jews were also barred from renting or buying property in some neighborhoods and staying in some hotels. Only rarely did antisemitism become violent. Perhaps the most shocking incident occurred in 1915, during the world war and about five years before the *Protocols* was published in the United States.

In 1913, Leo Frank, the manager of a pencil factory in Atlanta, Georgia, had been accused of murdering a 13-year-old girl, one of his employees. Even though the prosecution had a weak case, a jury found Frank guilty, as crowds outside the courthouse shouted, "Hang the Jew." Frank was not allowed in the courtroom when the jury gave its verdict, because the judge feared he would be attacked.

After the judge sentenced Frank to death, his attorneys appealed the conviction, but the higher courts, including the U.S. Supreme Court, voted against reopening the case. Only the governor of Georgia was willing to review the trial records. As a result of that review, he reduced Frank's sentence to life in prison. A few days later, a mob burst into the prison, kidnapped Frank, and lynched him.

The case shocked Jews throughout the nation. Many had believed that kind of antisemitic violence was impossible in the United States. Five years later, the publication of the *Protocols* added to their uneasiness. It was a time when vigilante groups like the one that had murdered Frank were being used to keep African Americans, Jews, and Catholics "in their place" not only in the South but also in many northern states. It was also a time when immigration was becoming an increasingly explosive issue, as a story in the *New York Times* revealed. On August 17, 1920, the newspaper reported:

> *Leon Kaimaky, [a commissioner of the Hebrew Immigrant Aid*
> *Society (HIAS) and] publisher of the* Jewish Daily News *of this city,*
> *returned recently from Europe, where he went, together with Jacob*
> *Massel, to bring about the reunion of the thousands of Jewish families*
> *who were separated by the war. Mr. Kaimaky has been abroad since*
> *last February. . . . In an article in the* Jewish Daily News *describing*
> *conditions in Eastern Europe Mr. Kaimaky declared that "if there*
> *were in existence a ship that could hold 3,000,000 human beings, the*
> *3,000,000 Jews of Poland would board it and escape to America."*[26]

Alarmed readers jumped to the conclusion that the HIAS was planning to bring over three million Polish Jews. So did members of Congress, who immediately called for a ban on all immigration. Albert Johnson, a Republican from Washington State and the chairman of the House Committee on Immigration, brought the matter to a vote without a hearing, and the House quickly passed the ban. By the time the vote was taken, many were fearful that as many as 15 million Jews—the estimated number of Jews in the world in 1920—would soon be arriving in the United States.

The Senate Committee on Immigration was more cautious. Its chairman told reporters, "This talk about 15,000,000 immigrants flooding into the United States is hysteria." He then called for hearings. The first witness was Johnson, who warned that unless an emergency act was passed, immigrants would "flood this country."

John L. Bernstein, the president of HIAS, also testified. He told Congress that HIAS had no plans to bring three million Polish Jews to the United States. He bluntly stated:

> *Now, gentlemen . . . during the year 1919 we obtained the largest*
> *contributions, both in membership and in donations, we have ever*
> *received . . . and the amount of the contributions was $325,000. . . .*
> *Now, I will leave it to you, gentlemen, how much of that $325,000*
> *will be left us to undertake this great plan that somebody is reading*
> *about?*[27]

In the end the Senate decided that there was no emergency, nor were there grounds for a general ban on immigration. Still, like their counterparts in the House of Representatives, many senators were uneasy about the "quantity" and "quality" of the nation's newest arrivals. In 1921, the House and the Senate passed the first of several laws limiting immigration.

In his testimony before the House Committee on Immigration, John Trevor, a New York attorney and member of a group called the Allied Patriotic Societies, proposed that Congress limit immigration country by country to two percent of the number of immigrants from that country living in the United States in 1890. He deliberately ignored the most recent census, from 1920, and chose an earlier one that predated the arrival of most Jewish immigrants. After much debate, a bill containing Trevor's plan passed by an overwhelming majority in both the House of Representatives (373 to 71) and the Senate (62 to 6). In May 1925, President Calvin Coolidge signed the National Origins Act into law. The new law effectively closed the United States to most Jewish immigrants.

During the debate, Coolidge told the American people,

> *Restricted immigration is not an offensive but purely a defensive action. . . . We cast no aspersions on any race or creed, but we must remember that every object of our institutions of society and government will fail unless America be kept American.*

Many Americans shared his views. The new law was extremely popular and seemed to solve the nation's "immigrant problem," at least for the time being. The problem in Europe was not as easily resolved. There, the notion that "the Jews" were a "nation within a nation" plotting world domination would lead to genocide—an effort to murder all of Europe's Jews.

[1] R. S. Churchill and Martin Gilbert, *Winston S. Churchill* (London, 1966-) 4:913-914, quoted in Paul Johnson, *Modern Times: The World from the Twenties to the Eighties* (New York: Harper & Row, 1983), 13.

[2] The American Jewish Committee, *The Jews in the Eastern War Zone* by the American Jewish Committee (New York, 1916), 7.

[3] S. Ansky, *The Enemy at His Pleasure: A Journey Through the Jewish Pale of Settlement During World War I*, ed. and trans. Joachim Neugroschel (New York: Henry Holt, 2004), 4-7.

[4] *Arkhiv Russkoi Revolutsii* (Berlin, 1926), 18:43-4; Michawel Cherniavsky, trans. and ed., *Prologue to Revolution* (Englewood Cliffs, NJ, 1967), 39-43, 56-72, 85-87, 121-123, 194-195, quoted in David Vital, *A People Apart: The Jews in Europe, 1789-1939* (New York: Oxford University Press, 1999), 655.

[5] Ibid.

[6] "Evreyakaya Zhizn," August 9, 1915, 19-20, quoted in The American Jewish Committee, *The Jews in the Eastern War Zone*, 62-63.

[7] Christian M. Rutishauser, "The 1947 Seelisberg Conference: The Foundation of Jewish-Christian Dialogue," *Studies in Christian-Jewish Relations*, 2, no. 2 (2007) http://escholarship.bc.edu/scjr/vol2/iss2/6.

[8] David Lloyd George, *The Truth About the Peace Treaties* (1938), 1119-1122, quoted in Sachar, *A History of the Jews in the Modern World*, 354.

[9] H. C. O'Neill, *The Royal Fusiliers in the Great War* (London: William Heinemann, 1922), 26; Ze'ev Jabotinsky, *The Jewish Legion in the World War* (New York, 1945), 164.

[10] Semosenko at Proskurov: Comité des Délégations Juives, Paris, *The Pogroms in the Ukraine* (Paris, 1927), 170-187, quoted in Ronald Sanders, *Shores of Refuge: A Hundred Years of Jewish Emigration* (New York: Schocken Books, 1988), 344.

[11] Ibid.

[12] Ibid., 345.

[13] Elias Heifetz, *Slaughter of the Jews in the Ukraine* (New York, 1921) 259, 262, 267, 308, quoted in Benjamin Lieberman, *Terrible Fate: Ethnic Cleansing in the Making of Modern Europe* (Chicago: Ivan R. Dee, 2006), 144.

[14] John Ernest Hodgson, *With Denikin's Armies* (London, 1932), 54-63, quoted in Sanders, *Shores of Refuge*, 356.

[15] Vladimir Burtsev, *Protokolov Sionskikh Mudrotsov* (Paris, 1938) 105-106, quoted in Norman Cohn, *Warrant for Genocide: The Myth of the Jewish World Conspiracy and the "Protocols of the Elders of Zion"* (London: Serif, 1996), 126.

[16] Hodgson, *With Denikin's Armies*, quoted in Sanders, *Shores of Refuge*, 356-357.

[17] Henry Morgenthau and French Strother, *All in a Life Time* (Garden City: Doubleday, Page & Company, 1922), 351.

[18] Joseph Tenenbaum, *In Search of a Lost People: The Old and the New Poland* (New York: Beechhurst Press, 1948), 176-177.

[19] David Lloyd George, *Memoirs of the Peace Conference* (New Haven, 1939), 2:881, quoted in Sanders, *Shores of Refuge*, 348.

[20] Quoted in Saul Friedländer, *Nazi Germany and the Jews* (New York: HarperCollins, 1997), 95.

[21] Quoted in Herman Bernstein, *The Truth about "The Protocols of Zion": A Complete Exposure* (New York: Covici-Friede, 1935), 283.

[22] *The Jewish Peril: Protocols of the Learned Elders of Zion*, 5th ed. (The Britons, 1921), ii.

[23] B. Segel, *Die Protokolle der Weisen von Zion*, 171, quoted in Cohn, *Warrant for Genocide*, 181.

[24] Advertisement, *New York Times*, January 16, 1921, 30-31.

[25] In Albert Lee, *Henry Ford and the Jews* (New York: Stein and Day, 1980), 106, quoted in Jonathan R. Logsdon, "Power, Ignorance, and Anti-Semitism: Henry Ford and His War on the Jews," http://history.hanover.edu/hhr/99/hhr99_2.html.

[26] *New York Times*, August 17, 1920.

[27] John L. Bernstein, testimony, *Jewish Immigration Bulletin, Hebrew Immigrant Aid Society Monthly Report* (January 1921), quoted in Sanders, *Shores of Refuge*, 385.

13

In the Face of Genocide

(1918–1945)

Henry Buxbaum was one of the more than 100,000 Jews who served in the German army during World War I. He returned home to Germany to find that antisemitism was sweeping the nation. He later recalled:

> *You could taste antisemitism everywhere; the air of Germany was permeated by it. All the unavoidable consequences of military defeat, revolution, a ruinous inflation, the Versailles [peace treaty], the loss of the territories in the east and west, the unsettling social changes following in their wake—each and every thing was blamed on the Jews and/or the Communists, who for the convinced Jew-hater were interchangeable.[1]*

At the end of World War I in 1918, Europe was home to more than 9.5 million Jews. At the end of World War II in 1945, Europe's Jewish population was approximately 3.5 million. Some had immigrated to other continents, but most—nearly 6 million children, women, and men—had been murdered by the German government solely because they were Jews. Those murders are now collectively known as the Holocaust.

Antisemitism did not begin in Germany, or anywhere else, in 1918; Jews had been regarded as dangerous outsiders for centuries, and anti-Jewish feeling usually intensified in times of war and other upheaval. But during World War II, for the first time in history, a government, with the support of many of its people, had systematically hunted and then murdered Jews for no reason other than the fact that their parents or grandparents were Jews.

Why was this time different? The years after World War I were a time of change almost everywhere in the world. Many of those changes had begun earlier and were speeded up by the war. Others were linked to innovations in science, art, and music that altered the way people saw themselves and the world around them. These innovations made some people uneasy; they suggested that things were not always as they had seemed in the past. Other people were bewildered by the modern world and longed for a return to simpler times.

In times of great change and uncertainty, many people want simple explanations for things they cannot explain. In the years between the two world wars, some found those explanations in tales of so-called Jewish conspiracies. Perhaps that is why Buxbaum described German antisemitism as motivated not by religious zeal or a fanatical racism (although both existed) but by a belief that Germans were being victimized by "the Jews."

"BACKSTABBING" IN A DEFEATED GERMANY

In a single week in November 1918, Germany experienced earth-shattering changes. On November 9, Kaiser Wilhelm II gave up his throne and fled to the Netherlands. Within hours, the Social Democrats, then the largest political party in Germany's parliament, replaced the monarchy with a republic. The new government faced incredible challenges, including the possibility of a revolution like the one in Russia (see Chapter 12). The capital, Berlin, was so unsettled that lawmakers met in Weimar (about 180 miles to the southwest), and the newly established government was therefore known as the Weimar Republic.

Then on November 11, just two days after Germany became a republic, World War I ended with a cease-fire. Only then did many Germans realize that they had lost the war. Some were even more stunned when they learned the terms of the peace treaty signed at Versailles just outside Paris in 1919. Germany had to give up its colonies abroad and some territory at home, and the size of its army was restricted. The treaty also held Kaiser Wilhelm responsible for the war and required that Germany pay reparations to the victors.

As anger over the terms of the treaty grew, Germans increasingly insisted that someone had "stabbed the nation in the back." General Erich Ludendorff, a war hero, told lawmakers that Germany had been betrayed not by the men who had led the nation into war but by some Social Democrats, the Catholic Center Party, the socialists, and of course, the Jews. At the time, Germany's 500,000 Jews accounted for less than one percent of a total population of about 61 million.

By 1922, Ludendorff was focusing almost entirely on Jews as "the enemy." He wrote, "The supreme government of the Jewish people was working hand in hand with France and England. Perhaps it was leading them both."[2] As proof, Ludendorff cited the *Protocols of the Elders of Zion*

Germans expressed their anger over their defeat in the war by protesting the Treaty of Versailles.

(see Chapter 12), even though he was aware that the *Times* of London had recently exposed the document as a hoax. He believed that the *Times* was wrong or misled. So did some members of Germany's parliament. As one explained, "The revelations of the *Times* cannot touch, let alone destroy, the genuineness of the *Protocols*."[3]

Despite such talk, most Germans in 1919 knew that Germany had lost the war because the United States gave France and Britain the advantage when it declared war on Germany in 1917. The United States had gone to war because of German attacks on its ships.

In the end, Germany's new constitution guaranteed equal rights to all citizens, including Jews. And some Jews took advantage of the opportunity that those rights afforded them. Outraged, extreme nationalists began to call the Weimar Republic the "Jew republic." Yet of the 250 Germans who served as ministers between 1919 and 1933, only four were Jews. For many nationalists, even one Jew in government was one too many.

The same was true in other fields. When Albert Einstein was awarded the Nobel Prize in Physics in 1921, he was attacked for introducing "Jewish physics" into "German science." In 1929, Einstein, who had once lived in Switzerland, wrote:

When I came to Germany fifteen years ago I discovered for the first time that I was a Jew; and I owe this discovery more to Gentiles than to Jews. . . .

I saw worthy Jews basely caricatured, and the sight made my heart bleed. I saw how schools, comic papers, and innumerable other forces of the Gentile majority undermined the confidence of even the best of my fellow Jews, and felt that this could not be allowed to continue.[4]

Among the extreme nationalists who saw Jews as a threat to Germany was a drifter who had moved to Munich from Austria just before the war. His name was Adolf Hitler. In the early 1920s, he, like many other veterans, was angry and bitter about the way the war had ended. Like some of them, he joined an extremist political group later known as the National Socialist German Workers' Party (the Nazi Party, for short). He quickly became its leader.

Hitler believed that world history was a struggle to the death between Germans and other members of the so-called "Aryan race" and "the Jewish race," with the world's future dependent on the outcome of that struggle. His views were based on the virulent racism of his own time as well as the romantic nationalism that evolved in Germany in the early 1800s (see Chapter 9). It was a nationalism that idealized the *Volk*—the word literally means "people," but it also came to mean a "race" with a distinct culture and soul. Jews were seen as the opposite of the *Volk*. Hitler viewed Jews as a dangerous force that drove other races to ruin, as well as a "subhuman" cause of disease, disintegration, and death.

The first step in "saving" Germany from the Jews and other inferior races, from this perspective, was the destruction of the Weimar Republic. Like other extremist groups, the Nazis hired thugs and organized a private army to kill supporters of the republic. Between 1919 and 1922, 376 political assassinations took place in Germany. German Communists were held responsible for 22 of the murders. The other assassinations were the work of extreme nationalists. Most of their victims were Jews, in part because German nationalists believed that all Jews were Communists regardless of their actual party affiliation.

Germany's foreign minister, Walter Rathenau, was among those targeted by extremist groups. Rathenau was a wealthy Jewish businessman, writer, and thinker. During the war, the kaiser had asked him to reorganize the German economy to ensure that the military had the resources it needed. Without his efforts, Germany would probably have lost the war sooner. Yet many Germans were outraged when he was appointed foreign minister in 1922. Never before (or since) had a Jew held such an important position in German government. Almost daily, mobs could be heard chanting, "Kill off Walter Rathenau, the greedy goddamn Jewish sow!"

On the morning of June 24, 1922, Rathenau was murdered on his way to work. The two gunmen and their co-conspirators were veterans who belonged to right-wing groups. In July, the police finally closed in on them and killed one assassin; the other committed suicide. The government then brought the 13 surviving conspirators to trial. The men justified the murder by arguing that they were defending the nation from Rathenau, whom they regarded as an "Elder of Zion."

Despite such attitudes, many Germans observed a day of mourning. In Berlin, "hundreds of thousands" of workers streamed out of factories and marched "silently along the great thoroughfare lined by immense crowds."[5] That day, Chancellor Josef Wirth told lawmakers: "The real enemies of our country are those who instill this poison into our people. . . . The enemy stands on the right."[6]

HITLER'S RISE TO POWER

After Rathenau's murder, the violence in Germany intensified as extreme inflation took hold. During a period of inflation, prices rise continuously as the purchasing power of money declines. By 1923, the value of a German mark, the country's unit of currency, was dropping almost hourly; no matter how high wages rose, they could not keep up with soaring prices.

Even though Jews suffered from this inflation along with everyone else, they were increasingly blamed for the crisis. On November 5, 1923, at a time when the mark was almost worthless, a mob rushed into a section of Berlin that was home to many Jews from Russia and Poland. For two days, the rioters attacked those Jews and ransacked their shops.

In that tense atmosphere, Adolf Hitler saw an opportunity. On the night of November 8, he and his private army of storm troopers (*Sturmabteilung*, or SA) burst into a Munich beer hall. They were accompanied by General Ludendorff, a recent ally. Hitler fired two shots into the air and announced that a revolution had begun. But within days the uprising was over, and Hitler, Ludendorff, and their comrades were charged with treason.

Reporters from newspapers across the country covered the trial, which gave Hitler a chance to present himself as a "war hero" committed to "saving" Germany from the Weimar Republic, which he repeatedly referred to as a "Jew government." When the prosecution challenged such remarks, the judge ruled that Hitler and the other defendants had been "guided in their actions by a purely patriotic spirit and the noblest of selfless intentions."

The court acquitted Ludendorff; most of the others, including Hitler received the minimum sentence, five years in prison. However, the judges offered Hitler the prospect of parole after serving only six months (with the remaining four and a half years considered a suspended sentence). As an Austrian citizen convicted of treason, Hitler should have been deported. But the judge refused to enforce the law, saying, "In the case of a man whose thoughts and feelings are as German as Hitler's, the court is of the opinion that the intent and purpose of the law have no application."[7]

While in prison, Hitler and an associate wrote *Mein Kampf* ("My Struggle"), an autobiography that included Hitler's beliefs and plans for Germany's future. The book romanticized the *Volk* by comparing them to the evil and "soulless" Jews. Although many Germans shared these views, few were willing to go as far as Hitler did. Nevertheless, soon after he left prison in the summer of 1924 after having served only a year of his sentence, he and other Nazis decided to come to power legally and then turn Germany into a "racial state"—one that would guard the purity of the "Aryan race." As Joseph Goebbels, a key Nazi official, later wrote, the plan was to act as "wolves in sheep's clothing."

By the time Hitler and his associates had been released from prison in 1924, the hyperinflation had ended and Germany was prospering. As a result, the Nazis did poorly in the elections that year, and their popularity did not increase until October 1929, when a worldwide depression began. Germans felt the effects almost immediately. By December 1929, 1.5 million workers were unemployed. A month later, that number jumped to 2.5 million, and it kept climbing. Once again, the Nazis took advantage of a crisis by blaming everything on the Communists and the Jews.

In the September 1930 election, the Nazis were expected to win 50 seats in Germany's parliament. To the surprise of many, they went from 12 seats to 107 seats. Hitler now led the nation's second-largest political party. Nevertheless, in the November 1932 elections—the last free elections in the Weimar Republic—the Nazis lost three million votes and 34 seats in parliament. Even with those losses, however, they were now the nation's largest party—and in January 1933, President Paul von Hindenburg appointed Hitler chancellor of Germany. He was to head a coalition government.

Hitler and other Nazis were now poised to destroy the Weimar Republic and "restore" Germany and the "Aryan race" to greatness by ending so-called Jewish racial domination and eliminating the Communist threat. The resulting government would become know as the Third Reich. (*Reich* is the German word for "empire.") For the Nazis, the First Reich was the Holy Roman Empire (952–1806), and the Second Reich was the empire established as the result of unification of the German states in 1871. The Nazis were confident that the Third Reich would be the greatest of all.

DISMANTLING DEMOCRACY

To build the Third Reich, Hitler and his Nazi Party had to destroy the Weimar Republic. The first step took place not long after Hitler became chancellor. A fire broke out in the *Reichstag* (Germany's parliament) on February 27, 1933. When the police arrived, they found Marinus van der Lubbe, a Dutch Communist, at the scene of the crime. After they tortured him, he confessed to setting the fire but insisted that he had acted alone. The Nazis ignored the confession. Within days, they imprisoned 4,000 Communists and called for emergency measures to "combat treason." Hitler soon had the right to censor mail, to search homes, and to confiscate property without a reason.

At about the same time, Hitler appointed Goebbels head of a new department in the government—the Ministry of Public Enlightenment and Propaganda. Goebbels's job was to make sure that every film, radio program, book, magazine, picture, and musical composition showed Hitler and the Nazis as heroic guardians of the German *Volk*. Goebbels's job was also to ensure that Jews were portrayed as evildoers who threatened humanity.

In March, not long after the Nazis failed to win a solid majority in parliament, they proposed a new law that would grant Hitler legislative power as well as increase his executive powers for the next four years. Two-thirds of the nation's lawmakers, present and voting, would have to approve the bill, because it would alter Germany's constitution. It passed easily despite the opposition of the Social Democrats—mainly because many lawmakers who opposed the Nazis, particularly the Communists, were unable to vote, as they were now in prison or in exile. Known as the Enabling Act, the new law was later extended for an indefinite period of time.

The same day that the Enabling Act was passed, the government opened Dachau, its first concentration camp. People could be held there indefinitely, usually without being formally accused of a crime. The first inmates were Communists.

In preparation for the boycott of Jewish businesses on April 1, 1933, the Nazis hung signs that targeted Jews as "the enemy of the German people."

With these measures in place, the Nazis focused on the "Jewish threat." As part of a campaign to isolate Jews, Goebbels's new department called for a one-day boycott of Jewish businesses on April 1, 1933. The government, which still included officials who did not belong to the Nazi Party, approved the boycott. Although it was not a total success, no Christian religious leaders publicly condemned it, and many openly supported it.

The morning of the boycott, Edwin Landau, a veteran of World War I, put on his military medals and walked through streets lined with posters that read, "Germans, defend yourselves—don't buy from Jews!" After watching Nazis turn shoppers away from stores owned by Jews, he realized,

This land and this people that until now I had loved and treasured had suddenly become my enemy. So I was not a German anymore, or I was no longer supposed to be one. That, of course, cannot be settled in a few hours. But one thing I felt immediately: I was ashamed that I had once belonged to this people.[8]

Landau and many other Jews now realized that they could not depend on the government for protection. It no longer protected their physical safety, their property, or their civil rights. As a Jew from Nuremberg explained, "Anybody could accuse you of anything—and you were lost."[9]

Marta Appel described what school was now like for her daughters:

> [T]he teachers denounced all the Jews, without exception, as scoundrels and as the most destructive force in every country where they were living. My children were not permitted to leave the room during such a talk; they were compelled to stay and to listen; they had to feel all the other children's eyes looking and staring at them, the examples of an outcast race.[10]

Little by little, the Nazis separated Jews of all ages from their non-Jewish neighbors. New statutes legalized racial discrimination. On April 7, 1933, the Law for the Restoration of the Professional Civil Service went into effect. It removed "non-Aryans" from jobs in government to "restore"

© United States Holocaust Memorial Museum, from "Trau Keinem Fuchs..."

The translation of this sign is, "Jews are not welcome here." Included in the Nazis' campaign against the Jews were children's books that depicted Jews as dangerous outsiders who threatened Germany.

the civil service to "true Germans." The only exceptions were Jewish veterans, their fathers, and their sons.

Before the month was over, Jewish doctors who worked in the national health system lost their jobs. At about the same time, the government sharply limited the number of Jews who could attend a public high school or teach in one. As a result of these and similar laws, about 20 percent of all German Jews were soon out of work.

By April, Hitler's ideas about "race" were being applied to the nation's Protestant churches. More than 65 percent of the German people considered themselves Protestants, and most attended Lutheran churches. Although Hitler never intervened directly in the operation of those churches, he did appoint a "Reich bishop" to lead a "German Christian" movement that tried to link Protestant traditions to Nazi beliefs—including the notion that Jesus was not a Jew but an enemy of the Jews. Hitler also maintained that conversion did not turn a Jew into a Christian. He therefore targeted Christians of Jewish descent as well as Jews.

Protestants who opposed some of those ideas organized the "Confessing Church." Its leaders insisted on the right to be independent on religious issues but did not oppose Nazi "race laws." As a result, Christians of Jewish descent could no longer attend some churches and were segregated in others. Only a few ministers raised even timid objections to the new laws.

About 30 percent of Germany's population was Catholic. As a minority, Catholics were sometimes accused of not being "true Germans" because they "took orders from Rome." Over the years, they had protected their rights by organizing and supporting the Catholic Center Party and the Bavarian People's Party. In the 1920s, a number of Catholic bishops had openly opposed the Nazis, but in 1933, Pope Pius XI and Cardinal Eugenio Pacelli, a *nuntius*, or ambassador, to Germany and later secretary of state of the Vatican, signed an agreement with Hitler to protect the freedom and rights of Catholics in Germany. That agreement was one of Hitler's first foreign-policy successes, and it greatly enhanced his prestige.

Edith Stein was a Jew who converted to Catholicism in 1922. She later became a nun and a respected Catholic educator. In April 1933, she wrote a letter to the pope. In it, she argued:

> *Everything that happened [in Germany] and continues to happen on a daily basis originates with a government that calls itself "Christian." For weeks not only Jews but also thousands of faithful Catholics in Germany, and, I believe, all over the world have been waiting and*

hoping for the Church of Christ [the Roman Catholic Church] to
raise its voice to put a stop to this abuse of Christ's name. Is not this
idolization of race and governmental power which is being pounded
into the public consciousness by the radio open heresy? . . . Is not
all this diametrically opposed to the conduct of our Lord and Savior,
who, even on the cross, still prayed for his persecutors?[11]

Pius XI did not respond to the letter, nor did his successor, Cardinal
Pacelli, who became Pope Pius XII in 1939. As for Stein, the Nazis considered her a Jew because she had Jewish grandparents. She was murdered as
part of the "final solution" to the "Jewish problem."

Hitler enacted 42 anti-Jewish measures in 1933 and 19 more the
following year. Each aimed at protecting "Aryan blood" from contamina-
tion with "Jewish blood." Then, in September 1935, Hitler announced
two new laws at a party rally in Nuremberg. These laws were designed
to turn Germany into a "racial state"—a country in which "race" determined citizenship. The first law defined a German citizen as a person "of
German or kindred blood who proves by his conduct that he is willing and
suited loyally to serve the German people and the Reich."[12] The second
statute, called the Law for the Protection of German Blood and German
Honor, outlawed marriages between Jews and those of "German or kindred
blood."[13] People of "German blood" who were already married to Jews were
encouraged to dissolve those marriages.

A third decree, dated November 14, addressed the question of who
was a Jew. A Jew was now defined as a person with three Jewish grandparents. A person with one Jewish parent was not considered a Jew unless
he or she belonged to a Jewish community, the non-Jewish parent was
dead, or the state did not approve of his or her behavior. According to
some estimates, Germany was home to as many as 300,000 *Mischlinge*—
persons of "mixed race"—and another 100,000 who were affected to some
extent by racial laws.[14]

In the years that followed, the government dissolved Jewish businesses. Jews who owned large companies had to turn over their holdings
"in trust" to "Aryans." Jews could no longer work as physicians, dentists,
lawyers, or accountants in Germany. Between 1933 and 1937, more
than 129,000 Jews left the country. Of those who remained, one in every
three had been reduced to extreme poverty by 1939. Jews were not the
only people targeted by the German government. They also singled out
the Sinti and Roma (the so-called "Gypsies"), individuals with physical,
mental, or social disabilities, Jehovah's Witnesses, and homosexual men.

THE SEARCH FOR REFUGE

As Jews and others were scrambling to leave Germany, Hitler began to take over neighboring countries. In March 1938, he annexed Austria, his homeland, and almost immediately applied German racial laws to Austrian Jews. He then turned his attention to the western part of Czechoslovakia. By 1939, it had become a German protectorate, and Slovakia, the eastern part of the country, was an "independent state" allied to Germany. Here, too, racial laws went into effect almost immediately. As a result, the number of Jews desperate to emigrate skyrocketed. However, most had nowhere to go. In the 1930s, the Nazis were not only ones who viewed Jews as an evil "race."

In July 1938, delegates from 32 nations met in Evian, France, to discuss the growing "refugee crisis." None of the delegates referred to it as the "Jewish refugee crisis," even though everyone there knew the truth. The delegate from Australia set the tone when he bluntly told the group, "As we have no real racial problem in Australia, we are not desirous of importing one."[15] Others were less openly hostile but equally reluctant to admit more "refugees." Golda Meir, who later became prime minister of Israel, attended the conference as the Jewish observer from Palestine. As an observer, she was not permitted to speak. She later wrote:

> I don't think that anyone who didn't live through it can understand what I felt at Evian—a mixture of sorrow, rage, frustration, and horror. I wanted to get up and scream . . . . "Don't you know that these so-called numbers are human beings, people who may spend the rest of their lives in concentration camps, or wandering around the world like lepers, if you don't let them in?" Of course, I didn't know then that not concentration camps but death camps awaited the refugees whom no one wanted.[16]

Hitler responded to the meeting in Evian by accelerating his campaign against Jews. He began by expelling Russian Jews who had lived in Germany for decades. Poland feared that the 70,000 Jews with Polish passports would be the next to go. To keep them from returning, the Polish government required a special stamp on their passports. Although few wanted to return to Poland, they needed valid passports. Yet when they tried to get stamps, they were turned away.

The crisis came to a head when Poland announced that no stamps would be issued after October 31, 1938. On October 26, the Germans expelled all Jews with Polish passports. When Poland refused to accept them, thousands ended up in makeshift camps along the border between the two nations. Among them were the parents of Herschel Grynszpan, a 17-year-old student in Paris. Frustrated by his inability to help his family, he marched into the German embassy in Paris and shot Ernst vom Rath, a low-level embassy official.

THE NIGHT OF THE POGROM

Ernst vom Rath died on November 9, two days after the shooting. That night, the Nazis claimed, the German people rose "spontaneously" to avenge his death. In fact, the Nazis had planned the violence. Police officers watched as Nazi storm troopers looted thousands of Jewish homes and businesses, set fire to more than 300 synagogues in Greater Germany (Germany and Austria), and killed about 90 Jews. The government also shipped approximately 30,000 Jewish men to concentration camps.

This pogrom was called *Kristallnacht* ("the night of broken glass"), because of the destruction it brought. Years later, many Jews would recall that night as a turning point in their lives. When they asked non-Jewish friends for help, most were turned away. This convinced even Jews who were reluctant to emigrate that they had no future in Germany.

Non-Jews also made choices. Some secretly came to the aid of their Jewish neighbors but feared speaking or acting openly on their behalf. More vocal were Germans who supported the Nazis but disapproved of the violence. One wrote:

> *Far be it from me to disregard the sins that many members of the Jewish people have committed against our Fatherland, especially during the last decades; also, far be it from me to deny the right of orderly and moderate proceedings against the Jewish race. But not only will I by no means justify the numerous excesses against Jewry that took place on and after November ninth of this year . . . but I reject them, deeply ashamed, as they are a blot on the good name of the Germans.*

> *First of all, I, as a Protestant Christian, have no doubt that the commitment and toleration of such reprisals will evoke the wrath of God against our people and Fatherland, if there is a God in heaven. Just as Israel is cursed and on trial because they were the first who rejected Christ, so surely the same curse will fall upon each and every nation that by similar deeds, denies Christ in the same way.*[17]

The writer thought Jews were rightly suffering for "rejecting Christ" but drew the line at killing them or destroying property.

In 1938, U.S. President Franklin D. Roosevelt was one of the few world leaders to recall his ambassador to Germany in order to express outrage at the pogrom. This is the traditional way that one nation shows disapproval of the policies of another. Despite the recall, Roosevelt did not offer to take in additional Jewish refugees from Germany. According to opinion polls, most Americans shared his disgust at the burning of synagogues but opposed even a small increase in immigration. Still suffering in the Great Depression, they feared that refugees might take American jobs.

By the end of 1938, Jews in Germany had been fined one billion marks for the damage done to them on the night of the pogrom. In addition, they could no longer own or even drive a car; attend theaters, movie houses, concert halls, or events at sports arenas; or use public parks and swimming pools. The Gestapo, the German secret police, even went door to door confiscating radios. Jewish children were banned from public schools, and every Jew had to adopt a "Jewish" middle name—Israel for the men and Sarah for the women.

Hitler also continued to eye neighboring countries. In the summer of 1939, his focus was on Poland. In preparation for an invasion, he signed a treaty with Joseph Stalin, the head of the Soviet Union. The two dictators vowed not to attack one another even if one declared war on an ally of the other. They also secretly agreed to divide up Poland.

After years of anti-Communist propaganda, many Germans were stunned by the pact. (So were many Russians.) Although Goebbels claimed that Hitler was opposed only to German Communists, not to Russian ones, many Germans felt uneasy. The uneasiness grew on September 1, 1939, when Germany invaded Poland. Two days later, Britain and France declared war on Germany: World War II had begun. On one side were the Allies. In 1939, they included not only Britain, France, and Poland but also the Netherlands, Luxembourg, and Belgium. On the other side were the Axis powers. In Europe, the Axis powers included Germany, Italy, Hungary, Romania, and Bulgaria; in Asia, Japan was part of the Axis. (The Soviet Union, despite its treaty with Germany, was not part of the Axis and did not declare war on the Allies.)

A RACIAL WAR WITHIN A WORLD WAR

Between September 3, 1939, and October 1941, the Axis powers enjoyed an almost unbroken string of military victories. Within months of conquering western Poland (the Soviets took over eastern Poland), the Germans defeated Denmark and Norway and then moved west to the Netherlands, Belgium, and Luxembourg. By June 1940, the Germans were marching triumphantly through the streets of Paris. That summer, Britain was Hitler's only remaining opponent. Yet despite daily bombings, the British refused to yield.

In every country the Germans occupied, they waged a "racial war" against Jews and other "racial enemies." They began by stripping Jews of all rights and confiscating their property. Hermann Göring, the head of the Gestapo until 1934, viewed these measures as essential. "In the final analysis," he argued, "it is about whether the German and Aryan prevails here, or whether the Jew rules the world."[18]

Jews were a small, powerless, and increasingly poverty-stricken minority almost everywhere in Europe. Yet the Nazis maintained that their "removal" was essential to Germany's future. Earlier, the Nazis had tried to make life so difficult for Jews that they would have little choice but to leave the country. With the conquest of Poland in 1939, however, the number of Jews under German rule more than doubled. At that time, Poland was home to more than three million Jews, and about two million of them were living in what had become German-occupied Poland. (The rest lived in what was now the Soviet-controlled part of Poland.)

In 1939, the Nazis addressed the "Jewish question" by calling for a new Pale of Settlement, a reservation to contain and isolate Jews much like the one in Russia in the 1800s (see Chapter 11). It would be located near the German-occupied city of Lublin, Poland. There, Germany would dump Jews from all of the areas it occupied. But within a month or two, the deportations suddenly stopped. According to a German report, officials in Lublin "were unable to cope with the difficulties which arose from the continuous dumping of thousands of Jews without any provision having been made for their housing and maintenance."[19] Those difficulties included a typhoid epidemic that could easily have spread to other parts of Poland and to Germany itself.

For a time, the Nazis thought about shipping Jews to Madagascar, a French colony off the east coast of Africa, but the extended war with Britain meant that Germany did not control the seas; Jews could not be shipped to Africa. Instead, the Germans expelled Jews from rural areas in Poland and concentrated them in crowded ghettos in large cities. The ghettos and the hundreds of concentration camps the Germans built in Poland quickly became a source of slave labor for the German occupation authorities as well as for large businesses.

1941: A TURNING POINT

Turning points in both World War II and Hitler's "great racial war" came in 1941. That spring, the Germans moved south into Greece and Yugoslavia in the hope of securing their rear areas and removing the possibility of British-led opposition. In June, despite the pact Hitler signed with Joseph Stalin, Germany invaded the Soviet Union. As part of that assault, the Germans drove the Soviet army out of eastern Poland. On the day the invasion began, Hitler escalated the war against the Jews. It was no longer a war of containment; increasingly, it was one of annihilation. The goal was the destruction of the Jewish people. There had been killings earlier, but the murders now became more systematic, deliberate, and routine.

In the summer of 1941, the *Einsatzgruppen*—four paramilitary units whose mission was to find and murder Jews—followed the German army as it advanced into previously held Soviet territory. They would enter a village or town and remove all Jews to a nearby isolated area, where they were shot and killed. In larger cities, the *Einsatzgruppen* could not kill

© United States Holocaust Memorial Museum / YIVO Institute, courtesy of Sharon Paquette

German soldiers and local residents took photographs of the mass murders. These pictures showed Jews taken to isolated areas where they were shot and killed.

everyone at once. Instead, they collected hundreds of people and trucked them to open pits, where they were slaughtered.

Historians estimate that 1.5 million Jews died in massacres like the one that occurred near Kiev on September 29–30, 1941. In two days, 33,771 Jewish children, women, and men were shot and buried in a ravine known as Babi Yar; this is believed to be the largest mass murder of the war.

Rivka Yosselevska, a survivor of one of those massacres, later testified about what happened when the *Einsatzgruppen* entered her town on a Sabbath afternoon in August 1942. She and other Jews were herded out of their homes while soldiers searched for valuables. Toward sunrise, a large truck took the Jews away. Those who could not fit into the truck— including Yosselevscka and her child—were forced to run behind it. When they arrived at their destination, they were ordered to undress and then line up. At that point the killings began.

The Germans murdered Yosselevscka's entire family, including her 80-year-old grandmother. Only she and her young daughter remained alive. Then it was their turn. She recalled:

> We turned towards the grave and then [a soldier] turned around and asked "Whom shall I shoot first?" . . . I did not answer. I felt him take the child from my arms. The child cried out and was shot immediately. And then he aimed at me. . . . I heard a shot, but I continued to stand. . . . Then I fell to the ground into the pit amongst the bodies. . . . I thought I was dead, that this was the feeling which comes after death. Then I felt that I was choking; people falling over me. . . . I was choking, strangling, but I tried to save myself, to find some air to breathe, and then I felt that I was climbing to the top of the grave above the bodies. . . . I came up on top of the grave. . . . I did not know the place, so many bodies were lying all over . . . not all of them dead, but in their last sufferings; naked; shot, but not dead.[20]

A few others emerged from the mass grave, and together they tried to pull out other survivors. Then, suddenly, the Germans returned. This time, Yosselevska was one of just four survivors.

> I was praying for death to come. I was praying for the grave to be opened and to swallow me alive. Blood was spurting from the grave in many places, like a well of water. . . . I cried out to my mother, to my father, "Why did they not kill me? What was my sin? I have no

one to go to. I saw them all being killed. Why was I spared? Why was I not killed?"[21]

Rivka Yosselevscka's questions have no answers. But historians and scholars have struggled to respond to other questions raised by the mass murders. How did the perpetrators come to accept as "necessary" or "good" what, until then, had been widely understood as "evil"—the murder of an entire people? Some historians have studied testimony given at trials in the 1960s and 1970s by 210 men from German Reserve Police Battalion 101. The men were specifically asked about their participation in the battalion's first mass killing on July 13, 1942.

Before the mission got under way, the battalion commander offered to reassign anyone unwilling to participate in the killings. About a dozen men stepped forward. They were not punished but were told to await further orders. Once the killing began, a few more asked to be relieved, but most continued to the end. Very few belonged to the Nazi Party, and not one described himself as an antisemite.

Why would a soldier kill an 80-year-old grandmother or a child in her mother's arms? Some people point to years of antisemitic propaganda and the teaching of contempt for Jews by both political and religious leaders. Others focus on the way war desensitizes soldiers. Still others stress the importance of obedience in wartime or the ambitions of soldiers eager to move up in the ranks. All of these factors may have come together in a "perfect storm."

Historian Christopher Browning, who studied interviews with the men of Police Battalion 101, has expressed doubt as to whether most of the men embraced the Nazi ideology, but he warned:

> *[I]t is also doubtful that they were immune to "the influence of the times," . . . to the incessant proclamation of German superiority and incitement of contempt and hatred for the Jewish enemy. Nothing helped the Nazis to wage a race war so much as the war itself. In wartime, when it was all too usual to exclude the enemy from the community of human obligation, it was also all too easy to subsume the Jews into the "image of the enemy."[22]*

Mass killings like the one Rivka Yosselevscka described were impossible to keep secret. Too many people participated in them. So the Germans looked for alternatives. Before long, they were testing the idea of using concentration camps as death camps. In these camps, the Germans would use a killing method that they were already secretly employing on Germans with physical or mental disabilities: gassing.

On December 7, 1941, as this plan was taking shape, Japan, one of the Axis powers, bombed the U.S. naval base at Pearl Harbor, Hawaii— then a U.S. territory. The next day, the United States declared war on Japan. On December 11, Germany, as an ally of Japan, declared war on the United States, and the United States responded with its own declaration of war.

By late 1942, the tide had turned in the war. Hitler had expected to easily defeat the Soviet Union. To his surprise, the Soviets fought fiercely and even put the German army on the defensive. At the same time, British and American forces began pushing the Germans out of North Africa, where they were threatening British colonies.

THE ACCELERATION OF THE "FINAL SOLUTION"

In January 1942, top Nazi and government officials met in the Berlin suburb of Wannsee to work out the details of their plans for "the final solution of the Jewish question." Although mass shootings continued, death camps, complete with gas chambers, would now play the major role in the genocide. Chelmno was the first; it opened in December of 1941, a few weeks before the meeting at Wannsee. By mid summer, three additional camps were ready—Belzec, Sobibor, and Treblinka. In these four camps alone, the Nazis murdered nearly two million Jews. Mass killings also took place at Majdanek (about 200,000 Jews and Poles) and Auschwitz-Birkenau, in German occupied Poland.

Auschwitz was the largest and the most infamous of the camps. At the peak of its operations, more than 12,000 people were murdered there each day—about one million in total, and all but about 122,000 were Jews. Rudolf Hoess, the commandant of Auschwitz, later described the "extermination procedure" there:

> *Jews selected for gassing were taken as quietly as possible to the crematoriums, the men being separated from the women. In the undressing rooms, prisoners of the special detachment, detailed for this purpose, would tell them in their own language that they were going to be bathed and deloused, that they must leave their clothes neatly together and above all remember where they had put them, so that they would be able to find them again quickly after the delousing. . . . After undressing, the Jews went into the gas chambers, which were*

furnished with showers and water pipes and gave a realistic impression of a bath house.[23]

Hoess' words made the process seem orderly and almost clinical. In fact, it was neither. Each day, hundreds of terrified children, women, and men were pushed into gas chambers. The Germans sometimes watched through peepholes as their victims gasped for air; the heavy doors muffled their screams. Within 20 minutes, everyone in the chamber was dead. The door was then opened so that Jewish prisoners who were kept alive for a time could dispose of the corpses, remove gold teeth, and cut off the hair of the women.

The Nazis melted down the gold, and they sent the women's hair to mattress factories to use as stuffing. Clothing and other possessions were also shipped to Germany. The German state railway company even charged fares for transporting Jews to their deaths, with children at half price. Officials at the Reich Security main office paid for the tickets with money and other property they confiscated from Jewish prisoners.[24]

Topf & Sons, an engineering firm, designed and maintained the furnaces used in the crematoria at Auschwitz. Medical researchers carried out medical "experiments" on the victims and reported their findings in scientific journals. For them and many other people the murders were a business or professional opportunity.

Not everyone brought to a camp like Auschwitz was killed immediately; some were used for slave labor. Filip Müller, a Slovakian Jew, was deported to Auschwitz and then assigned to a *Sonderkommado*, or special work unit. He later wrote:

> *The Ten Commandments . . . did not prevail here: Auschwitz had its own laws and macabre values. At Auschwitz gold teeth might buy a bowl of turnip soup; at Auschwitz a camp orchestra would play cheerful military music, not only in the morning when the prisoners marched out to work, but also at night when, bruised and battered, they struggled back carrying their dead comrades.*

> *. . . . Auschwitz was a place where every European language was spoken; it was also a place where people died, not only from starvation, sickness and epidemics, but from being battered to death, killed by having phenol [a poisonous acid] injected into their heart, or driven into the gas chamber. This wretched piece of land in eastern Europe was under the sway of the SS whose members regarded themselves*

as the elite of the German nation, a nation which had given to the world not only great writers and composers but also men like Adolf Hitler. The little Polish town of Oswiecim, which the Nazis called Auschwitz, had been turned into an inferno, and anyone taken there by an unkind fate might regard himself truly forsaken by God and his fellow men.[25]

Hitler was not satisfied with just eliminating Jews from German-occupied territory. He wanted his allies to turn over their Jews as well. In southern France, the Nazis had set up a puppet government under French leadership; it was known as Vichy France, because the town of Vichy served as its capital. In May 1942, Vichy's leaders voluntarily gave up Jewish refugees from Germany and central Europe, but they were more reluctant to expel French Jews.

Hungarians also resisted the idea of deporting their own Jews but willingly turned over to the Nazis 20,000 Jewish refugees from other parts of Europe. Italy was Germany's chief ally. It had its own racial laws and concentration camps but refused to take part in the genocide. Only after Germany took over the country in 1943 were Italian Jews shipped to death camps.

Bulgaria was also an ally of Germany. In March 1943, Bulgarian authorities deported all of the Jews from the territories Bulgaria had annexed in Macedonia (formerly part of Yugoslavia) and Thrace (formerly part of Greece). When the Germans pressured Bulgaria to deport its own Jews, the king initially agreed. He canceled the order only after receiving protests from thousands of ordinary citizens as well as leaders in the Bulgarian parliament and the Eastern Orthodox Church. As a result, most of Bulgaria's approximately 48,000 Jews survived the Holocaust.

RESISTANCE AND RESCUE

Events in the Warsaw ghetto, the largest in German-occupied Europe, reveal how antisemitism increased the risks of both resistance and rescue. Soon after the invasion of Poland in 1939, the Germans isolated Jews from their neighbors and initiated a propaganda campaign aimed at Poles. As part of that campaign, Jewish residential areas were routinely referred to as "plague-infected." In 1940, the Germans ordered Jews to build a wall around the "Jewish area." In June, they posted signs warning Poles of an "epidemic."

By November, every Jew in Warsaw was confined to a locked ghetto. There, one-third of the city's population was crammed into 2.4 percent

A German photographer took this picture during the final days of the revolt in the Warsaw ghetto. Notice that the fires are still burning, even as German soldiers march newly captured Jews to trains headed for Treblinka, a death camp in Poland.

of the land. Michael Mazor, a ghetto resident, disagreed with those who compared the Warsaw ghetto to those of the 1500s (see Chapter 7). He pointed out that in earlier times, ghettos "were not completely cut off from the world: Jews could leave them by day."[26]

It was only in the twentieth century, Mazor wrote, "especially in Warsaw," that the ghetto became "an organized form of death."[27] In January 1941, the Germans recorded 898 deaths in the Warsaw ghetto; in January 1942, the number of deaths was 5,123. The causes included starvation, disease, and exposure as well as punishment for "defying" the Nazis.

Then, on July 23, 1942, the Germans began to empty the ghetto by deporting 300,000 Jews to Treblinka, a death camp. Two days after the deportations began, the young members of the ZOB (the initials in Polish stand for Jewish Fighting Organization) called for armed resistance. They were joined at the last minute by a second organization known as the Jewish Military Organization. The two worked together under the leadership of Mordecai Anielewicz. When the Nazis began a new round of deportations in January 1943, the two groups attacked with handmade bombs and a few smuggled guns. They were heartened when, soon after, the deportations stopped for a time. What they did not know was that the Germans were preparing for a final assault on the ghetto.

On April 19, 1943, the eve of Hitler's birthday and the first day of Passover, General Jürgen Stroop arrived in Warsaw with 2,100 soldiers. He planned to present Hitler with a "Jew-free" city for his birthday. Once again, Warsaw Jews fought back. Yitzhak Zuckerman, a leader of the ZOB, said of their efforts:

> *This was a war of less than a thousand people against a mighty army, and no one doubted how it would turn out. This isn't a subject for study in a military school. Not the weapons, not the operations, not the tactics. If there's a school to study the* human spirit, *there it should be a major subject. The really important things were inherent in the force shown by Jewish youth, after years of degradation, to rise up against their destroyers and determine what death they would choose: Treblinka or Uprising. I don't know if there's a standard to measure that.[28]*

Jews in the Warsaw ghetto held out against the Germans for nearly a month. On May 16, after the Germans blew up the Great Synagogue in Warsaw, General Stroop proclaimed the end of "the Jewish Residential Quarter of Warsaw." Only a few Jews managed to escape. Among them was Krystyna Budnicka, the youngest of the eight children in her family. By the age of 11, she had lost two brothers, along with their wives and children. They were among the thousands shipped to Treblinka.

Aware that more deportations were to come, Krystyna's remaining brothers worked with neighbors to build a hiding place beneath their apartment building. They dug a tunnel connecting the hideout to the city's sewers and gathered whatever provisions they could find in a starving ghetto. The family and a dozen neighbors hid in the bunker shortly before the uprising. Krystyna recalled:

> *Many people in our bunker couldn't stand [being confined] and went out from the sewers straight into the bullets of Germans waiting by the manhole. Finally, convinced that they had killed the last Jew in the ghetto, the Germans calmed down a bit and stopped sniffing around and tracking so much. . . .*
>
> *Thus we survived several months, but even our starvation food rations came to an end at last. . . . Plans were made for gradually leaving the bunker.[29]*

The plans fell through, however, when the Germans discovered their hideout. Krystyna and her family managed to take shelter in the sewers. By the time they were rescued by Poles, it was September 1943 and Krystyna, her sister-in-law Anka, and her brothers Rafal and Itdl were all that remained of the family; all four were "living corpses" too weak to walk. Itdl died a short time later, at the age of 13. Then Rafal was betrayed by Poles who spotted him. He was then taken to Gestapo headquarters, where he was murdered.

Poles willing to resist the Nazis cared for Krystyna and Anka until August 1944, when the two had to flee Warsaw, which was in flames. As they left the city, they met a few nuns who were traveling with a group of orphans. Anka decided that Krystyna would be safer with them. The nuns accepted her, "although not even for a moment did they have any doubts about my origins."[30]

Krystyna's story highlights the complex relationship between Jews and non-Jews in war-torn Europe. The story was much the same in other places, where individuals like Oscar Schindler or groups like the Protestants in Le Chambon, France, tried to rescue Jews despite the risks. Even with their aid, however, the losses were staggering.

WORLD RESPONSES

Poland was not the only place where antisemitism complicated resistance and rescue. Soon after the German invasion of the Soviet Union in June 1941, the first rumors of mass murders in German-occupied Europe began to circulate, and reactions were varied.

Pope Pius XII knew about the mass killings as early as the fall of 1941. On Christmas in 1942, he gave a speech in which he referred to the "hundreds of thousands who, without any fault of their own, sometimes only by reason of their nationality or race, are marked down for death or gradual extinction."[31] Although he was clearly referring to Jews, he never mentioned them by name. Some historians believe that the pope, like many other Europeans during the war, guarded his words because he feared German retaliation.

Journalists were also reluctant to publish stories of mass murders that seemed too incredible to be true. So even when such stories were published, they were often buried in the back of the newspaper or labeled as rumors. Then, on December 13, 1942, Edward R. Murrow, a radio reporter, told listeners, "Millions of human beings, most of them Jews, are being gathered up with ruthless efficiency and murdered. . . . The phrase 'concentration camps' is obsolete. . . . It is now possible only to speak of extermination camps."[32] Four days later, the Allies confirmed a memo that documented the murders. It was issued by the Polish government-in-exile.

Although the Allies acknowledged the mass murders, they insisted that the best way to end them was by winning the war. A number of people, fearing that victory would come too late, organized protests and marches. Some placed ads in newspapers highlighting not only failures to help Jews but also successes. The biggest stumbling block turned out to be the U.S. State Department.

In January 1944, 13 months after the Allies had confirmed the genocide, Josiah DuBois, a lawyer in the U.S. Treasury Department, prepared a memo with the help of his colleagues John Pehle and Randolph Paul. It was sent to their boss, Henry Morgenthau, Jr., then secretary of the treasury. It stated, in part:

> *One of the greatest crimes in history, the slaughter of the Jewish people in Europe, is continuing unabated. . . .*
>
> *I am convinced on the basis of the information which is available to me that certain officials in our State Department, which is charged with carrying out [programs for saving European Jews], have been guilty not only of gross procrastination and wilful failure to act, but even of wilful attempts to prevent action from being taken to rescue Jews from Hitler.*
>
> *I fully recognize the graveness of this statement and I make it only after having most carefully weighed the shocking facts which have come to my attention over the last several months.*
>
> *Unless remedial steps of a drastic nature are taken, and taken immediately, I am certain that no effective action will be taken by this government to prevent the complete extermination of the Jews in German controlled Europe, and this Government will have to share for all time the responsibility for this extermination.*[33]

After reviewing the evidence, Morgenthau—one of the first Jews to hold a cabinet position in the United States—condensed the report and presented it to Roosevelt. The president responded by setting up the War Refugee Board, under Morgenthau's supervision. John Pehle, who headed the board later, described its efforts as "too little, too late." Nevertheless, it had some success.

In 1944, Hungarian Jews were the only large group of Jews still alive in German-occupied Europe. Earlier, Hungary, although an ally of Germany, had refused to send Jews to death camps. Now, with the Axis powers' defeat all but certain, the Germans (with the help of the Arrow Cross, a pro-Nazi group in Hungary) took over the Hungarian government with the intention of shipping all of that nation's Jews to Auschwitz. When two Jews from Slovakia—Rudolf Vrba and Alfred Wetzler—overheard guards in Auschwitz discussing the plan, they decided to alert the world.

With the help of other prisoners, the two men managed to escape from Auschwitz and eventually reach Slovakia, where they found an underground group willing to help them. Working with local Jewish leaders, they prepared a detailed description of Auschwitz, complete with diagrams locating the gas chambers and crematoria. They also spelled out everything they had learned about German plans to exterminate Hungarian Jews. In late April, their report reached the Jewish underground in Hungary. Copies were also sent to the Vatican and to officials in the United States and Britain, and excerpts from the document appeared in Swiss and American newspapers. The two men joined the resistance and waited for the world to respond.

In early June, two more prisoners escaped from Auschwitz and also found their way to Slovakia. They announced that despite the Vrba-Wetzler report, tens of thousands of Hungarian Jews had been murdered and that more were on their way to Auschwitz. They combined their account of recent activities at the camp with the earlier report, and the resistance movement used the new report to pressure Hungarian officials, who were now fearful of retribution after the war. As a result, the deportations ended in July of 1944.

As part of the American effort to save Hungarian Jews, the War Refugee Board, with the help of the Swedish government, sent Raoul Wallenberg to Hungary as a special agent. When the 32-year-old businessman arrived in July, more than 400,000 Hungarian Jews had already been sent to Auschwitz. Just 250,000 remained. Wallenberg presented himself as a Swedish passport officer and began issuing passports to Jews, much as diplomats like Charles Lutz of the Swiss embassy and the papal *nuncio* had done earlier on a smaller scale. Wallenberg issued 4,500 passports and honored thousands of others forged by Jewish youth groups in Hungary.

The Germans, however, would not let Jews use the passports to leave the country. So with money provided by the War Refugee Board,

THE HOLOCAUST

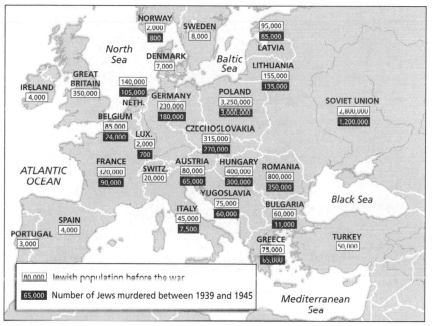

In 1939, Europe was home to about 9 million Jews; two out of every three of them were murdered during the war. In Germany, only about 20 percent survived; in Hungary, the percentage was a little higher, about 25 percent; but in Poland, only 8 percent were still alive.

Wallenberg bought or rented 32 buildings to house 20,000 Jews awaiting "emigration" to Sweden. Despite his efforts to save Jews, he was taken prisoner when the Soviet army liberated Budapest in January 1945. No one in the West knows why or exactly what happened to him, although documents that the Russians finally made public in 1991 reveal that he died while in their custody.

AT WAR'S END

In January 1945, as the Russians approached Auschwitz and other camps in Poland, the Germans forced thousands of prisoners to trudge through ice and snow to camps in Germany. About 250,000 died along the way. By spring, the Americans and the British were entering Germany. So were a number of war correspondents, including the American writer Meyer Levin. Within days of his arrival in Germany, a Polish refugee took Levin to see the camp outside Ohrdruf. He later described what he saw that day:

Gen. Eisenhower and other U.S. officials including Gens. Patton and Bradley viewed the charred remains of Jews and other prisoners. Those remains were burnt before German officials fled the camps.

We drove through the gate and halted. A circle of dead men lay there, in the striped slave uniforms which we now saw for the first time; these cadavers were fleshless; in back of each tight-skinned shaven skull was a bullethole.

The Pole opened the door of a shed. There was a cordwood stack of stiff naked human bodies, a stack as high as we stood. The bodies were flat and yellow as lumber. A yellow disinfectant was scattered over the pile.

We had known. The world had vaguely heard. But until now no one of us had looked on this. . . .

There is not often a meaning in being first, in getting somewhere first so as to rush out a moment ahead of the others with the "news"; but today I somehow knew that I had had to find and experience this without anyone's having told what it would be like. This was part of my personal quest. This was the source of the fear and the guilt in every human who remained alive. For human beings had had it in them to do this, and we were of the same species.[34]

A few days later, U.S. General Dwight D. Eisenhower, the supreme commander of the Allied forces in Europe, and Generals Omar Bradley and George S. Patton, Jr., also toured Ohrdruf. Eisenhower later described his response:

> *I visited every nook and cranny of the camp because I felt it my duty to be in a position from then on to testify at first hand about these things in case there ever grew up at home the belief or the assumption that "the stories of Nazi brutality were just propaganda."* . . . *I not only did so but as soon as I returned to Patton's headquarters that evening I sent communications to both Washington and London, urging the two governments to send instantly to Germany a random group of newspaper editors and representative groups from the national legislatures. I felt that the evidence should be immediately placed before the American and British publics in a fashion that would leave no room for cynical doubt.*[35]

Eisenhower insisted that Germans from a nearby town visit the camp so that they could see what had been done in their name. He also required that American soldiers tour the camp, so that they could see the evil they were fighting. Despite these efforts, many Jewish survivors found that they were still outsiders who were no more welcome in 1945 than they had been in 1939, the year the war began.

---

[1] Henry Buxbaum, "Recollections," in Monika Richarz, ed., *Jewish Life in Germany: Memoirs from Three Centuries*, trans. Stella P. Rosenfeld and Sidney Rosenfeld (Bloomington: Indiana University Press, 1991), 303.

[2] E. Ludendorff, *Kriegführung und Politik*, 2nd ed. (Berlin 1922), 51, quoted in Norman Cohn, *Warrant for Genocide: The Myth of the Jewish World Conspiracy and the "Protocols of the Elders of Zion"* (London: Serif, 1996), 149.

[3] *Deutches Tageblatt*, August 23, 1921, quoted in Cohn, *Warrant for Genocide*, 150.

[4] Albert Einstein to Willy Hellpach, Summer 1929, quoted in David E. Rowe and Robert Schulmann, *Einstein on Politics: His Private Thoughts and Public Stands on Nationalism, Zionism, War, Peace, and the Bomb* (Princeton: Princeton University Press, 2007), 170–171.

[5] Harry Kessler, *Walter Rathenau: His Life and Work* (New York, 1944), quoted in Howard M. Sachar, *Dreamland: Europeans and Jews in the Aftermath of the Great War* (New York: Alfred A. Knopf, 2002), 252.

[6] Quoted in Sachar, *Dreamland*, 252–253.

[7] State Archives, Munich, Staatsanw. Munich 3098, Decision 44, quoted in Ingo Müller, *Hitler's Justice: The Courts of the Third Reich*, trans. Deborah Lucas Schneider (Cambridge, MA: Harvard University Press, 1991), 16.

[8] Edwin Landau, "Recollections," in Monika Richarz, ed., *Jewish Life in Germany*, 310–311.

[9] Liselotte Kahn, Leo Baeck Institute (New York), 117, quoted in Marion A. Kaplan, *Between Dignity and Despair: Jewish Life in Nazi Germany* (New York: Oxford University Press, 1990), 20.

[10] Marta Appel, "Recollections," in Monika Richarz, ed., *Jewish Life in Germany*, 353–354.

11 "Letter of Saint Edith Stein to Pope Pius XI in 1933," accessed March 24, 2011, http://www.baltimorecarmel.org/saints/Stein/letter to pope.htm.

12 Reich Citizenship Law, September 15, 1935, quoted in Lucy S. Dawidowicz, ed., *A Holocaust Reader*, (New York: Behrman House, 1976), 45–47.

13 Law for the Protection of German Blood and German Honor, September 15, 1935, quoted in Dawidowicz, ed., *A Holocaust Reader*, 47–48.

14 Kaplan, *Between Dignity and Despair*, 75.

15 Quoted in Howard M. Sachar, *A History of the Jews in the Modern World* (New York: Vintage Books, 2005), 516.

16 Golda Meir, *My Life* (New York: G. P. Putnam's Sons, 1975), 158.

17 A Protestant clergyman from Berlin to Kitler, Goering, Goebbles, et al., December 1938, in Otto Dov Kulka, "Popular Christian Attitudes in the Third Reich to National Socialist Policies Towards the Jews," Papers Presented at the International Symposium on Judaism and Christianity Under the Impact of National Socialism, 1919–1945, June 1982 (Jerusalem: Historical Society of Israel, 1982), 252, trans. Paul R. Mendes-Flohr, quoted in Paul Mendes-Flohr and Jehuda Reinharz, eds., *The Jew in the Modern World: A Documentary History*, 2nd ed. (New York: Oxford University Press, 1995), 654.

18 In Jost Dulffler, *Deutsche Geschichte 1933–1945* (Stuttgart, 1992), 125, quoted in Michael Burleigh, *The Third Reich: A New History* (New York: Hill and Wang, 2000), 571.

19 *Jewish Chronicle*, December 15, 1939, quoted in Ronald Sanders, *Shores of Refuge: A Hundred Years of Jewish Emigration* (New York: Schocken Books, 1988), 477.

20 "Testimony by Mrs. Rivka Yosselevscka, Uncorrected English transcript of the Eichmann trial (mimeographed), May 8, 1961, section 30, pp. L1–N1," in Raul Hilberg, ed., *Documents of Destruction: Germany and Jewry, 1933–1945* (Chicago: Quadrangle Books, 1971), 59–62.

21 Ibid.

22 Christopher R. Browning, *Ordinary Men: Reserve Police Battalion 101 and the Final Solution in Poland* (New York: HarperCollins, 1998), 186.

23 Rudolf Hoess, *Commandant of Auschwitz: The Autobiography of Rudolf Hoess* (Cleveland: World Publishers, 1959), 223.

24 Claude Lanzmann, *Shoah: The Complete Text of the Acclaimed Holocaust Film* (New York: Pantheon, 1985), 141–143.

25 Filip Müller, *Eyewitness Auschwitz: Three Years in the Gas Chambers*, ed. and trans. Susanne Flatauer (New York: Stein and Day, 1979), 2.

26 Michel Mazor, *The Vanished City: Everyday Life in the Warsaw Ghetto*, trans. David Jacobson (New York: Marsilio, 1993), 19.

27 Ibid.

28 Yitzhak Zuckerman, *A Surplus of Memory: Chronicle of the Warsaw Ghetto Uprising*, trans. and ed. Barbara Harshav (Berkeley: University of California Press, 1993), xiii. Original emphasis.

29 Wiktoria Śliwowska, ed., Julian and Fay Bussgang trans., "Krystyna Budnicka," in *The Last Eyewitnesses: Children of the Holocaust Speak* (Evanston, IL: Northwestern University Press, 1998), 18–19.

30 Ibid., 20.

31 John Cornwell, *Hiter's Pope: The Secret History of Pius XII* (New York: Viking, 1999), 292, quoted in Carol Rittner and John K. Roth, eds., *Pope Pius XII and the Holocaust* (London: Leicester University Press, 2002), 3.

32 Edward R. Murrow, radio broadcast, December 13, 1942, quoted in Edward Bliss, Jr., ed., *In Search of Light: The Broadcasts of Edward R. Murrow, 1938–1961* (New York: Alfred A. Knopf, 1967), 56–57.

33 "Report to the Secretary on the Acquiescence of this Government in the Murder of the Jews," initialed by Randolph Paul for the Foreign Funds Control Unit of the Treasury Department, January 13, 1944.

34 Meyer Levin, *In Search: An Autobiography* (New York: Horizon Press, 1950), 232–233.

35 Dwight D. Eisenhower, *Crusade in Europe* (Baltimore: Johns Hopkins University Press, 1997), 409.

14

Antisemitism after the Holocaust

(1945–1979)

In the spring of 1945, Joseph Pulitzer, the editor of the *St. Louis Post Dispatch*, joined a group of American journalists on a tour of recently liberated concentration camps. At Buchenwald, Pulitzer entered a room filled with dying men. Only one was strong enough to lift his head. Pulitzer described him as "a Polish lad of perhaps 17." When asked why he was in the camp, the young man replied, "Because I am a Jew. You understand that? Because I am a Jew."[1]

Pulitzer did not say whether the young man recovered. He may not have; many died within a few weeks of liberation. For those who did not die—Jews who survived the camps, emerged from hiding, or returned from serving in the Soviet army or with various resistance groups—life after the war was difficult. "They very rarely located a relative or friend alive; they found whole Jewish communities destroyed; and they felt themselves unwelcome, despised, and hated in an atmosphere of virulent antisemitism."[2] Despite the Holocaust and efforts to bring those responsible for the murders to justice, antisemitism remained a force in the world.

"IS IT . . . ANTISEMITIC?" THE ALLIES AND JEWISH REFUGEES

By V-E Day—May 8, 1945, the day the Allies declared victory in Europe—about 30 million children, women, and men had been displaced across the continent. Some, like the young Jew that Pulitzer met, had been imprisoned by the Nazis. Other displaced persons (DPs) had fled their homes to avoid Communist rule as the Soviet army advanced through eastern Europe. Those who had collaborated with the Germans were also on the run, they feared they would be tried for treason or murdered if they returned home.

Among those millions of DPs were a few hundred thousand Jews. Most were physically and emotionally shattered. An eight-year-old orphan liberated from Buchenwald had to be "taught how to 'eat' again. . . . First, a quarter-slice of bread, then a half-slice."[3] A 16-year-old released from Bergen-Belsen felt "that something in me was frozen, numb. I heard there was a concept called 'a heart of stone,' and I thought this had happened to me, that I will no longer be able to laugh or cry."[4] In time, both boys relearned how to eat, laugh, and cry, but the process was slow, painful, and often complicated for them and thousands of other Jewish survivors, young and old alike.

Before the war ended, the Allies—led by the United States, Britain, France, and the Soviet Union—had tried to prepare for their occupation of "Greater Germany." They restored the national identities of Austria and Czechoslovakia. They also divided Germany and Austria into four zones of occupation (American, British, French, and Soviet). Every zone had the same goal: to send every DP home as quickly as possible. Until transportation became available, the Allies set up emergency centers to provide food, shelter, and medical care. Those who refused to go home were to be turned over to the United Nations Relief and Rehabilitation Administration (UNRRA) for resettlement elsewhere.

This massive effort was extraordinarily successful: millions of people were home within weeks of the war's end, including many Jews. Yet despite the Allies' best efforts, about 1.5 million DPs were still in emergency centers six months after the war, including about 75,000 Jews mainly from eastern and central Europe. Almost all of these DPs were in the American, British, and French zones of occupation. The Soviets shipped nearly all of the refugees in their zone to their home countries, whether they wanted to go or not.

Nationality determined how a refugee was treated. As a result, the Allies regarded German and Austrian Jews not as victims of the Nazis but as "ex-enemy nationals." And they, along with many other Jews, found themselves in DP camps alongside former concentration camp guards who now claimed DP status.

Not surprisingly, many Jewish DPs viewed with suspicion the very people who were trying to help them. One U.S. army intelligence agent saw their distrust as a sign of mental instability. He claimed, "The slightest remark or any official measure, be it one not even intended to apply to [Jewish DPs], would be discussed on a single criterion: 'Is it or is it not antisemitic?'"[5] He and other officers showed little understanding of the anguish and terror Jews had experienced or the depth of their losses. The battle-weary veterans who had witnessed conditions in the camps had been rotated home. The soldiers who dealt with the DPs were recent arrivals who had not seen the horrors of the camps.

Physicians and other relief workers were also unprepared for their encounter with survivors of genocide. One relief worker recalled how hard it was to get "these people" to shower. "Women screamed," the worker noted, and "quite a few" had to be "forcefully pushed or carried in."[6] Jewish DPs had good reason to fear communal showers. If the relief worker had asked, he might have learned that the Nazis had disguised gas chambers as showers. But the worker did not ask, and the Jews in his care did not know how to explain.

A number of American soldiers and army chaplains, particularly Jewish chaplains, were troubled by the treatment of Jews in DP camps. Some wrote letters home describing the refugees' plight. Many urged relatives and friends to pass on this information to reporters, politicians, and relief agencies. A few letters reached U.S. President Harry S. Truman. So did complaints from Jewish relief agencies that had been denied permission to enter the camps to help survivors.

At Truman's request, the U.S. State Department sent Earl G. Harrison to Germany and Austria to investigate. Harrison was the dean of the law school at the University of Pennsylvania and had served on various international commissions on the refugee crisis. The army prepared for his visit by arranging for him and his team to see the best-run camps. When that news reached Rabbi Abraham Klausner, an army chaplain assigned to Dachau, he saw to it that Harrison saw the worst camps as well as the best. As a result, Harrison and his advisers toured about 30 camps and interviewed dozens of officers, relief workers, soldiers, and Jewish DPs. On August 24, 1945, Harrison sent Truman a "bombshell":

> [W]e appear to be treating the Jews as the Nazis treated them except that we do not exterminate them. They are in concentration camps in large numbers under our military guard instead of S.S. troops. One is led to wonder whether the German people, seeing this, are not supposing that we are following or at least condoning Nazi policy.[7]

What prompted Harrison's bombshell? He provided Truman with the following explanation:

> Generally speaking, three months after V-E Day and even longer after the liberation of individual groups, many Jewish displaced persons and other possibly non-repatriables are living under guard behind barbed-wire fences, in camps of several descriptions (built by the Germans for slave-laborers and Jews), including some of the most notorious of the concentration camps, amidst crowded, frequently unsanitary and generally grim conditions, in complete idleness, with

no opportunity, except surreptitiously, to communicate with the
outside world, waiting, hoping for some word of encouragement and
action in their behalf.[8]

Harrison believed that conditions were unlikely to improve until the Allies treated Jews as a special group, even though it is "not normally desirable to set aside particular racial or religious groups from their nationality categories." He argued, "[T]he plain truth is that this was done for so long by the Nazis that a group has been created which has special needs. Jews as Jews (not as members of their nationality groups) have been more severely victimized than the non-Jewish members of the same or other nationalities."[9]

Truman sent U.S. General Dwight D. Eisenhower, the head of the Allied forces in Europe, a copy of Harrison's report along with a letter demanding that the armed forces do better. Although Eisenhower complained that Harrison had ignored the successes of the army in saving lives, he ordered his officers to set up separate camps for Jewish DPs and make their needs "a priority." But many officers had a different view of their priorities. As a result, how Jews were treated depended on who was in charge of a particular camp.

Most Jewish DPs in the American zone were in southern Germany—an area administered by General George S. Patton, Jr. In a diary entry dated September 15, 1945, Patton expressed his disdain for Harrison and the DPs. He wrote, "Harrison and his ilk believe that the DP is a human being, which he is not, and this applies particularly to the Jews who are lower than animals."[10]

A number of officers and ordinary soldiers shared Patton's prejudices, and their experiences with Jewish DPs reinforced their view of Jews as "different," even dangerous. Harrison also found that many soldiers and officers viewed "statelessness" as if it were "a loathsome disease." Others seemed to think that DPs were in camps because they had done something wrong, when in fact they were there only because they had no other place to go.

NO PLACE TO GO

Setting up camps for Jewish DPs was a stopgap measure. It did not address what Harrison saw as the central problem: Jewish DPs had nowhere to go. Little or nothing was left of their previous lives. Their families had been murdered and their communities destroyed.

Jewish Exodus from Europe (1945–1947)

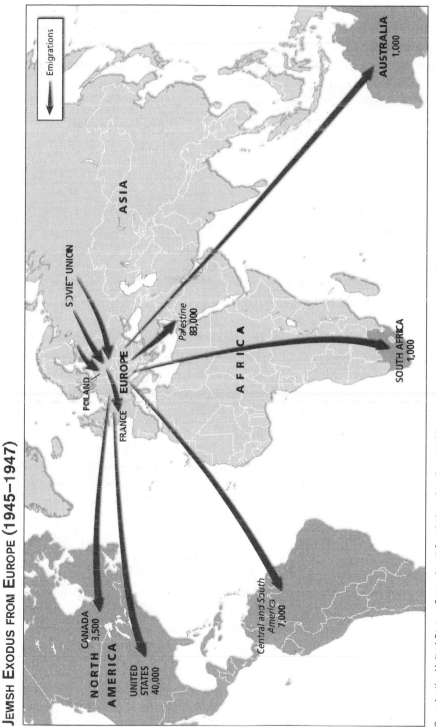

Canada, the United States, Central and South America, South Africa, and Australia took in about 52,500 Jews after the Holocaust. The other 83,000 refugees went to Palestine.

Emil Draitser was a Jew born just before the war in Odessa, a city in the Ukraine then under Soviet rule. In 1945, he and his mother returned from Uzbekistan (where they had hidden from the Germans) and discovered that "the war was still giving off smoke in the hearts of those children who had grown up in it." The parents of some of his classmates had aided the Germans. That collaboration, years of German propaganda (a media campaign that blamed the war on "the Jews" rather than the Nazis), and a deep-rooted antisemitism shaped the way many Ukrainians responded to Jews after the war. Draitser wrote:

> *For a long time after the war ended, in the quiet corners of Odessa streets, in the remote alleys of the parks, in the secluded places among the ruins, gangs of youngsters hunted for Jewish kids, survivors of the Holocaust, and harassed and beat them up, often till they bled.*[11]

Emmanuel Mounier, a leading French Catholic theologian, described a similar attitude in Poland in the spring of 1946. As a result, the few Jews he encountered were "gripped with terror. Survivors think only about leaving."[12] Some people attributed the virulent antisemitism in areas once occupied by Germany to guilt—for turning a blind eye to the murder of their neighbors, aiding the Germans, or taking the belongings Jews had left in their safekeeping. Others attributed the rise in antisemitism to the fear that Jewish survivors would seek revenge on those who had betrayed them.

This new outburst of antisemitism was not limited to eastern Europe. The Holocaust was one of many events that Europeans in the late 1940s wanted to forget. By focusing on wartime hardships, some Europeans cast themselves as victims to turn attention from other, more shameful memories.

Opinion polls in the United States also suggested that people who disliked Jews before the Holocaust did not like them any better after the Holocaust. In 1942, just weeks after Japan bombed Pearl Harbor, pollsters found that nearly 25 percent of Americans considered the Japanese the nation's greatest threat, 18 percent believed it was the Germans, and 15 percent the Jews. In June 1944, 11 months before the war ended, 24 percent identified Jews as the greatest threat, 9 percent the Japanese, and 6 percent the Germans.[13]

In 1945, yet another poll showed that 58 percent of Americans believed that "Jews have too much power in the United States."[14] When asked about European immigration, only 5 percent of Americans favored the idea of an increase.[15] Opponents of immigration wrote letters to Congress expressing their fears that changes in the law would result in "a flood of Jews." In their view, "we [already] have too many."[16] The story in Britain was much the same.

POLAND AFTER THE HOLOCAUST

Antisemitism affected the way Jews were treated almost everywhere after the war, but feelings ran particularly high in Poland. In the nine months after V-E Day, more than 350 Jews were murdered there, and countless others were assaulted.

When Germany and the Soviet Union had divided Poland in 1939 (see Chapter 13), many Poles believed that the Soviet Union was the greater threat. Jews in Poland strongly disagreed. Indeed, most of the Jews who survived the Holocaust did so because they found a safe haven in the Soviet Union. Tensions between Poles and Jews intensified after the Soviet Union, which had liberated Poland from the Germans, established a Communist government there. One of its first actions was a "population exchange" with the Soviet Union in the spring of 1946. That exchange returned to Poland an estimated two million Polish nationals who had been living in the Soviet Union for years. Among them were more than 150,000 Jews. In return, Poland shipped its Ukrainian population to the Ukraine even though many of them had lived in Poland for generations.

Concerned by the growing violence, Joseph Tenenbaum, the president of the American-based World Federation of Polish Jews, traveled to Warsaw in 1946 to meet with Cardinal August Hlond, the head of Poland's Catholic Church. He hoped to persuade the cardinal to aid Jewish survivors. The cardinal refused. He insisted that Jews were being killed in retaliation "for the murder of the Christian population by the Jewish Communist-run Polish Government."[17]

Tenenbaum pointed out that most of the Jews killed in Poland in 1946 were not Communists or government officials. As proof, he handed Cardinal Hlond a monthly bill for funeral expenses sent to the Jewish community in Krakow. It listed, by name and age, every Jew murdered in the city. Among those killed were two small children, one an infant. Tenenbaum asked:

> *Now, can anyone think that these children were killed by the bandits because they were Communists? Or is the common procedure of pulling suspected Jews out of trains and buses and stripping them to*

see if they are circumcised, and if proven to be so, murdering them
on the spot, while non-Jews are returned to the train with apologies;
is this political murder, or murder of Jews because they are Jews?[18]

The cardinal was not convinced. His stand confirmed what many Jews already believed: they had no future in Poland. Even before the war ended, a few young Jews who had led revolts in the ghettos made plans to take Jews out of the country. They organized an underground group known as *Brichah*—the Hebrew word for "flight." With the support of Palestinian Jews, especially members of the Jewish Brigade (a unit in the British army made up of Palestinian Jews, similar to the one that fought in World War I), *Brichah* helped Jewish refugees reach Italy and from there sail to Palestine. The group had the support of many individuals—non-Jews as well as Jews—despite British opposition.

The need to help Polish Jews took on new urgency in the summer of 1946. On July 4, a nine-year-old boy in Kielce, a small city 120 miles south of Warsaw, falsely claimed that "the Jews" had kidnapped him. He told the police that he had been taken to a basement, where he witnessed the murder of 15 Christian children "for their blood"—a reiteration of the ancient myth of ritual murder (see Chapter 5). Within hours, about 5,000 angry protestors had surrounded a building owned by the Jewish community and attacked every Jew inside. When the rampage ended, about 75 Jews were injured and 41 were dead, including a number of very young children. Both police officers and soldiers were on the scene, but none of them tried to stop the violence. Indeed, some participated in the rioting.

Cardinal Hlond claimed that the Jews had provoked the violence by accepting jobs in Poland's government in an "endeavor to introduce a governmental structure that a majority of the people do not desire."[19] And nearly 700 years after Innocent IV had become the first of many popes to confirm that Jews do not practice ritual murder, Hlond and his bishops insisted that the question had "not yet been definitively settled." By the end of 1946, tens of thousands of Jews had left Poland, and thousands more were eager to join them.

Jews in Poland were victims of ethnic cleansing—the use of violence and intimidation to expel an entire group of people from a nation. The term was not coined until 1993, but the practice is centuries old. Sometimes ethnic cleansing has been the work of a dictator like Adolf Hitler or Joseph Stalin. At other times and in other places, ordinary people have carried out ethnic cleansing on their own, much as the Poles who terrorized Jewish survivors did in 1946.

Jews were not the only group to experience ethnic cleansing after the war. In just 18 months, Czechoslovakia stripped nearly three million Czechs of German descent of their citizenship and then expelled them from the country, though some came from families that had lived in Czechoslovakia for generations. Germans were also forced out of Romania (nearly 800,000), Yugoslavia (500,000), Hungary (623,000), and Poland (1.3 million). When the Allies reduced the size of Germany, about seven million Germans suddenly found themselves living in Poland. They, too, were expelled. These governments treated all Germans as enthusiastic followers of Hitler and his Nazi Party. Although many had been supporters, some were not. Unlike Jews, however, these refugees were not victims of genocide. Moreover, they had somewhere to go; Jews did not.

ANTISEMITISM: AN INTERNATIONAL EMERGENCY

By the summer of 1947, many people feared that the rise in antisemitism since the war had reached a crisis level. Among them were 65 Christian and Jewish leaders and scholars from 19 nations. At a meeting in Seelisberg, Switzerland, they expressed their concerns:

> We have recently witnessed an outburst of antisemitism which has led to the persecution and extermination of millions of Jews. In spite of the catastrophe . . . antisemitism has lost none of its force, but threatens to extend to other regions, to poison the minds of Christians, and to involve humanity more and more in a grave guilt with disastrous consequences.[20]

The meeting the group held at Seelisberg was not the first interfaith conference. Some Jewish, Protestant, and Catholic leaders had been meeting formally as well as informally since the early 1900s. In the 1920s, for example, a group of Americans founded the National Conference of Christians and Jews in response to the threat posed by the Ku Klux Klan, which terrorized Jews and Catholics (as well as African Americans regardless of their religious affiliation). Events in Germany in the 1930s also prompted interfaith efforts to aid Jews fleeing Nazi persecution. However, the Seelisberg conference was the first to examine the roots of antisemitism by using as its starting point a critique written by a Jew. His name was Jules Isaac.

Before the war, Isaac had been France's inspector general for education and the respected author of the nation's official textbooks on French and world history. But once the Germans invaded France in 1940, he became a hunted man. Isaac and his family moved from one hiding place to another in a desperate effort to avoid arrest. Although he was never found, his wife, son, daughter, and son-in-law were discovered and shipped to Auschwitz. Only Jules Isaac and his son survived the Holocaust.

During his years in hiding, Isaac tried to understand why so many people in France and elsewhere collaborated with the Nazis. With the help of several Christian scholars, Isaac studied hundreds of church documents. In those documents he found what he called "the teaching of contempt" for Jews and Judaism in Christian churches. As a result of those findings, he came to believe that Christians had knowingly or unknowingly been spreading ideas that not only "departed from historical truth" but also distorted and contradicted truth to the point that those ideas "may justly be termed myths"—ideas "more appropriate to legend than to history." He traced those myths to "passionate controversies which took place, during the first centuries of the Christian era, between the scholars of the old Law [the rabbis] and those of the new Church, the men referred to as the Church Fathers [see Chapter 2]." He explained:

> *Christian theology, once started in this direction, never stopped. Utterly convinced of its rights, it has repeated and [spread] these mythical arguments tirelessly, with methodical thoroughness, through all the powerful means that were—and still are—at its disposal. . . .*
>
> *The result is that the myths . . . have eventually taken on the shape and consistency of facts, of facts that have become incontestable. They have ended up by being accepted as though they were authentic history. They have become an integral part of Christian thinking; nay, of the thinking of all educated people living in a traditionally Christian civilization.*[21]

Christians at the conference responded to his concerns by creating a document called the "Ten Points." The first four reminded Christians that their faith is deeply rooted in Judaism: "One God speaks to us all through the Old and the New Testaments." They also noted that "Jesus was born of a Jewish mother" and that the "first disciples, apostles and first martyrs were Jews." And they reiterated that "the fundamental commandment of Christianity, to love God and one's neighbor," came from the Hebrew scriptures and "is binding upon both Christians and Jews in all human relationships, without any exception."[22]

The six remaining points made it clear that Jews and Judaism must no longer be presented negatively in Christian teaching. For example, the fifth warned against praising Christianity by disparaging or mocking Judaism.[23]

Those who attended the conference did not see the Ten Points as a solution to the hatred that threatened Jews in 1947 but, rather, as the beginning of a process that they hoped would result in Christian thinking that was truer to the teachings of Jesus. It took more than 20 years before most churches accepted the principles outlined at Seelisberg. And even then, many of the old myths remained.

ANTISEMITISM AND NATIONALISM

Antisemitism was also on the rise in the Middle East and North Africa in the late 1940s. Some have attributed the increase in anti-Jewish sentiment to Zionism—the nationalist movement that began in Europe with the aim of establishing a Jewish homeland in Palestine. Conor Cruise O'Brien, an Irish diplomat then based in the Middle East, strongly disagreed with that assessment:

> As Britain and France disengaged from the Middle East and North Africa, around the middle of [the twentieth century], and were replaced by Arab nationalist Governments . . . Jews had to be at risk, throughout these vast regions, even if there had never been any Zionism. . . . Jews had helped the spread of Western influence, and had benefited from it. They had welcomed the coming of European rule, and benefited from that. With the withdrawal of the Europeans, and the coming to power of fervid Arab nationalist Governments, the Jews in every "decolonized" country were bound to be unpopular and in some danger.[24]

Jews in every country in the region have their own unique history, but a brief look at Iraqi Jews in the 1940s offers insight into the challenges Jews faced throughout the Middle East—challenges that had little to do with Zionism and everything to do with what O'Brien called "fervid" Arab nationalism. Naïm Kattan, an Iraqi Jew and writer, has described that nationalism as "wounded honor"—a fierce pride that was rooted at least in part in resentment and rage over colonial rule. To Kattan and other young Iraqi Jews in the 1940s, this nationalist pride was as central to their identity as it was to their Muslim classmates:

We were Iraqis, concerned about the future of our country and con-
sequently the future of each one of us. Except that the Muslims felt
more Iraqi than the others. It was no use for us to say to them, "This
is our land and we have been here for twenty-five centuries." We
had been there first, but they were not convinced. We were different.
Was our colouring not lighter than the Bedouins? Did we not know
foreign languages? The fact that the best students in Arabic in the
final examinations were Jews, that the Alliance Israélite School
produced the best Arabic grammarians, changed nothing. Our identity
was tainted.[25]

Despite that "taint," Kattan saw himself as an Iraqi patriot. He recalled
conversations with friends in Baghdad cafés:

We would liberate our country. Jews or Muslims, we had but one
enemy: the English. The Englishman would be crushed. And with
help from Germany we would be rid of him once and for all. The tall
blond Germans were mythical figures, valiant saviours of wounded
honor. Before the Muslims' overwhelming enthusiasm we kept silent,
but in the intimacy of our homes it was another story. My brother, my
uncle, our neighbors, spoke of the Germans in low voices and cau-
tiously, as of an imminent catastrophe. We knew how Hitler would
treat the Jews, and the Nazis' Iraqi disciples did not reserve a more
enviable fate for us. But I did not share these old people's fears. There
was no possible comparison between Iraqis and Germans. Once we
were independent, we would all work together, united in our desire
to build a new society.[26]

Despite the threat that Jews faced in Europe, Kattan was confident
that his classmates were attracted to the Nazis not because they were antisemitic but because the Germans were the enemies of Iraq's enemies—
the British. His brother, his uncle, and the family's Jewish neighbors were
less optimistic. They were aware that many Iraqi nationalists preached
a form of Arab nationalism that was intolerant of religious minorities. In
1933—just one year after Britain granted Iraq limited independence—the
Iraqi army had massacred 3,000 unarmed Assyrian Christians in northern
Iraq. Many Jews saw the massacre as a warning to every minority.

In 1940, the same year Kattan viewed himself as an Iraqi nationalist, Rashid Ali al-Gaylani, a popular Iraqi politician with strong Nazi

sympathies, became prime minister with support from the military. In April, he overthrew the regent who was ruling Iraq until the nation's future king (then just four years old) was old enough to take over.

Almost immediately, Rashid Ali allied Iraq with Germany and declared war on Britain. It was a very popular move. The only Iraqis who were not enthusiastic about it were Jews. As a result, their loyalty was suddenly in doubt. Young Muslims now roamed the streets arresting Jews as spies and sometimes executing them on the spot.

Despite such incidents, Jews were relatively safe until the end of May, when the British regained control of the country and Rashid Ali fled to Nazi Germany. In the time between his departure and the arrival of the former regent, the nation was supposed to be under the temporary rule of a three-person Council for Internal Security. But Rashid Ali's former minister of economics, Yunis al-Sab'awi, saw an opportunity to declare himself "the military governor of Baghdad."

On May 30, al-Sab'awi headed for Baghdad's radio station with plans to call for an uprising to rid the city of the "enemy within"—the Jews. Before he reached the station, the Council for Internal Security had him arrested and then forced him into exile.

Many Jews believed that the danger was now over; after all, the regent was on his way home and British troops were just outside the city. June 1 was the first day of Shavuot (the Jewish festival that marks the receiving of the Torah). That afternoon, a few Jews, still dressed in their holiday clothes, walked to the airport to welcome back the regent and their future king.

A number of Iraqis, who noticed how dressed up those Jews were, jumped to the conclusion that they were celebrating Iraq's defeat by the British. In revenge, they attacked the Jews, killing one and injuring others. This time, neither the police nor the army intervened. Kattan recalled:

> *The city was left to itself. . . . And it took just one hour to stir up a sleeping, pent-up people. The Bedouins had heard the signal and they were prepared. . . .*

> *They advanced. Armed with picks, daggers, sometimes with rifles, they unfurled in waves, surrounded the city, and beleaguered it. Rallying cries crackled on all sides. As they passed through, they brought along Muslims, spared the Christians. Only the Jews were being pursued. As they advanced, their ranks swelled, teeming with women, children, and adolescents.*[27]

During the rioting, 179 Jews were murdered, 242 children were left orphans, 586 businesses were looted and 911 apartment buildings—home to more than 12,000 Jews—were destroyed. Order was restored only when Iraqi troops entered the city on the evening of the second day. Iraqi Jews were outraged. Why, they asked, didn't British soldiers intervene? The British claimed that they did not want to "embarrass" the Iraqi army. Although peace was eventually restored, life was never the same for Jews in Iraq. Kattan noted that "[e]very year our chances dwindled and the screws were put on our prospects for the future."[28]

The Nazis were also popular with Egyptian nationalists in the 1930s and 1940s. In 1933, Ahmad Husayn, an Egyptian lawyer who wanted to free his nation from British influence, created a movement known as Young Egypt and modeled it after Hitler's Nazi Party. Approximately 2,000 members participated in the 1936 Nazi Party rally in Nuremberg, Germany. Although Husayn was somewhat disillusioned with Hitler after he invaded Austria and Czechoslovakia in 1938, Nazi ideas continued to influence Young Egypt.

Those same ideas also influenced the Muslim Brotherhood. Founded in 1928 by an educator named Hassan al-Banna, the Brotherhood, like Young Egypt, wanted the country to be independent of foreign rule. Unlike members of Young Egypt, the Brothers were suspicious of modern ways and determined to apply Islamic law to all parts of Egyptian life, including government. That combination of religious and national fervor struck a chord; by 1938, the group had about 200,000 members and had spread to other countries, including Lebanon and Syria.

During World War II, members of Young Egypt and the Muslim Brotherhood tried to overthrow Egypt's king, much as Rashid Ali did in Iraq. Among the conspirators were Gamal Abdul Nasser, a member of Young Egypt who would later become the second president of Egypt, and Anwar Sadat, a member of the Muslim Brotherhood who became the nation's third president. Although their effort failed, the movement continued to grow.

THE PALESTINIAN DILEMMA

The British, who controlled much of the Middle East, had been struggling to contain the wave of nationalism that had been sweeping the region since the 1920s. Nowhere was their task more difficult than in Palestine, where Arab nationalism collided with Jewish nationalism.

In 1919, the League of Nations divided parts of the old Ottoman Empire into "mandates"—territories held "in trust" by a European power until they were "ready" for independence. Palestine was one of those mandates; it was placed under British rule. At the time, it was home to approximately 512,000 Muslims, 66,000 Jews, and 61,000 Christians.[29]

Britain was the dominant power in the Middle East throughout the early 1900s. As a result, Arab and Jewish nationalists worked separately during World War I to persuade the British to recognize their claims to Palestine. Both succeeded to some extent. In 1917, Britain issued the Balfour Declaration, which promised Jews a national homeland (see Chapter 12). At about the same time, Britain made a similar promise to Hussein bin Ali, a descendent of Muhammad and the powerful head of the Arab clan that guarded Islam's holiest shrines in Mecca and Medina, in what is now Saudi Arabia (see Chapter 3). Hussein was told that he could establish an independent Arab kingdom under his family's rule.

In 1919, Hussein's son Faisal met privately with Zionists, including Chaim Weizmann, who later became Israel's first president. As a result of those meetings, the two groups agreed to aid one another in the development of a Jewish Palestine and an independent Arab state. The two also agreed to take "all necessary measures . . . to encourage and stimulate the immigration of Jews into Palestine on a large scale, and as quickly as possible to settle Jewish immigrants upon the land."[30]

Faisal described that meeting to Felix Frankfurter, a member of the American Zionist delegation to the Paris peace conference after World War I. Frankfurter was then a professor of law at Harvard University; he later became a justice of the U.S. Supreme Court. Faisal assured the professor that Jews and Arabs could work together to achieve their goals. Faisal's letter was later printed in the *New York Times*:

> With the chiefs of your movement, especially with Dr. Weizmann, we have had and continue to have the closest relations. He has been a great helper of our cause, and I hope the Arabs may soon be in a position to make the Jews some return for their kindness. We are working together for a reformed and revived [Middle East], and our two movements complete one another. The Jewish movement is national and not imperialist. Our movement is national and not imperialist, and there is room in Syria [Palestine had been part of the province of Syria in the Ottoman Empire] for us both. Indeed I think that neither can be a real success without the other.

People less informed and less responsible than our leaders and yours, ignoring the need for cooperation of the Arabs and Zionists have been trying to exploit the local difficulties that must necessarily arise in Palestine in the early stages of our movements. Some of them have, I am afraid, misrepresented your aims to the Arab peasantry, and our aims to the Jewish peasantry, with the result that interested parties have been able to make capital out of what they call our differences.

I wish to give you my firm conviction that these differences are not questions of principle, but on matters of detail such as must inevitably occur in every contact of neighboring peoples, and as are easily adjusted by mutual goodwill. Indeed nearly all of them will disappear with fuller knowledge.

I look forward, and my people with me look forward, to a future in which we will help you and you will help us, so that the countries in which we are mutually interested may once again take their places in the community of civilised peoples of the world.[31]

As the letter reveals, the ability of some Arab nationalists and Zionists to work together was complicated by two facts: both had associates who were unwilling to negotiate, and neither side had control over the British. Faisal recognized those facts when he added a condition to the agreement: it would be binding only if Britain kept its promises. Those promises were not kept, and in 1929, Faisal denied the agreement.

The British tried to quiet the outrage of Faisal and his family by making him king of Iraq. (He ruled until his death in 1933, when his son, and later his young grandson, became king.) The British also took land from Palestine to create a new country that they called Transjordan (now Jordan). They named Abdullah, one of Faisal's brothers, king of the new nation. Everyone knew, however, that Britain still controlled both nations. Britain's refusal to end colonial rule fueled resentment, anger, and a strong sense of betrayal throughout the region. In the late 1920s and 1930s, new leaders emerged; many of them, like their counterparts in Egypt and Iraq, found inspiration in the writings of Adolf Hitler and his Nazi followers.

One of Hitler's most vocal supporters in Palestine was the grand mufti of Jerusalem, Amin al-Husseini. A grand mufti is a religious official with considerable prestige but, traditionally, little power. Al-Husseini was the exception. The British had appointed him to the post because they saw

Amin al-Husseini, the grand mufti of Jerusalem, was an admirer of Adolf Hitler. He traveled to Germany during the war and gave speeches on the radio that called on Muslims to support the Nazis.

him as a potential "troublemaker" and hoped his new position would keep him quiet. They even enhanced his power by placing him on the Palestinian Arab Higher Committee—a group that spoke for Palestinian Arabs in much the way the Jewish Agency spoke for Palestinian Jews.

Al-Husseini made no secret of his admiration for the Nazis. He had particular praise for *Mein Kampf*, a book that combined Hitler's life story with his political views. In the book, Hitler insisted that Jews "do not at all intend to build a Jewish state in Palestine. . . . They only want an organization center for their international world-swindling."[32] It was a view the grand mufti embraced.

In the 1930s, Al-Husseini and many other Palestinians were alarmed by a sharp rise in Jewish immigration to Palestine. They did not place the blame on Adolf Hitler and his efforts to push Jews out of Germany for the increase; instead they blamed Palestinian Jews and the British. In 1936, anger over this issue had turned violent. Although Britain stopped the rioting, the fighting between Jews and Arabs never really ended.

In 1939, in an effort to quiet Arab protests, Britain limited Jewish immigration to Palestine to 15,000 people each year for a period of five years. That decision horrified those who were aware of the threat that Hitler posed to European Jews. Despite their protests, restrictions on Jewish immigration remained in effect even after the war.

With the publication of the Harrison report, many people in Britain and the United States urged British Prime Minister Clement Attlee to reconsider immigration policies in Palestine. He countered those demands by suggesting that the United States and Britain form a binational committee to determine the future of Jewish immigration to Palestine and the mandate. President Truman agreed.

Between January and April of 1946, this new binational committee heard testimony in Europe and the Middle East and reached a conclusion similar to the one Harrison had outlined. The committee also called on Britain to issue 100,000 certificates of immigration to Jewish DPs. And it urged other nations to accept at least some Jewish immigrants. In addition, the group recommended an end to British rule of Palestine and the creation of an Arab-Jewish state—an idea rejected by almost everyone in Palestine. In a letter to a London newspaper, Richard Crossman, a British representative on the committee, defended those recommendations:

> The tragedy of Palestine is that our obligations to the Jews and the Arabs are contradictory. We cannot do justice to the one without doing injustice to the other and at the moment we are doing grave injustice to both.

> When I weighed up the political objections of the Arabs against the human needs of the homeless survivors of Polish Jewry, I felt that the issuing of 100,000 certificates was a lesser injustice than the refusal to do so.[33]

Although the committee's recommendations were never carried out, Americans praised the plan. British officials responded by accusing the United States of hypocrisy at a time when the country itself was unwilling to increase its own immigration quotas. So did many Arab nationalists. Truman took the criticism seriously and issued an executive order that gave DPs preferential treatment under U.S. immigration laws. But that order had little impact, because most of the approximately one million DPs in Europe in 1946 were from eastern Europe. U.S. immigration laws limited the number of Poles who could settle in the United States in a single year to 5,982. Other eastern European nations had even smaller quotas—Romania, 603; Hungary, 473; and Lithuania, 344.

ARAB NATIONALISM AND A JEWISH STATE

With violence in Palestine growing, the British decided in 1947 to turn over their mandate to the newly formed United Nations. In May, the General Assembly set up the UN Special Committee on Palestine (UNSCOP) to recommend a solution to the conflict. Its 11 members were from Australia, Canada, Czechoslovakia, Guatemala, India, Iran, the Netherlands, Peru, Sweden, Uruguay, and Yugoslavia.

All 11 members traveled to Palestine to interview Jews, Arabs, and British officials. The British and the Jewish Agency cooperated, but the Arab Higher Committee refused to do so. Instead, committee members met informally with Palestinian Arabs.

In July, a dramatic incident altered the way some committee members saw the crisis. On July 11, an old American ferry boat that Zionists called the *Exodus* sailed from France with more than 4,500 Jewish refugees on board—including about 600 children. Those refugees had fled Germany and were planning to enter Palestine illegally because they had no other place to go. On July 18, four British destroyers surrounded and stormed the *Exodus*. The unarmed passengers and crew fought back with sticks and cans. The British killed 3 people and injured 28 others. They then brought the boat into the port of Haifa and transferred the passengers onto navy transports to take them back to Germany.

Four members of UNSCOP were in Haifa when the *Exodus* entered the port. As they watched in horror, the wounded and the dead were carried to shore. They saw the gashes the British had made in the ship and observed frightened children peeking out of portholes. And they heard the cries of anger and fear as passengers were shipped back to DP camps in Germany.

On August 31, with memories of the incident still fresh, UNSCOP sent its report to the UN. It recommended that Palestine be divided into two separate states, one a Jewish state and the other an Arab state. As UN delegates debated the proposal, the Palestinian Arab Higher Committee warned that if the resolution passed, the position of Jews in the Arab world "will become very precarious."

Despite that warning, on November 29, 1947, the General Assembly voted to create two states. The slightly larger one, about 56 percent of what was left of the mandate after the creation of Jordan, would be a Jewish state, with a population of about a million equally divided between Arabs and Jews; the smaller state, about 43 percent of the territory, would be an Arab state with a population of about 750,000 Arabs and 10,000 Jews.

The Jewish Agency accepted the plan, but the Arabs did not. Hassan al-Banna of the Muslim Brotherhood, an ally of the mufti, viewed the division of Palestine as "an international plot carried out by the Americans, the Russians, and the British, under the influence of Zionism."[34] He called for a holy war against the Jews. So did some members of the Arab League—which then consisted of Egypt, Iraq, Jordan, Lebanon, Saudi Arabia, Syria, and what is now Yemen.

Many Jews in Palestine and elsewhere viewed those harsh statements as antisemitic, particularly the false claims of an "international plot." But the strong language did not have the support of all Arabs. Neither Arabs nor Jews were completely united on any issue, including the proposed division of Palestine. King Abdullah of Jordan saw division as the "only realistic solution."[35] So did the prime minister of Iraq. He privately remarked that Iraq would have to accept Israel eventually but that "for now it is politically impossible to acknowledge this publicly. To do so would cause a revolt in Iraq."[36]

On May 14, 1948, the Jewish community in Palestine, headed by David Ben-Gurion (soon to be the new nation's first prime minister), proclaimed the establishment of the State of Israel. Within hours, the armies of Egypt, Iraq, Jordan, Syria, and Lebanon attacked the new nation. Other

European Jews came to Palestine in large numbers in the 1930s to escape antisemitism. They cleared land for farming, built new industries, and established schools and hospitals.

On November 29, 1947, the United Nations voted to divide Palestine into an Arab and a Jewish state. In December, Britain announced that it would end its rule of Palestine on May 15, 1948. On May 14, David Ben Gurion and other leaders established the state of Israel.

members of the Arab League supported the war financially but did not send troops.

Why were some Arab leaders willing to fight for a single Palestinian state even though they thought partition was a more practical solution? One answer lies in their strong commitment to nationalism. Arab nationalists believed that the Arab people were bound by more than a common language, religion, and history. They also shared a goal—ending Western influence in the Middle East. They saw a Jewish state as a continuation of Western influence.

Many Jews in Palestine had only recently been victims of European antisemitism. They found it difficult to understand how anyone could regard them as European colonists in what they considered their ancestral home; after all, many Jews traced their roots to the Biblical Israelites. At the same time, the anti-Jewish feelings on the Arab side were often mirrored on the Jewish side. Some Jewish settlers regarded Palestinian Arabs as "backward" or "treacherous." Both sides were outraged by the violent acts committed by the other. And gradually, each side came to view its own people as victims and its opponents as powerful, aggressive, and dangerous. Those views made reaching a compromise extremely difficult.

Yet another force driving the Arabs' decision to go to war rather than accept a Jewish state was the unrelenting effort of leaders like the grand mufti and groups like the Muslim Brotherhood. In speeches, books, and radio broadcasts, they repeatedly labeled "the Jews" as "the enemy of Islam."

When the fighting in Palestine ended in January 1949, Israel controlled all of the territory the UN had allotted to it plus about half of the land set aside for an Arab state. The other half of that land was divided between Jordan and Egypt. Jordan held east Jerusalem and the West Bank (of the Jordan River), and Egypt controlled Gaza (a strip along the Mediterranean Sea that lies on Egypt's eastern border).

By the spring of 1949, Israel had signed cease-fire agreements with Egypt, Lebanon, Jordan, and Syria. Even though the four agreed to a truce, they refused to recognize Israel, negotiate borders, or set terms for a lasting peace. Even the hint of a peace agreement could be dangerous. On July 16, 1951, such rumors led to the assassination of Riad Bey al-Solh, a former prime minister of Lebanon, and, four days later, to the murder of King Abdullah of Jordan.

In the course of the fighting, many Palestinian Arabs became refugees. There is no agreement on their numbers—the lowest number is 520,000, an Israeli estimate, and the highest is 800,000 to 850,000, an Arab estimate. United Nations agencies in 1948 placed the number at 726,000. There was no agreement then or now on how they came to be refugees or how best to repatriate or resettle them. For more than 60 years, the two sides have struggled to negotiate solutions to these and a host of other problems.

In 1948, with no solution to the refugee problem in sight, the UN took charge of Palestinian refugees, which it defined as individuals who had lived in Palestine between June 1946 and May 1948 and had lost their homes and means of livelihood as a result of the conflict. That definition now includes the descendants of those individuals, regardless of where they live. In many respects, they became hostages in a political game in which they had little say.

In that sense, Palestinian Arabs had much in common with refugees in other parts of the world immediately after World War II. But in at least one way, they have been unique: they have never been repatriated or officially resettled. Instead, many have remained in camps administered by the United Nations for more than 60 years. The conditions in which these

Palestinians lived varied greatly. Jordan allowed Palestinians to become citizens, but Palestinians in Lebanon had no civil rights, access to public services, or the right to work in more than 70 trades and professions. In Syria, refugees had the right to education and employment but not to citizenship.

Much attention has been deservedly focused on the plight of these refugees over the years. Less attention has been paid to another group of refugees who were also forced from their homes as a result of the Arab-Israeli conflict—the approximately 875,000 Jews who lived outside Palestine in the Middle East and North Africa. Most came from families that had lived in the region for more than 2,500 years. By the 1960s, all but a handful had been forced into exile, including the Jews of Iraq. Growing antisemitism in the Middle East intensified the problems these Jews faced, as did the Cold War—a fierce competition for military, political, and economic superiority between the United States and the Soviet Union.

---

[1] Joseph Pulitzer, "Report on German Murder Mills," in *Army Talks*, Vol. 4 (July 10, 1945), 9.

[2] I. F. Stone, *Underground to Palestine* (London: Hutchinson, 1979).

[3] Yisrael Meir Lau, "The Orphan Who Became Chief Rabbi of Israel," *Jewish Press*, May 7, 1993, quoted in Benjamin Blech, ed., *Eyewitness to Jewish History* (Hoboken: John Wiley & Sons, 2004), 263–266.

[4] Ibid.

[5] Wolfgang Jacobmeyer, "Polnische Juden in der Amerikanischen Besatzungzone Deutschlands 1946/7," *Vierteljahrshefte für Zeitgeschichte*, 26 (January 1977). 129–132, quoted in Michael R. Marrus, *The Unwanted: European Refugees in the Twentieth Century* (New York: Oxford University Press, 1985), 332.

[6] Quoted in Leonard Dinnerstein, *America and the Survivors of the Holocaust* (New York: Columbia University Press, 1982), 66.

[7] Report of Earl G. Harrison to President Harry S. Truman, enclosed in letter from President Truman to General Eisenhower, August 31, 1945, White House News Release (September 29, 1945), http://www.sunsite.unc.edu/pha/policy/1945/450929a.html.

[8] Ibid.

[9] Ibid.

[10] George Patton, *The Patton Diaries, 1940–1945*, 137–139, quoted in Abram L. Sachar, *The Redemption of the Unwanted: From the Liberation of the Death Camps to the Founding of Israel* (New York: St. Martin's/Marek, 1983), 164.

[11] Emil Draitser, *Shush! Growing Up Jewish under Stalin: A Memoir* (Berkeley: University of California Press, 2008), 16.

[12] Emmanuel Mounier, "L'ordre regne-t-il à Varsowie?," 999–1000, quoted in Jan T. Gross, *Fear: Anti-Semitism in Poland after Auschwitz, An Essay in Historical Interpretation* (New York: Random House, 2006), 35.

[13] Charles H. Stember, *Jews in the Mind of America* (New York: Basic Books, 1966), 128, cited in Leonard Dinnerstein, *Antisemitism in America* (New York: Oxford University Press, 1994), 131.

[14] Cited in Leonard Dinnerstein, "Anti-Semitism Exposed and Attached, 1945–1950," AJH 71 (September 1981): 135; Samuel H. Flowerman and Marie Jahoda, "Polls on Anti-Semitism," *Commentary* 1 (April 1946): 83, cited in Dinnerstein, *Antisemitism in America*, 146.

[15] Ronald Sanders, *Shores of Refuge: A Hundred Years of Jewish Emigration* (New York: Schocken Books, 1988), 573.

[16] In David Kennedy, *A Political Passage: The Career of Stratton of Illinois* (Carbondale: Southern Illinois Press, 1990), 52-53, quoted in Dinnerstein, *Antisemitism in America*, 161.

[17] Joseph Tenenbaum, *In Search of a Lost People: The Old and the New Poland* (New York: Beechhurst Press, 1948), 238.

[18] Ibid., 238-239.

[19] Ibid., 241.

[20] *Reports and Recommendations of the Emergency Conference on Anti-Semitism,* International Council of Christians and Jews (London/Geneva, 1947), 14, quoted in Christian M. Rutishauser, "The 1947 Seelisberg Conference: The Foundation of Jewish-Christian Dialogue," *Studies in Christian-Jewish Relations*, 2, no. 2 (2007): 42-43, http://escholarship.bc.edu/scjr/vol2/iss2/6.

[21] Jules Isaac, *The Teaching of Contempt: Christian Roots of Anti-Semitism* (New York: Holt, Rinehart and Winston, 1964), 42.

[22] *Reports and Recommendations of the Emergency Conference on Anti-Semitism*, 14ff, quoted in Rutishauser, "The 1947 Seelisberg Conference," 44-45.

[23] Ibid.

[24] Conor Cruise O'Brien, *The Siege: The Saga of Israel and Zionism* (New York: Simon & Schuster, 1986), 341-342.

[25] Naïm Kattan, *Farewell Babylon: Coming of Age in Jewish Baghdad*, trans. Sheila Fischman (Boston: David R. Godine, 2007), 11.

[26] Ibid., 16-17.

[27] Ibid., 18.

[28] Ibid., 53.

[29] Doreen Ingrams, ed., *Palestine Papers, 1917-1922: Seeds of Conflict* (New York: George Braziller, 1973), 44.

[30] Walter Laqueur and Barry Rubin, eds., "Emir Feisal and Chaim Weizmann: Agreement (January 3, 1919)," in *The Israel-Arab Reader: A Documentary History of the Middle East Conflict* (New York: Penguin Books, 2008), 17.

[31] Walter Laqueur and Barry Rubin, eds., "Emir Feisal and Felix Frankfurter: Correspondence (March 3-5, 1919)," in *The Israel-Arab Reader*, 19-20.

[32] Adolf Hitler, *Mein Kampf* (Munich: Verlag Franz Eher Nachfolger, 1925), 2:356, quoted in Matthias Küntzel, *Jihad and Jew-Hatred: Islamism, Nazism and the Roots of 9/11*, trans. Colin Meade (New York: Telos Press, 2007), 29.

[33] Richard Crossman to *Times*[?] (London), May 25, 1946, in Richard Crossman, manuscript, quoted in Dinnerstein, *America and the Survivors of the Holocaust*, 98.

[34] Abd Al-Fattah Muhammad El-Awaisi, *The Muslim Brothers and the Palestine Question 1928-1947* (London: Tauris Academic Studies, 1998), 195, quoted in Küntzel, *Jihad and Jew-Hatred*, 48.

[35] Thomas Mayer, "Arab Unity of Action and the Palestine Question 1945-1948," *Middle Eastern Studies*, 22, no. 3 (July 1986), 344, quoted in Küntzel, *Jihad and Jew-Hatred*, 50.

[36] Bruse Maddy-Weitzman, *The Crystalization of the Arab State System 1945-1954* (New York: Syracuse University Press, 1993), 80, quoted in Küntzel, *Jihad and Jew-Hatred*, 50.

15

Antisemitism and the Cold War

(1945–2000)

The Cold War was a 46-year standoff between two superpowers—the United States and the Soviet Union. It began at the end of World War II and continued until 1991, the year the Soviet Union's Communist government collapsed. During those years, the two nations and their allies competed fiercely for military, political, and economic superiority. Although there were many regional conflicts throughout this period, neither side was willing to risk a world war at a time when its opponent had weapons that could destroy the world.

The Cold War was a time of heightened nationalism. In the 1950s and 1960s, the great empires built by European nations in earlier centuries were crumbling. In their place, dozens of new nations emerged. Each of the two superpowers tried to bring those nations into its sphere of influence. That competition turned the Middle East into a major battlefield in the Cold War—and antisemitism was increasingly used as a weapon in that war.

CHANGING ATTITUDES

Before World War II, Europe was home to most of the world's Jews; by 1950, just five years after the Holocaust ended, the United States had the world's largest Jewish population (between 4.5 and 5 million), even though the number of Jews in the nation grew only slightly during the 1940s. The Soviet Union ranked second, despite the fact that about half of the approximately three million Jews who lived there in 1939 had been killed during the Holocaust.

American Jews had been safe from the genocide, but many did not feel safe. Antisemitic attacks rose sharply during the war, and discrimination in housing, employment, and education continued to limit opportunities for Jews (see Chapter 12).

Yet by the 1950s, attitudes toward Jews were changing. More Americans now viewed Jews in a positive way; as a result, antisemitic violence fell sharply. Historians have attributed much of that shift to a

Experiences with discrimination and persecution during and after World War II led many in the United States to demand equal rights for all Americans. Dr. Martin Luther King, Jr. (center) and Rabbi Abraham Joshua Heschel (second from right) were among those who believed they had a moral responsibility to bring the nation closer to its ideals.

growing prosperity in the United States in the postwar years. Many Americans were more confident about the future and less fearful of minorities, including Jews. Some historians have also credited the thousands of GIs who experienced discrimination in the American armed forces during the war and returned home, in the words of one veteran, "far less willing to tolerate the traditional, often dehumanizing, ethnic snobberies of the pre-war years."[1] Some, particularly African-American and Hispanic veterans, were now determined to bring the United States closer to its ideals by overturning discriminatory laws. Although neither racism nor other hatreds disappeared, they did become less socially acceptable.

Antisemitism also increased in the Soviet Union during the war, but it did not decline after the war. Indeed, when Soviet Jews turned to the government for protection, officials refused to help. Instead they accused the victims of "unleashing Jewish nationalism." Many Soviet Jews were shocked by the charge. During the war, they had shown great loyalty. About 500,000 Jews had served in the Soviet army, and 200,000 of them died in battle. More than 170,000 were awarded medals for their service.

Hirsh Smoliar, a Communist activist who was also a Jew, was proud of that history. And yet everywhere he turned in 1945, he saw signs of a fierce hatred for Jews—a hatred that the government made no effort to curb. Deeply troubled by what he saw and heard, Smoliar consulted Ilya Ehrenburg, a popular journalist who was also a Communist and a Jew.

Ehrenburg pointed to the huge piles of letters written by Jews that lined his office—letters from "all corners of the Soviet Union." He suggested that Smoliar read a few at random. Each complained of a mindless, all-encompassing antisemitism. Smoliar recalled, "I felt as though an abyss had opened at my feet and each letter was pushing me deeper into the bottomless pit."[2]

A few days later, Smoliar spoke to a high-ranking official about the letters. The official explained that once Joseph Stalin had questioned the loyalty of Jews or any other group, government workers were free to treat them as unwanted outsiders.[3] Stalin ruled the Soviet Union from 1929 until his death in 1953. In a brutal dictatorship such as his, attacks on a group were allowed to continue only if they had the support of the nation's leader. And Stalin considered what he called "Jewish nationalism" a crime.

Still, though Stalin attacked Zionism within the Soviet Union, he supported the creation of a Jewish state in Palestine. In 1947, Andrei Gromyko, the Soviets' chief delegate to the United Nations, reminded the General Assembly that Jews in German-occupied Europe had been subjected to "almost complete . . . annihilation." He added, "[N]o western European State was able to provide adequate assistance for the Jewish people in defending its rights and its very existence."

That "unpleasant fact," Gromyko argued, "explains the aspirations of the Jews to establish their own State. It would be unjust not to take this into consideration and to deny the right of the Jewish people to realize this aspiration."[4] With those words, the Soviets acknowledged the Holocaust and recognized the right of Jews to have a state. Stalin's support for Israel as a Jewish state did not mean that he had changed his mind about Zionism or Zionists. His treatment of Soviet Jews strongly suggests that he simply saw an opportunity to undermine British influence in the Middle East.

IN SEARCH OF "TRAITORS"

While Gromyko and others defended the idea of a Jewish state at the UN, Stalin was on the hunt for so-called "Zionist traitors" at home. Among the first to be attacked were members of the Jewish Anti-Fascist Committee (JAC), a group Stalin created during the war to improve the image of the

Soviet Union and raise money abroad for the war effort. The JAC was one of five anti-fascist committees; the others appealed to women, youth, scientists, and Slavs.

The JAC was a success, but its members quickly learned that the more successful they were, the more certain Stalin was of their disloyalty. The fact that they were all devoted Communists made no difference. Although they had no ties to Judaism as a religion, many had been deeply affected by the mass murder of Jews at places like Babi Yar (see Chapter 13). The group documented those murders by gathering eyewitness accounts in the hope of bringing those responsible to justice after the war. The accounts were collected into a volume known as *The Black Book*. Stalin refused to allow it to be published, even though the information was used as evidence at international trials of Nazi officials held after the war in Nuremberg, Germany.

Stalin may have feared that the book would reveal that the Germans were not the only ones involved in the genocide. A number of Russians, Ukrainians, and other Soviet citizens had taken part in the mass murders. Stalin may have also feared that the book would promote "ethnic nationalism." He insisted that everyone had suffered equally during the war. In fact, however, they had not: Jews accounted for about half of all Soviet civilians murdered by the Germans, even though Jews made up less than 1 percent of the population.

The Black Book was not the only reason the JAC was in trouble. Some of its members wanted to turn Crimea (a part of the Ukraine) into a Jewish "autonomous republic"; it would be a place where Soviet Jews could live without fear of antisemitism. Nikita Khrushchev, who headed the Ukrainian Communist Party in 1948, described Stalin's reaction:

> *He had [committee members] arrested, arbitrarily and without any regard for legal norms, regardless of the important and positive role which the accused had played during the war in helping to bring to light the atrocities committed by the Germans. Theirs had been constructive work, but now it counted for nothing. . . . Stalin could have simply rejected their suggestion and rebuked them. But no, he had to destroy all those who actively supported the proposal.*[5]

In January 1948, Stalin began the process of destroying the JAC by ordering the "accidental death" of its chairman, Solomon Mikhoels. Then, one by one, other members were executed or shipped to forced-labor camps in Siberia on Stalin's order.

Golda Meir, who was born in the old Russian Empire, returned in 1948 as Israel's first ambassador to the Soviet Union. When she tried to attend services at a Moscow synagogue, she was mobbed by Jewish well-wishers. Stalin saw their pride in her as evidence of their disloyalty to him.

That summer, Golda Meir, who would later become prime minister of Israel, came to Moscow as Israel's first ambassador to the Soviet Union. Meir had been born in Russia, and many Jews there were extraordinarily proud of her accomplishments. In early fall, when she arrived at one of the few synagogues left in Moscow to observe Rosh Hashanah (the Jewish New Year), she found nearly 30,000 Jews gathered just to catch a glimpse of her. She recalled that "within seconds they had surrounded me, almost lifting me bodily, almost crushing me, saying my name over and over again."[6] Golda Meir later wrote of the consequences of that joyous outburst:

> *By January, 1949, it was apparent that Russian Jewry was going to pay a heavy price for the welcome it had given us, for the "treachery" to communist ideals that was—in the eyes of the Soviet government— implicit in the joy with which we had been greeted. . . . Within five months there was practically no single Jewish organization left in Russia, and the Jews kept their distance from us.*[7]

Stalin's campaign against the Jews was not limited to those who welcomed Golda Meir. It also focused on Jews in the arts, particularly those who expressed themselves in Yiddish or used Jewish themes in their work. These artists were accused of being "rootless cosmopolitans"—unpatriotic people with no attachment to their homeland. Many lost their jobs or were expelled from the Communist party, while others were imprisoned.

At about the same time, a number of even more unlikely "Zionist traitors" were put on trial: government officials of Jewish descent in the Soviet bloc (nations that the Soviets liberated in 1945 and turned into "democratic republics"). Hundreds were demoted or fired. Others were tried for treason. Among the accused was Rudolf Slansky, the former secretary-general of Czechoslovakia's Communist Party. In 1951, he and 13 colleagues were indicted for shielding "Zionist criminals," conspiring against the state, and taking part in a "Zionist plot" that supposedly included U.S. President Harry Truman and Israeli Prime Minister David Ben-Gurion.[8]

Throughout the trial, prosecutors referred to Slansky and the 10 other Jewish defendants as "swine." As "proof" of their "treachery," prosecutors revealed that the accused had sold arms to Israel in 1948. They had, in fact, provided weapons to Israel, but what the government failed to acknowledge was that Stalin had approved the sale. All were found guilty of treason and sentenced to death.

According to the *New York Times*, the proceedings were a "show trial"—a trial whose outcome is determined in advance. The accusations were also based at least in part on the long-discredited *Protocols of the Elders of Zion*. Reporters noted that Slansky and his fellow defendants were convicted of betraying their country to "American imperialism" in order to serve the State of Israel. The *Times* feared the trial was "the beginning of a major tragedy as the [Soviet Union] swings further and further towards anti-Semitism masked as anti-Zionism."[9]

In December 1952, Stalin heightened that fear when he told party officials, "Every Jew-Nationalist is an agent of American intelligence. . . . Among the doctors are many Jew-Nationalists."[10] A month later, the government arrested nine physicians for trying to "poison" Stalin and other leaders. The doctors were also charged with promoting Zionism—a crime in the Soviet Union.

The well-publicized arrests created a panic. Suddenly millions of people in the Soviet Union were terrified of Jewish doctors. Rumors swirled across the nation, one more fantastic than the next. Some claimed that Jewish physicians were injecting poison into food as well as medicine.

Others claimed that all Jews were involved in the "conspiracy." As a result, tens of thousands were fired, demoted, or denied employment.

Many in the Soviet Union believed that after the trial, all Jews would be shipped to Siberia for "security reasons." Before that could happen, Stalin died suddenly. A month later, in April 1953, the government announced that the doctors had been arrested "incorrectly" and "without any lawful basis." By then, two physicians had been tortured to death, but the rest were released.

Although the "doctors' plot" had been discredited, hostility toward "Zionist traitors" and "Jewish conspirators" continued. In 1956, Nikita Khrushchev, who had become the leader of the Soviet Union, denounced Stalin at a party meeting, but antisemitism was not on the list of crimes he attributed to the former leader. Khrushchev and his successors were not as hostile to Jews as Stalin was, but they were just as willing to use Jews as scapegoats.

In the early 1960s, Khrushchev and other leaders repeatedly blamed almost every economic crisis on what they called "Zionist conspirators." In the Soviet Union, treason included smuggling and other "economic crimes."

The title of this cartoon is "Proof of the Crime: the Jew Is Unmasked." The "crime" was the so-called plot by Jewish doctors to poison Stalin and other leaders and to promote Zionism.

Between 1961 and 1963, the government executed about 200 individuals for such crimes. About two-thirds were Jews, and lurid accounts of their activities in the Soviet press often included antisemitic slurs.[11]

The Soviet government supported its claims against the "Zionist traitors" with propaganda that falsely linked Soviet Jews to Israel or the United States. One of the most widely distributed was a book called *Judaism without Embellishment* by Trofim Kichko. Kichko claimed that "Zionists, Israelis, Jewish bankers, and Western capitalists" were taking over the world. Barukh Podolsky, an Israeli scholar who grew up in Moscow, recalled some of the ways Jews responded to the Soviet Union's anti-Zionism campaign:

> *Some tried not to stick out, [while] others "went into hiding," changed their passports and were passing for anything but Jews to get rid of the cursed "point five" [the place where "nationality" was indicated on every citizen's internal passport].*

> *There were others, who wore their Jewishness openly and with pride; but Yiddish was hardly ever heard in the streets.*[12]

As a teen, Podolsky knew very little about Zionism or Judaism. But one day he entered a synagogue near his home, out of curiosity, and he soon became a regular visitor. On one occasion, he noticed a small group that stood apart. An elderly Jew, noticing his interest, whispered that they were from the Israeli embassy.

On another visit, Podolsky approached the Israelis. They gave him a prayer book, which he showed to his parents. His mother later asked him to introduce her to the embassy people, and Podolsky arranged a meeting. At that meeting, the Israelis gave the boy and his mother a few books. The encounter also inspired Podolsky to study Hebrew. In most nations, no one would have paid attention to the gift of a few books or participation in a Hebrew language class. But in the Soviet Union, those activities prompted an investigation. Podolsky recalled:

> *The Embassy people were kept under constant surveillance, and we were tracked down and photographed, in spite of the precautions we were taking and, on April 25th 1958, all of us were arrested. All of us—meaning my parents and myself, Tina Brodetsky [a fellow Hebrew student] . . . , her stepfather, Yevsei Drobovsky, and Zilberman the Hebrew teacher.*[13]

Podolsky, his parents, and the others were eventually charged with "anti-Soviet agitation and propaganda using national/ethnic prejudices" and "participating in an anti-Soviet organization." Podolsky's parents were also accused of high treason for supposedly passing military secrets to Israel. His mother worked at a school near an aircraft plant, and the government claimed that her knowledge of the plant's existence "proved" she was a spy, despite the fact that everyone in the city knew about the plant. Streetcar conductors even announced the stop near the school as "aircraft plant."

In March 1959, a military board of the high court of the Soviet Union acquitted Podolsky's parents of high treason and sentenced them to seven years in prison. Podolsky got five years; his fellow student got two; her stepfather received one and a half; and the Hebrew teacher, who was 82 years old, got one year in prison.[14]

CONFRONTING THE PAST

Although the Podolskys may not have been aware of it at the time, they were part of a movement among Soviet Jews to reclaim a Jewish identity. In

After the war, Jews gathered at Babi Yar and other sites of mass murder to mourn loved ones, but there was no monument until 1974.

©United States Holocaust Memorial Museum, courtesy of Babi Yar Society.

many places, that movement was inspired by the need to remember loved ones murdered during the Holocaust. Some Jews put up small memorials at the places where relatives had been murdered. Often, these were little more than a sign nailed to a tree or a few stones surrounding a photograph or other artifact. Each year, people would gather to mourn and remember. From the start, Soviet officials viewed these gatherings as disloyal and insisted that Jews put the past behind them.

Holocaust survivors in other nations had similar experiences. When an Italian Jew returned from Auschwitz, she "encountered people who didn't want to know anything, because the Italians, too, had suffered." They told her, "For heaven's sake, it's all over." And so she remained quiet for a long time, as did many survivors in the Americas and other parts of Europe.[15]

By the 1950s and 1960s, however, a growing number of survivors were finding it difficult to move on with their lives without confronting the past. And some perpetrators and bystanders were also feeling the need to face not only the Holocaust but also centuries of antisemitism. The work initiated at interfaith conferences like one at Seelisberg in 1947 (see Chapter 14) now began to shape a deeper understanding of that history, and activists who took part in those conferences often led the way. Among them was Jules Isaac, a French Jew who had challenged Christian teachings of contempt for Jews at Seelisberg.

After meeting with Isaac, Pope Pius XII agreed to make a few changes in those teachings but balked when Isaac insisted that far more was needed. After Pius's death, Isaac met privately with the new pope, John XXIII. After three days of intense discussion, Isaac asked, "Can I leave with hope?" The pope responded, "You are entitled to more than hope."

That meeting contributed to Vatican II, a council of leaders in the Roman Catholic Church that met between 1962 and 1965 to reform church teachings. Among the issues these leaders dealt with was the "teaching of contempt." In 1965, two years after the death of Isaac and Pope John, the council approved a document known as *Nostra Aetate* (a Latin phrase meaning "in our time"). It and a number of related statements renounced the myth that today's Jews are responsible for the crucifixion and reaffirmed the church's belief that God has an "eternal covenant" with the Jewish people. In years to come, other churches would take a similar stand. Changes in doctrine were reinforced by changes in religious practice. For example, many Roman Catholics no longer spoke of the "perfidious Jews" on Good Friday.

BREAKING THE SILENCE

The Vatican II reforms were just a few elements in a series of seemingly unrelated events that led many individuals and nations to confront both the history of the Holocaust and antisemitism. Those events included the 1961 trial of Adolf Eichmann, Hitler's "expert" on the "Jewish question." Eichmann was responsible for the deportation of hundreds of thousands of Jews to death camps during the Holocaust (see Chapter 13). He hid after the war to avoid prosecution but was captured in Argentina by Israeli agents. Israel charged him with war crimes, crimes against the Jewish people, and crimes against humanity.

James Parkes, an Anglican priest and expert on early Christianity, attended the Eichmann trial. In Parkes's view, the trial revealed that "there is an unbroken chain which goes back from Hitler's death camps to the denunciations of [Jews by] the early Church."[16] Not long after the trial ended, the Protestant World Council of Churches issued a document condemning antisemitism and stating that contemporary Jews were in no way responsible for the death of Jesus.

Immediately after the war, the Allies had tried a number of Nazi leaders for war crimes and crimes against humanity in Nuremberg, Germany. Those trials were based on the literally thousands of detailed records that the Germans kept. At Eichmann's trial, however, the emphasis was not on the written record but on the testimony of survivors. Ariana Melamed, an Israeli writer and a child of survivors, said of those who testified:

> *Most of them had no direct relation to Eichmann's doings, and in an ordinary trial their testimonies would have been disqualified due to lack of relevance. But their cries, their despair, the exposing of secrets they had carried inside them like malignant tumors—all those were much more important than the trial itself. They enabled the Israelis . . . to understand something that [had] until then remained out of the public eye: The power of the personal account over that of the official narrative."[17]*

Melamed was not the only young Israeli who found the trial eye-opening. Gideon Hausner, the Israeli prosecutor, said of the letters he received during and after the proceedings:

> *It was the overwhelming popular reaction of a nation shocked to the core. Many, probably youngsters, too ashamed to reveal themselves*

but still wishing to react somehow, expressed their emotions in various ways . . . . A girl wrote saying she had no uncles and aunts to visit on Saturdays and holidays, like other children, but had never understood before why they were all dead. . . . A girl of seventeen from Ramat Gan went further. "I could not honor all my relatives about whom I heard from my father. I loathed them for letting themselves be slaughtered. Thank you for opening my eyes to what had really happened."[18]

Most young American Jews in the 1960s also knew very little about the Holocaust. Brooks Susman, who would later become a rabbi, told an interviewer, "My parents hid it from us. They didn't want us to be injured or brutalized by it. 'We went to war. We beat Hitler. It can never happen again. You don't need to know about it.'" His parents were not alone; many Jews in the years after the Holocaust were reluctant to discuss the genocide with their children. And yet, as adults, many of those children recalled that it "was hard not to stumble upon the Holocaust" in the

© McNamee / CORBIS

Jews in the United States and Western Europe held rallies demanding that the Soviet Union allow Jews to freely emigrate.

1950s and 1960s through books like *The Diary of Anne Frank* or films like *Judgment at Nuremberg.*[19]

As these young Jews became more aware of the Holocaust, some formed study groups at synagogues and community centers to deepen their knowledge. Louis Rosenblum, a NASA scientist in Cleveland, Ohio, attended one of those groups. By the time the course ended, he and his classmates were convinced that their parents' generation had not done enough to save European Jews. They were determined not to make the same mistake. So they decided to find out where Jews were still at risk. They quickly focused on the plight of Jews in the Soviet Union.

Rosenblum and other Jewish activists worked with many Catholics and Protestants to build a network that publicized the obstacles faced by Soviet Jews, pressured the Soviets to allow Jews to emigrate, and helped those permitted to leave to find new homes.[20] These efforts were complicated by the Cold War. American officials endorsed the movement, but their Soviet counterparts viewed the calls for emigration as proof of Jewish disloyalty and even treason.

EGYPTIAN ANTISEMITISM AND ANTI-ZIONISM

Jews in Arab countries were also seen as potential traitors. But the antisemitism they experienced was not exactly like the hatred that Soviet Jews encountered. In the Soviet Union, anti-Zionism was little more than a mask for antisemitism and a convenient tool for diverting attention away from problems at home and abroad. In Arab nations, many people opposed Zionism because they believed that the UN had no right to establish a Jewish state on what they considered Arab land. They also saw the Zionist claim to Israel as a continuation of Western domination. And, for some, anti-Zionism was increasingly rooted in a belief that God had given Muslims ownership and responsibility for all of the Middle East.

The fact that Arabs had reasons for opposing Zionism did not mean that their opposition was free of antisemitism. A closer look at Egypt between 1945 and 1967 suggests how an opposition to Israel as a Jewish state became entangled with antisemitism.

At the end of World War II, Egypt was independent in name only; the British controlled much of the nation's foreign policy. Most Egyptians wanted real independence. Some took to the streets to express those feelings. On November 2, 1945—the anniversary of the Balfour Declaration, a document that promised British support for a Jewish homeland in Palestine (see Chapter 12)—Hassan al-Banna, the head of the Muslim Brotherhood (see Chapter 14), gave a fiery speech at a rally in Cairo. Soon after, violence broke out as angry protestors went on a rampage in the city's Jewish neighborhoods.

Why did anger at a declaration issued in 1917 result in an attack on Egyptian Jews 28 years later? Perhaps it was because the British had power and Egyptian Jews did not and so they were easier to attack. The answer may also have had something to do with the way Egyptians had come to define citizenship. In 1919, the slogan of one of the first nationalist uprisings was "Religion is for God and the homeland is for all." That slogan included everyone in Egypt. By 1945, the motto had become "Egypt for the Egyptians," and it referred only to Egyptians who were Muslim and Arab. Some groups, like the Brotherhood, wanted to narrow the meaning further to include only those who wanted an Islamic state—one governed according to Islamic religious principles.

The Brotherhood believed that European ways had corrupted Egyptians and degraded Egyptian society. Members called for a jihad to restore Egypt to "God's rule." The word *jihad* literally means "struggle" or "striving." It traditionally refers to the struggle of believers to carry out God's will. However, the Brotherhood used the term to refer to an armed struggle against the enemies of Islam.

The enemies in that struggle were "the Jews," according to Sayyid Qutb, one of the Brotherhood's leading thinkers. In his view, they had been the "enemies of the Muslim Community from the first day." He added, "This bitter war which the Jews launched against Islam . . . is a war, which has not been extinguished, even for one moment, for close on fourteen centuries, and which continues until this moment, its blaze raging in all corners of the earth."[21]

The war to which Qutb referred was the conflict that resulted from the refusal of Jewish tribes in Medina to accept Islam in the 600s (see Chapter 3). In Qutb's view, "the Jews were still fighting that war with the help of 'agents,'" whom he defined as those who lead "the Muslim Community away from its Religion and its Qur'an."[22] As more and more imams (prayer leaders) and mullahs (religious scholars) incorporated Qutb's ideas into their teachings, those ideas began to shape the way ordinary people regarded Jews.

In 1945, however, few Egyptians supported such ideas. Indeed, a number of Egyptians tried to protect Jews from the rioters. King Farouk and other officials expressed sympathy for the victims and offered to rebuild a synagogue burned in the riots. Despite such expressions of concern, however, one observer noted, "The critics of the riots did nothing to stop the distribution of anti-Jewish propaganda in Egypt."[23]

Despite—or perhaps because of—the propaganda, Farouk offered Jews his protection soon after Egypt led an Arab attack on the newly declared State of Israel in May 1948. But his prime minister, Mahmud Fahmi al-Nugrashi, did not. Instead, claiming that all Jews were "potential Zionists" and "potential traitors," he ordered that every Jewish organization provide the names and addresses of its members. The Muslim Brotherhood went further by calling for a boycott of all Jewish businesses. Some members went further still. In July, they set off a bomb in Cairo that killed 22 Jews and wounded 41 others.[24]

At first officials blamed the explosion on "an aerial torpedo from Jewish aircraft." But witnesses disagreed. As more bombings took place over the next few months, the prime minister had to confront the Muslim Brotherhood. He banned the group, and the Brotherhood retaliated by assassinating him. In response, government agents killed al-Banna, the group's leader.

Nevertheless, soon after Egypt signed a formal cease-fire agreement with Israel in 1949, about 20,000 Jews—25 percent of the nation's Jewish population—emigrated. Among them were a few Zionists, but most were from families that had lived in Egypt for generations and regarded it as their home but could no longer earn a living there. A 1947 law required that 90 percent of workers in almost every business and 51 percent of owners had to be Egyptian—and this now meant a person born in Egypt who was Arab and Muslim.

In July 1952, the revolution that King Farouk and his supporters had long feared finally came. It was led by a group known as the Free Officers, nearly all of whose members had fought in the 1948 war against Israel. They blamed the king and his advisers for their losses. Now the Free Officers declared Egypt a republic with Muhammad Naguib as its first president; in 1954, he was ousted by Gamal Abdul Nasser.

Before the revolt, Naguib, Nasser, and 8 of the other 14 leaders of the revolution had vowed to carry out the goals of the Muslim Brotherhood. Once in power, however, they concentrated on promoting Arab nationalism. Nasser also wanted Egypt to become a socialist state much like the Soviet Union.

In 1956, Nasser nationalized hundreds of foreign-owned businesses, including the Suez Canal Company (most of whose stockholders were British and French). Almost immediately, he closed the canal to ships going to or from Israel. Israel viewed the closure as an act of war. On

October 29, the nation invaded Egypt's Sinai Peninsula and pushed toward the Suez Canal. Two days later, Britain and France joined the invasion.

As the Suez crisis was turning into a war, a revolt against Communist rule was taking place in Hungary. Although the Soviets brutally crushed that uprising, they loudly condemned France, Britain, and Israel for their occupation of the Canal Zone and threatened to use "modern weapons of destruction" if the fighting continued. U.S. President Dwight Eisenhower also expressed disapproval. He thought that the invasion was ill-considered and should be undone. Within days, the fighting ended.

During the Suez crisis, Egyptian Jews were not harassed by mobs as they had been in 1948. This time the threat came from a government that no longer distinguished Zionists from other Jews. As Lucette Lagnado, an Egyptian Jew, explained, "Families who had lived in Egypt for genera-tions, whose children were born there and knew no other way of life, were escorted to the airport and, as squads of rifle-toting soldiers watched, put on planes bound for Europe."[25]

Within a year, another 30,000 Jews had left Egypt. By 1967, only 4,000 remained. Even as Jews fled or were pushed from the nation, antisemitism increased. The spread of Arab nationalism, the influence of groups like the Muslim Brotherhood, and the ongoing conflict with Israel all played a part in blurring the line between anti-Zionism and antisemitism.

Bookstalls in Egypt now featured the writings of Qutb along with dozens of newspapers, books, and magazines that demonized Jews. There were also Arabic translations of the *Protocols of the Elders of Zion* and Hitler's *Mein Kampf,* as well as Soviet propaganda. Arab leaders like Nasser praised these works. He claimed that the *Protocols* proved "beyond a shadow of doubt that three hundred Zionists, each of whom knows all the others, govern the fate of the European continent."[26] Although Egypt and Saudi Arabia were at odds during these years, King Saud of Saudi Arabia also recommended the *Protocols* to foreign visitors.

POLITICS AND WAR IN THE ARAB WORLD

In the late 1940s and the 1950s, Egypt, Jordan, and other Arab nations in the Middle East took the lead in the continuing conflict with Israel. They claimed that it was only a matter of time until they drove out the Israelis and established an Arab state (see Chapter 14). By the early 1960s, however, some Palestinians were tired of waiting and decided to take matters into their own hands by raiding Israeli settlements. In time, these raids became a new "front" in the Cold War.

Israel tried to convince Arab leaders of the need to stop the violence by retaliating after each raid. The strategy persuaded President Nasser of Egypt and King Hussein of Jordan; neither wanted another war. But the Soviet Union and Syria saw the raids as an opportunity to expand their influence in the region, so they provided the Palestinians with money and arms.

Fatah was one of the groups the Soviet Union and Syria supported. It had been founded in the 1950s by Yasir Arafat and several other young Palestinians; by the early 1960s, the group was taking credit for dozens of raids into Israel. Its popularity and the rise of even more extreme groups worried Egypt and other members of the Arab League. In 1964, the Arab League decided to unite those groups into a single organization under their leadership—the Palestine Liberation Organization (PLO). The league hoped the new group would keep young Palestinians in check.

If the Arab League had been united, the plan might have worked. However, Syria had no interest in halting the raids on Israel. In 1965, with its help, Fatah claimed responsibility for 35 raids; in 1966, 41; and in the first four months of 1967, 37. As the attacks continued, Israel clashed not only with Fatah but also with Syrians in the Golan Heights (which bordered Israel). The Soviets also contributed to the rising tensions by supplying Fatah and similar groups with money and arms and spreading false rumors that Israeli troops were gathering near the Syrian border.

By mid-May, Nasser was convinced that war was inevitable and began making plans for the coming conflict. He closed the Straits of Tiran to ships going to or from Israel, demanded that UN troops leave the Sinai Peninsula, and stationed troops along Egypt's borders with Israel. Those acts, in turn, convinced the Israelis that war was inevitable. On June 5, 1967, war began. It became known as the Six-Day War, or the 1967 War. By the time the UN arranged a cease-fire on June 11, Israel held Egypt's Sinai Peninsula, Jordan's West Bank and East Jerusalem, and Syria's Golan Heights.

As news of Israel's victory spread through the Middle East and North Africa, angry mobs attacked the few Jews who remained in Arab nations. When the UN and the Red Cross tried to intervene, they were turned away. The leaders of Egypt, Syria, and Iraq responded to the anti-Jewish violence by expelling nearly every Jew within their borders. Only King Hassan of Morocco and President Habib Bourgiba of Tunisia condemned the riots.

Not long after the war ended, a number of Arab leaders made plans for yet another war. On October 6, 1973, Egypt led a surprise attack against

Israel. Although Israel was caught unprepared, in less than three weeks its army had gained the initiative. On October 26, the UN imposed a cease-fire to prevent a regional war from escalating into a world war.

Although Egypt did not win the 1973 War, its success in the early battles showed that Israel was not invincible. The war also revealed the power of a new factor in the conflict—oil. The leaders of Saudi Arabia and other oil-producing states raised the price of oil for nations they considered pro-Israel. The sharp increases hit many countries hard. Some began to rethink their support for Israel.

Arab losses in the two wars gave groups like Fatah new legitimacy. Fatah took over the PLO soon after Yasir Arafat became chairman in 1969. By the 1970s, the group was not only raiding Israeli settlements but also attacking Jews abroad. Its 1968 charter described Zionism as "racist and fanatic in its nature, aggressive, expansionist, and colonial in its aims, and fascist in its methods" and called for the destruction of Israel. The charter also claimed that the Zionists were using Israel as "a geographical base for world imperialism."[27] To many Israelis, the document was proof that anti-Zionism was a form of antisemitism.

The Muslim Brotherhood saw the Arabs' defeat in the two wars as evidence that Arab leaders had strayed from the "pure teaching of Islam." Some leaders, including Nasser, agreed. Nasser once again aligned himself with the group, telling his followers that "Almighty God wanted to give us a lesson."[28] After Nasser's death in 1970, Anwar al-Sadat became president. He continued to support the radically conservative Islamic ideology that marked Nasser's final years.

CONSEQUENCES ABROAD

The Middle East and North Africa were not the only places where the two wars had an impact. Israel's victories shattered old stereotypes about the "cowardliness of the Jews." In Western Europe, those old stereotypes were quickly replaced with new ones. In a 1967 press conference, French President Charles de Gaulle described Jews as "an elite people, self-confident, and domineering" and claimed that they were responsible for "provoking ill will in certain countries and at certain times."[29] In Britain, novelist Colin MacInnes observed:

> Before the battle started most Englishmen thought of Jews only as the oppressed, the victims, "Little Israel"; surrounded by foes dedicated to its destruction. After their swift victory, the Jews seemed transformed

THE EMIGRATION OF JEWS FROM MUSLIM NATIONS (1948–1967)

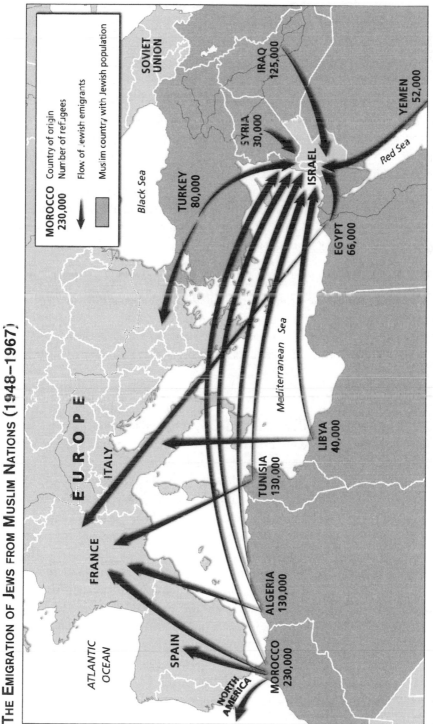

Legend:
- MOROCCO 230,000 — Country of origin / Number of emigrants
- Flow of Jewish emigrants
- Muslim country with Jewish population

SOVIET UNION

IRAQ 125,000

YEMEN 52,000

SYRIA 30,000

Red Sea

TURKEY 80,000

Black Sea

ISRAEL

EGYPT 66,000

Mediterranean Sea

LIBYA 40,000

TUNISIA 130,000

EUROPE

ITALY

FRANCE

ALGERIA 130,000

SPAIN

MOROCCO 230,000

ATLANTIC OCEAN

NORTH AMERICA

Jews have lived in the Middle East and North Africa for thousands of years. By the 1960s, most of these communities were gone. Some Jews left because they no longer saw a future for themselves in the country of their birth. Many others were forced out by extreme nationalists or governments that increasingly saw all Jews as potential traitors.

into the conquerors, even oppressors. And Arabs, who were thought of
as arrogant attackers, seemed to have become overnight the victims,
the wronged, the weak.[30]

Leaders of the Soviet Union and its allies in Eastern Europe insisted
that Israel's victories were the result of a "powerful international conspiracy" linked to the Nazis. Several brochures promoting that lie appeared
in the Ukraine. According to the *New York Times*, they "accused Zionist
leaders of conspiring against the Government of the Soviet Union and
charged that they had collaborated with the Nazi regime in Germany."[31]

Similar accusations appeared in government-controlled media throughout
the Soviet bloc. In 1968, British philosopher Bertrand Russell expressed
his outrage at those charges in a letter to Wladyslaw Gomulka, the first
secretary of Poland's Communist Party:

Over the past eighteen months in Poland, the Press, the secret police
and the Government have instigated anti-Semitism quite deliber-
ately. By some twisted logic, all Jews are now Zionists, Zionists are
fascists, fascists are Nazis, and Jews, therefore, are to be identified
with the very criminals who only recently sought to eliminate Polish
Jewry.[32]

Despite such criticism, the Soviet Union continued to provide Arab
nations with military and economic support. That aid persuaded the United
States to supply Israel with arms in order to "balance" Soviet influence in
the region. To many Soviet and Arab leaders, American support for Israel
was proof that the Israelis were "in league with" the Americans.

The Soviet Union, along with its allies in the Soviet bloc (except for
Romania), broke off diplomatic relations with Israel immediately after
the Six-Day War and launched a new anti-Zionist campaign at home and
abroad. That campaign marked a turning point for many Soviet Jews. They
were now more eager than ever to leave the Soviet Union and reclaim
their Jewish identity. Boris Kochubiyevsky, a young radio engineer from
Kiev, attributed their eagerness to antisemitism—"the new brand which
was implanted from above and, as a means of camouflage, is called
anti-Zionism."[33]

To emigrate, a Soviet citizen needed permission from the government,
and Soviet officials routinely denied almost all such requests. In 1970,
eleven Soviet activists—eight Jews and three non-Jews—took the matter
into their own hands. They planned to hijack a plane and fly it to Finland.

They were arrested before they could do so, however, and charged with treason. Ten of the eleven were found guilty. Two received the death penalty; the others were sentenced to 5 to 15 years in prison.

In New York City, Mayor John Lindsay spoke at a rally attended by more than 2,000 people. He said: "We meet this afternoon as Jew and Gentile, black and white, young and old . . . to speak out for thousands of Soviet Jews who cannot speak for themselves."[34] Similar rallies were held in cities across the United States and Western Europe.

In the end, Soviet leaders gave in and reduced the sentences issued at the Leningrad trials. Jews had found a way to be heard. In the 1970s, only a few hundred Jews were allowed to emigrate each year. Throughout the 1980s, the numbers grew. More than 8,000 left in 1987, about 70,000 in 1989, and nearly 300,000 in 1990.

CONFRONTATION AT THE UNITED NATIONS

Throughout the 1970s, Soviet and Arab leaders falsely linked Zionism to racism and imperialism by arguing that Zionism was "an imperialistic militant ideology of racial hatred which should be universally condemned."[35] That language had a powerful impact on nations that had only recently been under colonial rule and were still struggling with the consequences of racism and imperialism. As a result, many people in the world's newest nations (most of whom had never met a single Jew) came to believe that "Zionist organizations" and "Zionist capital" dominated the world. Zionism was increasingly viewed as a huge, invisible power linked to American imperialism.

The Soviets and the Arabs also used the United Nations to promote anti-Zionism. In 1948, the year Israel declared its independence, the UN had 58 members; by 1965, it had 117. Over the next ten years, an additional 27 nations would join the UN. Many of them supported a 1975 UN resolution backed by the Soviet Union and Arab nations that defined Zionism as a "form of racism."

Still, after listening to the debate, a delegate from Sierra Leone reminded his colleagues that Kwame Nkrumah, a leader of the African nationalist liberation cause, used the term *black Zionism* to describe a movement to return to Africa those people whose African ancestors had been sold into slavery. He noted that Nkrumah did not consider black Zionism racist. Israeli ambassador Chaim Herzog began his speech on a similar note:

Zionism is to the Jewish people what the liberation movements of Africa and Asia have been to their own people. . . .

Historically it is based on a unique and unbroken connection, extending some four thousand years, between the People of the Book and the Land of the Bible. In modern times, in the late nineteenth century, spurred by the twin forces of anti-Semitic persecution and of nationalism, the Jewish people organized the Zionist movement in order to transform their dream into reality. . . .

Zionism is our attempt to build a society, imperfect though it may be, in which the visions of the prophets of Israel will be realized. I know that we have problems. I know that many disagree with our government's policies. Many in Israel too disagree from time to time with the government's policies . . . and are free to do so because Zionism has created the first and only real democratic state in a part of the world that never really knew democracy and freedom of speech.[36]

In the end, the resolution passed with 72 votes in favor, 35 against, 32 nations abstaining. Jews in many places were immediately branded as "racists worse than the Nazis," and anti-Zionism was incorporated into UN documents. It took Israel and its allies, including the United States, 16 years to overturn the resolution. They succeeded in part because of the collapse of the Soviet Union's Communist government in 1991.

Despite the resolution, some progress toward peace took place in the Middle East. In November 1977, Anwar al-Sadat flew to Israel to meet with Israeli Prime Minister Menachem Begin. As a result of that journey and the support of the United States, Sadat and Begin signed a peace treaty in March 1979. It aroused fierce opposition not only in other Arab nations but also in Egypt. On October 6, 1981, Sadat was assassinated by the Muslim Brotherhood, a group to which he had once belonged. Although the new leaders who governed Egypt after Sadat's death did not revoke the treaty, they continued to support the antisemitic propaganda that made the conflict so difficult to resolve.

THE PALESTINIAN-ISRAELI CONFLICT

By 1987, Israel had occupied the West Bank and Gaza for 20 years, and one effort after another to negotiate a settlement had failed. That year, young Palestinians expressed their frustration with the continuing occupation by rioting, throwing stones at Israeli soldiers, and setting off homemade bombs. These attacks were known as an *intifada*, an Arabic word that means "shaking off," in the sense of shaking off the power of an oppressor.

As the rioting continued, Palestinians formed new factions that challenged the PLO. Hamas, with its ties to the Muslim Brotherhood, was the most popular. Both Hamas and the Muslim Brotherhood viewed Israel as the enemy not just because it held land that Palestinians claimed but because "Israel, by virtue of its being Jewish and of having a Jewish population, defies Islam and the Muslims."[37] In their view, the conflict was a religious as well as a political struggle.

During the fighting, the United States and several European nations encouraged Israel and the PLO to negotiate a peace agreement. The two sides met publicly in Madrid, Spain, and then secretly in Oslo, Norway. In 1993, they agreed on a course of action known as the Oslo Peace Process, with the goal of establishing two separate states—Israel and Palestine. The following year, Israel and Jordan signed a peace treaty.

As part of the peace process, Israel transferred administrative power over the territories to an elected Palestinian Authority headed by Yasir Arafat. The next step was to work out solutions to the issues that continued to divide Israelis and Palestinians—including the rights of Palestinian refugees, the status of Jerusalem, the future of Israeli settlements in the West Bank and Gaza, and security arrangements on both sides.

Even though most Israelis and Palestinians favored a two-state solution to the conflict, some Palestinians and some Israelis opposed any compromise. Hamas was among the most vocal opponents of the peace process, and it played a major role in the violence that defined the second intifada, which began in 2000.

The first intifada was dominated by young Palestinians who threw stones at soldiers, the second was marked by young people who exploded bombs that killed civilians within Israel's borders. Within Israel, the attacks hardened distrust of Palestinians. There were other differences between the two intifadas as well. Significantly by the second intifada, the Cold War was over, and the Soviet Union no longer existed. In the Middle East, several nations scrambled to take its place as a powerful benefactor. Perhaps the most aggressive was Iran, an oil rich Muslim nation with a Shi'a majority.* In 1979, Islamists had overthrown the shah, or monarch, of Iran and created a new government strictly based on Islamic law.

---

* The Shi'a and Sunni are the two great branches within Islam. Their separation grew out of a dispute over who was the legitimate successor to the Prophet Muhammad (see Chapter 3). The Shi'a are a majority in four Muslim nations—Iran, Azerbaijan, Bahrain, and Iraq. The Sunni are the majority in the others.

The new Iranian government supported Hamas, which shared its views of Israel and "the Jews." Those views included the notion that the Jews were an evil force in the world and that Israel was the "greatest enemy" of Islam. Such views were echoed in the 1988 Hamas charter, which declared, "The Zionist plan is limitless. After Palestine, the Zionists aspire to expand from the Nile to the Euphrates. . . . Their plan is embodied in the *Protocols of the Elders of Zion* and their present conduct is the best proof of what we are saying."[38]

This extreme language had—and continues to have—consequences. As in earlier times, it has spurred a rise in violence against Jews; this violence has reawakened many to the fact that antisemitism is still a very convenient hatred.

[1] Joe McCarthy, "GI Vision of a Better America," *New York Times Magazine*, August 5, 1945, 10; E. Digby Baltzell, "Foreword," in Murray Friedman, ed., *Philadelphia Jewish Life, 1940–1985* (Ardmore, PA: Seth Press, 1986), ix, quoted in Leonard Dinnerstein, *Antisemitism in America* (New York: Oxford University Press, 1994), 151.

[2] Quoted in Nora Levin, *The Jews in the Soviet Union since 1917: Paradox of Survival, vol.1* (New York: New York University Press, 1988), 1:444.

[3] Levin, *The Jews in the Soviet Union*, 1:445.

[4] Andrei Gromyko, United Nations General Assembly, 77th Plenary Meeting, May 14, 1947, http://unispal.un.org/UNISPAL.NSF/0/D4126DF1132AD6BE052566190059E5F0.

[5] Nikita Khrushchev, *Khrushchev Remembers: The Last Testament*, trans. and ed. Strobe Talbott (Boston: Little, Brown & Company, 1974).

[6] Golda Meir, *My Life* (New York: G. P. Putnam's Sons, 1975), 250.

[7] Ibid., 254.

[8] Levin, *The Jews in the Soviet Union*, 1:524.

[9] "Tragicomedy in Prague," *New York Times*, November 22, 1952.

[10] V. A. Malyshev diary, *Istochnik* no. 5 (1997), 140–141, quoted in Geoffrey Roberts, *Stalin's Wars: From World War to Cold War, 1939–1953* (New Haven: Yale University Press, 2006), 341.

[11] Howard M. Sachar, *A History of the Jews in the Modern World* (New York: Vintage Books, 2005), 715.

[12] Barukh Podolsky, "How I Became a Zionist," Soviet Jews Exodus, accessed March 25, 2011, http://www.angelfire.com/sc3/soviet_jews_exodus/English/Memory_s/MemoryPodolsky.shtml.

[13] Ibid.

[14] Ibid.

[15] Giuliana Tedeschi, interview by Nicola Caracciolo, *Uncertain Refuge: Italy and the Jews During the Holocaust*, trans. and ed. Florette Rechnitz Koffler and Richard Koffler (Urbana: University of Illinois Press, 1995), 121.

[16] James Parkes, "After the Eichmann Verdict," *Observer*, December 17, 1961, 8, quoted in David Cesarani, *Becoming Eichmann: Rethinking the Life, Crimes, and Trial of a "Desk Murderer"* (Cambridge, MA: Da Capo Press, 2006), 329.

[17] Ariana Melamed, "The Year the Silence Was Broken," *Israel News,* April 22, 2008.

[18] Gideon Hausner, *Justice in Jerusalem* (New York: Harper & Row, 1966), 433.

[19] Myrna Katz Frommer and Harvey Frommer, *Growing Up Jewish in America: An Oral History* (New York: Harcourt Brace, 1995), 122, 124.

[20] Louis Rosenblum, "Involvement in the Soviet Jewry Movement," Cleveland Jewish History, accessed March 25, 2011, http://www.clevelandjewishhistory.net/sj/lr-beginnings.htm.

[21] Sayyid Qutb, essay reproduced in Ronald L. Nettler, *Past Trials and Present Tribulations: A Muslim Fundamentalist's View of the Jews* (Oxford: Pergamom Press, 1987), 72–87, quoted in Matthias Küntzel, *Jihad and Jew Hatred: Islamism, Nazism and the Roots of 9/11*, trans. Colin Meade (New York: Telos Press, 2007), 83.

[22] Ibid., 85.

[23] Thomas Mayer, *Egypt and the Palestine Question, 1936–1945* (Berlin, 1983), 300, quoted in Norman A. Stillman, *Jews of Arab Lands in Modern Times* (Philadelphia: Jewish Publication Society, 2003), 143.

[24] Stillman, *Jews of Arab Lands in Modern Times*, 153.

[25] Lucette Lagnado, *The Man in the White Sharkskin Suit: A Jewish Family's Exodus from Old Cairo to the New World* (New York: Harper Perennial, 2007), 92.

[26] Quoted in Küntzel, *Jihad and Jew Hatred*, 70.

[27] Walter Laqueur and Barry Rubin, eds., "The Palestinian National Charter, July, 1968," in *The Israel-Arab Reader: A Documentary History of the Middle East Conflict* (New York: Penguin Books, 2008), 119.

[28] Quoted in Küntzel, *Jihad and Jew Hatred*, 72.

[29] Charles de Gaulle, quoted in Jon D. Levenson, "Closeness and Its Enemies," *Commentary*.

[30] Colin MacInnes, *Sunday Telegraph*, June 18, 1967.

[31] Raymond H. Anderson, "Soviet Again Excoriates Zionism As Instigator of Anti-Semitism; Anti-Zionist Brochures Racist Activity Charged," *New York Times*, December 31, 1967.

[32] Bertrand Russell, "Open Letter to Wladyslaw Gomulka," in *World Jewry* 11, no. 6 (Nov.–Dec. 1968): 8, first quoted in Possony, *Waking Up the Giant*, 473.

[33] Boris Kochubiyevsky, quoted in Allan Levine, *Scattered among the Peoples: The Jewish Diaspora in Twelve Portraits* (Woodstock, NY: Overlook Duckworth, 2003), 383.

[34] "Protests Here and Abroad Continue on Soviet Jews," *New York Times,* December 30, 1970.

[35] Weekly News Summary, UN Press Release WS/760, April 30, 1976.

[36] Chaim Herzog, "Speech to the General Assembly of the United Nations, November 10, 1975," in *Who Stands Accused? Israel Answers Its Critics* (New York: Random House, 1978), 6–9.

[37] "Hamas Charter (1988)," *Selected Documents Regarding Palestine*, The Jerusalem Fund, http://www.thejerusalemfund.org/carryover/documents/charter.html.

[38] Ibid.

16

Antisemitism Today:
A Convenient Hatred

In the 1990s, many Jews came to believe that widespread antisemitism no longer limited what they could achieve or how far they could go in life—that unlike Jews at earlier times in history, they had no need to deny or mask their identity in order to realize their dreams. And yet, by the turn of the twenty-first century, a growing number of Jews and non-Jews were uncomfortably aware that antisemitism was still a force in the world. In 2002, journalist Jonathan Rosen wrote:

> When I was growing up, my father would go to bed with a transistor radio set to an all-news station. Even without a radio, my father was attuned to the menace of history. A Jew born in Vienna in 1924, he fled his homeland in 1938; his parents were killed in the Holocaust. I sometimes imagined my father was listening for some repetition of past evils so that he could rectify old responses, but he may just have been expecting more bad news. In any event, the grumbling static from the bedroom depressed me, and I vowed to replace it with music more cheerfully in tune with America. These days, however, I find myself on my father's frequency. I have awakened to anti-Semitism.[1]

In many respects, the antisemitism to which Rosen awoke is similar to the antisemitism explored in earlier chapters of this book. As Nicholas Weill, a French journalist, noted, "Synagogues are still set on fire" and "Jews are still blamed for their supposed excessive money or power, and the cartoon and newspaper caricatures revive the oldest clichés of antisemitism: vampirism, ritual murder, and so on."[2] And hate speech still sparks bloodshed. Words have power, and the link between the language of extremism and actual violence remains as strong as ever. So is the scapegoating that has turned antisemitism into a convenient hatred.

And yet antisemitism today is not exactly like the hatred that Rosen's father experienced, or even like the antisemitism his ancestors knew. Like other hatreds, antisemitism is almost always a current event—one that is triggered by the fears and anxieties of the moment. And in an age when anyone almost anywhere can stir anger with a lie broadcast widely and repeated endlessly on satellite TV or the Internet, today's antisemitism is frequently an international affair.

WHEN "THE IMPOSSIBLE BECAME POSSIBLE"

In the 1990s, Rabbi Jonathan Sacks, Britain's chief rabbi, was among those who believed that widespread antisemitism no longer threatened Jews. In 2005, he explained why he changed his mind:

> It happened in a little place called Durban [South Africa] one week before September 11 [2001], [at] the United Nations Conference Against Racism. Mary Robinson [the UN high commissioner on human rights], who convened that conference, knew that it was going to be a catastrophe, and she asked me and [Prince El Hassan bin Talal of Jordan] several months before it began [to rewrite the draft of the conference declaration] in a way to do justice [to] Palestinian aspirations without doing injustice to Jews, Israel, and the Holocaust. And we did. We got together a think tank . . . in King's College, London, and we got Muslims—the World Council of Churches—we got a lot of people. We did it in three days. We sent it in, and it was rejected at the preconference in Geneva.[3]

That pre-conference meeting took place during the second intifada (see Chapter 15). Mary Robinson and other UN officials had turned to Rabbi Sacks and Prince Hassan of Jordan for help because they feared that the ongoing conflict between Israelis and Palestinians would dominate the World Conference Against Racism (WCAR). The refusal of many delegates to even consider a compromise confirmed those fears. Nevertheless, nearly 4,000 non-governmental organizations (NGOs) sent representatives to Durban. Among them was the European Union of Jewish Students (EUJS). About a dozen members of the group attended the two forums that overlapped with the governmental conference—one for youth organizations and the other for NGOs.

Joëlle Fiss, then chair of the EUJS, kept a diary throughout her stay in Durban. To her surprise, she and her colleagues found themselves the focus of angry demonstrations by Palestinian activists and their supporters. The demonstrators insisted that they were not antisemitic; they were simply showing their outrage at Israel's treatment of the Palestinians in the territories it occupied after the Six-Day War in 1967 (see Chapter 15).

Yet as Fiss and her colleagues repeatedly pointed out, they were not Israelis, nor did they have any influence on Israeli policies. But they found no one willing to listen.

As the harassment continued, Fiss looked forward to a session on antisemitism. According to the rules of the NGO forum, it would be an opportunity for Jews to tell their story without interruption. Despite the rules, the audience heckled every Jewish speaker. Then, suddenly, several dozen people standing just outside the tent in which the session took place mounted an assault. Fiss wrote:

> *They storm into the tent and scream at the top of their lungs: "You are all murderers! You have Palestinian blood on your hands!" They approach us as we gather at the center of the room around the table where the panelists are seated. Panic drives some to run away. "You don't belong to the human race!" "Chosen people? You are cursed people! I won't speak to you, as long as you do not remove this thing," a man yells at David, who is wearing a kippa [a skullcap traditionally worn by religious Jewish men].*

> *The assault continues. "Why haven't the Jews taken responsibility for killing Jesus? They have sucked our blood, all these years. We don't want you here. Jews don't belong in Jordan. Jews don't belong in Israel." "I believe in a Jewish state . . . on Mars!" "[Ariel] Sharon [the Israeli prime minister], Golda Meir [a former Israeli prime minister]. . . . They are all the same. We cannot convince Sharon to be a human being."*

> *. . . The anger against us can no longer be contained. We have no refuge. The violence becomes physical.*[4]

Nearly every slander hurled at Jews over the centuries was expressed in that moment. And, as in the past, the mob's anger was directed not just at Israel or at "Zionists" but at all Jews everywhere.

Although the forums were sponsored by the UN, officials did not intervene at that session or any other. Nor did they remove the antisemitic literature, banners, and posters on display throughout the WCAR. They were not the only ones who failed to take a stand. About 18,000 activists from 166 nations attended the conference. Although most did not participate in the catcalls, chants, or physical intimidation of Jewish participants, they too failed to intervene.

ICARE (Internet Centre Anti Racism Europe), a virtual network that provides information on issues related to human rights, issued daily reports throughout the conference. Its staff was struck by the fact that "antisemitism against and intimidation of anyone who was thought to be Jewish, friendly to Jews, or a member of a Jewish organisation ran wild. It was a hijack and we all let ourselves be hijacked, some even fully assisted the hijackers."[5]

The NGO forum was supposed to produce a declaration and a plan of action. Both would then be submitted to the governmental conference for approval. Claiming that Zionism was a form of racism, the two documents singled out only one nation in the world as "racist"—Israel. In doing so, they deliberately challenged the 1991 UN resolution that renounced the idea that Zionism was racist (see Chapter 15).

The vote to approve the two documents was by caucus. A caucus in this context was a group of NGOs that shared a theme (such as "human rights"), belonged to the same victim group, or lived in the same region (such as Africa or Eastern and Central Europe). Delegates could join and vote in more than one caucus, and many did.

In the end, just four caucuses—the Jewish, European, Roma, and Eastern and Central European ones—opposed the draft. After the vote, the Jewish and Eastern and Central European caucuses walked out of the NGO forum in protest. The Roma (a group sometimes referred to as "Gypsies") stayed briefly to explain why its members opposed the "blatantly intolerant anti-Semitic spirit plaguing the entire process."[6] As a result of that "anti-Semitic spirit," the governments of the United States and Israel refused to participate in WCAR. Members of the European caucus stayed to negotiate a more tolerant declaration and plan of action at the governmental conference.

After the UN conference, ICARE summed up what its staff had learned:

> The fact that racism was allowed to run rampant during the WCAR is astonishing. What is even more astonishing, shameful, and harmful for the antiracism cause and for the victims of racism is that the majority of the organisers and participants let that happen, did nothing to stop it and did not speak out during or after the WCAR. The fight against racism and discrimination is a fight against all forms of racism and discrimination. The moment antiracists tolerate or even promote one kind of racism and only fight the other kinds they are no longer antiracists.[7]

In reflecting on what she had learned, Joëlle Fiss wrote in 2008, "The UN Conference teaches us that the impossible is still possible."

Before Durban [she noted], the large majority of public opinion basked comfortably in the peaceful days of the '90s, when, despite the fragile situation in the Middle East, today's younger generation of Diaspora Jews no longer suffered from any existential threat. Durban reminded [us that] hatred can resurface with no prior notice.[8]

A TERRORIST ATTACK AND AN AGGRESSIVE LIE

On September 11, 2001, just two days after the Durban conference ended, 19 men—15 from Saudi Arabia, one each from Egypt and Lebanon, and two from the Arab Emirates—hijacked four passenger planes in the United States. They flew two of the planes into the World Trade Center in New York City and one into the Pentagon in Washington, DC. The fourth plane crashed into a field in Pennsylvania, killing everyone on board. That day, approximately 3,000 men, women, and children of many religions and more than 60 nationalities were murdered.

The perpetrators belonged to a terrorist group known as al-Qaeda. Its members were Islamists who, like the Muslim Brotherhood and Hamas (see Chapter 15), were motivated at least in part by hatred of the modern world, which they associated with the West in general and the United States in particular. The 2002 trial of a member of an al Qaeda cell in Hamburg, Germany—the same cell to which Mohammed Atta, the ringleader of the September 11 attacks, belonged—suggested that antisemitism played a part in those attacks. Shahid Nickels, a former member of that cell, testified that he, Atta, and other members regarded New York City as "the center of world Jewry." They believed that from that center in New York, Jews controlled the U.S. government, the media, and the economy.[9]

Conspiracy theories are rarely logical. It is not surprising, then, that even as al-Qaeda "took credit" for the September 11 attacks, the group did nothing to stop a rumor claiming that "the Jews" were really responsible. That rumor alleged that Israel—specifically Mossad, Israel's intelligence agency—was behind the plot and had warned Jews not to go to work at the World Trade Center on the day of the attacks.

On September 18, an editor for a website known as the Information Times posted a message claiming that the "terrorist government of Israel . . . cannot be ruled out" as a suspect.[10] The editor did not identify a motive or provide evidence in support of his allegation. In his words, he was simply raising a "reasonable question." Five days later, al-Manar, a TV station based in Lebanon, stated that Mossad had indeed warned 4,000 Jews who worked at the World Trade Center to stay home on September 11.

Al-Manar is owned by Hezbollah, a radical Shi'a group based in Lebanon that is inspired by the revolution that turned Iran into an Islamic state. A number of journalists questioned officials at both al-Manar and Hezbollah about the station's claim that Jews were to blame for the attacks. In a December 2001 interview, Sayyid Hasan Nasrallah, Hezbollah's secretary general, told journalists that al-Manar "didn't make that story up." He went on to say that the station "just limited itself to reproducing what was being said, even if we're not totally sure that the theory is true."[11] Al-Manar presented the rumor as a fact, however, not a theory. Within days, that rumor appeared in newspapers and electronic mailing lists around the world. People continued to believe the lie despite the fact that about 18 percent of the known dead were identified in obituaries as Jews.

When an editor in Pakistan was asked why people there blamed the attacks on Jews, he replied that it might have had something to do with the Internet: "When you see something on a computer, you tend to believe it is true."[12] The same has been said about images seen on TV. Perhaps that is why Hezbollah and other Islamist groups have used both to spread their ideas.

In 2001, al-Manar was one of the most-watched TV stations in the Middle East. Many traced its popularity with young viewers to the music videos that the station showed between programs. Those videos combined violent images with music that incited hatred toward not only Israel but also Jews as a people.[13] In 2006, with help from Saudi Arabia, Hamas launched its own television station modeled after al-Manar. It too used both religion and popular culture to promote hatred of Jews. That message was also featured on its website and reinforced in the sermons heard in many mosques and the lessons taught in many madrassas (religious schools or seminaries).

That propaganda also appealed to many young people around the world—particularly in nations with a significant Muslim population. In 2007, the German Interior Ministry found that young Muslims in Germany were more likely to express "anti-Semitic attitudes" than non-Muslims, whether immigrants or native-born.[14]

"RITUAL MURDER" IN THE TWENTY-FIRST CENTURY

About five months after the attacks of September 11, many Jews experienced yet another "awakening to antisemitism." In January 2002, a correspondent for the *Wall Street Journal*, Daniel Pearl, was kidnapped in Pakistan. Despite efforts by the governments of the United States and Pakistan to keep the reporter's Jewish identity a secret, the kidnappers clearly knew that Pearl was a Jew. A group that called itself the National Movement for the Restoration of Pakistani Sovereignty recorded his beheading in a video entitled "The Slaughter of the Spy-Journalist, the Jew Daniel Pearl." It showed a carefully staged ritual murder.

On video, the kidnappers forced Pearl to repeat their demands and then state, "My name is Daniel Pearl. I'm a Jewish American. I come from . . . a family of Zionists. My father's Jewish. My mother's Jewish. My family follows Judaism. We've made numerous family visits to Israel. In the town of B'nei Brak in Israel, there's a street called Haim Pearl Street, which was named after my grandfather, who was one of the founders." Moments later, Pearl was beheaded. Journalist Thane Rosenbaum later noted:

> It must have been a tremendous coincidence for [his killers] to learn that the Pearls had a street named after them in Israel. Indeed, his murderers had hit the hostage jackpot: a Jewish-American journalist with Zionist roots. But they would have killed him anyway, even if he had never been to Israel, even if he didn't know what a Zionist was. . . . His murderers marked him for death because of one central truth in his biographical data: Stripped down to his essence, Daniel Pearl was a Jew.[15]

"INFECTION"

Pearl's murder, the UN conference in Durban, and the attacks of September 11 occurred within a six-month period. Each was motivated at least in part by antisemitic propaganda. In the months after September 11, that propaganda struck a chord even in countries that were home to few, if any, Jews. One such nation was Spain. In the early 2000s, Spain had one of Europe's smallest Jewish communities—approximately 12,000 people out of a total population of 42 million.

In 1492, Spain expelled its entire Jewish population (see Chapter 6), and it did not officially overturn that order of expulsion until 1968. In 2005, Pilar Rahola, a journalist and a former Spanish lawmaker, described her country as one that has "never confronted its responsibility with regards to antisemitism—neither in the past, nor present." She then cited a survey conducted in Spain that same year. It showed that 78 percent of the public would not accept a Jewish neighbor, 69 percent believed Jews are too powerful, and 55 percent attributed "dark intentions" to them.[16]

That survey suggested that more than 500 years after Jews had been forced out of Spain, antisemitism was still deeply embedded in Spanish culture. The media has helped keep that prejudice alive. A report issued by the European Union Monitoring Centre on Racism and Xenophobia revealed that coverage of the Middle East conflict in the Spanish media included the same antisemitic slurs that the Nazis had leveled against Jews in the 1930s (including the lies that Jews engage in ritual murder and that they conspire to control the world). The group saw a link between "the tremendous wave of anti-Israel sentiment in Spain" and the "antisemitic content in the news."[17]

British journalist Howard Jacobson comes from a nation where Jews have long been an integral part of national life. Yet he, too, worries that old slurs are once again becoming part of England's culture. He explains:

> *Most English Jews walk safely through their streets, express themselves freely, enjoy the friendship of non-Jews, and feel no less confidently a part of English life than they ever have. . . .*
>
> *And yet, in the tone of the debate, in the spirit of the national conversation about Israel, in the slow seepage of familiar anti-Semitic calumnies into the conversation—there, it seems to me, one can find growing reason for English Jews to be concerned. Mindless acts of vandalism come and go; but what takes root in the intellectual life of a nation is harder to identify and remove. . . .*
>
> *The language of extremism has a malarious dynamic of its own, passing effortlessly from the mischievous to the unwary, and from there into the bloodstream of society. And that's what one can smell here. Infection.*[18]

How does the "language of extremism" enter the "bloodstream of society"? In 2007, the Community Security Trust, the defense agency of Britain's Jewish community, explained:

> *Messages that start out as attacks on alleged Israeli policy or behaviour often conclude with abuse of, or threats to, all Jews, the wish that all Jews were dead, claims of Jewish conspiracy, or the accusation that Jews killed Christ. The antisemitism is compounded if the incident*

*is targeted at a Jewish person or institution—such as a synagogue—
that is then held responsible for the alleged actions of the Israeli
government. This charge of collective responsibility and collective
guilt, whereby every Jew in the world is supposedly answerable for
the behaviour of every other Jew, is one of the fundamental building
blocks of all racism.*[19]

This was the process that left Joëlle Fiss and her colleagues angry,
frightened, and frustrated at the Durban conference in 2001; it motivated
the September 11 terrorists and inspired the rumors that swirled after the
attacks; and it played a critical role in the murder of Daniel Pearl.

In the years since those events, a number of individuals and groups
have pressed for better ways of identifying and combating antisemitism
nationally and internationally. As a result, more than a dozen countries
have passed laws designed to reduce antisemitic violence through
education and programs that raise awareness of the problem and improve
law enforcement. Although some of these programs have been successful, the "language of extremism" has continued to infect one nation
after another. In France, it created an atmosphere that contributed to yet
another murder. This time the victim was Ilan Halimi, a 23-year-old cell-
phone salesman.

On February 13, 2006, more than three weeks after Halimi's family
notified the authorities that he was missing, the Paris police found him
half-naked, stabbed, and with cigarette and acid burns covering much of
his body. He died on the way to the hospital. The 27 individuals charged
with his murder were members of a criminal gang known as the Barbarians.
All but two were found guilty; their sentences ranged from six months to
life in prison.[20]

Why did the gang torture Halimi? That question troubled Judea Pearl,
the father of Daniel Pearl. After noting that many politicians and civic
leaders attended Halimi's funeral, he wrote:

*They always talk about "them"—the criminals, the Barbarians—
rarely about THEMSELVES.*

*They do not talk about the silence and tacit encouragement that
have created this climate in France where a gang of youngsters would
choose to target Jews. . . . A climate in which torturing a Jew is considered a lesser form of cruelty. . . . "We tortured him because he was
a Jew," said one of the abductors last week.*

How did this climate of inhumanity infiltrate a country that gave the world liberty, equality and brotherhood?[21]

The continuing violence against Jews in France in the weeks that followed Halimi's murder seemed to support Pearl's argument. Although some in Paris and other cities publicly protested the violence, many others just shrugged and turned away. Those attitudes had consequences.

In 2010, the Stephen Roth Institute for the Study of Contemporary Antisemitism and Racism reported a significant rise in antisemitic incidents in the first decade of the twenty-first century—even in years "when there was no significant Middle East trigger."[22] (A trigger is the spark that sets off violence but is not necessarily the cause of that violence.) The worst year was 2009 "in terms of both major antisemitic violence and . . . verbal and visual expressions against Israel and the Jews."[23]

Experts attributed some of the increase in antisemitism to widespread opposition to an Israeli military action in Gaza during the winter of 2008–2009.[24] But it was not the only factor. Elisa Massimino, president of the group Human Rights First, explained why:

> *Contemporary antisemitism is multifaceted and deeply rooted. It cannot be viewed solely as a transitory side-effect of the conflict in the Middle East. Antisemitic incitement and violence predate the Middle East conflict and continue to be based in large part on centuries-old hatred and prejudice. The branding of Jews as scapegoats for both ancient and modern ills remains a powerful underlying factor in the antisemitism hatred and violence that continues to manifest itself today.*[25]

Massimino also reminded her audience that antisemitism was not the only hate-motivated violence in Europe. Similar attacks were directed "against members of a range of communities because of their ethnicity, religion, sexual orientation, or other similar factors."[26] And, as in other times in history, when one group is threatened, everyone is at risk. Pilar Rahola explained:

> *Canaries are brought into coal mines to measure contamination. When they die, the level of contamination is very high. When Jews die because they are Jews, the contamination of democracy has reached a dangerous level. Jews are democracy's canaries: they live and die to the extent that liberty lives or dies. Thus, whenever the enemies of*

democracy have increased in number, Jews have died. Jews first, then
everyone else.[27]

NATIONALISM, XENOPHOBIA, AND ANTISEMITISM

Some experts have linked part of the rise in antisemitism and xenophobic
violence to fears about globalization—the opening of national borders to
ideas, people, and investments. Many feel threatened by the enormous
increase in international connections and fear the loss of their national
identity and their independence. As in other times of rapid change, they
sometimes latch onto old myths as they search for easy solutions to tough
problems. For example, several Spanish newspapers responded to the
economic downturn that began in 2008 with editorial cartoons showing
"the Jews" using "their money" to manipulate the world for evil purposes.
Extreme nationalist groups in Russia have taken a similar stand by blaming
the nation's economic problems on a "Zionist-influenced commercial-
financial mafia."[28] To many people, those images and slogans evoke
memories of Nazi propaganda (see Chapter 13). The rise of an extreme
nationalist political party in Hungary offers insights into similarities and
differences between that time and now.

In the first decade of the twenty-first century, Gabor Vona, a former
history teacher, founded a student movement that quickly became a
political force in Hungary. That group, Jobbik Magyarországért Mozgalom,
or Jobbik for short (in English, "the Movement for a Better Hungary"), has
repeatedly claimed that it is "not against anything but only *for* Hungary."
The group vehemently denies that it is extremist: "We do not believe in
the division between left and right. The true division is between those who
want globalization and those who do not. We are a patriotic party."[29]

Despite such remarks, party officials have repeatedly inflamed audiences
by warning that "a crumbling country, torn apart by Hungarian-Gypsy civil
war, could easily be claimed by rich Jews. That is why we should expect
a Hungarian-Gypsy civil war, fomented by Jews as they rub their hands
together with pleasure."[30] By 2007 Jobbik had its own private army, known
as the Hungarian Guard. Its leaders claimed that the guard was needed to
"maintain public order, preserve Hungarian culture, and defend the nation
in extraordinary situations."

Many Hungarians disagreed. They saw similarities between the
Hungarian Guard and the Arrow Cross, a Hungarian pro-Nazi party that
helped the Germans ship about 500,000 Jews and between 5,000 and
10,000 Roma to Auschwitz and other camps during World War II. Their

Jews in Hungary were troubled by the establishment of the Hungarian Guard–a paramilitary group that reminded them of the Nazi-inspired Arrow Cross during World War II. A few Jews demonstrated at the group's swearing-in ceremony; some carried mementoes of loved ones targeted by the Arrow Cross.

concerns increased in 2010, when Jobbik signed an agreement with the Independent Police Trade Union, a radical group with nearly 5,000 members. As a London newspaper observed, the pact between the two groups meant that thousands of armed police officers were now allied with an extremist political party with its own uniformed guard. The paper noted, "There is a whiff of the Weimar Republic here."[31]

As in Weimar Germany, the call for "protection" from an imaginary threat appealed to many people at a time when the economy was slowing and unemployment was on the rise. In Hungary, the angry rhetoric led to the murder of five Roma between 2008 and 2010 by so-called "patriots" and at least 30 firebomb attacks on the homes of Roma families. At the same time, Jobbik supporters barraged Hungary's Jewish community with antisemitic chants, posters, and acts of vandalism.

The supporters of Jobbik have not been people on the fringes of society; they have been in the mainstream. Moreover, the party has had particular appeal for young Hungarians; nearly one out of four voted for Jobbik in 2010. Thousands of them visited the party's website, watched rallies on YouTube, and purchased Jobbik and National Guard T-shirts and other merchandise. As one observer noted, "even those who don't agree with their ideology, they [the Jobbick party] catch them also by creating this fashion trend."[32]

Krisztian Szabados, head of the Political Capital Institute, attributed the success of the party to its ability to use racism to its advantage. He told a reporter, "Jobbik [has] simply delivered extremism to an electorate that demands it. No mainstream party has seriously tackled the antagonism towards minorities that has been here for decades."[33]

In 2009, many people thought that support for Jobbik would diminish. That year the courts banned the National Guard (a ban that was later overturned). And yet, just a few months later, Jobbik won 15 percent of the vote in elections to the parliament of the European Union and 47 of the 386 seats in the Hungarian parliament—about 12 percent of the total. Although Fidesz, the conservative party, held a solid majority, Jobbik became the nation's third-largest party.

Jobbik was not the only political party in the early 2000s to win votes by arousing fears and anxieties. France's National Front and the British National Party also appealed to stereotypes and myths of the "other," but these parties focused more on Muslims and immigrants than on Roma and Jews. In 2009, those parties also won seats in the parliament of the European Union. They also tend to support one another. Both Nick Griffin of the British National Party and Jean Marie Le Pen of the National Front have stirred the crowds at Jobbik party rallies.

ANTISEMITISM AND HOLOCAUST DENIAL

The antisemitism that has marked the early twenty-first century was rooted in ancient anti-Jewish slurs. Some were applied to Israel in an attempt to delegitimize the nation. Others, including the myth of a Jewish conspiracy, were recycled to address fears of globalization, financial disaster, and other crises. Perhaps one of the most incredible examples of such recycling is the false claim that the Holocaust is a hoax or, in the words of Nick Griffin of the British National Party, "a mixture of Allied wartime propaganda, an extremely profitable lie, and latter-day witch-hysteria."[34] Why would he and a number of other politicians and activists deny the most documented mass murder in history? Walter Reich, former head of the United States Holocaust Memorial Museum, offered one answer:

> *The primary motivation for most deniers is anti-Semitism, and for them the Holocaust is an infuriatingly inconvenient fact of history. . . . What better way to . . . make anti-Semitic arguments seem once again respectable in civilized discourse and even make it acceptable for governments to pursue anti-Semitic policies than by convincing*

As Holocaust deniers from countries around the world met in Iran in 2006, some Iranians took to the streets to show their support for those who claimed the murders never happened.

the world that the great crime for which anti-Semitism was blamed simply never happened—indeed, that it was nothing more than a frame-up invented by the Jews, and propagated by them through their control of the media? What better way, in short, to make the world safe again for anti-Semitism than by denying the Holocaust?[35]

Those who question or deny the Holocaust see themselves as "revisionists." Most historians strongly disagree. They point out that although historians debate the causes and the consequences of the Holocaust, there is no debate as to whether Germany under Adolf Hitler systematically put to death millions of Jews, "Gypsies," political radicals, and other people.

Perhaps the most prominent Holocaust "revisionist" has been Mahmoud Ahmadinejad, who became president of Iran in 2005. In 2006, he hosted a conference to "neither deny nor prove the Holocaust" but "to provide an appropriate scientific atmosphere for scholars to offer their opinions in freedom about a historical issue."[36] On the guest list were 67 "Holocaust deniers" from the United States, Germany, Canada, France, and other nations, but not a single scholar who regarded the Holocaust as a fact.

Although Iran is a Muslim nation, it differs from its Arab neighbors in language and culture. It is also home to more Jews than any other Muslim nation in the Middle East. Despite the fact that the government has often treated those Jews as second-class citizens, Iran has long protected their religious rights. Furthermore, the nation has never been at war with Israel. Indeed, before the Iranian revolution, the two countries had a good working relationship. What, then, has motivated Ahmadinejad and his followers to deny the Holocaust? David Menashri, director of the Center for Iranian Studies and dean of special programs at Tel Aviv University, offered some possible answers:

> *The immediate explanation may simply be a sincere belief in the need to eliminate Israel and a conviction that the Holocaust was a primary tool used to establish the Jewish state and justify the suppression of the Palestinians. America's involvement in Iraq and growing Iranian oil income may have contributed to a perceived sense of strength. In addition, Ahmadinejad may hope to consolidate his political position at home by giving voice to extremist views against Israel. With Iran's domestic problems continuing to multiply, he may also be trying to divert attention away from economic issues and toward an external enemy in order to mollify public opinion. Finally, voicing such opinions and taking the lead in supporting the Palestinian cause may be Ahmadinejad's way of promoting Iranian leadership in the Islamic world. Regardless of the reasons for his frequent harangues on the Holocaust, the strong sentiments held against Jews (although not necessarily against the Jews of Iran) by the president and the media serve to further radicalize such views in Iranian society.[37]*

In other words, Ahmadinejad and other Iranian leaders view antisemitism as a very convenient hatred, even though that policy has been criticized both at home and abroad. Sadegh Zibakalam, a political science professor at Tehran University, wrote of the 2006 conference,

> *I don't know what is the honor of gathering a group of anti-Semites, neo-Nazis, Ku Klux Klan members, and racists—and [bringing] them to Iran, for what? . . . And this is happening at a time when our nuclear case is at the UN and we have to do our best to gain the trust of the international community.[38]*

Haroun Yahaya'i, the head of Iran's Jewish community, also spoke out. Describing the Holocaust as one of the twentieth century's "most obvious and saddest events," he wondered: "How is it possible to ignore all the undeniable evidence existing for the killing and exile of the Jews in Europe during World War II?"[39]

Others have noted that too many people in far too many nations have been willing to believe that the facts have been "embellished" because they know very little about this period in history. A Hungarian activist pointed out that the history books used in his nation's schools "are without a word of criticism regarding the role of Hungary in the Second World War"[40]— or, he might have added, the Holocaust. Sociologist Maria Vasarhely conducted a survey that showed the consequences of that failure to teach history as more than a set of heroic tales: in Hungary, 15 percent of college students held racist views and one-third of history majors were prejudiced against Jews. Thirty-five percent believed that criminality is in the blood of the Sinti and Roma.[41]

Iranians, Hungarians, and Spaniards are not the only people who have difficulty confronting the facts of the Holocaust. In 2006, Pope Benedict XVI was one of many religious leaders who spoke out against Holocaust denial at the Iranian conference on the Holocaust.[42] Yet just three years later, he lifted the 1988 excommunication of four bishops excluded from the Catholic Church because of their association with the Society of St. Paul X, which was founded in 1969 by priests opposed to all church reforms. One bishop, an Englishman named Richard Williamson, was a Holocaust denier who repeatedly referred to the *Protocols of the Elders of Zion* as "proof" that "the Jews" were preparing "the Anti-Christ's throne in Jerusalem."

The Vatican insisted that the pope was not aware of Williamson's views when he lifted the excommunication, but many people wondered why his staff had not investigated more carefully. Perhaps the pope's most prominent critic was Angela Merkel, the chancellor of Germany. As a German, she felt that she and other Germans had an obligation to challenge any attempt to deny the Holocaust.

Merkel, a Protestant, did something that political leaders rarely do: she publicly criticized a religious leader of another faith—Pope Benedict. She insisted that as a person who grew up in Nazi Germany, Benedict had a duty to make it "absolutely clear" that he opposed all Holocaust denial. In the end, he agreed.

Merkel was not alone in insisting that leaders have a responsibility to take a stand against Holocaust denial. Patrick Desbois, a French Roman Catholic priest, founded a group called *Yahad in Unum* (which means "together as one" in Hebrew and Latin) to identify the mass graves of Jews and Roma murdered by the Germans. By 2010, his group had documented

850 extermination sites in Belarus and Ukraine, many previously unknown. Desbois explained why he has taken on this task:

> *First of all, to give [the victims] dignity and so they can finally receive a* Kaddish *[a memorial prayer for the dead]. They were killed like animals and buried like beasts. Today, thieves quite often open the graves to look for gold teeth.*

> *But also, because today, on our planet, there are some individuals and groups that create propaganda that pretends that the Holocaust never existed, that it's a lie to justify the birth of the State of Israel. Denial is not an intellectual position. There is no denial without anti-Semitism. Denial odiously tries to remove all legitimacy from the Jewish people. The Holocaust was the black fruit of anti-Semitism. "Antisemitism is a sin against God and against humanity," [said] Pope John Paul II. . . .*

> *We do not want to, we cannot, condemn the children murdered during the Holocaust to silence; we do not want to, we cannot create a modern world on the thousands of unknown mass graves of murdered Jews.* [13]

MEMORY AND EDUCATION

Why do leaders like Angela Merkel and Patrick Desbois vigorously oppose attempts to minimize, diminish, or deny the Holocaust? Elie Wiesel, a Holocaust survivor and recipient of the Nobel Prize for Peace, offered one answer in a speech to the German Reichstag. He addressed his remarks to young Germans. He told them that he had "neither the desire nor the authority" to judge them for "the unspeakable crimes" committed by Hitler and other Nazi leaders. "But," he added, "we may—and we must—hold [today's generation] responsible, not for the past, but for the way it remembers the past. And for what it does with the past." He continued:

> *To remember is to create links between past and present, between past and future. To remember is to affirm man's faith in humanity and to convey meaning on our fleeting endeavors. The aim of memory is to restore dignity to justice. . . .*

In remembering, you will help your own people to vanquish the ghosts that have been hovering over their history. Remember: a community that does not come to terms with the dead will find that the dead will continue to perturb and traumatize the living. Reconciliation can be achieved through and in memory.[44]

To those who fear that memory perpetuates hatred, Pilar Rahola pointed out that "lack of memory leads to ignorance, ignorance produces prejudice, and prejudice breeds intolerance. Who said there is nothing more dangerous in the world than sincere ignorance?"[45] Perhaps that is why the European Union Agency for Fundamental Rights responded to the rise in antisemitism by creating a working definition of the term. It describes antisemitism as a "certain perception of Jews that may be expressed as hatred." To aid in law enforcement, the group included examples of modern-day expressions of hatred. It also recognized that today's antisemitism comes from new and different directions and therefore encouraged member nations to legislate against those who incite hatred in new ways—including those who promote Holocaust denial.

These efforts have not always been successful, but, despite setbacks, progress has been made. That progress would not have been possible without the determination of a handful of individuals, Jews and non-Jews. In 2003, for example, Judea Pearl, father of the murdered journalist, and Akbar S. Ahmed, former high commissioner of Pakistan to Great Britain and professor of Islamic studies at American University in Washington, DC, began a series of public discussions that tackled the religious and ethnic hatred that divided their own communities.

As children, both men had witnessed the terrible consequences of hatred. Ahmed was born in India. In 1947, when the subcontinent was divided into two nations—a predominantly Hindu India and a Muslim Pakistan—he and his family were among the millions of people uprooted by the conflict. Judea Pearl grew up in British Palestine and saw the violence that erupted there immediately after the establishment of the nation of Israel in 1948 (see Chapter 14). Those memories and the murder of Pearl's son inspired their conversations. In reflecting on their first encounter in 2003, Ahmad wrote:

What was I to say to a man whose son had been killed in the city where I grew up, and at the hands of those belonging to my own faith? In turn, how could I communicate the political anarchy and social implosion that provided the setting within which we are to understand the murder? And what purpose would dialogue serve in the first place?

WHERE MOST JEWS LIVED IN 2010

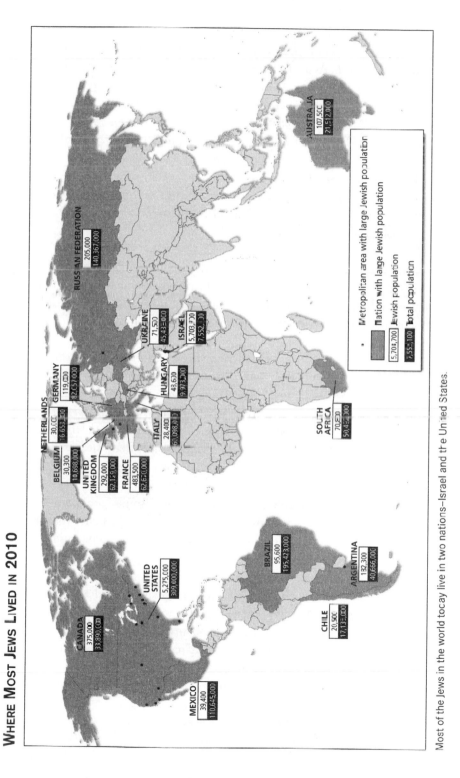

Most of the Jews in the world today live in two nations–Israel and the United States.

I agreed to go to Pittsburgh in order to express my support to the Pearl family for creating in Daniel a symbol of compassion in spite of the personal tragedy. As a Pakistani I felt it would also allow me to express my deep sympathy. As a Muslim I could make the point that Danny's murder was un-Islamic. Indeed Danny's death symbolized that far too many innocent people—Muslims and non-Muslims in different places, in different societies—were being brutally killed in our world.

In explaining why he agreed to the dialogue, Dr. Pearl said that he was a scientist who wished to avenge Danny's murder by attacking the hatred that took his son's life and by challenging the ideology that permitted the hatred to bloom.[46]

At that session and those that followed, Ahmed and Pearl did not speak as Muslim or Jew, Pakistani or Israeli, but rather as concerned individuals. They shared memories, fears, and dreams. Not everyone who heard them thought that these conversations were a good idea. Ahmed noted:

Many [Muslims] felt that the victimization and killing of Muslims around the world provided no reason to talk to the Jews. Others pointed out that the Pearl family was associated with Israel and therefore no dialogue or reconciliation could take place unless the problem of the Palestinians was resolved. Still others distrusted dialogue attempts because they felt they had been let down too many times in the past. The criticism made my task of public dialogue even more difficult.[47]

Pearl encountered similar criticism from some in the Jewish community. Nevertheless, the two men persisted in their belief that their public conversations were "tiny steps toward mutual understanding and dialogue."[48]

A number of observers have wondered how much two grandfathers on a stage can accomplish. Can speaking to several hundred people in the United States or Europe lead to significant change? To Ahmed, the value of such conversations cannot be measured by the number of people in an auditorium. He noted that thousands more read about these events in newspapers or see portions of them on TV or the Internet and begin to see "the other" as individuals rather than as stereotypes. Ahmed insisted:

Dialogue by itself is empty. . . . Two people talk, they go home and nothing happens. But dialogue that leads to understanding [is

Members of a soccer team from Abou Gosh, a village in Israel, include both Israeli Jews and Arabs. They are often invited to play in Europe to demonstrate that Arabs and Jews can get along.

different]. I've gotten to know Judea. I've come to know the pain, the history and the traditions of his people. From this dialogue we have seen the possibility of friendship and friendship changes everything. When people become friends. . . . [t]hey are prepared to make compromises, to change, to accommodate.[49]

The journey in which the two men have been engaged requires mutual respect, empathy, and a willingness to honestly confront the past as well as the ability to compromise, change, and accommodate. As Elie Wiesel noted, "Although we today are not responsible for the injustices of the past, we are responsible for the way we remember the past and what we do with that past." Only through the process of facing history and ourselves can we hope to reduce the hatred and prevent further violence.

[1] Jonathan Rosen, "Waking Up to My Father's World," in *Best Jewish Writing, 2002*, ed. Michael Lerner (San Francisco: Jossey-Bass, 2002), 77.

[2] Nicolas Weill, "Antisemitism in France and 'Holocaust Fatigue,'" in *Not Your Father's Antisemitism: Hatred of the Jews in the 21st Century*, ed. Michael Berenbaum (St. Paul: Paragon House, 2008), 11.

[3] "Address by Chief Rabbi: Speech to Washington Institute for Near East Policy," Office of the Chief Rabbi, accessed March 25, 2011, http://www.chiefrabbi.org/ReadArtical.aspx?id=320.

[4] Joëlle Fiss, *The Durban Diaries: What really happened at the UN Conference against Racism in Durban (2001)* (New York: American Jewish Committee/European Union of Jewish Students, 2008), 24–25.

[5] "The Adoption of the NGO Declaration and Program of Action," ICARE, accessed March 25, 2011, http://www.icare.to/wcar/main.html.

[6] David Matas, "Civil Society Smashes Up," B'nai Brith Canada, accessed March 25, 2011, http://www.bnaibrith.ca/institute/articles/dm020107.html.

[7] Ronald Eissens, "Editorial," ICARE, accessed March 25, 2011, http://www.icare.to/wcar/main.html.

[8] Fiss, *The Durban Diaries*, 43.

[9] Matthias Küntzel, "Islamic Antisemitism and Its Nazi Roots," April 2003, http://www.matthiaskuentzel.de/contents/islamic-antisemitism-and-its-nazi-roots.

[10] Bryan Curtis, "4,000 Jews, 1 Lie, Tracking an Internet Hoax," October 5, 2001, http://www.slate.com/id/116813/.

[11] Jorisch, "Al-Manar: Hizbullah TV, 24/7.

[12] Ayesha Haroon, interview by John Daniszewski, quoted in Harold Evans, "The View from Ground Zero" (lecture, Hay-on-Wye Literary Festival, June 2, 2002), http://www.mideastweb.org/evansmedia.htm.

[13] Jorisch, "Al-Manar: Hizbullah TV, 24/7."

[14] Matthias Küntzel, "'Wipe Out the Jews': Anti-Semitic Hate Speech in the Name of Islam," *Spiegel Online International,* May 16, 2008, http://www.spiegel.de/international/world/0,1518,553724,00.html.

[15] Thane Rosenbaum, "Danny Pearl," in *Those Who Forget the Past: The Question of Anti-Semitism*, ed. Ron Rosenbaum (New York: Random House, 2004), 127.

[16] Pilar Rahola, "'Democracy's Canaries': Jews and Judeophobia in Contemporary Europe," June 13, 2005, http://www.pilarrahola.com/3_0/CONFERENCIAS/default.cfm?ID=116.

[17] Ibid.

[18] Howard Jacobson, "Pox Britannica: Anti-Semitism on the March," *The New Republic*, April 20, 2009.

[19] "Antisemitic Incidents Report, 2006," Community Security Trust, 14, http://www.thecst.org.uk/docs/Incidents_Report_06.pdf.

[20] Craig S. Smith, "Torture and Death of Jew Deepen Fears in France," *New York Times*, March 5, 2006; "Gang Leader Receives Life in Prison for Killing," Associated Press, July 10, 2009.

[21] Judea Pearl, "Remembering Ilan Halimi," Israel Jewish Scene, *Ynetnews,* March 19, 2006, http://www.ynetnews.com/articles/0,7340,L-3229504,00.html.

[22] "Antisemitism Worldwide 2009: General Analysis," Stephen Roth Institute for the Study of Contemporary Antisemitism and Racism, 2, http://www.tau.ac.il/Anti-Semitism/asw2009/general-analysis-09.pdf.

[23] Ibid., 1.

[24] Ibid., 6.

[25] Human Rights *First*, Testimony of Elisa Massimino, Hearing on "Combating Anti-Semitism": Protecting Human Rights, United States House Committee on Foreign Affairs, Subcommittee on International Organizations, Human Rights and Oversight, April 14, 2010.

[26] Ibid.

[27] Rahola, "Democracy's Canaries."

[28] Konstantin Ostashvili, interview in *Izmailovskii vertnik*, no. 2 (1990): 3, quoted in Zvi Gitelman, *A Century of Ambivalence: The Jews of Russia and the Soviet Union, 1881 to the Present*, 2nd ed. (Bloomington: Indiana University Press, 2001), 245.

[29] Zsolt Varkonyi, quoted in Leigh Phillips, "A Far-Right for the Facebook Generation: The rise and rise of Jobbik," *EUobserver*, April 19, 2010, http://euobserver.com/843/29866.

[30] Yehuda Halav, "Proud Hungarians Must Prepare for War against the Jews," *Haaretz*, January 6, 2009.

[31] Adam LeBor, "Jobbik: Meet the BNP's Fascist Friends in Hungary," *The Sunday Times*, June 9, 2009.

[32] Megan K. Stack, "Jobbik: In Hungary, Far Right Is Making Gains," *Los Angeles Times*, October 11, 2009.

[33] Bojan Pancevski, "Anti-Semitism Stirs as Hungary Goes to Polls," *The Sunday Times*, April 11, 2010.

[34] Tom Baldwin and Fiona Hamilton, "Times interview with Nick Griffin," *Times*, October 22, 2009, http://www.timesonline.co.uk/tol/news/politics/article6884722.ece.

[35] Walter Reich, "Erasing the Holocaust," *New York Times*, July 11, 1993.

[36] Rasoul Mousavi, quoted in "Berlin Counters Holocaust Conference," *Spiegel Online International*, December 11, 2006, http://www.spiegel.de/international/0,1518,453691,00.html

[37] David Menashri, "Iran, the Jews and the Holocaust," Steven Roth Institute for the Study of Contemporary Antisemitism and Racism, accessed March 25, 2011, http://www.tau.ac.il/Anti-Semitism/asw2005/menashri.html.

[38] Ibid.

[39] Ibid.

[40] Vilmos Hanti, quoted in Phillips, "A Far-Right for the Facebook Generation."

[41] Paul Hockenos, "Inside Hungary's Anti-Semitic Right-Wing" GlobalPost, June 1, 2010, http://www.globalpost.com/dispatch/europe/100520/hungary-jobbik-far-right-party.

[42] "Iran's 2006 Holocaust Denial Conference: A Gathering of Nazi Sympathizers & Racists," Réalité-EU, January 16, 2007, http://www.realite-eu.org/site/apps/nlnet/content3.aspx?c=9dJBLLNkGiF&b=2315291&ct=3447651.

[43] Patrick Desbois, speech, April 21, 2009, http://www.holocaustbybullets.com/en/about-patrick-desbois/durban-ii-april-20-24-yom-hashoah.

[44] From "When Memory Brings People Together," in Elie Wiesel, *From the Kingdom of Memory. Reminiscences* (New York: Schocken Books, 1990), 194–200.

[45] Rahola, "Democracy's Canaries."

[46] Akbar S. Ahmed, "A Small Step toward Interfaith Dialogue," *Pakistan Daily Times*, November 1, 2003.

[47] Ibid.

[48] Ibid.

[49] "Pew Forum: Five Years After 9/11, 'Dialogue' with Islam Cause for Hope," interview with Akbar Ahmed, August 22, 2006, The Pew Forum on Religion & Public Life, http://pewforum.org/Politics-and-Elections/Five-Years-After-911-Dialogue-with-Islam-Cause-for-Hope.aspx.

SELECTED BIBLIOGRAPHY

1. BEGINNINGS

Josephus, Flavius. *The Complete Works of Josephus*. Translated by William Whiston. Grand Rapids: Kregel Publications, 1960.

Modrzejewski, Joseph Mélèze. *The Jews of Egypt from Ramses II to Emperor Hadrian*. Translated by Robert Cornman. Philadelphia: Jewish Publication Society, 1995.

Schäfer, Peter. *Judeophobia: Attitudes toward the Jews in the Ancient World*. Cambridge, MA: Harvard University Press, 1997.

2. SEPARATION: SYNAGOGUE AND CHURCH, JEW AND CHRISTIAN

Boys, Mary C. *Has God Only One Blessing? Judaism as a Source of Christian Self-Understanding*. New York: Stimulus, 2000.

Carroll, James. *Constantine's Sword: The Church and the Jews*. Boston: Mariner Books, 2002.

Fredriksen, Paula and Adele Reinhartz, eds. *Jesus, Judaism, and Christian Anti-Judaism: Reading the New Testament after the Holocaust*. Louisville: Westminster John Knox Press, 2002.

Internet Jewish History Sourcebook. Fordham University, Paul Halsall. Last modified May 31, 2007. http://www.fordham.edu/halsall/jewish/jews romanlaw.html.

Levine, Amy-Jill. *The Misunderstood Jew: The Church and the Scandal of the Jewish Jesus*. New York: Harper Collins, 2006.

University of Pennsylvania, Department of History. *Translations and Reprints from the Original Sources of European History*. Vol. 4. Philadelphia: The Department of History of the University of Pennsylvania, 1897–1907.

Wilken, Robert L. *John Chrysostom and the Jews: Rhetoric and Reality in the Late 4th Century*. Berkeley: University of California Press, 1983.

3. CONQUESTS AND CONSEQUENCES

Ben-Sasson, H. H., ed. *A History of the Jewish People*. Translated by George Weidenfeld and Nicolson Ltd. 9th ed. Cambridge, MA: Harvard University Press, 1994.

Catherwood, Christopher. *A Brief History of the Middle East: From Abraham to Arafat*. New York: Carroll & Graf, 2006.

Durán, Khalid. *Children of Abraham: An Introduction to Islam for Jews.* Hoboken: Ktav, 2001.

Hourani, Albert. *A History of the Arab Peoples.* New York: Warner Books, 1992.

Lewis, Bernard. *The Jews of Islam.* Princeton: Princeton University Press, 1984.

Stillman, Norman A. *The Jews of Arab Lands: A History and Source Book.* Philadelphia: Jewish Publication Society, 1979.

4. HOLY WARS AND ANTISEMITISM

Chazan, Robert, ed. *Church, State, and Jew in the Middle Ages.* West Orange: Behrman House, 1980.

Chazan, Robert. *In the Year 1096: The First Crusade and the Jews.* Philadelphia: Jewish Publication Society, 1996.

Glick, Leonard B. *Abraham's Heirs: Jews and Christians in Medieval Europe.* Syracuse: Syracuse University Press, 1999.

Kriwaczek, Paul. *Yiddish Civilisation: The Rise and Fall of a Forgotten Nation.* New York: Vintage Books, 2005.

Lopez, Robert S. *The Commercial Revolution of the Middle Ages, 950–1350.* Cambridge, UK: Cambridge University Press, 1976.

Marcus, Jacob Rader, ed. *The Jew in the Medieval World: A Source Book, 315–1791.* Rev. ed. Cincinnati: Hebrew Union College Press, 1999.

Peters, Edward, ed. *The First Crusade: "The Chronicle of Fulcher of Chartres" and Other Source Materials.* 2nd ed. Philadelphia: University of Pennsylvania Press, 1998.

Sachs, Stephen E. "New Math: The 'Countinghouse Theory' and the Medieval Revival of Arithmetic." 2000. Last modified May 25, 2000. http://www.stevesachs.com/papers/paper_90a.html.

5. THE POWER OF A LIE

Chazan, Robert, ed. *Church, State, and Jew in the Middle Ages.* West Orange: Behrman House, 1980.

Dundee, Alan, ed. *The Blood Libel Legend: A Casebook of Anti-Semitic Folklore.* Madison: University of Wisconsin Press, 1991.

Glick, Leonard B. *Abraham's Heirs: Jews and Christians in Medieval Europe.* Syracuse: Syracuse University Press, 1999.

Kriwaczek, Paul. *Yiddish Civilisation: The Rise and Fall of a Forgotten Nation.* New York: Vintage Books, 2005.

Langmuir, Gavin I. *Toward a Definition of Antisemitism.* Berkeley: University of California Press, 1996.

Marcus, Jacob Rader, ed. *The Jew in the Medieval World: A Source Book, 315–1791.* Rev. ed. Cincinnati: Hebrew Union College Press, 1999.

6. REFUGEES FROM INTOLERANCE

Blech, Benjamin, ed. *Eyewitness to Jewish History.* Hoboken: John Wiley & Sons, 2004.

Chazan, Robert, ed. *Church, State, and Jew in the Middle Ages.* West Orange: Behrman House, 1980.

Edwards, John. *The Jews in Christian Europe, 1400–1700.* New York: Routledge, 1991.

Glick, Leonard B. *Abraham's Heirs: Jews and Christians in Medieval Europe.* Syracuse: Syracuse University Press, 1999.

Kriwaczek, Paul. *Yiddish Civilisation: The Rise and Fall of a Forgotten Nation.* New York: Vintage Books, 2005.

Marcus, Jacob Rader, ed. *The Jew in the Medieval World: A Source Book, 315–1791.* Rev. ed. Cincinnati: Hebrew Union College Press, 1999.

7. IN SEARCH OF TOLERATION

Braudel, Fernard. *Civilization & Capitalism, 15th–18th Century.* Vol. 1, *The Structures of Everyday Life. The Limits of the Possible.* Translated by Sian Reynolds. New York: Harper & Row, 1979.

Chazan, Robert, ed. *Church, State, and Jew in the Middle Ages.* West Orange: Behrman House, 1980.

Edwards, John. *The Jews in Christian Europe, 1400–1700.* New York: Routledge, 1991.

Flannery, Edward H. *The Anguish of the Jews: Twenty-Three Centuries of Antisemitism.* Rev. ed. New York: Stimulus, 1999.

Glick, Leonard B. *Abraham's Heirs: Jews and Christians in Medieval Europe.* Syracuse: Syracuse University Press, 1999.

Hsia, R. Po-chia. *The Myth of Ritual Murder: Jews and Magic in Reformation Germany.* New Haven: Yale University Press, 1988.

Kriwaczek, Paul. *Yiddish Civilisation: The Rise and Fall of a Forgotten Nation.* New York: Vintage Books, 2005.

MacCulloch, Diarmaid. *The Reformation: A History.* New York: Viking, 2003.

Marcus, Jacob Rader, ed. *The Jew in the Medieval World. A Source Book, 315–1791.* Rev. ed. Cincinnati: Hebrew Union College Press, 1999.

Nicholls, William. *Christian Antisemitism: A History of Hate*. Lanham, MD: Rowman & Littlefield, 1993.

Oberman, Heiko A. *The Roots of Anti-Semitism: In the Age of Renaissance and Reformation*. Translated by James I. Porter. Philadelphia: Fortress Press, 1984.

Roth, Cecil. *Doña Gracia of the House of Nasi*. 2nd ed. Philadelphia: Jewish Publication Society, 1977.

8. SAFE HAVENS?: POLAND AND THE OTTOMAN EMPIRE

Dubnow, S. M. *History of the Jews in Russia and Poland*. Vol. 1, *From the Beginning until the Death of Alexander I (1825)*. Translated by I. Friedlaender. Philadelphia: Jewish Publication Society, 1916.

Eban, Abba. *Heritage: Civilization and the Jews*. New York: Summit Books, 1984.

Gilbert, Martin. *In Ishmael's House: A History of Jews in Muslim Lands*. New Haven: Yale University Press, 2010.

Hanover, Nathan. *Abyss of Despair (Yeven Metzulah)*. Translated by Abraham J. Mesch. New Brunswick: Transaction Books, 1983.

Levine, Allan. *Scattered Among the Peoples: The Jewish Diaspora in Twelve Portraits*. Woodstock, NY: Overlook Duckworth, 2003.

Lewis, Bernard. *The Jews of Islam*. Princeton: Princeton University Press, 1984.

Roth, Cecil. *Doña Gracia of the House of Nasi*. 2nd ed. Philadelphia: Jewish Publication Society, 1977.

Weinryb, Bernard D. *The Jews of Poland: A Social and Economic History of the Jewish Community in Poland from 1100–1800*. Philadelphia: Jewish Publication Society, 1972.

9. THE AGE OF ENLIGHTENMENT AND THE REACTION

Arendt, Hannah. *The Origins of Totalitarianism*. San Diego: Harvest, 1976.

Craig, Gordon A. *The Germans*. New York: Meridian, 1991.

Elon, Amos. *The Pity of It All: A Portrait of the German-Jewish Epoch, 1743–1933*. New York: Picador, 2002.

Glassman, Bernard. *Protean Prejudice: Anti-Semitism in England's Age of Reason*. Atlanta: Scholars Press, 1998.

Goldfarb, Michael. *Emancipation: How Liberating Europe's Jews from the Ghetto Led to Revolution and Renaissance*. New York: Simon & Schuster, 2009.

Lossin, Yigal. *Heine: His Double Life*. New York: Schocken Books, 2000.

Mendes-Flohr, Paul, and Jehuda Reinharz, eds. *The Jew in the Modern World: A Documentary History.* 2nd ed. New York: Oxford University Press, 1995.

Muller, Jerry Z. *Capitalism and the Jews.* Princeton: Princeton University Press, 2010.

Vital, David. *A People Apart: The Jews in Europe, 1789–1939.* New York: Oxford University Press, 1999.

Wistrich, Robert S. *Antisemitism: The Longest Hatred.* New York: Schocken Books, 1991.

10. ANTISEMITISM IN AN AGE OF NATIONALISM

Florence, Ronald. *Blood Libel: The Damascus Affair of 1840.* New York: Other Press, 2006.

Foner, Philip S., ed. *The Life and Writings of Frederick Douglass.* Vol. 2. New York: International Publishers, 1950.

Frankel, Jonathan. *The Damascus Affair: "Ritual Murder," Politics, and the Jews in 1840.* Cambridge, UK: Cambridge University Press, 1997.

Graetz, Michael. "Jewry in the Modern Period: The role of the 'rising class' in the politicization of Jews in Europe." In *Assimilation and Community: The Jews in Nineteenth-Century Europe,* edited by Jonathan Frankel and Steven J. Zipperstein, 156–176. Cambridge, UK: Cambridge University Press, 1992.

Mendes-Flohr, Paul, and Jehuda Reinharz, eds. *The Jew in the Modern World: A Documentary History.* 2nd ed. New York: Oxford University Press, 1995.

Mosse, George L. *Toward the Final Solution: A History of European Racism.* New York: Howard Fertig, 1978.

Sachar, Howard M. *A History of the Jews in the Modern World.* New York: Vintage Books, 2005.

Vital, David. *A People Apart: The Jews in Europe, 1789–1939.* New York: Oxford University Press, 1999.

11. ANTISEMITISM IN FRANCE AND RUSSIA: "THE SNAKE . . . CREPT OUT OF THE MARSHES"

Bartal, Israel. *The Jews of Eastern Europe, 1772–1881.* Translated by Chaya Naor. Philadelphia: University of Pennsylvania Press, 2006.

Berk, Stephen M. *Year of Crisis, Year of Hope: Russian Jewry and the Pogroms of 1881–1882.* Westport: Greenwood Press, 1985.

Dawidowicz, Lucy S., ed. *The Golden Tradition: Jewish Life and Thought in Eastern Europe.* New York: Schocken Books, 1967.

Herzen, Alexander. *My Past and Thoughts: The Memoirs of Alexander Herzen.* Translated by Constance Garnett, revised by Humphrey Higgins. Berkeley: University of California Press, 1982.

Levine, Allan. *Scattered Among the Peoples: The Jewish Diaspora in Twelve Portraits.* Woodstock, NY: Overlook Duckworth, 2003.

Lindemann, Albert S. *The Jew Accused: Three Anti-Semitic Affairs (Dreyfus, Beilis, Frank), 1894–1915.* Cambridge, UK: Cambridge University Press, 1991.

Mendes-Flohr, Paul, and Jehuda Reinharz, eds. *The Jew in the Modern World: A Documentary History.* 2nd ed. New York: Oxford University Press, 1995.

Sachar, Howard M. *A History of the Jews in the Modern World.* New York: Vintage Books, 2005.

Wengeroff, Pauline. *Rememberings: The World of a Russian-Jewish Woman in the Nineteenth Century.* Translated by Henny Wenkart. Bethesda: University Press of Maryland, 2000.

12. LIES, STEREOTYPES, AND ANTISEMITISM IN AN AGE OF WAR AND REVOLUTION

The American Jewish Committee. *The Jews in the Eastern War Zone.* New York: The American Jewish Committee, 1916.

Ansky, S. *The Enemy at His Pleasure: A Journey through the Jewish Pale of Settlement During World War I.* Edited and translated by Joachim Neugroschel. New York: Henry Holt, 2004.

Bernstein, Herman. *The Truth about "The Protocols of Zion": A Complete Exposure.* New York: Covici-Friede, 1935.

Bronner, Stephen Eric. *A Rumor about the Jews: Antisemitism, Conspiracy, and "The Protocols of Zion."* New York: Oxford University Press, 2000.

Cohn, Norman. *Warrant for Genocide: The Myth of the Jewish World Conspiracy and the "Protocols of the Elders of Zion."* London: Serif, 1996.

Hebrew Immigrant Aid Society. *Jewish Immigration Bulletin (HIAS Monthly Report),* January, 1921.

Lieberman, Benjamin. *Terrible Fate: Ethnic Cleansing in the Making of Modern Europe.* Chicago: Ivan R. Dee, 2006.

Morgenthau, Henry, and French Strother. *All in a Life-Time.* Garden City: Doubleday, Page & Company, 1922.

O'Neill, H. C. *The Royal Fusiliers in the Great War*. London: William Heinemann, 1922.

Sachar, Howard M. *A History of the Jews in the Modern World*. New York: Vintage Books, 2005.

Sanders, Ronald. *Shores of Refuge: A Hundred Years of Jewish Emigration*. New York: Schocken Books, 1988.

Tenenbaum, Joseph. *In Search of a Lost People: The Old and the New Poland*. New York: Beechhurst Press, 1948.

Vital, David. *A People Apart: The Jews in Europe, 1789–1939*. New York: Oxford University Press, 1999.

13. IN THE FACE OF GENOCIDE

Bauer, Yehuda. *Rethinking the Holocaust*. New Haven: Yale University Press, 2001.

Bliss, Edward Jr., ed. *In Search of Light: The Broadcasts of Edward R. Murrow, 1938–1961*. New York: Alfred A. Knopf, 1967.

Browning, Christopher R. *Ordinary Men: Reserve Police Battalion 101 and the Final Solution in Poland*. New York: HarperCollins, 1998.

Burleigh, Michael. *The Third Reich: A New History*. New York: Hill and Wang, 2000.

Cohn, Norman. *Warrant for Genocide: The Myth of the Jewish World Conspiracy and the "Protocols of the Elders of Zion."* London: Serif, 1996.

Dawidowicz, Lucy S., ed. *The Golden Tradition: Jewish Life and Thought in Eastern Europe*. New York: Schocken Books, 1967.

Eisenhower, Dwight D. *Crusade in Europe*. Baltimore: Johns Hopkins University Press, 1997. First published 1948 by Doubleday.

Friedländer, Saul. *Nazi Germany and the Jews*. 2 vols. New York: HarperCollins, 1997–2007.

Gilbert, Martin. *The Holocaust: A History of the Jews of Europe during the Second World War*. New York: Holt, Rinehart, & Winston, 1986.

Hilberg, Raul, ed. *Documents of Destruction: Germany and Jewry, 1933–1945*. Chicago: Quadrangle Books, 1971.

Hoess, Rudolf. *Commandant of Auschwitz: The Autobiography of Rudolf Hoess*. Cleveland: World Publishers, 1959.

Kaplan, Marion A. *Between Dignity and Despair: Jewish Life in Nazi Germany*. New York: Oxford University Press, 1998.

Lanzmann, Claude. *Shoah: The Complete Text of the Acclaimed Holocaust Film*. New York: Pantheon, 1985.

Levin, Meyer. *In Search: An Autobiography*. New York: Horizon Press, 1950.

Mazor, Michel. *The Vanished City: Everyday Life in the Warsaw Ghetto*. Translated by David Jacobson. New York: Marsilio, 1993.

Meir, Golda. *My Life*. New York: G. P. Putnam's Sons, 1975.

Mendes-Flohr, Paul, and Jehuda Reinharz, eds. *The Jew in the Modern World: A Documentary History*. 2nd ed. New York: Oxford University Press, 1995.

Müller, Filip. *Eyewitness Auschwitz: Three Years in the Gas Chambers*. Edited and translated by Susanne Flatauer. New York: Stein and Day, 1979.

Müller, Ingo. *Hitler's Justice: The Courts of the Third Reich*. Translated by Deborah Lucas Schneider. Cambridge, MA: Harvard University Press, 1991.

Richarz, Monika, ed. *Jewish Life in Germany: Memoirs from Three Centuries*. Translated by Stella P. Rosenfeld and Sidney Rosenfeld. Bloomington: Indiana University Press, 1991.

Rittner, Carol, and John K. Roth, eds. *Pope Pius XII and the Holocaust*. London: Leicester University Press, 2002.

Rowe, David E., and Robert Schulmann, eds. *Einstein on Politics: His Private Thoughts and Public Stands on Nationalism, Zionism, War, Peace, and the Bomb*. Princeton: Princeton University Press, 2007.

Sachar, Howard M. *Dreamland: Europeans and Jews in the Aftermath of the Great War*. New York: Alfred A. Knopf, 2002.

Sanders, Ronald. *Shores of Refuge: A Hundred Years of Jewish Emigration*. New York: Schocken Books, 1988.

Śliwowska, Wiktoria, ed. *The Last Eyewitnesses: Children of the Holocaust Speak*. Translated by Julian and Fay Bussgang. Evanston, IL: Northwestern University Press, 1998.

Zuckerman, Yitzhak. *A Surplus of Memory: Chronicle of the Warsaw Ghetto Uprising*. Translated and edited by Barbara Harshav. Berkeley: University of California Press, 1993.

14. ANTISEMITISM AFTER THE HOLOCAUST

Bickerton, Ian J. *The Arab-Israeli Conflict: A History*. London: Reaktion Books, 2009.

Blech, Benjamin, ed. *Eyewitness to Jewish History*. Hoboken: John Wiley & Sons, 2004.

Dinnerstein, Leonard. *America and the Survivors of the Holocaust*. New York: Columbia University Press, 1982.

———. *Antisemitism in America*. New York: Oxford University Press, 1994.

Draitser, Emil. *Shush! Growing Up Jewish under Stalin: A Memoir*. Berkeley: University of California Press, 2008.

Gross, Jan T. *Fear: Anti-Semitism in Poland after Auschwitz, An Essay in Historical Interpretation*. New York: Random House, 2006.

Ingrams, Doreen, ed. *Palestine Papers, 1917–1922: Seeds of Conflict*. New York: George Braziller, 1973.

Isaac, Jules. *The Teaching of Contempt: Christian Roots of Anti-Semitism*. New York: Holt, Rinehart and Winston, 1964.

Kattan, Naïm. *Farewell, Babylon: Coming of Age in Jewish Baghdad*. Translated by Sheila Fischman. Boston: David R. Godine, 2007.

Küntzel, Matthias. *Jihad and Jew-Hatred: Islamism, Nazism and the Roots of 9/11*. Translated by Colin Meade. New York: Telos Press, 2007.

Laqueur, Walter, and Barry Rubin, eds. *The Israel-Arab Reader: A Documentary History of the Middle East Conflict*. New York: Penguin Books, 2008.

Lewis, Bernard. *The Middle East: A Brief History of the Last 2000 Years*. New York: Scribner, 1995.

Marrus, Michael R. *The Unwanted: European Refugees in the Twentieth Century*. New York: Oxford University Press, 1985.

Morris, Benny. *Righteous Victims: A History of the Zionist-Arab Conflict, 1881–2001*. New York: Vintage, 2001.

O'Brien, Conor Cruise. *The Siege: The Saga of Israel and Zionism*. New York: Simon & Schuster, 1986.

Rutishauser, Christian M. "The 1947 Seelisberg Conference: The Foundation of the Jewish-Christian Dialogue." *Studies in Christian-Jewish Relations* 2, no. 2 (2007). http://escholarship.bc.edu/scjr/vol2/iss2/6.

Sachar, Abram L. *The Redemption of the Unwanted: From the Liberation of the Death Camps to the Founding of Israel*. New York: St. Martin's/Marek, 1983.

Sanders, Ronald. *Shores of Refuge: A Hundred Years of Jewish Emigration*. New York: Schocken Books, 1988.

Stillman, Norman A., ed. *Jews of Arab Lands in Modern Times*. Philadelphia: Jewish Publication Society, 2003.

Stone, I. F. *Underground to Palestine*. London: Hutchinson, 1979.

Tenenbaum, Joseph. *In Search of a Lost People: The Old and the New Poland*. New York: Beechhurst Press, 1948.

15. ANTISEMITISM AND THE COLD WAR

Caracciolo, Nicola. *Uncertain Refuge: Italy and the Jews During the Holocaust*. Translated and edited by Florette Rechnitz Koffler and Richard Koffler. Urbana: University of Illinois Press, 1995.

Cesarani, David. *Becoming Eichmann: Rethinking the Life, Crimes, and Trial of a "Desk Murderer."* Cambridge, MA: Da Capo Press, 2006.

Chehab, Zaki. *Inside Hamas: The Untold Story of the Militant Islamic Movement*. New York: Nation Books, 2007.

Dinnerstein, Leonard. *Antisemitism in America*. New York: Oxford University Press, 1994.

Frommer, Myrna Katz and Harvey Frommer. *Growing Up Jewish in America: An Oral History.* New York: Harcourt Brace, 1995.

"Hamas Covenant 1988: The Covenant of the Islamic Resistance Movement." The Avalon Project: Documents in Law, History, and Diplomacy. http://avalon.law.yale.edu/20th_century/hamas.asp.

Hausner, Gideon. *Justice in Jerusalem*. New York: Harper & Row, 1966.

Khrushchev, Nikita. *Khrushchev Remembers: The Last Testament*. Translated and edited by Strobe Talbott. Boston: Little, Brown & Company, 1974.

Küntzel, Matthias. *Jihad and Jew-Hatred: Islamism, Nazism and the Roots of 9/11*. Translated by Colin Meade. New York: Telos Press, 2007.

Lagnado, Lucette. *The Man in the White Sharkskin Suit: A Jewish Family's Exodus from Old Cairo to the New World*. New York: HarperPerennial, 2007.

Laqueur, Walter, and Barry Rubin, eds. *The Israel-Arab Reader: A Documentary History of the Middle East Conflict*. New York: Penguin Books, 2008.

Levin, Nora. *The Jews in the Soviet Union since 1917: Paradox of Survival* Vol. 1. New York: New York University Press, 1988.

Levine, Allan. *Scattered Among the Peoples: The Jewish Diaspora in Twelve Portraits*. Woodstock, NY: Overlook Duckworth, 2003.

Lewis, Bernard. *The Middle East: A Brief History of the Last 2000 Years*. New York: Scribner, 1995.

Meir, Golda. *My Life*. New York: G. P. Putnam's Sons, 1975.

Montefiore, Simon Sebag. *Stalin: The Court of the Red Tsar*. New York: Vintage Books, 2003.

Oren, Michael B. *Six Days of War: June 1967 and the Making of the Modern Middle East*. Oxford: Oxford University Press, 2002.

Podolsky, Barukh. "How I Became a Zionist." *Soviet Jews Exodus*. Last modified February 22, 2011. http://www.angelfire.com/sc3/soviet_jews_exodus/English/Memory_s/MemoryPodolsky.shtml.

Roberts, Geoffrey. *Stalin's Wars: From World War to Cold War, 1939–1953*. New Haven: Yale University Press, 2006.

Sachar, Howard M. *A History of the Jews in the Modern World*. New York: Vintage Books, 2005.

Stillman, Norman A., ed. *Jews of Arab Lands in Modern Times*. Philadelphia: Jewish Publication Society, 2003.

Vaksberg, Arkady. *Stalin Against the Jews*. Translated by Antonina Bouis. New York: Alfred A. Knopf, 1994.

16. ANTISEMITISM TODAY: A CONVENIENT HATRED

Berenbaum, Michael, ed. *Not Your Father's Antisemitism: Hatred of the Jews in the 21st Century*. St. Paul: Paragon House, 2008.

The Community Security Trust. "Antisemitic Incidents Report, 2006." http://www.thecst.org.uk/docs/Incidents_Report_06.pdf.

Desbois, Patrick. Speech on Holocaust Remembrance Day, Geneva, April 21, 2009. http://www.holocaustbybullets.com/en/about-patrick-desbois/durban-ii-april-20-24-yom-hashoah.

Fiss, Joëlle. *The Durban Diaries: What really happened at the UN Conference against Racism in Durban (2001)*. New York: American Jewish Committee/European Union of Jewish Students, 2008.

Gitelman, Zvi. *A Century of Ambivalence: The Jews of Russia and the Soviet Union, 1881 to the Present*. 2nd ed. Bloomington: Indiana University Press, 2001.

Jacobson, Howard. "Pox Britannica: Anti-Semitism on the March." Originally published in *The New Republic*. *NationalPost.com*, April 20, 2009. http://network.nationalpost.com/np/blogs/fullcomment/archive/2009/04/20/pox-britannica-anti-semitism-on-the-march.aspx.

Jorisch, Avi. "Al-Manar: Hizbullah TV, 24/7." *Middle East Quarterly*, Winter 2004. http://www.meforum.org/583/al-manar-hizbullah-tv-24-7.

Küntzel, Matthias. "Islamic Antisemitism and its Nazi Roots." April 2003. http://www.matthiaskuentzel.de/contents/islamic-antisemitism-and-its-nazi-roots.

———. "'Wipe Out the Jews': Antisemitic Hate Speech in the Name of Islam." *Spiegel Online International*, May 16, 2008. http://www.spiegel.de/international/world/0,1518,553724,00.html.

Lerner, Michael, ed. *Best Contemporary Jewish Writing, 2002*. San Francisco: Jossey-Bass, 2002.

Lévy, Bernard-Henri. *Left in Dark Times: A Stand against the New Barbarism*. New York: Random House, 2009.

Menashri, David. "Iran, the Jews and the Holocaust." Steven Roth Institute for the Study of Contemporary Antisemitism and Racism. http://www.tau.ac.il/Anti-Semitism/asw2005/menashri.html.

Rahola, Pilar. "'Democracy's Canaries': Jews and Judeophobia in Contemporary Europe." From the World Jewish Conference, June 13, 2005. http://www.pilarrahola.com/3_0/CONFERENCIAS/default.cfm?ID=116.

Rosenbaum, Ron, ed. *Those Who Forget the Past: The Question of Anti-Semitism*. New York: Random House, 2004.

Stephen Roth Institute for the Study of Contemporary Antisemitism and Racism. *Antisemitism Worldwide, 2008/9*. Stephen Roth Institute for The Study of Contemporary Antisemitism Racism: 2010.

Stern, Kenneth S. *Antisemitism Today: How It is the Same, How It is Difference, and How to Fight It*. American Jewish Committee, 2006.

Wiesel, Elie. *From the Kingdom of Memory: Reminiscences*. New York: Schocken Books, 1990.

ACKNOWLEDGMENTS

We are deeply grateful for all of the support, help, and advice we received in creating this book. We wish to thank Leonard Stern for sponsoring the book and serving as a valued adviser throughout the process.

No one involved with Facing History and Ourselves advocated for a book on the history of antisemitism more than Father Robert Bullock, who served on our board of directors and as chair of our board of scholars until his death in 2004. He was a loyal friend and a trusted teacher to us all.

Seth Klarman, the chair of our board of directors, also was deeply involved in this project. He read every word and repeatedly engaged us in deep conversations about the content.

The book owes much to a dedicated a group of colleagues who met regularly to discuss chapters. The suggestions, criticisms, and concerns of Marc Skvirsky, Marty Sleeper, Adam Strom, Dimitry Anselme, Jan Darsa, and Doc Miller influenced the final product in small ways and large. So did the helpful comments we received from other interested readers.

On this project, like on so many others, we benefited from the extraordinary staff at Facing History and Ourselves. They provided a broad array of special services ranging from project management to aid in research, editing, and production. Among them were Michael Durney, Brooke Harvey, Tracy O'Brien, Eva Radding, Catherine O'Keefe, and April Lambert.

We also valued the help we received from the book's content editor, Carol Barkin. Her attention to detail, pointed questions, and thoughtful advice strengthened the manuscript. So did the services we received from photo researcher Carol Frohlich of Visual Connection Image Research, Inc., and her associate Elisa Gallagher. International Mapping Associates and the designers and copy editors at Six Red Marbles also have contributed greatly to the final product. We are most appreciative of the cover design created by Rodrigo Corral Design.

We also wish to express our gratitude to Yehuda Bauer, Michael Berenbaum, Lawrence Langer, and John Stendahl for their honest critiques of the manuscript, their helpful advice, and wise counsel. They improved the book. We are grateful to Paula Fredriksen, Mary C. Boys, and Ahmed al-Rahim for sharing their expertise on key aspects of this complicated history. And we would like to thank Sir Martin Gilbert for his many works that over the years have become part of the intellectual background and historical understanding at Facing History and Ourselves. His books on Jewish history, the Holocaust, and antisemitism, as well as his incredible atlases, have informed the modern world.

Margot Stern Strom
Phyllis Goldstein

CREDITS

Reproduced by permission of ABC-CLIO, Inc. from Steve M. Berk, *Year of Crisis, Year of Hope: Russian Jewry and the Pogroms of 1881–1882* (Westport: Greenwood Press, 1985), 35–36, 48, 49, 66-67, 68, 69, 72–73.

Reproduced by permission from Pauline Wengeroff, eds. Bernard Dov Cooperman, Henny Wenkart, *Rememberings: The World of a Russian-Jewish Woman in the Nineteenth Century* (Bethesda: University Press of Maryland, 2000), 221, 223.

Reproduced by permission from Lucy S. Dawidowicz, *The Golden Tradition: Jewish Life and Thought in Eastern Europe* (New York: Henry Holt and Co., 1967),128–129.

Reproduced by permission from Georges Borchardt on behalf of translator, *The Enemy at His Pleasure: A Journey Through the Jewish Pale of Settlement During World War I,* ed. and trans. Joachim Neugroschel (New York: Henry Holt, 2004), 4–7.

Reproduced by permission from Naïm Kattan, *Farewell Babylon: Coming of Age in Jewish Baghdad,* trans. Sheila Fischman (Boston: David R. Godine, 2005).

Reproduced by permission from Barukh Podolsky. "How I Became a Zionist" (Soviet Jews Exodus, http://www.soviet-jews-exodus.com, 2002).

Reproduced by permission from Jonathan Rosen, *Waking Up to My Father's World,* in "Best Jewish Writing 2002," ed. Michael Lerner (San Francisco: Jossey-Bass, 2002), 77.

Reprinted by permission from the Washington Institute for Near East Policy from Chief Rabbi Jonathan Sacks, *Muslims and Jews in Europe Today.* Speech given at the Washington Institute for Near East Policy on November 28, 2005.

Reproduced by permission from Joëlle Fiss, *The Durban Diaries* (New York: American Jewish Committee, 2008), 24–25.

Reproduced by permission from Howard Jacobson, "Pox Britannica: Anti-Semitism on the March," *The New Republic*, April 20, 2009.

Reproduced by permission from Walter Reich, "Erasing the Holocaust," *New York Times*, July 11, 1993.

Reproduced by permission from David Menashri, *Iran, the Jews and the Holocaust* (Tel Aviv: the Steven Roth Institute for the Study of Contemporary Antisemitism and Racism, http://www.tau.ac.il/Anti-Semitism/asw2005/menashri.html, 2006).

Map Credits: Map, p. 10: Data from: Scheindlin, *A Short History of the Jewish People: From Legendary Times to Modern Statehood*, 48. Map, p. 27: Data from: Barnavi, *A Historical Atlas of the Jewish People: From the Time of the Patriarchs to the Present*, English ed., 55. (All subsequent source lines refer to this edition). Map, p. 49: Data from: *A Historical Atlas of the Jewish People*, 81. Map, p. 66: Data from: *A Historical Atlas of the Jewish People*, 105; Gilbert, *The Atlas of Jewish History*, rev. ed., 38. (All subsequent source lines refer to this edition). Map, p. 83: Data from: *A Historical Atlas of the Jewish People*, 107. Map, p. 94: Data from: *A Historical Atlas of the Jewish People*, 111. Map, p. 130: Data from: *The Atlas of Jewish History*, 44. Map, p. 137: Data from: Ahitiv, *The Jewish People: An Illustrated History*, 249. Map, p. 180: Data from: *A Historical Atlas of the Jewish People*, 159; *The Atlas of Jewish History*, 59. Map, p. 193: Data from: *The Jewish People*, 361. Map, p. 221: Data from: *A Historical Atlas of the Jewish People*, 191. Map, p. 234: Data from: *A Historical Atlas of the Jewish People*, 211. Map, p. 285: Data from: *A Historical Atlas of the Jewish People*, 233. Map, p. 293: Data from: *A Historical Atlas of the Jewish People*, 240. Map, p. 331: Data from: *A Historical Atlas of the Jewish People*, 259; *The Jewish People*, 380. Map, p. 357: Data from. *World Jewish Population, 2010*, 19.

INDEX

Passport stamped with "J" for Jew (top)   Survivors of the Holocaust, 1945 (bottom)